Finis Jennings Dake

His Life and Ministry

By

Leon Bible

Dake Publishing

Lawrenceville, Georgia
2006

Finis Jennings Dake
His Life and Ministry

By
Leon Bible

Published by
Dake Publishing, Inc.
P.O. Box 1050
Lawrenceville, Georgia 30046–1050
1 (800) 241–1239
http://www.Dake.com

First Printing 2006
Printed in the United States of America

Library of Congress Catalog Card Number: 2005907396
ISBN 1–55829–156–3

For more information or to order additional copies of this or other books, see the order form in the back of this book or contact the author at the address below.

Leon Bible
746 Vern Cora Road, Laurens, South Carolina 29360
E–mail: leon@DakeBible.com

FORWARD

Finis Jennings Dake's extraordinary life was grounded in his exquisite commitment to God and His Word. This abiding passion was reflected in all aspects of Dake's ministry. Whether as pastor, evangelist, writer, or educator, Dake powerfully impacted the lives of countless believers.

Fittingly, Dake's ministry continues today. Through his exhaustive, decades-long work in compiling The Dake Annotated Reference Bible, he continues to impart his thirst for Scripture to contemporary believers.

I count myself one of those happily 'infected' with Dake's love for the Word. Since the early 1960s, I've owned a copy of The Dake Annotated Reference Bible, wearing out four sturdy copies and giving away hundreds of others. How I appreciate the years of study and revelation that went into this outstanding resource! I have yet to exhaust its depths – and I continue to be amazed by the brilliance of the notes and study helps found in its pages. To this day, I tell Christians, "If you're going to be a good student of the Word, you need a Dake's Bible."

It is no wonder that God inspired Dake, a man truly dedicated to His Word, to produce what is, in my opinion, the best study Bible available. I remember the day almost forty years ago when he ministered at our church; Finis Dake quoted scriptures on a multitude of topics, without once opening his Bible! His example inspires me to this day, and has become a foundation stone in the Bible teaching ministry to which I have been called.

I am forever grateful to Finis Jennings Dake for his profound influence upon my heart and on the Body of Christ as a whole. This biography, full and rich in detail and discovery, is an apt testament to his extraordinary life and ministry, and a work that is sure to light the fire anew in the heart of today's believer.

~ Marilyn Hickey

DEDICATION

As with any man God uses, there are always those who are behind the scenes, of whom we hear very little. Most often these are the very dedicated and loyal family members who have made sacrifices, often as great or greater than the man of God himself. But what happens when the man of God goes to his reward and his life's work is left behind? In many cases the ministry had its effect and was used of God, yet at death the ministry was stopped.

Thank God this was not the case with the ministry of Finis J. Dake, for there are three that bear record of his life and ministry. Through their diligent efforts, hard work, great sacrifices and relentless determination, even in the midst of persecution, the ministry goes on.

For their great love of the ministry of their dad . . . and yet an even greater love for their Lord, Jesus Christ . . . and for their desire to make available to the world the Word of God . . . I dedicate this book to the three children of Finis and Dorothy Dake.

Finette Dake Kennedy

Annabeth Dake Germaine

Finis Jennings Dake, Jr.

Your love and service to your father is only eclipsed
by your love and service to God!

The Author

TABLE OF CONTENTS

Forward 3

Dedication 5

Chapter One—*Childhood Days* 9

Chapter Two—*I Want To Be A Cowboy* 19

Chapter Three—*Home For A Visit* 23

Chapter Four—*The Bible School Years* 37

Chapter Five—*Her Name Was Dorothy* 57

Chapter Six—*Dake Finds A Wife* 63

Chapter Seven—*From Pastor To College Principle* 67

Chapter Eight—*Controversy At Southwestern* 91

Chapter Nine—*Dake's Teaching On The Pre–Adamite World* 103

Chapter Ten—*Dake's Teaching On The Sons Of God* 111

Chapter Eleven—*The Battle Rages At Southwestern* 121

Chapter Twelve—*Zion* 131

Chapter Thirteen—*John Alexander Dowie And The City He Built* 137

Chapter Fourteen—*Dake Pastoring In Zion* 143

Chapter Fifteen—*Dorothy Dake Is Quite A Preacher* 155

Chapter Sixteen—*Dake Builds Another Bible School* 165

Chapter Seventeen—*Shiloh Bible Institute* 169

Chapter Eighteen—*The Shiloh Scroll* 193

Chapter Nineteen—*The Halls Remember Dake* 207

Chapter Twenty—*Lester Sumrall Remembers Dake* 215

Chapter Twenty–One—*Crisis In Zion* 219

Chapter Twenty–Two—*The Baptism In The Holy Spirit* 229

Chapter Twenty–Three—*Dake Leaves Zion* 245

Chapter Twenty–Four—*St. Paul And Bristol* 251

Chapter Twenty–Five—*Church Of God Preacher* 257

Chapter Twenty–Six—*Atlanta* 273

Chapter Twenty–Seven—*God's Plan For Man* 283

Chapter Twenty–Eight—*Dake On The Radio Again* 291

Chapter Twenty–Nine—*New Testament Church* 297

Chapter Thirty—*Dake And His Bible Notes* 305

Chapter Thirty–One—*Dake Bible Sales* 313

Chapter Thirty–Two—*The Accident* 323

Chapter Thirty–Three—*The Seventy's* 329

Chapter Thirty–Four—*The Man Of The Word Goes Home* 335

Chapter Thirty–Five—*Conclusion* 343

TABLE OF CONTENTS (CONTINUED)

Chapter Thirty–Six—*A Lasting Memorial* 349

Appendix One—*Graduation Sermon* 353
Appendix Two—*Genealogies* 365
Appendix Three—*Dake's Testimony* 367
Appendix Four—*Women Preachers* 373
Appendix Five—*Religious Emotionalism* 377
Appendix Six—*The Potter's Masterpiece* 381
Appendix Seven—*Like A Rose* 384
Appendix Eight—*Dake and Doctrine* 385
Appendix Nine—*The Trinity* 393
Appendix Ten—*Tri–Theism* 399
Appendix Eleven—*The Mormon Doctrine Of God* 403
Appendix Twelve—*Personal Recollections* 407

Bibliography 419
Index 425

CHAPTER ONE

CHILDHOOD DAYS

A BIRTH IN IBERIA

In 1900, Iberia of Miller County was a small town located in the middle of the state of Missouri, about 117 miles west of St. Louis. The 1990 United States Census reported that Iberia had a total population of only 650 residents. Henry Dake, Dake's[1] father, was born in Missouri. His parents had come east from Tennessee and were living in Missouri at the time of the 1870 census. It was in this small mid–western town of Iberia, on Saturday, the eighteenth day of October, 1902, that Finis Jennings Dake was born. As Dake put it himself: "I was born in a little town down in the sticks."

Dake was born the son of James Henry (7/10/1869–7/18/1912) and Mary Ellen Dake (5/16/1870–1948). At the ages of twenty and nineteen respectively, James and Mary were married on Thursday, June 13, 1889, in the state of Tennessee. Dake was the eighth child in a large family of eleven children.[2] He was an unusual child, having an ancestry which included Scotch, Irish, Dutch, French and even Cherokee Indian from his mother's side of the family. Not only was he born with a diverse heritage, he was also born with unusually large hands and big feet. A large child such as this truly needed a big name, and that must have been what his parents had in mind when they named him after the famous American lawyer and politician, William Jennings Bryan.[3]

1901

Agnes Ozman speaks in tongues in Topeka. Charles Parham calls tongues the "Bible evidence" for baptism in the Spirit.

THE DAKE'S MOVE TO SPRINGFIELD

It wasn't long after his birth in 1902 that the Dake family moved about 85 miles south to Springfield, Missouri. Henry Dake made this move understanding that it would take the resources of a large–sized town to feed

---

[1] While it may seem lacking in respect to some to refer to Finis Dake as simply "Dake," this was the name he was known by his entire life. To this day all over the world students of the Bible refer to his ministry and writings, and when doing so it is always simply "Dake." This work will continue respectfully that tradition.

[2] See the Appendix for the Dake family tree.

[3] William Jennings Bryan, 1860–1925. American lawyer and politician.

his thirteen–member family. Dake himself did not remember, with any degree of certainty, how old he was at the time of this move. He said: "I don't even remember when we moved to Springfield; I was just a little lad at the time."

In Springfield, Henry Dake showed himself to be an industrious and hard–working father. He became very successful in building and contracting, and even ran his own general store of sorts. He and his building crew built two wood–frame buildings in Springfield from which he would operate his businesses.

In the first wood–frame building he ran his construction business. From one end of the building to the other, he mounted a large sign on the roof that read: *J. H. Dake, Contractor and Builder, Houses for rent or sale, Terms to suit buyer.* The housing industry was a booming business in Henry Dake's day. At the turn of the century, 25 percent of all Americans

J.H. Dake office and employees

lived in their own home.[4] Land was cheap, construction methods were inexpensive, and taxes were only 1 percent of the annual income for couples earning more than $4,000.00.[5] Henry Dake's contracting business was no small concern, on the contrary, he met the payroll for more than sixteen employees. At the time of his death in 1912 he had thirty–seven houses under construction. With the financing of homes going for $100.00[6] down and $10.00[7] per month, it was easy to see that Henry Dake was providing a very profitable lifestyle for his family and was well on his way to becoming quite wealthy.

In the second wood–frame building, Henry Dake ran his general store. A wooden sign hanging from a steel rod over the front door read: *J. H. Dake, Groceries, Flour & Feed, Meat Market.* Groceries, like most goods, were sold on credit. "Cash and carry" was a phrase that was to come

---

[4] *Victorian America*, by Thomas J. Schereth, Harper Pernnial, New York: New York, page 101.

[5] Ibid. page 79.

[6] Or about $1,858.00 in year 2005 dollars.

[7] Or about $185.00 in year 2005 dollars.

much later. Henry Dake's store was arranged like most general stores of his day. Customers could see, feel, and even taste the merchandise. The counters on the right side of the store were filled with dry goods and those on the left side with groceries, sundries, and patent medicines. In the rear of the store you would find kerosene and the meat barrels. On occasion you might even find a luxury item such as a cuckoo clock!

J. H. Dake

Henry Dake was quite a businessman, and for the times, Henry Dake and his large family were really doing quite well. Henry Dake was a generous man as well. He worked hard and expected such from his workers, but he rewarded them well and was known as a giver in the community. Dake said of his father:

> Every Sunday and on every holiday, without exception, my father would make a great feast for his workers and his friends. He would invite our neighbors and would provide meals for crowds of people.

Dake's recollection of this prosperous time was that:

> Things were looking bright for us in those days, as far as our natural life was concerned, for we were being well cared for, receiving an education and looking forward to many opportunities in life.

As a father, Henry Dake was very strict with his children. A practical and hard working man, he required such with his children. While not being religious himself, one of the many things he demanded of his children was that they attend church each and every Sunday. Dake recalled:

> I remember that, from my earliest days, we were all taught through the years that Sunday was the Holy day, the Holy sabbath, and we were to be so sanctimonious, so godly, so consecrated, so righteous, so still and sacred, about everything we thought or did on that day. But on other days we could do anything we wanted to do. We had a special

cloak we put on that particular day. The other days we took it off and lived like we wanted to live.

For the most part, the Dake children attended the Methodist church, but on regular intervals they attended the Baptist church as well. Dake recalls that "when only a very small boy, I was obliged to put on shoes, stockings and a hot suit to attend the services." This was quite a task for a little boy to endure who enjoyed the freedom of overalls and bare feet for the rest of the week.

DEATH IN SPRINGFIELD

The days in Springfield were not all good, however. The eleventh child of Henry and Mary Ellen Dake, born on April 22 of 1910, did not fare well. Sadly, Flomarie Etta Dake (4/22/1910–9/26/1910) passed away as an infant of just five months and four days. Then, just two years later, the unthinkable happened. At forty–three years and eight days of age, on Monday, July 8, 1912, Henry Dake, the husband, father and sole provider for his family, passed away. The family recalls this being a heart attack. Dake noted:

> Suddenly, and without a single day's warning, my father was seized with an attack of the heart and died. It was a dark cloud indeed that seemed to shadow our home.

Sadly, the very large Dake family laid their dad to rest, in a graveyard where his body would lay next to that of his dad and their grandfather, George W. Dake.

After the death of Henry Dake things turned bad financially—really bad. Mary Ellen Dake had been spending most of her time raising this large family and was not accustomed to handling business matters. Mary Ellen Dake had always been a sickly woman. Dake recalled: "As a child I never remember my mother having a well day in her life; there were medicines and doctors all the time."

Most of the children who were still at home were young and unable to help with Henry Dake's businesses. Dake himself was not quite ten years old. Under these circumstances, it was only a few days before the businessmen and lawyers in whom Mary Ellen Dake had placed her confidence had the homestead and other property in their possession. Mary Ellen Dake was left homeless, penniless and physically unfit to work.

Yet this mother now had the task of caring for, and raising, the large Dake family.

Alone, without her husband of twenty–three years, Mary Ellen Dake was to take her family to a new home. She became a renter rather than an owner. The older children did their best to work and help defray expenses. Dake himself, barely twelve years of age, secured a job as a newspaper boy and did his part to help the struggling family keep food on the table and a roof over their heads.

Growing up Without a Father

Doing the right thing sometimes has problems associated with it. It was a good thing for a young boy to help with the family expenses. Dake proved to be a hard worker just like his dad. He worked his way up from delivering and selling newspapers on the street to becoming a messenger boy. While this meant an increase in pay, the new job required longer hours. To help meet the needs of his family, Dake dropped out of school.

Gravesite of J. H. Dake

While certain aspects of Dake's early boyhood are to be commended, he was still just a boy. Like most of the boys his age, he loved to attend the movies. In the first few years after the turn of the century, the movie industry was booming. There were 10,000 movie theaters playing to a nationwide audience of over 10 million people weekly. Movies at this time were more popular than dime museums, concert halls, circuses and even street carnivals.[8] Dake didn't like watching just any movie; he preferred the shoot–'em–up cowboy type. His favorite movie cowboy was Hop–A–Long Cassidy, though he also enjoyed watching Buffalo Bill and Annie Oakley working around the ranch, fighting Indians, and even "tangling" with other cowboys from time to time. It was an exciting way for a little boy to spend his Saturday afternoons; especially when the average price of a movie was only about seven cents. Later in his life

---

[8] *Victorian America*, by Thomas J. Schereth, Harper Pernnial, New York: New York, page 202.

he would admit to one of his shortcomings connected to his love for the movies:

> In my young days after father's death I went to many moving picture shows, especially to those of the wild west type. Often I would sell old coats and clothing left by my father, for enough money to buy my ticket. The idea of being a cowboy, a real movie cowboy, seized me; and in fact held me until God intervened in my life.

Dake's wayward activities were not only confined to movie–going, an acceptable activity even in the early 1900's. Actually, he really was a rowdy young boy. Dake himself said: "After father's death the Dake boys were the meanest boys in the whole country." It seems that the values and teachings of the Methodists had very little affect upon his life. No blame should be associated with the Methodist or Baptist churches here; after all, how much of an effect can a church have on a little boy who is "sent" to church for just one hour each week? While God was respected in the Dake home and the family was morally good, it cannot be said that it was a Christian home.

To illustrate the absence of God in Dake's life, a story written in *The Sparkling Fountain* concerning Dake and his brother Arthur, who was eight years older than himself, will be of some interest:

> While we were meeting in the wooden tabernacle on Boonville Street, the crowds would often come to find out about Pentecost. We also would attract quite a crowd of rowdies on the outside. They would cut the harness off of our old horses. They would stand at the windows and holler, pound on the walls, and carry on. Often times, the crowd on the outside looking in was almost as big as the crowd on the inside seeking the Lord. In Springfield, we seemed to be regarded as castoffs. But the power of God would come down and it seemed like the Glory Cloud of old would fill the tabernacle.
>
> One night, while Sister Lula France from Joplin was preaching, a young boy ran halfway down the center aisle and threw an egg. It soared through the air, hit the pulpit a perfect bull's eye and splattered all over the platform, the

preacher, and those near the front. The young man stood there with a great big grin, pretty proud of his aim. Mother jumped up, ran over to him, pointed her finger at him and said, "I saw you throw that egg." He arrogantly snorted, "What of it?" Mother said, "I'm going to pray that you won't be able to sleep nights until you get saved. I'm going to pray that the Lord will make you miserable until you give your life to Christ. I'm going to pray that God will make you a preacher and a winner of souls—that you will lead many to Christ." Well, he just stood there, grinned, then swaggered out of the tabernacle. I can remember Mother praying about this many times afterward.

1914

300 people gather to form the Assemblies of God in Hot Springs, Arkansas.

Years later, after Central Bible Institute had been started in the basement of our church (which was located on the same spot where the tattered tent had stood), a tall, well–dressed, handsome, young man came to my Mother one morning and said, "Mrs. Corum, do you remember me?" Mother looked at him and somewhat confusedly said, "No, I don't think I know you." The young man said, "I'm the one that threw the egg." He began to weep and related, "I couldn't sleep nights and I remembered that you said you were going to pray that I couldn't sleep. In my misery, I sought God and He saved me, and I'm here at Central Bible Institute to become a minister." He later wrote a Bible Commentary and pastored a church in Texas. His name was Finis Jennings Dake. And so, God used a humbling incident to make a preacher.

The Lord dealt with other members of the crowd that hollered in the windows and pounded on the walls of that tabernacle on Boonville Street. There was one little boy that was terribly mean. He wore a yellow shirt and we called him "yellow jacket." He would shout and throw stones at the people at the altar and run and hide. He would torment us any way he could. Martha Childers was a radiant young Christian then. She had a beautiful velvet dress and all the girls were envious of her. Just before church one night, while she was praying at the altar, this rascal threw a rotten egg and hit her in the middle of the back. One of the saints grabbed him and said, "Look here. The Lord's going to get hold of you and use you for His glory." Martha was full of the joy of the Lord and she got up and sang and testified anyway. By the way, "yellow jacket" became a Christian, got the Holy Ghost, and ten years later, he was the contractor that built the first building (Bowie Hall) at Central Bible Institute. His name was Arthur Dake and his brother was Finis Dake.[9]

DEATH COMES TO THE DAKE FAMILY AGAIN

On Friday, February 22, 1918, Joseph Franklin Dake was killed. The sixth child in the Dake family, Joseph had gone to war at the age of nineteen, serving his country proudly in the United States Navy. Again, death had dealt a terrible blow to the Dake family. But learning from the loss and hardship his father's death had brought, Joseph Franklin Dake had taken out a life insurance policy in the Navy. With the proceeds from this policy and his pension plan, Mary Ellen Dake was left enough money to move her family to the country and rent a farm. The farm was located about eight miles from Marshfield, Missouri. There was also enough money to equip the farm with the necessary team of mules and farm implements that would be needed to raise crops, both for eating and for sale. Dake, about fifteen years old at the time, accompanied the family to Marshfield and secured work on a nearby farm.

It was also during this period of Dake's life that he and his brothers went on what he called a "notable fishing trip." From the time he was just a very small child Dake had always liked to fish. He always had an intense desire to live in the open. In his own words:

> Hunting, fishing and swimming seemed a part of me. Many was the time before father's death that I had slipped off for a swim, only to receive a whipping for my disobedience upon my return.

---

[9] *The Sparkling Fountain,* by Fred T. Corum and Hazel E. Bakewell. Corum & Associates, Inc. Windsor: Ohio.

On this occasion Dake and some of his brothers left for a fishing trip in the farm wagon. While they were enjoying themselves fishing, it began to rain. In fact, it began to pour. Having the ingenuity of their father flowing through their veins, they came up with a remarkable idea. They would take the bed off of the wagon and use it for a shelter! Heavy as it was for the Dake brothers to disassemble, they managed to take apart the wagon. They turned the bed upside down and—with torrents of rain pouring down throughout the night—the Dake boys slept in the shelter they had made. While young boys are very courageous and willing to try anything for an adventure, they sometimes don't think things through. When morning came, Dake found that he could barely move. In lifting the wagon bed he had sprained his back. Sadly, this back sprain later developed into sciatic rheumatism, and while still a young teenage boy, Dake walked with a limp and used a cane.

1916

The Oneness Movement splits the Assemblies of God.

This condition eventually forced him to leave the farm and go back to Springfield where he sought treatment for his ailment. Later in his life, Dake would experience healing for himself and see many thousands of others healed through simple prayer and faith in God's Word. Yet at this time in his life Dake lamented:

> Jesus Christ as the healer of sick and afflicted bodies was not a reality to me at that time. I managed finally to do without the cane, but was still more or less disabled at times.

CHAPTER TWO

I WANT TO BE A COWBOY

TRYING TO MAKE A LIVING

In his mid–teens Dake moved from Springfield to the northern part of Missouri. There he joined one of his brothers who worked on a ranch. His work during this time was hard and strenuous. He baled hay, broke the ice on the rivers so that the cattle could drink and herded the livestock. His work was not only confined to traditional ranching activities, he also worked in the logging camp harvesting lumber for use on the ranch and for sale. Clearing fields, and digging up and burning stumps, were all part of his daily task. And for this very strenuous work he received the grand sum of $1.00 per day.[10] The poverty level at this time was about $660.00[11] per year.[12] That meant that the average person, even at the poverty level, would make about $2.00 per day for a six–day week.[13] But for a teenager who had always dreamed of being a cowboy one day and loved the outdoors, Dake was glad to be paid anything at all for doing what he loved.

1919

Pentecostal Assemblies of the USA (now Pentecostal Church of God) is formed.

The job in northern Missouri didn't last long however. In just a matter of months Dake moved west to Kansas City. In this thriving town the young boy who wanted to be a cowboy found work as a dishwasher. Unfortunately, his lack of enthusiasm and experience quickly brought about his termination. This experience led him from one job to another. Eventually, he found work as a busboy at the Harvey House. He quickly moved his way up to head busboy, but was just as quickly fired following a heated argument with his supervisor. The quarrel ended with Dake removing his shoe and throwing it at his supervisor! Needless to say, Dake was soon looking for work again. It is often said that when a man of God has a call on his life, he will be successful at nothing until he surrenders to

---

[10] Or about $11.00 per day in year 2005 dollars.

[11] Or about $7,500.00 per year in year 2005 dollars.

[12] *Victorian America*, by Thomas J. Schereth, Harper Pernnial, New York: New York, page 34.

[13] Or about $22.00 per day in year 2005 dollars.

that call. In Dake's own words he said: "I was proving to be a 'jack of all trades and master of none,' shifting here and there, unsettled, unsatisfied and without God."

Go West Young Man

It was about this time in his life that his desire to become a cowboy came to him more forcibly than ever before. He felt that the time to launch out as a real–life "Hop–A–Long Cassidy" had finally come. With no money and a lot of determination, he set out traveling west.

Leaving Kansas City, Dake passed through the rest of Kansas. Not having an automobile or other means of transportation, he decided to travel by rail—not as a paying passenger, but, as he described it later in his life, as a hobo. "I proceeded like a professional 'bum' and boarded a train, riding on the tender of the engine to a point in Kansas," Dake recounted. The "tender" was the car that was attached to a steam locomotive for the purpose of carrying a supply of fuel and water.

Dake as a cowboy

Traveling north through Kansas he wound up in Omaha, Nebraska. This was only a temporary stop however, just long enough to work, earn some money, and buy some needed food and clothing. Riding the rails had not been pleasant, and for three full days he had been without food. Finding a place to sleep in Omaha was also a problem—where does a man with no money find a bed? Dake slept wherever he could; sometimes even in a boxcar. On a few fortunate occasions, he slept in the stockyard on the hay with the horses and other animals.

Facing hardship and difficulty for a just and righteous cause is something to be admired, but Dake later regretted that he had sacrificed for such a worldly ambition as the desire to be a cowboy. Reflecting on the hardships and suffering Paul endured for the sake of the Gospel, in regard to this period of his life, Dake wrote: "I am sorry to say, these hardships were not passed through in behalf of the noble cause for which Paul suffered."

After staying in Omaha for about a month, he headed further west toward Wyoming, looking for work. Here he found a job on a sheep ranch. It wasn't quite what he was looking for—after all, those sheep really smelled bad—but this job would do, and he would earn a little money for food and clothing. Now, for the first time in his life, he had made enough money to buy some of the things he really wanted. In the way of clothing, of course, what he wanted was an outfit that a cowboy would wear. He purchased a shirt that had fancy leather cuffs attached to it. The cuffs were made of leather and had a large star design, which was made from tin brads. The boots he bought were complete with jingling, jangling spurs. A large and bold handkerchief was purchased to tie around his neck. Leather chaps adorned both of his legs, complete with tin stars and leather strips swinging in the wind as he would ride. He added a large brimmed black hat to cover his head and, to top it all off, he wore a six–shooter on his hip. At the age of sixteen, Dake may have never worked as a cowboy, but he sure looked like one!

1921

First Christian radio broadcast is aired by Calvary Episcopal Church, Pittsburgh, Pennsylvania.

A COWBOY AT LAST

Leaving Wyoming he went south into Colorado. There he met a man who took him for an experienced cowhand. After all, he sure looked the part! The man offered him work on a ranch that was just west of Denver. Without a second thought, Dake accepted. It was there he spent his first full season herding cattle. Finally, he was a real working cowboy. His dream he had from a child, had finally come true. For Dake life could not have been more complete. He said:

> At last my desire for life in the open was being satisfied.
> Riding, shooting and roping became important features of
> my life. I felt sure that I had found my life's work.

But it seemed that God had other plans.

CHAPTER THREE

HOME FOR A VISIT

OH NO! MY FAMILY GOT RELIGION!

After being away for almost two years, Dake wanted to go home for a visit. After all, he had arrived at his chosen profession and no doubt wanted to show his family that he had become a success. In fact, he had plans to go to Mexico after the visit with his family. He had heard about the Mexican bandit Pancho Villa, and wanted to join the outlaws in order to make a name for himself. Then, Dake reasoned, he would be ready to head to Hollywood and make his mark in the movies. But what was supposed to be a brief, but joyful, reunion with his family turned into something quite different.

> *"One can only become holy in Christ by full obedience to the Gospel."*
>
> *Finis Dake*

Upon arriving back in Springfield he found that his mother had fallen ill and was bedridden. His short visit turned into several weeks as he helped out around the farm. It was during this time that he realized that his whole family had changed. After being away for over a year, things were different. While the Dake family had always been honest, hard–working, charitable and had a respect for God and the Bible, they had never really been religious. When Henry Dake was alive, sending his children to the Methodist and Baptist churches was the extent of the family's religious commitment. None of them had ever been truly saved or born again. But now a change had taken place in the family. Many members of the family, including his mother, had made commitments to Christ. Furthermore, there was a desire in the home to read the Bible and attend church. This was completely new to Dake, who had never enjoyed reading the Bible and hated being forced to attend church when he was younger. While away on the range he had never attended church, and he hadn't had the time for God or His Word. Even now, at this juncture of his life, he still had no time for religion or God. In his own words he said:

> The whole family had been stirred concerning religious matters. I myself was a disinterested party!

Their "religion," as Dake put it, was not something his family was willing to keep private. They were eager to share it with him and would constantly find ways to bring the subjects of God and the Bible into conversations in an attempt to bring him to Christ.[14] It was here in Springfield that the seeds of the New Birth were first planted in Dake's life. While he did not receive salvation at this time he did say:

> Religion began to get a hold of me, or at least I began to think about it. When the family would talk about religion I would leave the room, and sometimes the house, trying to get away. But I would never let my family know that God was dealing with me.

Not only had Dake's family become religious, but, in his mind, they had become religious in the worst way—the group of people that he and his brother Arthur had thrown eggs at just a few years earlier were the same group that his family had began to associate with—Pentecostals!

To get away from all this "religion talk," as Dake put it, he decided to leave Springfield and go to Tulsa, Oklahoma, which was about 173 miles southwest of Springfield. He would stay with one of his brothers who was living there at the time. But, to his amazement, Dake found that "they were talking about religion down there too!"

Revival was springing up all around Tulsa at this time. There were prayer meetings and cottage meetings going on everywhere, and the first place his brother took him was to a Pentecostal prayer meeting. To say that this religious gathering was quite different from his brief experiences in the Methodist and Baptist churches would be an understatement. Dake had little preparation for what was happening in this Pentecostal meeting. He spoke of his childhood days:

> In the little church there was only one Methodist elderly woman that would get up and shout every Sunday morning. This was the only thing that I remember that was really spiritual. And most of the congregation were ashamed and made fun of the woman. And so did I.

Dake was not used to any kind of church service, especially one where there was dancing, loud singing, shouting, and choruses of "amens" and "hallelujahs" that followed the preacher as he preached. Dake recalled:

---

[14] For a detailed study of witnessing and personal work see the *Dake Annotated Reference Bible*, Compact Edition, by Finis Dake. Dake Publishing, Inc. Lawrenceville: Georgia, Old Testament, page 1596, Compact edition.

I shall never forget the peculiar impression that the first service made upon me. Indeed, it was an interesting time when they danced, sang, and shouted all around me. God was surely working with those folks.

WITNESSING GOD'S HEALING POWER

It was here in Tulsa that Dake saw God's healing power manifest for the first time. Dake's brother had a small daughter who suffered from what he called "sore eyes." In fact, she was losing her eyesight rapidly, and at this time was almost totally blind. To Dake's amazement she was healed. Her healing was instant and complete. This miracle was so profound in the Dake family that both Dake's brother and wife came to the Lord in a powerful salvation experience.

While this was the first miracle Dake ever saw, it would not be the last. In fact, it would only be the beginning. Faith had come to the Dake family and Dake himself found that, surprisingly, he himself was being drawn toward this healing God—a God whom he had never met and who he knew next to nothing about.

His mother, Mary Ellen Dake, was still in Springfield and was still sick when this miracle occurred. Everyone's faith was growing, and Mary Ellen Dake, who had already become a Christian at this time, wanted to be healed. She called for one of the saints, Mrs. Welch, and several of the brethren who worked at the newly–founded Gospel Publishing House[15] in Springfield, to come to her home and pray that God would heal. God, who is always faithful, honored the prayers of those faithful brothers and sisters and restored Mary Ellen Dake to health. This was a notable healing for Mary Ellen, who had spent most of her life in pain and misery from bad health and heartbreak. God was merciful and true to His Word. In fact, Mary Ellen was so well and full of health that in the midst of a snowstorm she made a trip to Tulsa to participate in the revival that was taking place there.

> *"You can get healed as easily as you can be forgiven of sins."*
>
> *Finis Dake*

---

[15] Gospel Publishing House is the publishing house for the Assemblies of God and is dedicated to providing resources to help churches further the cause of Christ and proclaim the Gospel. It was founded in 1915.

In 1920 Tulsa was known as a boomtown. Like their father before them, who left the small town of Iberia for the larger town of Springfield, the Dake family was now moving from Springfield to the large city of Tulsa. This time, they were not moving in order to enjoy a more secure financial future, but for the promise of a richer spiritual life. The family pooled their resources and managed to purchase a small piece of land. There they built a small cottage in which Mother Dake would now make her new home.

"God will not make a special pet out of you or anyone else."

Finis Dake

It was just a short time later that Brother E. F. Cunningham launched a revival at the Full Gospel Church, located at 8th and Florida Street in Tulsa. Seeing the great change that had taken place in so many of his family members, Dake himself was one of the most regular attendees of the revival.

Still, Dake did not fully surrender his life to the Lord during this meeting. Dake said: "In the revival meetings they would try to get me to give my heart to God or 'join the church' as they put it in those days." Dake was not ready for such a step of faith. While most of the family had already come to Christ, Dake's conversion was to take a little while longer.

Dake's problems centered around his desire to see genuine Christianity lived, practiced and experienced in the everyday life of the people. In his early boyhood days he recounted:

> I saw very little Christianity lived. I saw the deacons, the best members and preacher leave the church smoking, chewing their tobacco, dipping snuff, and going to shows and other places of amusements. In my childhood mind I said, 'If that is Christianity I don't want it!' I wanted to see something real in Christianity before I ever gave my life to God and devoted myself to the Christian cause.

While later Dake confessed it was wrong to do so, at this time in his life he used this as an excuse for not coming to Christ. He said:

> I wandered in sin, rejecting Christianity, more or less, because I had stumbled over the inconsistent and unchristian lives of professing Christians.

As a youth, Dake had never made a confession of faith, but he had chosen to remain free from smoking and drinking. He spoke about himself as an "honest–hearted sinner."

THE COWBOY FINALLY TURNS TO JESUS

He had seen the change in his family. He had seen the incredible joy and happiness they now experienced. Dake's difficulty in surrendering to the Lord was that he was seeking an experience with Christ more than the person of Christ. Dake later wrote about this time in his life:

> Night after night found me at the revival under such deep conviction that my body trembled and my teeth chattered. The Spirit of the Living God was striving with my heart and I was rejecting His pleadings. One night I had courage enough to go to the altar, but sat down on my leg in a most uncomfortable way and was afraid to move. When I got up I had no victory but possessed a lame leg and could scarcely walk. I partly decided not to go back if that was the effect the procedure was to have on me, but my decision didn't last long and I was at the altar the next night. For two weeks I went forward looking for a feeling, but no feeling came.

When we fail to receive one way, God, who is longsuffering and faithful, speaks to us through another. When a real revival is in progress and lives are truly being changed and strengthened in the Lord, there is always more happening outside the church than inside! This was the case here as well. A Christian brother by the name of Otto French, who lived in Tulsa, was having prayer meetings at his home. Dake heard about these and decided to attend. It was here that, for the first time in his life, Finis J. Dake received Christ and was born again. In his own words:

> Finally, in a prayer meeting at the home of Brother Otto French of Tulsa, the battle was fought, the victory won and the power of God fell upon me. My second birth had actually taken place and I was a new creature in Christ with new desires and new ambitions. It had been several weeks of struggling with my conscience and the conviction for my sins by the Holy Spirit, but after the fact was

made clear that there was a reality in Christianity, I made a complete surrender of my life to God; to serve Him the rest of my life and to do His will, whatever it may be.

It was the winter of 1920 and Dake was 17 years of age. Later Dake recalled:

> I had always believed it was possible to live a Christian life free from sin and bubbling over with joy, but some of the professors I watched were poor specimens indeed—especially my young companions who were supposed to have been saved in a Baptist revival I attended. One dear old Methodist sister however, made a real impression upon my mind. She really did have an experience with God and her life proved it. That was the kind I wanted and thank God, it was the kind I got when I did turn and seek Him with my whole heart.

"One must experience salvation the 'Bible way' or be lost."

Finis Dake

Dake's desire for banditry and Hollywood fame had radically changed. Just how much of a change Dake had yet to find out. There was no way of knowing what God had in store for this young cowboy who had just traded his six–shooter and spurs for a genuine relationship with the almighty God!

DAKE IS BAPTIZED IN WATER

It was just a matter of weeks before Dake followed the Lord in Christian water–baptism, which is a symbol of the crucifixion of the old man.[16] It was brother S. A. Jamieson who baptized Dake, taking him one step closer to a lifetime of dedication and commitment, as he sought to walk in obedience to Christ in every way.

DAKE IS BAPTIZED WITH THE SPIRIT

After his conversion, Dake began to ask the Lord for the Spirit baptism that his family had told him so much about. This also proved to be a

---

[16] *God's Plan for Man*, by Finis Dake. Dake Publishing, Inc. Lawrenceville: Georgia, Page 633.

difficult experience for him to receive. He prayed, fasted and sought God at every possible occasion. In fact, it was three months after his conversion experience that he finally yielded to the Spirit. Dake said:

> For three months after my conversion to Christ, there was a constant hunger in my life, day and night, for a closer walk with God and a complete understanding of the will of God for my life. I spent most of my time in prayer, seeking to be filled with the Holy Spirit. I knew nothing of the spiritual blessings that God had promised, other than the truth that all true Christians could have all the experiences that were received by early Christians. Hours of waiting on God seemed like minutes. My very soul, with all its feelings, emotions and desires became centered upon God and absorbed in ever–deepening prayer and consecration to the end to which I was hungering. I lived wholly for God. All my sins and bad habits were renounced and all worldly pleasures rejected once and for all. My entire waking moments were spent in worship and prayer and seeking God.

"True New Testament prayer is always heard of God and the answer is always sure."

Finis Dake

It was May, 1920, and a group of African–American Pentecostals were conducting a tent revival. A Hindu evangelist was preaching and many familes from the surrounding communties were attending. A meeting like this was not an ordinary event to be taking place in America during the 1920's. But, when people have Jesus in their hearts, walls and barriers are broken down. Dake loved worshiping and fellowshipping with all of God's children, and he had fond memories of saints of God who would, as he referred to it, "get after the devil":

> In those days, the saints would "get after the devil" when anybody was attacked. They would pray for the sick. They were determined to see that person healed, and the whole prayer group would go, not just the elders. We used to have some wonderful experiences. Many times we would see the sun rise up in the morning.

It was in this tent meeting, after several nights of seeking God, that Dake was filled with the Holy Spirit in what he called "the old time way." In Dake's own words he said:

> I was in prayer about two o'clock one morning when sud-denly there came over my being a cool and rushing wind. It seemed I could hear the fluttering of the wings of a dove settling down upon my body. Instantly, there came from the very depths of my innermost being "the rivers of living water" that Jesus said "they that believe on Him should re-ceive."[17] Rivers of praise and glory began to flow from my lips as I gave vent to the unutterable gushings of my soul. I received in a measure what the disciples received on the Day of Pentecost. My experience was one like that on the Day of Pentecost with the Spirit of God filling and thrill-ing me even to the extent of using my tongue to speak in a language entirely new to me and one I had never learned. I shall never forget it! The hour was about two in the morn-ing but I was far from asleep; I was seemingly in the very presence of the Lord Himself, and His marvelous glory fairly thrilled my being. It was indeed good to be there.

A SPECIAL ABILITY COMES WITH THE SPIRIT BAPTISM

After receiving the baptism of the Holy Spirit, Dake found himself possessing a new and surprising ability. He was able to quote Bible verses—hundreds of them—without ever having memorized a single one! Later in life Dake wrote:

> At the end of three months of whole–hearted surrender of my life to God and seeking to be filled with the Holy Spirit, I received a great anointing of the Spirit in my life. I was immediately able to quote hundreds of Scriptures with-out memorizing them. I also noticed a quickening of my mind to know what chapters and books various verses were found in. Before conversion, I had not read one full chapter of the Bible. This new knowledge of Scripture was a gift to

---

[17] John 7:37-39.

me, for which I give God the praise. From the time of this special anointing until now, I have never had to memorize the thousands of Scriptures I use in teaching. I just quote a verse when I need it, by the anointing of the Spirit.

Throughout Dake's life he would describe this wonderful gift he had received. Like the writers of the Gospels filling in various and different details of the life of Christ, so another account of Dake's testimony concerning this rare gift will be helpful in understating just what God had wrought in his life. This is a portion of testimony taken from Dake's personal writings in 1949 which describes this gift in more detail:

What I know is solely of God by the anointing of the Holy Spirit. I take no credit for the things I am able to do. I give to God all the praise and humbly live in gratitude to Him for this ability He gave to me over thirty years ago. The fact is, I could quote Scripture from the very beginning under the anointing of the Holy Spirit, by the hour. On any Bible subject that would come to my mind, I could automatically quote Scriptures from all parts of the Bible on that doctrine.

It has become one of the great pleasures of my life to quote Scriptures as the Spirit moves me. Not only has the Spirit quickened me to quote Scriptures on various subjects, but it is also perfectly natural for me to know the books, chapters and verses where they are found.

> *"A person under the control of the Holy Spirit will be gentle, humble, honest, and open–minded to truth."*
>
> *Finis Dake*

The nearest approach I can make to illustrate this ability and operation of the Spirit in my life, is what took place on the Day of Pentecost, and on other occasions when men were baptized in the Spirit.

In the Bible it is plainly recorded that when the Holy Spirit came upon the early disciples, they began to speak in other languages as the Spirit gave them utterance; they began to speak in new languages that they had never learned and that they did not even understand.

31

My quoting Scripture was by divine anointing as the Spirit gave me utterance. The Scriptures were in my own language and similar to God speaking "by the mouth of all his holy prophets since the world began."[18]

When the Spirit gave me this gift, I had not read the Bible through one time. I do not recall ever reading one chapter of the Bible before my conversion. During the three months I was seeking the Holy Spirit, I read very little of the Bible, due to constantly seeking God in prayer. After the anointing of the Spirit, I began to read and study the Bible, but it mattered not whether I had read some Scriptures, they would roll out of me like rivers of living water. Naturally, the more I read and studied the Bible, the more I would retain of what I had read. Since then, Scriptures were brought to my remembrance, just as Jesus promised all disciples in John 14:26.

From the very beginning of my Spirit–filled life and after receiving this gift, I could quote from any and all parts of the Bible as I would yield to the Spirit. The whole Bible as I read it became literally simple and clear. It became just as clear in all its parts, as if I had known it all my life. It became as easy for me to understand and remember Scripture, as it was for me to understand and know my name, address and other details of my life. The Bible became a part of my mental and spiritual equipment, exactly like the divine gift of Knowledge given to Solomon. As a boy newly–converted, I could always help people finish quoting Scriptures they would forget and even tell them where they would be found. I interpreted so–called difficult passages in prophecy and other parts of the Bible to ministers and laymen alike, when they seemed to misunderstand some Scripture.

Dake often spoke of his gift as an impartation of the Spirit such as men and women received throughout Bible days. In 1954 he said:

---

[18] Acts 3:21.

The Holy Spirit came down upon my life and gave me the ability to quote Scripture something like the prophets of old—just out of my innermost being flowed Scripture after Scripture.

As the Spirit of God moved on his life he was empowered to answer Bible questions with a vast knowledge of the Scriptures at his command. One need only to look at his monumental *Dake Annotated Reference Bible* and it is easy to see, as you note all the Scripture references, that this had to have been a gift from God. What a blessing indeed!

MUCH STUDY WAS TO FOLLOW

A gift of knowledge of the Scriptures is one thing, putting it all together is another. The fact that Dake had hundreds, even thousands, of Scriptures at his command did not mean that he was an instant theologian. But this did give him a wonderful head start.

Each of us can only base our doctrine on what we know of God's Word. If we knew only one verse of Scripture, then our doctrine would be based on that one verse. Of course, knowing ten verses of Scripture would result in a more complete and thorough understanding of a particular doctrine. This was the case with Dake. Knowing so many Scriptures did not mean that he at once understood them all, but it did mean that, with his analytical mind, he was able to process a large number of Scriptures and formulate doctrine at a very early age.

Dake knew this and, just after receiving this "gift of Scriptures," as he called it, said:

"When we study God's Word, we hold a map stretching from eternity past to eternity future."

Finis Dake

I then began to study the Bible without ceasing, and spent hours digging into the wealth of its teachings. From the first of my studies, I found the Bible to be simple and clear. Daily study, coupled with my ability to quote the Bible as I yielded to the Spirit, helped me "rightly divide the word of truth" (2 Timothy 2:15). Difficult passages in prophecy and elsewhere did not seem mystifying to me, for what was unclear in one passage was made clear by other Scriptures on the same subject. Hours of study provided a rich storehouse to draw from as I yielded to the Spirit.

BACK TO MAKING A LIVING

After receiving the Holy Spirit baptism, Dake turned his attention to making a living in a new line of work. He secured a job as a crane man in a machine shop. Among the employees, Dake found that two of them were believers and had received the Holy Spirit just as he had. Needless to say, revival fires began to break out at the work place. First a draftsman, then a timekeeper and finally a machinist were saved and filled with the Spirit.

Every day at the noon hour, during lunch, they held a Bible study in the timekeeper's office. With Dake's baptism had come a mighty gift. He used his newly–found knowledge of the Scriptures to teach and share with all who would listen, which was sometimes quite difficult, seeing that he was still just a lad of seventeen. Notwithstanding his age, however, many of the workers were amazed at the knowledge of the Scriptures he possessed, as they heard him freely quote from nearly any section of the Bible. Dake also proved to be a real student of the Word. During this time, though he had never really read or studied the Scriptures in the past, Dake found that he had an intense desire to know the God of the Bible, whose words had been implanted into his soul. He later wrote:

> The Bible became my constant companion. I took it daily to work with me and every spare moment was spent in reading and studying its pages.

He made a special study of prophecy during this time, which was to become a hallmark of his ministry for the rest of his life. This was a grand time for Dake; he later recalled:

> They were happy days while working with God's Holy book by my side and I was contented and satisfied because Jesus dwelt in my heart.

Not only was Dake a dedicated young man now, but rather than selling off his father's clothing to go to the movies, as he had done as a child, he was now giving his weekly earnings from the machine shop to his mother to help pay her expenses. Yes, Jesus had really made a change in this young man's life, and he was starting out in a walk of obedience to the Word of God. "Let him that stole steal no more: but rather let him labour, working with his hands the thing which is good, that he may have to give to him that needeth." *Ephesians 4:28*

The work in the machine shop lasted only a short time, however. The machine shop went out of business and Dake was out of work once again. At this time, Dake began to feel the call to the Gospel ministry. His father had taught him at a young age the value of hard work and discipline. He was offered an opportunity to go into fulltime ministry with another young minister, but decided that he needed preparation before launching out into such a weighty task for the Lord. He had spent the last year earning a living, conducting Bible studies, seeking and waiting on God, but now he had come to the conclusion that God's will for him was that he should attend Bible college.

> *"The study of the Bible is one of the best ways to help God's work."*
>
> *Finis Dake*

Even from this early age, Dake knew the challenges he would face. A gift from God was wonderful. But not everyone would accept this young man who was quoting all these Scriptures. Dake thought about it like this:

> Being young and likely to be unaccepted in the ministerial realm from the mere fact that I was young, I decided at the age of eighteen to enroll in a Bible institute to prepare for the ministry.

So off to Bible school he would go . . .

35

CHAPTER FOUR

THE BIBLE SCHOOL YEARS

OFF TO HIS FIRST YEAR OF BIBLE SCHOOL

While he began making plans to go to Bible school, Dake met another young man by the name of Otto Iverson, who also lived in Tulsa, Oklahoma. Brother Otto had also planned to enter Bible school. Dake borrowed what money he could and, with what he already had amassed, he had the grand sum of $50.00.[19] He used this money to purchase an extra pair of trousers—not cowboy clothing this time, but dress pants. The cowboy in Dake was dead and, in his place, a man of the Word had come alive. He packed up his few belongings and headed for California. Not knowing what lay ahead, he and Brother Otto were on their way in Brother Otto's Ford Model T, to give their all to the Lord in Gospel ministry. Their destination? Glad Tidings Bible Institute in San Francisco, California, over 1,600 miles away. At the time, the institute was being run by Brother R. J. Craig.

"Being a young man of at least ordinary ability and intelligence, I knew what the Bible said on many points and withstood the professors."

Finis Dake

DAKE RECEIVES A VISITATION

About 1,100 miles into their journey, the two stopped in Salt Lake City, Utah, where a Full Gospel tent meeting was in progress. At the leading of the Lord and seeing the need of these two young travelers, the preacher in charge of the meeting offered them his living tent to sleep in. Needless to say, they gladly accepted and retired for a much–needed night of sleep.

The two boys were sound asleep when something strange happened in the night. It wasn't a visitation of the Lord, but a visitation from a robber! A thief came in the night and took what was left of Dake's $50.00 and the new trousers he had purchased, and left his wallet lying empty in the sawdust shavings just outside the tent.

When Dake awoke the next morning he found himself penniless and absent one new pair of trousers. Now, all that he had left was one old summer suit, one extra pair of old trousers and an old coat. Undaunted,

---

[19] Or about $547.00 in year 2005 dollars.

he was determined to make it the rest of the way to San Francisco, which was now over 700 miles away. He was going to Bible school!

Lessons in Humility

During this time, Dake would have surely had to go back home, had it not been for Brother Iverson loaning him money until school started, at which time he could get work. This was not easy however, for the proud young Dake who had started out life in a very prosperous family. He recalled:

> On one occasion, I felt so ashamed for having had to borrow so often that I went three days without food. Upon Brother Iverson's discovery of this fact, he proceeded to give me $5.00[20] and I sat down to an inviting meal.

In the past Dake had been a very proud cowboy, sporting his sparkling cowboy attire and trusting in his six–shooter. Now, however, it seemed as though he was learning two very valuable lessons at one time—a lesson in humility and a lesson in trusting God!

Dake arrived in San Francisco in the fall of 1921, about two weeks before the fall semester was to begin. Glad Tidings Bible Institute was really a blessed school in those early days of the Pentecostal revival with its six–story concrete building and its 2,500 seat auditorium.

Glad Tidings Bible Institute

During the next two weeks, Dake arranged to attend classes and found what work he could. Arriving in very poor circumstances, as cold weather set in, the school must have had compassion on Dake as they saw him in his very meager circumstances. Dake said:

---

[20] Or about $54.00 in year 2005 dollars.

My shoes were ragged, I had no overcoat for the cold weather and no warm winter suit. For several weeks I was obliged to stand around chilling in my summer Mohair suit, but I could not, and would not, give up. As colder weather came on, money was again advanced by my companion from Tulsa and I purchased a winter suit for $20.00.[21]

Dake Enters The News Business Once Again

In an attempt not to become totally destitute, Dake acquired his first job in San Francisco. The job was not one that was unfamiliar to him, however, for as a 12 year–old he had had the same job! Dake was once again in the paper business. He joined ranks with the much younger children and became a San Francisco paperboy, delivering to the downtown business section. This proved to be yet another humbling experience. Dake recalled:

To me it was quite humiliating as a grown man to carry the papers around like a little newsboy, but I threw back my shoulders and performed my duties until after Christmas.

A New Line Of Work On His Knees

The next job Dake acquired was that of cleaning a barber shop. Each Monday morning he and another student would make their way to the "hair trimming parlor." Once there, they would sweep the floor and then get down on their knees and scrub the floor, woodwork, and bottom of the chairs. Then they cleaned the mirrors, the front windows and took turns cleaning the red and white barber pole. For this work they were paid $2.00 each.[22]

Many think of Bible college as a time for Bible study and prayer. But men and women pay the price to earn their degrees, and Dake was no exception. While he was much more fond of being on his knees in prayer than scrubbing the floor, the bills had to be paid, and eating was a necessary fact of life.

---

[21] Or about $219.00 in year 2005 dollars.
[22] Or about $22.00 in year 2005 dollars.

DAKE ATTEMPTS A CLEAN SWEEP

In an effort to help students earn their way through college, many companies offered sales opportunities to diligent students. A broom manufacturer had just introduced a new broom into the market and sought out several of the students from Glad Tidings Bible Institute to help with door–to–door sales. Indeed, Dake was first in line to sell this new broom. The students began to canvas the city block by block and house by house. Much like today, in 1921 not many people were interested in hearing from door–to–door salesmen. Dake became discouraged rather quickly. He recalled:

> My success was not much, for most of the doors said "no peddlers allowed," and others would not even answer when I knocked.

Even though the part–time jobs did bring in some money, it took all of it for Dake simply to have a place to live and food to eat. But there was also Bible college tuition to consider, and books and other expenses to be paid. In a great blessing that was much needed at the time, a little money came in from his brother. This was enough to pay for his books and buy a decent pair of shoes. It may not have seemed like much, but to a young man with virtually nothing, it was heaven sent. After completing the first school year, with all the odd jobs he could handle and stretching every dollar as far as it would go, Dake ended up with a $200.00[23] debt for his first year in Bible school.

PROBLEMS WITH DOCTRINE

While Dake enjoyed his first year in Bible school and truly learned much about God and His Word, he still faced problems with contradictions between what he was being taught and what the Bible actually said. Dake had difficulties with one doctrine in particular. He understood the Bible to teach that God has form—that He has a spirit body. This was something the professors at Glad Tidings strongly rejected. Dake gives an account of his memories concerning this situation:

> When I went to a Bible Institute as a young man, out on the west coast, they taught me that God was an invisible noth-

---

[23] Or about $2,190.00 in year 2005 dollars.

ingness;[24] that God was just as invisible and nothing as the light, as far as tangibleness was concerned. They pictured God as being an invisible something, floating around in nowhere; that he did not have a spirit body with bodily parts.

I brought to them many of the Scriptures about God's bodily parts[25] and they explained them this way: "That's a mere human expression trying to convey some idea of God." I argued back at them: "What kind of a human expression could it be or what kind of an idea does it convey about God—that he *doesn't* have these bodily parts, or that he *does*?" "Oh," they said, "God is a spirit." They did have the knowledge of that one thing about God; that God was a Spirit.[26] But they refused to recognize all these many hundreds of other Scriptures, describing God's spirit body as being real, having bodily parts like a human being.[27]

> *"I argued that if the Bible is God's Word in human language, then it means exactly what it says. Then no Bible teacher or minister or layman has any right to change one word of it."*
>
> *Finis Dake*

So I said to them: "Is that the way you would tell me you didn't have hands? To talk about your hands? What you did with your hands? What you can do with your hands? What you're going to do with your hands? You're really trying to get across to me you didn't have any such things?" They said: "Oh no, that isn't the way we would say it."

So, I asked: "How would you say it?" They said: "If I didn't have hands I would tell you right out, I do not have hands." I said: "If God had ever said that one

[24] See *God's Plan For Man*, Page 51 where Dake discusses *"The Invisibility of God."*

[25] See *God's Plan For Man*, Page 56 where Dake discusses *"God has a spirit body with bodily parts like a man."*

[26] See *God's Plan For Man*, Page 52 where Dake discusses *"True interpretation of God as Spirit, John 4:24."*

[27] See the notes on John 4:24 in the *Dake Annotated Reference Bible* for a discussion of God's spirit body.

time in the Bible that He didn't have hands, He didn't have feet, He didn't have hair, He didn't have a body, He couldn't wear clothes, He couldn't sit on a seat, He couldn't walk, He couldn't talk, He couldn't see, He couldn't hear; if the Bible ever said one thing like that about God, then that would be sufficient. I would take all these so–called 'human expressions' as being figurative language about God."

"Any interpretation that is the least bit out of harmony with that which is written must be rejected as being the theories of men and not the truth of the Word of God."

Finis Dake

But I have learned that all figurative language expresses literal truth, just like the figures themselves. In other words, figures of speech convey real ideas, not unrealities. So, when we read in the Bible of God having a body of bodily parts,[28] of soul passions,[29] and that He goes from place to place,[30] He eats food,[31] He wears clothes,[32] He rests,[33] He dwells in a mansion[34] and lives in heaven,[35] He sits on a throne,[36] He walks[37] and rides on chariots[38] and on clouds[39] and He does other real things, then what is wrong in believing in the reality of a God of this nature? Why do we have to question Him every time He says anything about Himself? Why not believe everything just like we read it in the Bible?

---

[28] Daniel 10:5-19
[29] Hebrews 10:38
[30] Genesis 11:5
[31] Genesis 18:1-8
[32] Daniel 7:9-14
[33] Hebrews 4:4
[34] John 14:1-3
[35] Revelation 21
[36] Isaiah 6
[37] Genesis 3:8
[38] Psalms 68:17
[39] Isaiah 19:1

Decisions That Last a Lifetime

Dake faced decisions in reconciling what he knew the Scriptures said, against some of what he was being taught. He expressed it in these words:

I soon learned that one must either believe what the Bible alone teaches, or spend his life wrestling with the confusion and varied interpretations of men. One teaching was that there was not a Jew in the body of Jesus Christ— that the Church was made up exclusively of Gentiles. The professor quoted Acts 15:13. That professor would even take us to his room sometimes and cry like a crocodile and beg us to accept this. We did not.

> *"I soon learned that one must either believe what the Bible teaches, or believe the many and varied interpretations of men."*
>
> *Finis Dake*

The professors did not agree among themselves on some of the basic truths, and a number of them even disagreed with what the Bible itself plainly stated on certain subjects. I became acquainted with the perplexing array of doctrines set forth by present–day leaders of Christianity. Some of it was in agreement with Scripture, as could be proved when all passages dealing with the subject were brought together and examined. But much turned out to be hand–me–down theology of a former generation of preachers, many of whom were great—not *because of* their doctrinal errors—but *in spite of* their doctrinal errors.

Dake reasoned that he had a decision to make:

Should I go along with the crowd, winning its applause by accepting all it taught, including the uncontested and unchallenged doctrines of former leaders, whom even I admired because of their zeal? God has given me a gift. Should I respect and depend upon God and the knowledge of the Word of God He has given?

A decision was made:

My decision was clean–cut and firm, and was expressed in a promise I made to God. I vowed to my Lord never to teach one thing in private or in public that I could not prove by the Bible, giving two or three plain Scriptures as required in 2 Corinthians 13:1, realizing also that "no prophecy of the Scripture is of any private interpretation" (2 Peter 1:20). I further resolved not to change or attempt to change what the Scripture plainly says. I reasoned that if the Bible is God's Word in human language, then it means exactly what it says and no teacher, minister or layman has a right to change one word of it. I concluded that any interpretation which is the least bit out of harmony with what is plainly written must be rejected as the theory of man and not the truth of God.

1922

Central Bible Institute starts in the basement of Central Assembly of God in Springfield, Missouri.

So with that firm commitment of a lad of only eighteen years of age, Dake established one of his core values that would remain with him for the rest of his life and ministry.

Looking back, one might ask: "For a young man who had such a wonderful gift of the knowledge of the Scriptures, was it worth it to go to Bible college?" Dake felt it was. He knew the Scriptures and their locations, but the application of them and the doctrines they taught all came by diligent study. In regard to the value of Bible college and the hardships that are sometimes encountered, Dake later wrote:

> The trials had been severe and numerous but the knowledge I gained of God's Word was enough to pay me for every effort put forth.

The first year of Bible college was filled with study, meditation and searching the Scriptures. For Dake, this was the delight of his life and would prove to be a lifestyle that he would continue throughout his entire ministry.

At Glad Tidings Bible Institute it was not all study, however. As the name implies, they sought to give the students on–the–job training and practical application of what they were learning. The school felt that practical ministry was vital to the education of young ministers. For this reason, as a part of the training, the students would hold street meetings every day in the slum district of San Francisco. Every Saturday night a meeting was held in China Town. What a sight that would have been to behold—the young Dake, with his middle America, country Missouri accent, ministering to a predominately Chinese speaking audience. These experiences in ministry were valuable to Dake who later wrote:

> Thus, I learned to come to handle the Word and gained many a profitable experience along the lines of personal work.

It was during this time that Dake compiled many of his notes for ministering to the lost, as found in the Dake Bible.[40]

SCHOOL IS OUT FOR SUMMER

After a year full of study, work and little sleep, the end of the first year finally came and school let out for the summer of 1922. During the summer months Dake spent his time roaming around the school campus and was blessed to find work as a janitor in a large department store. The pay he received allowed him to pay off a few of his smaller debts and buy some desperately needed clothing.

Though most of the jobs Dake held during this time were low paying and, really, the only jobs that struggling students like himself might accept, he did them the best that he could and always managed to keep a good attitude about his work. This kind of work ethic, taught to him by his father at a very early age, is one that management and owners appreciate. Dake wrote:

"There can be no excuse for misunderstanding the Bible concerning anything it says."

Finis Dake

> One day the General Manager met me on the elevator and, being impressed with the courtesy I showed him, asked me what position I held in the store. He then invited me to his office for a more formal interview. In his office he revealed a desire to take me into his sales department and give me training along that line.

---

[40] See *Dake's Annotated Reference Bible*, Dake Publishing, Inc. Lawrenceville: Georgia, 1963, page 943 of the Standard Edition, for *A Guide For Personal Work.*

For a young man who had very little and often wondered where his next day's meals would come from, this could have proved to be a very tempting opportunity. Dake said:

> For a few days I considered it, but the desire to go through Bible School and equip myself for God's service continued to hold me. I was obliged to give the manager my thanks, but no thanks.

A LETTER OF HOPE

It was about that time that a letter came from his brother John, who was living back in Springfield. The letter spoke of the possibility of a new school being located there and, if such came to fruition, Dake's brother would be glad to help him attend. Dake began to pray for the school's success as his hopes mounted high. The burden of a place to live and food to eat would be lifted if the school opened in Springfield, for not only did his brother John live there, but so did his brother Arthur. While he would surely help with the expenses of the family where he would be staying, the amount of money needed would be very small compared to the financial burden he was now carrying.[41]

"The Bible is the most simple book in the world to understand."

Finis Dake

It was just a few weeks later that a second letter came, informing Dake that a decision had been made and it was official—Central Bible Institute would be located in Springfield, Missouri. Upon receiving this joyful word, Dake borrowed enough money to cover the expenses for the 2,000 mile journey back to Springfield. The young man who had originally come with him to Glad Tidings also decided to go as well, thus he and Brother Iverson were on their way back home.

THE SECOND YEAR OF BIBLE SCHOOL—WHAT A BLESSING

Upon arriving in Springfield in late summer of 1922, Dake's brother Arthur fulfilled his promise of financial help. He paid the necessary reg-

---

[41] Author's note: Bible college is a great challenge for many. When we as family and friends, can give aid and help, it is such a blessing to those in need, and God will surely reward us for doing so.

istration fee and gave him room and board in his home free of charge. At last, a bit of financial relief had come Dake's way. He was able to devote himself entirely to study and prayer as he sought the Lord through dedicated Bible studies.

Central Bible Institute

Needless to say, his second year of Bible college (his first year at Central Bible Institute) proved to be another valuable time in the study of God's Word. At this time, the school was under the dedicated and faithful supervision of Brother D. W. Nerr and Brother Willard Pierce.

After two years of Bible college in the summer of 1923, Dake was in debt about $300.00[42], which included the balance due on his return trip from California. The job Dake acquired this summer was different than that of the summer before. This time, he found a job doing something he had been trained to do and was very good at—operating a crane. He had located a job in Granite City, Illinois, which was about 225 miles northeast and just outside of St Louis. He definitely saw this job as a gift from God. He recalled:

> God supplied my needs in a wonderful way. He honored
> my determination to go through school at any cost, gave

---

[42] Or about $3,228.00 in year 2005 dollars.

me work as a crane man with a firm in Granite City, Illinois, where I received $5.00 a day.[43] Meals were provided and I was allowed to stay in the home of a brother and sister of the Lord, free of charge! I was able to pay off all of my debts and even save enough to go through the next school year, thanks to the fact that room and board was again supplied by my brother.

THE THIRD YEAR OF BIBLE SCHOOL AND A NEW BUILDING

Until this time, the students at Central Bible Institute roomed in private homes, and classes were held in the basement of a church. But sometime during the previous year, work had begun on the building that was to house Central Bible Institute, and Dake's brother (who learned the trade from his father) took charge of some of the work. The building was completed and ready for occupancy in time for Dake to begin his third year of Bible school training in the fall of 1923.

After his third year of schooling, under Brother Frank M. Boyd, Dake again returned to Granite City, Illinois, and worked for the same firm as the last summer, saving what he could for his upcoming fourth year of Bible school. Again, sacrifice and commitment was the rule of the day.

During that time I made every possible sacrifice, often making a meal of a can of pork and beans with a loaf of bread or of cornbread and milk, for economy's sake. The battle was too near the end to give up.

DAKE BEGINS MINISTRY AS AN EVANGELIST

It was also during this summer of 1924 that the conviction to minister God's Word became the strongest that he had ever felt. While he was working daily operating the crane, his friend, Brother Iverson, stopped by to pay him a visit. Brother Iverson was on his way northeast to Ohio, about 500 miles away, to a revival that was being conducted by E. F. Cunningham, the evangelist under whose ministry both of them had been converted. Dake did not have the luxury of quitting work, but did manage to take the weekend off in order to accompany Brother Iverson on the trip.

---

[43] Or about $54.00 per day in year 2005 dollars.

During this meeting Dake was stirred more than ever to be in full–time ministry for the Lord. He recalled:

> Being in the gospel services with Brother E. F. Cunningham was just enough to revive the fires in my soul and put the finishing touch to my conviction of God's call. I began to pray for God to close the door of opportunity He had opened for me in the work as a crane man, should it be His will, and started home with a heart that was happy and free.

God honored Dake's prayer and his commitment to the ministry of the gospel, for when he arrived back at the job, the manager under whom he worked informed him that the slow season had forced the company to discharge five crane men. Dake was one of the five. This was an answer to his prayer and, with a light heart, he went back to help Brother E. F. Cunningham for a few days more with his Ohio campaign. From there he headed for Chicago, along with his traveling companion and friend, Brother Iverson.

"Prayer is seeking help from God in matters that are beyond our power."

Finis Dake

Prior to this time, Dake had been in correspondence with the saints in Joliet, Illinois, who wanted a pastor for their church. So, after a short visit to Chicago with Brother Iverson, he headed South to Joliet, about 50 miles away. With the church in Joliet, Dake began a revival. During the first service he found only about eight people in attendance. For several nights following, the same little crowd came—until Sunday, when attendance increased slightly. Dake was asked to continue the meetings another week and was then asked to stay for a third week. Believing this to be God's will, he agreed. During this time the crowds grew considerably. People were eager to hear this young man of only twenty–one, who it seemed could quote the whole Bible from cover to cover.

EVANGELIST DAKE BECOMES PASTOR DAKE

A church vote led to the election of Dake as their pastor. He was to receive the sum of $20.00[44] per week, with free room and board. After accepting this call, he launched a revival campaign. He followed the revival

---

[44] Or about $215.00 in year 2005 dollars.

with two weeks of nightly Bible teaching, later to become the hallmark of his ministry.

Though the church in Joliet was still small, Dake saw this as an excellent start, one which presented a great opportunity for a young minister such as himself. He was faced with the option of remaining as the full–time pastor of the Joliet church, rather than returning for his fourth and final year of Bible college in Springfield. He lamented:

> For a while I thought I would not return to school to graduate, since God was so blessing my efforts in His active service, but an encouraging letter from Brother Boyd, who was over the school, caused me to change my mind.

After prayer and seeking the Lord on this matter, he determined that it was God's will for him to finish the course he had started over three years ago. He decided he would return and finish his Bible college education.

He left the work in Joliet to the charge of a young man who was to keep things going until the spring. At that time, according to the wishes of the people, he would return and resume his pastoral ministry.

RAISING MONEY FOR THE LAST YEAR OF BIBLE COLLEGE

The church at Joliet was still in its infancy, and the pay he had received was just enough to get by. Needless to say, there was a great need for tuition for his fourth year in Bible college. Once again God was faithful.

The church, though having very little, did their part. On the afternoon of his departure the congregation gave him an offering of $85.00.[45] He gratefully accepted this loving gift and applied it to his school fund. However, more was still needed. To raise the necessary funds, he sold everything that was not absolutely essential, including his raincoat, overcoat, suits, Bibles, books, calendars, galoshes, cook aprons, and of course, his collection of religious books of all kinds.

It was a difficult time for Dake, living through those early days of Bible college, but not unlike most students of his day. Pentecostal schools, institutes, and colleges were all very new and in their infancy. Most of them involved sacrifices from everyone, students and professors alike.

---

[45] Or about $915.00 in year 2005 dollars.

Nothing in the way of government grants or loans were available as they are today. Most of the Pentecostal denominations were doing all they could to just keep the churches going. Besides this, in some Pentecostal circles, Bible colleges were not well received. Some believed that the anointing and gifting of the Spirit was all that the Christian worker needed. This was not Dake's view, however. While he believed strongly in the empowerment of the Spirit and had experienced the same in his own life, he always regarded biblical knowledge and study as a top priority for all Christians. Later in life he would present his monumental work, the *Dake's Annotated Reference Bible,* to the world, and in the preface he would admonish its readers with a verse which would be the most quoted of his entire life: "Study to shew thyself approved unto God, a workman that needeth not to be ashamed, rightly dividing the word of truth" (2 Timothy 2:15). In regard to his financial difficulties he wrote:

> *"Unwavering faith is faith taking God at His Word without question."*
>
> Finis Dake

> I had become accustomed to financial struggles by this time, so I tried to put forth an extra effort in order to make the goal. Indeed, the benefits received were worth it. Besides the wonderful store of knowledge gained during those years in the classroom, there was many an interesting experience on the outside in doing practical work.

THE LAST YEAR OF BIBLE SCHOOL IS FILLED WITH MINISTRY

After traveling the 500 miles to Springfield, Dake started back to college in the fall of 1924. During this fourth and last year he managed to continue to minister. For a short time he served as a pastor in Miller, Missouri, which was about 30 miles away. In Miller, he preached three times every Sunday. On Monday nights, after traveling back to Springfield, he accepted the invitation to preach in a black church. He and the congregation hit it off so well that this meeting turned into a weekly Bible study and lasted throughout his entire fourth year of Bible college. Mixed congregations were rare in those days of segregation, and while there was not a lot of fellowship between whites and blacks in the church world in general, Dake did not allow this to stop him from fellowshipping with and ministering to his black brothers and sisters in the Lord.

This last year of schooling was a year filled with ministry. Dake preached in schoolhouses, on street corners and anywhere else that an opportunity presented itself. No doubt this early experience proved to be a great help in ministry after his departure from Bible school.

THE CLOSING WEEK AT CENTRAL BIBLE INSTITUTE

For Dake, the closing days of Central Bible Institute were precious days indeed. He had faithfully finished his course of study and would be off to do his best for his Lord. With a sense of sadness he would leave his many new–found friends, but with a sense of mission he would go out into the world to do something for God. Exactly what he was going to do he didn't quite yet know, but was sure that God would lead him.

Just a few days before the closing of the school year and the first graduation class, the faculty surprised the students by giving them a picnic. The entire graduation class hiked to a beautiful park about two miles away. They enjoyed the afternoon together and were then served supper at 5:00 o'clock. They were back with plenty of time to prepare for the next day of classes.

On Saturday, May 16, 1925, the students packed up their belongings in preparation for leaving on the Tuesday following. They placed their trunks in the halls, leaving their rooms almost empty, making it convenient for the thorough cleaning they were to give every room. The standard and tried motto: "leave it as clean as you found it," was strictly observed, as the students faithfully and respectfully cleaned their rooms, making them a welcoming site for the future students who would take their place in their beloved school of learning.

In the evening, the students gathered in the west dining room and held their last fellowship meeting. There they gave testimonies of how their lives had changed as a result of attending Central Bible Institute. With great appreciation for the dedication of the faculty, the graduating class, led by Brother Myer Pearlman,[46] presented the school with a beautiful

---

[46] Pearlman, Myer (1898–1943) Educator and author. Born in Edinburgh, Scotland, a Jew, who immigrated to New York City in 1915. After converting to Christianity and receiving the baptism in the Spirit in San Francisco, he moved to Springfield, graduating from Central Bible Institute in 1925, where he became a part of the faculty. Best known for his work, *Knowing the Doctrines of the Bible*, (1937). (*Dictionary of Pentecostal and Charismatic Movements*, published by Zondervan Publishing House, 1988.)

picture of *Christ and the Rich Young Ruler.* The evening was adjourned
with all the students joining hands and embracing one another singing:
Blest Be the Tie:[47]

> Blest be the tie that binds
> Our hearts in Christian love;
> The fellowship of kindred minds
> Is like to that above.
>
> Before our Father's throne
> We pour our ardent pray'rs;
> Our fears, our hopes, our aims, are one,
> Our comforts and our cares.
>
> We share our mutual woes,
> Our mutual burdens bear;
> And often for each other flows
> The sympathizing tear.
>
> When we asunder part,
> It gives us inward pain;
> But we shall still be joined in heart,
> And hope to meet again.
>
> This glorious hope revives
> Our courage on the way;
> That we shall live in perfect love
> In God's eternal day.
>
> From sorrow, toil, and pain,
> And sin we shall be free:
> And perfect love and friendship reign
> Through all eternity.

GRADUATION DAY ARRIVES

After four years of hard work, diligent Bible study and practical ministry, the time finally came for the first graduating class of the Central
Bible Institute to receive their diplomas. It was Monday, May 18, 1925.

---

[47] *Blest Be The Tie* hymn written by: *John Fawcett, 1782 (1740–1817)*

Dake and the other students had spent most of three years together in the study of the greatest book in the world, the Bible itself.

For the graduating exercises, three speakers were selected. Meyer Pearlman, a converted Jew, spoke on the subject, *Israel the Everlasting People*. After graduation he was privileged to join the faculty of Central Bible Institute. Mrs. Arthur Wilson, later sent as a missionary to the French Sudan, West Africa, spoke on *Unafraid*, which was a missionary challenge to the graduating class. Then, of course, Dake himself spoke. His theme was the *Second Coming of Jesus Christ*, a subject that, over the years, would be one of his favorite and most often preached messages.

Finis Jennings Dake, Central Bible Institute

The written copy of Dake's sermon was over 4,200 words long and was included in *The Pentecostal Evangel;* the official organ of the Assemblies of God.[48] At 23 years of age, Dake put together a classic doctrinal statement on the Second Coming. One of his first written works, it carries a great deal of weight, and is a look forward at this young man's theology during the first part of his ministry. For that reason, it is included in it's entirety in Appendix Twelve.

The time finally came for which all the students had been studying, praying and waiting—the presentation of the diplomas. In all, fourteen students received their diplomas in that first graduating class of Central Bible Institute. Among them, standing humbly, yet head and shoulders above them all, was Finis Jennings Dake, the little boy who wanted to be a cowboy!

---

[48] *The Pentecostal Evangel, A Family and Missionary Paper:* Number 602, June 20, 1925, page 5. A Special thanks goes out to the Assembly of God archive for a copy of this historic document, as well as other issues used throughout this work.

You Won't Leave Here Like You Came

The speeches were made, the exercises were over, the diplomas distributed, and the trials of Bible school life were over and gone. Dake had truly come a long way in the last four years. Later in life he recalled:

> I had started to school without shoes, overcoat, money or a good suit, but I pressed into the battle four years, came out with shoes, suit, a few pennies in my pocket, free from debt and with a knowledge of God's Word I can never forget. The only real difficulty facing me was that of securing enough funds to get away from school on, and I did that by selling my overcoat for $15.00.[49]

---

[49] Or about $158.00 in year 2005 dollars.

CHAPTER FIVE

HER NAME WAS DOROTHY

DOROTHY IS BORN

On Friday, April 10, 1903, Dorothy Virginia Dobbins was born on 15th and Moffatt Avenue, in the mid–western town of Joplin, Missouri, to the proud parents of Neel (7/25/1874–1/1/1951) and Hattie May Dobbins (10/31/1879–8/23/1960). Dorothy was the oldest of four children: Pauline (3/5/1906), Neel (4/4/1910), and Jonathon (3/5/1912). At her birth Dorothy . . .

> became the pride and joy of the whole family—a beautiful baby she was and above average intelligence. Her light brown, almost blonde hair was never cut and at age twenty–two months hung in ringlets down to her shoulders.[50]

A SIMPLE LIFE

Dorothy's household was a simple midwestern family. Her father, Neel, worked hard as a concrete finisher and bricklayer, and her mother, Hattie May, was a homemaker, taking care of the family and the home. Maybe a little old fashioned today, but in the 1900's this represented the average home. The Dobbins family was a close and happy family. Both parents were healthy, strong and at ease about showing affection to all their children. Hattie May was of average height, a little on the plump side, with long, thick, chestnut–brown hair and bluish–gray eyes. Neel (whom Dorothy always called "Papa") was all muscle, a little under average height, with brown eyes and black hair. In the evenings, Dorothy and her sister would sit in their dad's lap and take turns combing his hair,

1902

First congregation of the Church of God formed at Camp Creek, North Carolina.

---

[50] McAfee, Pauline. *One Life to Live Forever*. An undated life story written by Dorothy's sister, which as of yet, remains unpublished. Most of the early childhood information concerning Dorothy and her family was gleened from this work. The author extends heartfelt thanks and appreciation for this wonderful account of a precious and godly family.

all the while Dad was trying to read the evening paper. Yes, an average family indeed!

As a child, Dorothy and her sister would go to the nearby bakery and stand in line on certain days of the week to buy "day old" cookies. Pauline remembers:

> Never has anything tasted as good as those brown "Mama" cookies we carried back in the cloth flour bag we kept just for that purpose.

Sometimes Dorothy would go next door to the Bentleys to "touch" their new automobile, or perhaps squeeze the rubber bulb that honked the horn. And on one occasion, the Bentleys even took Dorothy for a ride!

BAPTIST AND METHODIST COME TOGETHER

Spiritually, however, the family was divided. Neel was a Methodist, attending his family church—Byers Avenue Methodist. Hattie May now attended a Full Gospel church. Earlier in her Christian walk she had been Baptist, but when the outpouring of the Holy Spirit had come to Joplin, Hattie May's father was the first person in town to receive the experience. It was quite natural that when a little Full Gospel Mission opened (which was later to become an Assembly of God), she was one of the first persons to associate with this new movement.

Hattie May had been open to the fulness of the Spirit for a long time now. When Dorothy was just a little baby, Hattie May tells of how she made the trip to Topeka, Kansas, and wheeled Dorothy in a baby buggy up to a Gospel tent for one of the first Full Gospel meetings in the nation. In fact, it was in this meeting that she came to accept Jesus as her Lord and Saviour. The meeting was conducted by none other than Charles Parham, a famous leader at the time, and the individual whom some credit with founding the Pentecostal movement in America in the early 1900's.

DOROTHY LEADS THE WAY

From an early age Dorothy showed strong leadership abilities. Her sister Pauline remembers:

> When I was about five and Dorothy eight, mother got us dolls alike and dressed mine in pink and Dorothy's in blue. When mother put us to bed on Christmas Eve she told us

our dolls would be on the kitchen table in the morning. Do you think we slept with such knowledge in our heads? At about midnight when we thought our parents were asleep, Dorothy got up, got me up, took my hand and said: "Come, let's go see our presents." A thing I would never have dreamed of doing on my own. So the pattern was set—if my sister said it was alright, it was, and I did it!

Even in these early years, we see the development of the strength and leadership which Dorothy possessed—character traits that would make her an indispensable part of the husband–and–wife team that were later to create *Dake's Annotated Reference Bible*.

Six years of age is an exciting time for a little girl. After all, what little girl wouldn't enjoy spending her days pushing her baby carriage around with her favorite kitten dressed in baby clothes! But alas, at six years of age, public school also becomes part of a child's life. The shock of school was lessened a little by the fact that Mrs. Belva Lett, Dorothy's first grade teacher, was also the sister of her aunt. Dorothy would prove to be a capable student. In fact, although her first day in school had begun, it was really the first day of a lifetime of education; both for herself and for everyone she would meet.

1906

"Azusa Street revival begins in Los Angeles under William J. Seymour."

DISAPPOINTMENT IN NEW MEXICO

In 1913, when Dorothy was ten years old, her father Neel made a difficult decision. Times were hard for his family of six, and his meager income as a concrete finisher was not enough to support them as he felt he should. To Dorothy's surprise and dismay, he packed up his family, sold their home, and moved to New Mexico.

In New Mexico, Neel laid stake to a "claim" and planted a crop of pinto beans. Their home wasn't much: only a one–room house with one bed, a three–burner oil stove, and a water bucket, which in order to be filled had to be carried from the neighbor's well. The house was snake infested, the nearest school was over ten miles away and, to Hattie May, this was not working out. So, less than three months after they arrived in New Mexico, they packed up and went back to Joplin, Missouri.

Somehow, though the family had only been away for three months, times were better when they returned to Joplin. Neel was able to purchase some land and began building their new four–room house. Dorothy and her family loved their new home, even though there was no electricity and water had to be carried from about a block away. But the cold winters would be bearable as the family kept warm by a coal stove set up in the living room. With all these hardships faced and then overcome, the children could once again continue their education. That year Dorothy enrolled in Emerson School, about a mile away from their new home.

Back To School

The years passed quickly and Dorothy grew up to be a beautiful and intelligent young woman. She was always an industrious soul, quick and eager to learn, and always willing to use her gifts for the good of others.

Dorothy Dobbins

At the young age of seventeen she felt the desire to help those in need. Her deeply–felt compassion may have had its roots in a sickness she had suffered earlier in her life. After coming home sick from school one day, it was diagnosed that she had smallpox—a serious, contagious, and sometimes fatal infectious disease. She wasn't alone; her father and five other members of the family also contracted the disease. Thanks to the graciousness of the Lord and a praying mother, they all survived.

In 1921, not quite knowing the direction her life would take, she enrolled in, and completed, a course in *Home Hygiene and Care of the Sick,* which was taught by the American Red Cross. True to form, she was always reaching out to help others, and usually this help involved some type of "take charge" role.

On June 17, 1921, Dorothy finished her high school education at Joplin High School. Dorothy was involved in a great many activities during her high school years. She was a member of both the Glee Club and the Hi Club. The Hi Club was a club sponsored by the YWCA and was the largest and most active organization for girls in the high school. It is interesting to note that Dorothy's favorite saying, as quoted in her high school yearbook, was: "Anything for a quiet life." One has to wonder if Dorothy had any idea that her "quiet life" would be a dream that only heaven could fulfill, for soon she was to start on a wonderful journey for the Lord that would be anything but quiet!

HER FIRST PAYING JOB

After graduation, Dorothy was hired by Mr. Edgar Wallower as his private secretary. Edgar Wallower was the president of a mining company in Oklahoma. This, Dorothy's first job, paid $100.00 per month.[51] With this salary, she began to help out around the house with a number of home improvements. Soon there was a new carpet for the living room, a record player, and a number of other items that Dorothy gladly purchased for her parents. With a generous heart, Dorothy did not leave out her brothers and sister. She decided that this family, now that a little money was available, was going to move into the world of music. For her sister Pauline she bought a saxophone, for Neel there was a clarinet, and for Johnnie a trombone. Not only did she buy the instruments for the family, but she also enrolled them in music classes—and paid for the lessons! What about Dorothy? . . . She had a little trouble making up her mind. First, she purchased a trombone, but later switched to a mellophone.[52] Other relatives also got into the act. Their cousin Jo bought a saxophone, and Philip and John purchased trombones. Together they formed an orchestra and began to play in church. At first it was, as you might imagine, just a "joyful noise," but soon the ministry of music they provided became a valued part of every church service.

DOROTHY IS CALLED TO THE MINISTRY

It was during this time that Dorothy began to feel the call to the ministry. She began by accepting speaking engagements in nearby churches on the weekends. Her sister Pauline, or "Pat" as everyone began to call her (Dorothy had given her this nickname), joined her, adding her musical ability. Dorothy also took what would turn out to be her lifelong nickname: "Dot." By this time, Pat could play the piano, saxophone and xylophone. They were billed as the *Dobbins Sisters Evangelistic Party.* Soon, however, the duo became a trio when their cousin Jo joined them. Now a full–fledged trio, they felt the need to dress alike. They appeared for their engagements all dressed in white, even down to their shoes!

---

[51] Or about $1,021.00 in year 2005 dollars.

[52] A mellophone is a valved brass instrument similar in form and range to the French horn.

A NEW CAR FOR THE LADIES IN WHITE

The girls had musical ability and were certainly well–dressed, but they needed a way to get to the meetings. The trio had finally launched out into full–time ministry, and they had to have transportation. They purchased a couple of used cars, but the repairs and lack of mechanical ability for three young girls proved to be too much. In May of 1925 they purchased a brand new Ford Touring Car. Because of Mr. Ford's ingenuity with the assembly line, the car that cost about $850.00[53] in 1908 was now being sold for the unheard of price of $290.00.[54] Only because of the production line were they able to afford such a fine new automobile.

1923

Aimee Semple McPherson founds International Church of the Foursquare Gospel in Los Angeles.

There were five automobiles offered by Ford during this time, and the Touring Car was the second from the bottom of the line in price. It was a simple black car with black fenders. How these three young ladies must have stood out in their open–air Touring Car all dressed for church in their white dresses, hats and shoes. With this new Ford they held revival campaigns in Chetopa and Iola, Kansas; Reeds and Joplin, Missouri; and a city–wide tent revival in Eureka Springs, Arkansas. Indeed, this new car was going to really take them places, but God had greater plans for Dorothy, and He was going to take her a lot further!

It was about this time that Dot and the *Dobbins Sisters Evangelistic Party* made their way to the Assembly of God General Assembly, being held in Eureka Springs, Arkansas. There they would meet many important people and acquire many more meetings for the work of the Lord. However, a meeting was about to take place that would change Dot's life forever.

---

[53] Or about $8,936.00 in year 2005 dollars.
[54] Or about $3,049.00 in year 2005 dollars.

CHAPTER SIX

DAKE FINDS A WIFE

DAKE DISCOVERS HIS TEACHING GIFT

During Dake's final days at school, news had reached him concerning the young man whom he had left to take care of the church in Joliet, Illinois. It seems that this young minister had acted unwisely in a few business affairs and, as a result, the congregation had split. The church property had been sold, and the church was disbanded.

Not having a church to return to as he had planned, Dake headed home for a visit. When he was seventeen he had returned home a cowboy—complete with six–shooter, boots, spurs and hat. Now, at the age of 23, he was coming home quite a different man. His cowboy clothes had been replaced with a suit and tie. In place of his six–shooter, he had something much more powerful—his trusted *Scofield Reference Bible*[55] and his newly acquired *Companion Bible.*[56]

1924

Maria B. Woodworth–Etter dies at age 80.

After a short visit with family he went north, stopping off for a visit in Iberia, Missouri, his birth place. There he gathered a crowd and preached a sermon at the old home place of his mother. Traveling still further north to St. Louis, he joined some acquaintances from school who were driving to Chicago, Illinois. On the way he stopped for a visit in Joliet, at the church he had planned to pastor until things had taken a wrong turn.

Conditions in Joliet were bad indeed. The young minister's mishandling of several situations had brought an end to the work that Dake had left prospering. Reluctantly, Dake felt it best not to get involved in the problems that remained. He determined to seek the Lord for His will concerning his future ministry. It seemed clear that, for now, he would return to an evangelistic ministry.

His first stop on the evangelistic trail west was about 550 miles away in Milford, Nebraska. From there he traveled north 470 miles to Belle

---

[55] *The Scofield Reference Bible*, edited by C. I. Scofield. New York: New York, Oxford University Press, 1909.

[56] *The Companion Bible*, edited by E. W. Bullinger. Kregel Publications, Grand Rapids: Michigan, 1922.

Fourche, South Dakota. In both of these cities he saw wonderful results. However, Dake knew, even at this early age, that his calling was not that of an evangelist, but of a teacher. He recalls:

> God blessed me abundantly in these efforts and although I had some few dreams of being an evangelist, it seemed that my soul was more blest and thrilled in the Bible teaching that I did.

THE 1925 GENERAL COUNCIL MEETING

In the fall of the year, being an ordained minister in the Assembly of God, Dake felt it necessary that he attend the 1925 General Council meeting that was being held in Hot Springs, Arkansas. Little did he know at the time, but events taking place at this meeting were to alter the pattern of his life. It was here that he would meet and marry his wife.

The Assemblies of God was founded in 1914, and as a new association each General Council meeting had profound importance in shaping the future and direction of this still–young group of Full Gospel churches.

1925

John T. Scopes is found guilty of teaching evolution in a Dayton, Tennessee high school.

On Thursday morning, September 17, 1925, the Eleventh General Council Meeting was called to order by Elder D. Kerr.[57] There were 360 delegates attending this opening session and another 500 visitors would be making their way to the evening session. The presence of the Lord was made consciously real from the very beginning of the meeting. The primary focus of the meeting was an emphasis on remaining a missionary organization.

In gratitude and praise for the work of God, both the schools Dake had attended were mentioned—Glad Tidings Bible Institute in northern California, with its six–story concrete building and its 2,500 seat auditorium, and Central Bible Institute in Springfield, Missouri, now valued at over $101,000.00[58] and debt free! Both of these schools were reported to be filled to capacity.

---

[57] See the *Pentecostal Evangel*, Number 617, dated October 10, 1925 for a complete record of the meeting.

[58] Or about $1,061,914.00 in year 2005 dollars.

The ministry of Gospel Publishing House was also mentioned, noting the prosperity that was being enjoyed by the newly–founded publishing house. The remainder of the afternoon session was devoted to fellowship. Various speakers spoke during this time, of which one was Pastor W. E. Moody of Zion, Illinois. Pastor Moody spoke of the great worldwide revival that he believed was on the brink. He encouraged the attendants to continue in prayer and intercession—the only way to bring about this great revival. Perhaps this speaker inspired Dake, for the day would come when Dake would also pastor in this town of Zion, Illinois.

Then came the evening service, when the pulpit was shared by both a man and woman. This was unusual for many churches of the day, but not in the Pentecostal camp! Pastor Jonathan F. Perkins, of Tulsa, Oklahoma, gave a splendid Pentecostal message, and Sister Blanche Appleby of Lo Pau, South China, gave a remarkable missionary address: *Give Us Thy Vision Lord, That We Perish Not.*

Sister Blanche Appleby's message concerning missionary vision must have touched Dake's heart, but there was another vision that touched him more. There, on that Thursday evening, for the first time, he laid eyes on a young lady named Dorothy Virginia Dobbins, of Joplin, Missouri. When Dot laid eyes on this "tall, blond minister from Tulsa, Oklahoma, it was love at first sight." Dake himself later wrote:

> I attended, and during the course of the first evening met the young lady who some twenty days later became my wife. She was a musician and an evangelist and the very help I needed in Gospel work.

Neither of them had any questions about spending the rest of their lives together, for they met on Thursday, September 17, and by the end of the council meeting on Wednesday, September 23, they were engaged.

When the meeting came to a close the "Dobbins Sisters Evangelistic Party" made their way to the town of Des Arc, Missouri, for a revival. Due to the rain and muddy roads, this 180–mile trip turned out to be a three–day journey. In fact, on the way there, they suffered a wreck in their new Ford. They turned over in a ditch, ruined the top, bent two fenders and broke the windshield. Thankfully, with the hand of God on their lives, they were lifted out of this wreck by some road workers with barely a scratch on them. This event led these three young ladies to believe that they really needed "a man" in their party.

It had only been a few days, but Finis Dake could not stay away from his beloved Dot, so he paid them a visit in this revival meeting. It was during this meeting that Pastor Talcutt and his wife, Jo, Earl Steveson and Pat, all drove with Finis and Dot to the county seat in Greenville, Missouri. And just twenty days after meeting, on Wednesday, October 7, 1925, Finis and Dorothy became man and wife.

Immediately following their wedding, they returned to Des Arc and continued the revival meeting.

CHAPTER SEVEN

FROM PASTOR TO COLLEGE PRINCIPAL

PASTORING ONCE AGAIN

Since the summer of 1924, when Dake had pastored the little church in Joliet, Illinois, he had maintained a correspondence with them by mail. The people had continued to plead with him to return once again to the work there. Not having a strong desire to pastor, yet wanting to see the people and help where he could, Dake agreed to go back for a brief period of time.

Throughout the winter of 1925, Dake did his best to minister to the congregation and to establish himself as a family man with his new bride, Dot. These were happy days for the young Dake family. Dot was an evangelist at heart and Dake was a scholar of the Word. Together they began a pattern of ministry that would continue for the rest of their lives. Dake would preach the Sunday morning services; Dot would preach Sunday evenings. On Wednesday night, Dake would fulfill the driving desire of his heart; he taught a series of lessons which would later come to be known as *God's Plan for Man*.[59] The young couple even found time for an evangelistic campaign during their short pastorate. And who was the guest speaker? Evangelist Dorothy Dake, of course.

> *"God has a personal plan for your life that will fit perfectly into His larger plan for man."*
>
> *Finis Dake*

THE EVANGELISTIC FIELD

In the summer of 1926, the Dakes felt the call to launch out as full–time evangelists. The Dake meetings were much different than the traditional services held by many of the evangelists of their day. The traditional evening services consisted of Pentecostal choirs, spontaneous singing and shouting, evangelistic preaching (mostly by Dorothy), nightly altar calls—with many coming to the Lord crying tears of joy—prayer for the sick, and the moving of the Spirit accompanied by tongues and interpretations. But there was more . . .

---

[59] *God's Plan For Man*, by Finis J. Dake, (Lawrenceville, Georgia: Dake Bible Sales, Inc. 1949)

DAKE'S FIRST CHART

Along with these nightly meetings, Dake began to hold afternoon services where he would teach from the Bible and his *Plan of the Ages* Bible chart. In that day, when there was no television, this was a rare and interesting treat indeed. In fact, by modern standards, and even by Dake's own admission, it was a crude drawing, but for those folks in 1926 who were

Dake and the Plan of the Ages chart

eager to learn God's Word, it was state of the art! The chart was four feet high and eighteen feet long. Dake was very proud of his first little chart, for he wrote:

> My first chart of the ages was quite a crude one made on blackboard cloth with chalk, but the Lord blessed my soul in giving forth the Word to believers. Little did I realize at that time the field that God had awakened in me on that line.

The Plan of the Ages Bible chart was literally the *Bible on Canvas,* as Dake became accustomed to saying at the beginning of all his teachings from this chart. "Now this is what we call the Bible on canvas, or *God's Plan for Man,*" Dake would say, [60]

> Somewhere on this one chart here is illustrated and made clear for you all the doctrines of the entire Bible, including the books of Daniel and Revelation. This chart takes you from the eternal past to the eternal future. And all these

---

[60] *God's Plan for Man: The Pre–Adamite World,* 8–tape series, tape 4801.

balls drawn on this line represent periods of time from the time that God created His original kingdoms to the time that Jesus Christ reigns on the planet earth forever, even forever and ever.

A Description of the Chart

The chart was basically a dispensational[61] chart. After graduating Bible school and as a result of a great deal of study, Dake adapted the basic dispensational model as found in the Scofield Bible.[62] This included the nine distinct dispensations found in Scripture:

1 – God's rule in eternity past
2 – The Dispensation of Innocence
3 – The Dispensation of Conscience
4 – The Dispensation of Human Government
5 – The Dispensation of Promise
6 – The Dispensation of Law
7 – The Dispensation of Grace
8 – The Dispensation of Divine Government or Millennium
9 – God's rule with Faithful Angels and the Redeemed

Dake Teaching From His Bible Chart

In addition to the framework, which the Scofield model provided, Dake added much more to make the plan of God even more clear for serious Bible students. He divided these nine dispensations into four divisions consisting of:

1 – The origin of all things
2 – God's historical dealings with man
3 – God's present dealings with man
4 – God's future dealings with man

---

[61] Dake defined a dispensation as: "an administration, stewardship, dispensation, or guardianship. It refers to a moral or probationary period in angelic or human history during which God dealt with angels or human beings according to a particular test or responsibility, under which each was to remain true to his trust of administering affairs for God under His direction." See the *Dake Annotated Reference Bible*, Compact Edition, Old Testament Section, page 86.

[62] Genesis 1:28, note 5: *The Scofield Reference Bible*, with notes by Dr. C. I. Scofield.

Within these four divisions he saw five ages:
    1 – The Ante–Chaotic Age
       (from the Creation to the Flood of Lucifer)
    2 – The Ante–Diluvian Age
       (from the Restored Earth to the Flood of Noah)
    3 – The Present Age
       (from the Flood of Noah to the 2nd Coming)
    4 – The Age to Come
       (The Millennium)
    5 – The Age of the Ages
       (Eternity, time without end)

Along the bottom of the chart there are five departments of the underworld:
    1 – Tartarus
    2 – Paradise
    3 – Hell
    4 – The Bottomless Pit
    5 – The Lake of Fire

At the top of the chart Dake displayed five major events taking place in heaven:
    1 – Paradise since the Resurrection
    2 – The Throne of God in Heaven
    3 – The Judgment Seat of Christ
    4 – The Marriage Super of the Lamb
    5 – The Great White Throne Judgment

To round out the chart, Dake also included images depicting Lucifer's rebellion; the translation of Enoch and Elijah; the books of Daniel and Revelation; the Tabernacle and a host of other biblical subjects and doctrines.

MORE TEACHING FROM THE CHART

It was also in this same summer of 1926 that Dake and his minister friends, Pastor Jonathan Perkins and Brother J. Edgar Freeman, traveled to Amarillo, Texas, for a tent campaign. Brother Perkins pastored in Tulsa, and Dorothy was happy to be left to fill his pulpit during his absence. It was during this time that Dake noted the deep feelings in his heart for the teaching ministry:

> Again I had afternoon services to teach the Bible. It seemed that everywhere I went people were reaching out for the Word and that was what I longed to give to them.

During that summer there were wonderful results as they ministered under the big tent that had been set up. Amarillo was a leading oil town in its day, and there was a great work for the Lord to do. Many were saved as they received Jesus as Lord and Saviour, leaving a life of sin and wickedness. Dake and his party preached a total Gospel, however, and even more were filled with the Spirit and healed from all manner of sickness and disease.

REVELATION EXPOUNDED IS BORN

While Dake loved teaching from all of his chart, his favorite section was the latter part which concerned end–time events. Along with the book of Daniel, the book of Revelation was where Dake would spend hour after hour of intense study and prayer. During this time, Dake penned the manuscript for what would later become known as *Revelation Expounded*.[63] It would be several years before he would get this book to print, but the study and foundation had been laid during the early days of his ministry. In fact, at just 24 years of age, Dake had written his first commentary on the Bible and he started with the book of Revelation! Truly, the writing of this book would show the extent of God's gift in Dake's life. And this was just the beginning.

"The Revelation had its origin in the mind of God."

Finis Dake

THEY JUST WOULDN'T LET HIM LEAVE

At the end of the summer, the people simply wouldn't let Dake leave. After much prayer, everyone concerned felt that it was the will of the Lord for him to take on the pastoring of the North Side Assembly of God in Amarillo. So, Dake drove the 366 miles back to Tulsa to pick up his beloved Dot, once again returned to pastoring—this time in Amarillo, Texas.

---

[63] *Revelation Expounded*, by Finis Dake. Dake Publishing, Inc. Lawrenceville: Georgia, 1977.

At the time, Amarillo was a large, prosperous town of about 40,000 people, according to the U.S. Census of 1930. Located in the Texas panhandle, Amarillo maintained a strong flavor of the Old West, which suited Dake just fine!

In every church there are certain people who just stand out. Many of these are great blessings to the pastor and his family. Often, many of the illustrations used by pastors in their sermons are the result of interactions with the members of the church.

On one particular topic—the eternality of hell—Dake owes one of his favorite sayings to a lady from this Amarillo church. Dake later recalled:

> A lady in Amarillo, Texas, some years ago got up in my church and said, "Bless God! Just as sure as there is an eternal bliss, there is an eternal blister." This is one way of saying what the Bible plainly teaches on eternal hell.[64]

The next year was filled with wonderful results. Dake writes:

> We had a most profitable year in Amarillo. It was our pleasure to see many a soul saved, and a number receive the Holy Ghost. My wife was the Sunday night evangelist and usually spoke to a packed house. This was quite a contrast to the small audience that filled the first row or two when I preached my first sermon in the church. We were made to believe that the smile of God's approval was upon us.

THE DAKE COUPLE BECOME A FAMILY

Spiritual births were not the only kind of birth the Dake's saw while at Amarillo, for it was here that their first child was born. This infant was a great surprise to Dake who wrote:

> According to my own desires this child was supposed to have been a boy! Yes, he should have had big feet, big hands, white hair and should have been called "Finis Jennings, Jr."

---

[64] *God's Plan For Man*, by Finis Dake. Dake Publishing, Inc. Lawrenceville: Georgia, Page 755.

To Dake's surprise, her hands and feet were very little indeed, and though she did have white hair, they felt they just could not call her "Finis Jennings, Jr.!" Instead, they did the next best thing and named her "Finette Janelda Dake."

In those days, before the invention of ultrasound and the advancements in medicine which allow couples to know the sex of their child months before its birth, many couples had in their mind what they wanted the child to be. It wasn't until birth that the truth was revealed. And, like most fathers of his day, Dake wanted his first child to be a boy. The fact that the Dake's first child was a girl was soon accepted with great joy. Dake himself wrote of Finette:

> *"If men are not holy, they are not saved; if they are saved, they are holy."*
>
> *Finis Dake*

> She has proved a delight to our home and we thank God for the hundreds of happy little smiles she has given us day by day.

The Dakes had come to Amarillo as a couple, but with the birth of Finette their lives had changed forever—they were now a family.

DAKE IS FILLED WITH POSSIBILITIES

Now that Dake was a daddy, life was fuller than ever. He was settling down to a teaching ministry and having the time of his life. He later said of this time:

> I continued my teaching of the Bible in the church and God prospered me in doing so. I was so happy in fulfilling the ministry that God had given me.

It was during this time that Dake was able to create his first color chart of *The Plan of the Ages*. It was painted in oil and in full color, which made Bible teaching much more interesting to his church. He then purchased a mimeograph machine and began printing his notes on the Bible lessons he was teaching. Filled with so much of God's Word, he felt a strong desire to share it with as many people as he could, in whatever ways he could. It was indeed a small beginning, but to this young family it was a beginning of enormous potential. He later wrote that "it seemed that I would never be able to exhaust the possibilities ahead of me."

Teaching and ministering to his church was the joy of his life, but it seemed to him that there must be more. His message was changing lives, making stronger Christians and having an impact on his community, but he felt that God was preparing him for something beyond his present ministry. He recalled:

> I was so happy in the work that I often told my wife I would certainly like to be in a Bible school next winter where I could teach to my heart's content. I felt somehow, sometime, somewhere in the near future, I would be in that kind of work and quite unconsciously I was making Bible school notes. In reality however, there was no Bible school in sight.

What men cannot see with the natural eye is often seen through the eyes of faith. And for Dake, this was happening. He couldn't see the possibility of a Bible school ministry but, in his spirit, it was a vision that propelled him forward.

It was about this time that Dake was asked to meet with the chairman of the Texas District Council of the Assemblies of God. They wanted to talk with him about a Bible school!

DAKE STARTS A BIBLE SCHOOL

A Bible school is a work of the Lord, and as such, takes dedication and commitment from those who are willing to make sacrifices. Thus, Dake would write that "the Texico Bible School was born after many months and years of anxiety and travail."

It seems that the Texas and New Mexico brethren had planned for a school for several years, but the plans did not sufficiently materialize to warrant an immediate start. In fact, when Brother A. P. Collins (one of the brothers who was so interested in a school) died, the proposition was temporarily dropped, as there was no one to champion the cause. The District Council brought up the idea now and again, for the idea remained fresh in the hearts of those desiring to see a training school for the work of the ministry. In God's providence, however, Dake's heart was being made ready to champion this cause.

In June of 1927, the District Council met in Dallas, Texas. It was in this meeting that the school once again came up before the house, and a resolution was read—unanimously adopted—which gave full power to the Executive Committee to work out the details connected with a school, having the standard course of study as recognized by other schools of the Council fellowship.

Brother Cadwalder, the chairman of the Texas District Council of the Assemblies of God, came to meet with Dake concerning the possibility of starting a Bible school in the area. He was so impressed with the studies and notes Dake had compiled that he encouraged him to hold steady before God in the matter, committing to pray and see what the Lord would do. As the Lord worked it out, Brother Cadwalder was able to bring this idea up at the very next meeting of the council.

The council, in agreement that the formation of a Bible school was indeed the will of God, granted the authorization for the opening of a new Bible school. With this decision of the council, Dake's dreams and visions were coming to pass. He had enjoyed pastoring and evangelizing, but it was the teaching ministry that had always captivated his heart. Dake remembered this time by saying:

> *"It is 'unbelief and hardness of heart' that causes men to question what the Bible says."*
>
> *Finis Dake*

I was to be principal of the institution. It was like a dream coming true.

DAKE THE TEACHER

In the early part of the twentieth century, Christian churches were consumed with preachers. The ministry of the teacher had not achieved the prominence in the body of Christ that it has today. Teachers, for the most part, were confined to children and the Sunday School classroom. In the Pentecostal churches of Dake's day, preachers were fiery, loud, emotional and very demonstrative. Dake, for some time, had been concerned about whether he was really aligned with the will of God in this matter. After all, to be devoted to a full–time teaching ministry was quite a departure from the norm of his day.

In this regard, the Lord was gracious to confirm His leading and direction in Dake's life. It was about this time that Brother E. F. Nuir gave him the opportunity to travel to California to teach in a Bible school there.

Dake noted:

> I was made more sure than ever that my previous convictions in regard to teaching were of the Lord.

DAKE'S CHART GOES INTO PRINT FOR THE FIRST TIME

It was in the summer of 1927 that Dake had the opportunity to travel 350 miles northeast to Tulsa, Okalahoma, where he was to participate in a large tent meeting with Rev. J. Edgar Freeman. Dake was very excited about this trip, for he was able to teach from his new, full–color, freshly painted oil chart in the 6:00 p.m. service that was held just before the nightly evangelistic meetings. Just to be allowed to teach from the chart to a large crowd was all Dake expected, for this was more of his vision coming to pass. But there was more in store for Dake.

1927

Dake's Bible chart "The Plan of the Ages" is first printed.

Dr. J. F. McCutcheon was in attendance in these Tulsa meetings. Listening to Dake teach, he was overcome by his wealth of Scripture knowledge, as well as the plain and simple way the Bible seemed to come alive. But he was more than just excited. He was willing to help. It was here that he advanced Dake the funds to have the big chart reduced in size so that it could be folded and carried in a Bible. For the first time, Dake's chart went into print. This was a great day indeed! God was moving. Dake later recalled:

> It seemed that God was working on every hand "His wonders to perform." In fact, the Lord, Himself was supplying my needs for Bible school work.

BACK TO AMARILLO

Greatly encouraged by the Tulsa meeting, Dake headed back home to share the good news with Dorothy. She had been in the Amarillo church performing all the duties of the pastorate during Dake's absence. While Dorothy always supported her husband in every way she could, it was not totally one–sided, for she loved to preach as well. While Dake was a teacher, Dorothy was a gifted preacher.

Aware of this, Dake presented her with an extended opportunity for ministry. It was his plan to travel throughout the district and begin to raise the needed money for the Bible school. Dorothy agreed to take on all the responsibilities of the church while Dake was plunging forward, full of determination to begin the building of the Bible college as soon as possible. Sacrifice was the order of the day, and both Dake and his wife were willing to pay the price.

God was continuing to bless their endeavors. Many came to Dake's aid with support for the Bible college, as they testified of the presence of the Lord filling their hearts with a desire to help. In only a few short weeks, Dake raised enough money to obtain a twenty–two room house which was completely furnished. With this, students began to come in from every direction. Encouraged by the generosity of God's people, Dake wrote:

> God certainly blessed every effort put forth to establish a
> Bible school in the district and we are sure the thing was
> of Him.

In Amarillo, the first schoolhouse was built in 1889, followed by West Texas State University in 1909 and Amarillo Junior College in 1929. But it was on Tuesday, November 1, 1927, just fourteen days after his 25th birthday, that Finis Dake opened the doors of the Texico Bible School for the first day of class. There were thirty–six students from eight different states that came to learn the Word of God under Dake's ministry. So successful was the school's opening that more would soon have to be done, for the twenty–two room house was very crowded with as many as four and five students to a room. Because of this limited space, Dake had to turn many applicants away.

In the notes to the *Dake Annotated Reference Bible,* Dake would later make an interesting comment. Concerning the woman in 2 Kings 4 who was told to borrow vessels, which were then miraculously filled with oil at the word of Elisha in order to pay off debts, Dake wrote:

> All the vessels were filled and countless others could have
> been filled if she had borrowed more.[65]

---

[65] Finis J. Dake, *Dake's Annotated Reference Bible,* (Lawrenceville: Georgia, Dake Publishing), 2 Kings 4:1 note.

One wonders if maybe Dake's notes on this passage were a fond remembrance of this Bible school opening. If only he had built more rooms!

THE BIBLE SCHOOL IS OPENED

Proper arrangements were made, catalogues and application blanks were distributed in August, and the first advertisement went forth in the September 17, 1927, edition of the *Pentecostal Evangel.*[66] The write–up reads as follows, after which time Dake said, "immediate replies started to come in from far and near."

New Bible School in Texas

The Texas and New Mexico District Council in session at Dallas, Texas, June 7 to 10, voted unanimously to start a new Bible school to meet the pressing need of training evangelists, pastors, missionaries and Christian workers for effective service for God. The District Council autho-rized the Executive Committee of the District to work out all details necessary in connection with the undertaking and report at the earliest possible date. The details have been worked out and . . . school will start November 1, 1927. Some of the details are as follows:

Name. – Texico Bible School of the Texas and New Mexico District Council of the Assemblies of God.

Establishment. – This school is authorized by the District Council but is not exclusively a District school. It is for all men and women everywhere who feel the call to the ministry and feel that they cannot afford to go to other Bible schools that are higher in price, farther away and longer in school terms than this will be. The school is not an individual experiment but is backed by the states

---

[66] The *Pentecostal Evangel* is the official weekly magazine of the Assemblies of God. It was first published in 1913 as *The Weekly Evangel* one year before the formation of the Assemblies of God. J. Roswell and Alice Flower established *The Weekly Evangel* to report on revivals and missions activities. For more information contact: The General Council of the Assemblies of God, 1445 Boonville Avenue, Springfield, MO 65802–1894.

of Texas and New Mexico and by many individuals and assemblies.

Board of trustees. – Hugh H. Cadwalder, president; C. M. Ward, secretary; H. E. Bowley, treasurer; Finis Jennings Dake, principal; J. C. Wilder, State Presbyter; and Hugh H. Wray, State Presbyter.

Purpose of the school. – The purpose of the school is not to compete with other good, established schools but to fill up a gap in our Council fellowship. Everywhere there are young people who are desirous of going to Bible school but are hindered because of finances. Many of these students have been one year and some two years to school somewhere but were not able to finish because of the short time in summer months to earn sufficient with which to go back to school. It is these young people we want to help, giving them the same opportunities as are given to them who finish in other schools. Our plan to help these, will by no means exclude anyone whom God leads to come to this school.

> *"One should get up every morning and pray and have faith in God's help through the day."*
>
> *Finis Dake*

We plan on having a three year course of good, solid, Scriptural teachings given by capable teachers who have been through all the ups and downs of student life. The course will be given in three years of six months each. Other schools have about 7½ to 8 months to the year. We are to have six days a week for classes during the six months which will make us get in seven school months in six months, thus leaving the student six months to earn the small amount necessary to enable him to come back to school. The school will open November 1 and close about May 1.

Cost. – There will be a registration fee of $50.00 to be paid as soon as possible so as to get the buildings rented and everything arranged for school. The charge for board and room will be $4.00 a week. The school year will cost

$146.00 besides a few dollars for laundry and notes. If you cannot get this amount before school opens write us and we will see what can be done.

Location. – The school will be located at Dallas, Texas, a city of nearly 300,000 inhabitants. There are scores of shops, factories, schoolhouses and churches, which will afford excellent opportunity for the practical work of the school and also be beneficial to students who wish to work part time. Two large dormitories will be rented this year, one for men and one for women. The class room and dining room will be in the buildings. The Dallas assembly has a gospel truck which will be turned over to the school to hold street meetings with and to use in the practical life of the school.

"We promise to provide a wealth of clear Scriptures as we seek to unmask truths that have been hidden for generations."

Finis Dake

Let all the saints pray that God will supply every need of the school this year till it gets on its feet. Any furniture for rooms, class room and dining room, etc., will certainly be appreciated by the school. You can furnish a room or part of a room as you can afford.

Please write for a catalog which will tell you all necessary details concerning the school. Any question concerning this school will be answered promptly. Send for catalogs and application blanks to Finis Jennings Dake, principal, 900 N. Pierce St., till Sept. 13th and after that 4910 Gurlcy Ave., Dallas, Texas.[67]

THE FIRST YEAR BEGINS

On November 1, 1927, on 111 North Crawford Street, Dallas, Texas, the Texico Bible School began its first year of training young men and women for the work of the ministry.

In addition to the students, there were two teachers with their wives,

---

[67] *The Pentecostal Evangel, A Family and Missionary Paper*: Number 715, September 17, 1927, page 9.

as well as the cook with his wife and daughter. The students came from eight different states and Canada. Dake was greatly encouraged with this new work. He would later write:

> From the present outlook we will have to provide for seventy–four or one hundred students next year, by securing a larger building and enlarging the faculty.

THE SCHOOL COURSES

The school course consisted of a three–year plan. It included the following subjects: Dispensational Truth, Typology, Bible Introduction, Bible Atlas, Old and New Testaments Synthesis, Prophecy Epistles, Doctrine, Personal Work, Effective Speaking, Parliamentary Law, Hermeneutics, Missions, Homiletics, English, Music, Church History, Greek, Reading, Spelling, Pastoral Epistles, General Epistles, and two or three miscellaneous subjects.

IT'S PRAYER TIME ALL THE TIME

The spiritual life of the school was to be given the best of attention. The students had prayer from 6:30 a.m. to 7:00 a.m., and at 8:15 a.m. to 9:00 a.m. they would take turns in leading morning chapel. Each class began with an attitude of contacting God. At noon, prayers for missionaries were offered from 12:00 p.m. to 12:30 p.m. Each day prayer would be offered for a different mission field around the world. Dake commented:

> The needs of each field were brought before the students and prayers were answered time and time again.

Students prayed for the Jewish diaspora on Monday, South America on Tuesday, Africa on Wednesday, China and Japan on Thursday, India on Friday, Russia and all of Europe on Saturday and the islands of the sea on Sunday. These prayer times took care of the daytime, but the night was not left out. The evenings were a time for personal spiritual commitment to the Lord. Dake said:

> At night the students have a special time for prayer and we can safely say that all are being blessed in their spiritual life and are growing fat like calves in the stall.

PRACTICAL LIFE

The daily life of the students was organized as efficiently as possible. Just as quickly as opportunities for ministries opened for the school, whether it was in a factory, shop, schoolhouse, church, jail, or street, students were ready to fill the call. The goal was to have every student involved in some work for God every week.

STUDENTS AWAY FROM HOME YET AT HOME

Concerning the home life of the students Dake wrote:

> *"You may struggle at first to realize that the benefits we promise you, according to Scripture, are true and really for you."*
>
> *Finis Dake*

The home atmosphere is wonderful here in every part of the school life. The rooms are all furnished with carpets on every floor, nice beds, tables, chairs and dressers. Then, too, there is a large closet and mantel and mirrors just over the mantels in almost every room. The two reception halls, classroom, kitchen and dining room are all so homey till it all goes to take away most of the homesickness from the students. Above all, we have a nice mother for the school in Mrs. Harned, who has been through all the ups and downs of life for more than threescore years and who is a wonderful help to all when things are a little hard.

No doubt, this precious lady helped to encourage Dake himself—who was only about twenty–five years old at this time. How wonderful it must have been for the Dakes to be in a home like this, enjoying the fellowship of the saints and the household of God.

DISCIPLINE

During his days at Bible school in California, Dake had learned much about the need for college students to lead a disciplined lifestyle. From the very beginning, Dake made up his mind that Texico Bible School was to be a school that practiced discipline and order. Dake wrote:

> Every student knows his place and just what he is to do. The home is kept clean by the students, who are assigned

something new to do every week. Promptness in every phase of school life can be seen throughout the day and God is blessing us in many lessons to learn along this line as well as any other part of the work. Everything is kept clean and sanitary and the food is just wonderful, due to the fact that we have one of the best cooks in the South, who knows how to put the finishing touches on every table comfort.

Mission–Minded

In the early days of Pentecost, foreign missions was always on the heart of every believer. In the first year of the school, Dake invited several missionaries and guest speakers to impress upon the students the great need around the world. Dake was convinced that the exposure to those who had been on the mission field would . . .

always make the students determined to make just as great sacrifices and would cause them to consecrate their all to God for any part of the world.

Moral Code

The moral code of the school was very strict by design. Dake himself said they were the "strictest and best that are obtainable." This, of course, was no modern coed school. The boy's and the girl's quarters were in two different parts of the building and no association between them was permitted at any time during the school year, either on or off the grounds!

The study periods were from 2:00 p.m. to 5:30 p.m. in the afternoon and from 7:00 p.m. to 10:00 p.m. at night, during which time absolute quietness would reign throughout the entire building. Dake said this helped the students to "study the deeper truths of the Word of God and get grounded in the Rock of Ages."

> *"Everyone must have this faith to receive anything from God."*
>
> *Finis Dake*

School Cost A Walk Of Faith And Prayer

One of the most difficult parts of any work for God seems to be finances. The cost for the school year, including registration, tuition, books, notes, laundry, board, room, was between $150.00 to $175.00.[68] In regard to raising the necessary funds for students who were unable to pay, Dake did his best to help. An article was written for a Christian magazine which read as follows:

> We certainly would appreciate the cooperation in prayer from all the saints everywhere that God would bless the school beyond all expectations and supply the needs of some of our students who have come this year trusting God for their support. This might not have been the case if they had known of the school in time to prepare for it. We have about ten such needy students that will need help all along.
>
> If the assemblies who have some student here in that condition would take up an offering for them God would bless you for it. If you do not know how your student is getting along, write us and we will be able to furnish you with all the information you need.
>
> We are taking the liberty here to mention that we would appreciate any canned goods, fruits, vegetables, meats or any other edible that any one at any time would like to give to the Lord. We have had to furnish and equip the school this year, and it has drained our resources considerably. Would you stand with us in prayer that God will supply our every need this year until the school is established on a paying basis and gets fully equipped to do as we would like to do for God? Would you kindly pray with us about the matter of a larger and more permanent place for the school for next year? We are overflowing already this year and could not take care of one more in our present quarters. Some have come in recently and had to get a room outside the school, which is very inconvenient for us all. The more we think of all God has done for us in getting the

---

[68] Or about $1,586.00 to $1,850.00 per year in 2005 dollars.

school started and how He has answered prayer here and there, we are made to lift our hearts in praise and gratitude to God for His abundant love. We believe God is in this if He was ever in anything and are looking forward to better and more profitable years in the future, knowing "that He which has begun a good work (among us) will perform it until the day of Jesus Christ."

CORRESPONDENCE COURSES

With the problems of finances and the limited space available for the school, it was clear that other methods of biblical education had to be explored. So, in the very first year of the school, a Bible correspondence course was begun. All of the same subjects offered in the school were also offered through correspondence courses. The total cost of each course by mail was $3.00.[69] This cost included study notes, questions covering the notes in detail, a Bible chart and the examinations.

FIRST YEAR JUST A BEGINNING

Indeed, this first year was a great year in Dake's life. If his life had been full before, it was even more so now. In his own words he wrote:

The experiences of that first year will never be forgotten. I was, at the age of twenty–five, having fulfilled in my life the one great desire of my heart: that of really teaching the Bible to students who are eager to learn. Each day was full and the work heavy, for besides my class work and preparation of notes for the same, I began to combine notes on every subject into correspondence courses for those who could not attend the school in person. Every minute was enjoyed, however, for I was digging deep into the depths of that dear old book, the Bible.

"Wavering faith is faith doubting God and refusing to believe."

Finis Dake

It is interesting to note that some readers of the Dake Bible have wrongly thought that Dake was opposed to a Bible school education.

---

[69] Or about $32.00 in 2005 dollars.

This, however, could not be further from the truth. Dake always felt that his own bible school days were an important part of his Bible education. He was always quick to commend anyone to the study of God's Word in any venue in which learning the truth could take place. Later in his life Dake commented:

> How I thank God for this (Texico Bible College) and the many other efficient Bible schools in our land! Those I have attended have meant so much in the molding of my

Texico Bible School 1927–1928

> spiritual life and the teachers still remain an inspiration to me. I pray God will permit me to be just as valuable and helpful to others in the study of His Holy Word.

Dake's prayer would most certainly be answered—in the Bible school at Texico, and in many other Bible schools which would use his material for years to come, right up to this present time.

Dorothy Dake also looked back at this season of life as a pleasant and wonderful time. She saw it as a fulfillment of the call of God that was placed upon their lives. So moved by this work of God, she wrote a lovely poem that gave expression to the feelings deep inside her heart.

THE TEXICO BIBLE SCHOOL

'Twas in the month we call November,
I'm sure you all can well remember,
When students came with such bright faces,
And one by one soon found their places.

The School was called the "Texico."
The Town was Dallas, as you know.
One nine two seven was the year,
When came the class God's Word to hear.

The house itself was rented bare,
But soon the furniture was there.
For all the rooms of more than twenty,
The Lord Himself sent in a plenty.

The subjects studied were not few,
About the Gentile and the Jew.
From Personal Work to Synthesis,
We took the Bible—all it says.

Then there was English—Music too.
To leave out Spelling wouldn't do.
And then our Dispensational Truth,
Helped us in giving sinners proof.

The Hermeneutics made us work,
If that we learned we could not shirk.
And Bible Introduction too,
With Reading gave us much to do.

Our teachers were the rarest kind,
The best, I'm sure, that you could find.
Our Brother Harned, first in age,
Taught us the lessons page by page.

His wife, a mother, oh so sweet,
Helped make our home–life quite complete.
And then the Principal—Brother Dake,
Would many notes and questions make.

The Principal's wife, our Sister Dake,
Would teach us to some music make.
Her little girl we called "Finette,"
As good a baby as you've met.

And then the "Harts" would always cook,
Such excellent meals that just a look,

Would make you hungry to partake,
Of all the food from meat to cake.

The student body was the kind,
Whose ears were to the Lord inclined.
The small, the great, the young, the old,
Were asking God their lives to mould.

Our Brother Hines and Ira Bryce,
Had both been saved and paid the price.
Our Brother Little—Boteler too,
Were seeking God—His will to do.

McCutcheon, Foster and Liebee,
Were boys who long'd their Lord to see.
De Vasher, Tucker, Robinson,
Prepared to hear the good "Well Done."

Miss Kelly, Mensel, Brown and Vass,
Had studied the Bible in order to pass.
Miss Ansohn and Doderer—Cochran too,
Were searching the Word to learn who's who.

Miss Goss, her mother, Miss Shelton and Smith,
Stood firm by the Bible as more than a myth.
A Sister McCamey—and Summers came,
To lift up Christ and exalt His name.

The Partons and Anthonys all were there,
In trials and blessings their part to share.
Brother Killion, De Merchant and Henderson,
Had called on God—the victory won.

Brother Arch L. Newby, with Sam Woodbury,
About the world had ceased to worry.
Miss Swarts, Brother Markum and Livingston too,
Desired their best for Christ to do.

And there was Brother Cadwalder, God had sent,
To head the School as President.
And then Brother Bowley, the Treasurer too,
Would record all the dollars—whether many or few.

Brother Wray, Brother Wilder, Brother Ward, they say,
Make the best trustees, in every way.
And then Brother Dunn, the best would do,
When buying the food or equipment new.

Thus was the starting of such a School,
That never is surpassed as a general rule.
For the students were aflame with the fire of God,
The armour put on and their feet all shod.

By Dorothy Dobbins Dake

CHAPTER EIGHT

CONTROVERSY AT SOUTHWESTERN

ENID, OKLAHOMA

About two years after founding the Texico Bible School, in the fall of 1929, Dake and Dorothy were invited to help with the newly–founded Bible college that had recently opened about 300 miles to the north in Enid, Oklahoma. In addition to his teaching responsibilties, Dake would also serve as the Dean for the male students. This school was founded by noted Bible scholar, P. C. Nelson.[70]

"Faith is simple."

Finis Dake

While Garfield County, where Enid was located, was not the largest county in Oklahoma, it was a well–populated area of 45,000 people. Enid had grown to be the center of commerce for all of northwest Oklahoma. It was the cornerstone for the development of arts and culture in the area, and a regional center for healthcare services. From its beginnings as a prairie town, Enid had become known as "The Bright Star of the Great Plains."

While at Southwestern, the Dakes were as busy as ever. Dorothy was writing sacred songs,[71] as music continued to be a big part of their lives. She also taught and played music while Dake, with his baritone voice and slide trombone—and on a few rare occasions his banjo—would join in at every opportunity.

In addition to their music ministry, Dake and Dorothy were also writing. Songs, bible studies, books, and charts began to roll off the press. Dake may not have known it at the time, but the work that he and Dorothy were now doing would one day be published around the world. On the next page, an ad for some of their work is reproduced. This ad appeared in 1929.

---

[70] Peter Christopher Nelson (1868–1942) was born in Denmark and immigrated to the U.S. in 1872. He started out as a Baptist, but left in 1920 after receiving the baptism in the Holy Spirit. For a while he traveled as an evangelist, but finally settled in Enid, Oklahoma in 1927 where he opened Southwestern Bible School. (*Dictionary of Pentecostal and Charismatic Movements*, published by Zondervan Publishing House, 1988.)

[71] See the Appendix for a sampling of the many songs Dorothy wrote during her ministry: *The Potter's Masterpiece,* published in 1929 and *Like A Rose*, published in 1935, by Dorothy Dake.

SACRED SONGS

Words and music by Dorothy Dobbins Dake

"I Have the Sunshine of His Smile."

"The Potter's Masterpiece" (Duet)

"I Cannot Afford to Miss Heaven"

Price each 20c   2 copies for 35c   3 copies for 50c

"Stories of the Bible in Verse"

A book of poems by Dorothy Dobbins Dake and Pauline Dobbins McAfee. Many of the most prominent and interesting Bible Stories are put in verse form. Makes a most appropriate gift. Instructive and attractive.

Price 35c

Bible Study Courses By Finis Jennings Dake

1. Dispensational Truth (God's plan of the ages)............$2.50
2. Bible Introduction (Inspiration, genuineness and authenticity of the Bible) 1.00
3. Hermeneutics (Fundamental principles of Interpretation)........ 1.00
4. Old Testament Synthesis (The Old Testament book by book)........$1.50

Charts Designed By Finis Jennings Dake

Chart of the Ages (Illustrating Dispensational Truth Courses)............$ .50

Same chart 6 ft. long on paper........ 2.00

Cloth Chart 7 ft. long (good for class work)........ 7.00

Just Coming Off The Press!

A volume by Finis Jennings Dake on the Book of Revelation. Interesting and complete in every detail. Contains up to date facts in world events which help simplify the Book of Revelation.

Send all orders to:

Finis Jennings Dake,
828 N. St. Louis St.,
Tulsa, Okla.

DAKE THE TENT PREACHER

While Dake and Dorothy were ministering at the school, they continued with their revival meetings. Dake taught and Dorothy preached. Doctrine and biblical teaching was an important part of their ministry, but their heart's cry for souls was never dampened by their studies and scholarship.

With a passion for the lost, they set up a tent in the town of Sand Springs, Oklahoma, just outside of Tulsa and a little over a hundred miles away to the east. Here they saw the salvation of many, and a number of miracles and healings took place. It was a very successful meeting that lasted for forty–two days. During this event, Dake tells the interesting account of a man who came to their tent meeting and shared a testimony of a genuine encounter with God.

We pitched a tent in Sand Springs, Oklahoma, for a revival meeting. Nearly every night during the testimony meetings when opportunity was given for Christians to tell what God had done for them, an old man by the name of George Nye would get up with tears running down his cheeks and make comment on his favorite hymn. He described it as: "There ain't a friend like the lowly Jesus, no, not one! no, not one!" He would then tell the following story, as well as I can remember it.

> *"God is not the author of sin."*
>
> *Finis Dake*

"About eight years ago Jesus Christ saved me from a life of sin. I used to tramp the streets of Tulsa (about eight miles from Sand Springs) and steal milk bottles, rakes, hoes, lawn mowers or anything that I could get my hands on in order to get a little more dope to keep me alive. I was a dope fiend and one of the lowest kind of sinners. I had such a record of arrests in Tulsa until they would seldom bother me any more. I was always getting into jail and out again. I had to have dope or I could not live. The craving for dope was so strong until it would force me to do anything to get more of it. I never will forget my last friend. He was an old black dog that followed me through the streets of Tulsa. I would live out of the garbage pails and sleep in the streets at nights.

"One day I lay in the gutter at the corner of First and Main streets. I was under the influence of dope and whiskey until I hardly knew what I was doing. I got so low that my last friend left me. My old black dog looked at me and wagged his tail and walked off. I never saw him again. After some time I got up and staggered down the street. I heard the Salvation Army singing, 'There ain't a friend like the lowly Jesus.' I went with them to the hall and there I staggered up to the altar and gave my heart to Jesus Christ. He saved me from all my sins. I had no more desire for tobacco, whisky, dope, or any other sin. I have been serving the Lord for about eight years and He is so good to me. I am always happy and am working every day. I now have a nice place to stay and plenty to eat and wear. He is such a wonderful Saviour. He can save anyone that will come to him."

We soon learned that "old George" (as he was called) was a trusted servant of the multi–millionaire oil man, Charlie Page, who was also a great philanthropist of Tulsa and Sand Springs, Oklahoma. George was the private mail carrier for this man, traveling between Tulsa and Sand Springs. Mr. Page had a widow's colony and an orphan's home that he supported besides many other projects to help the poor. One day Mr. Page invited us to eat Sunday dinner at the orphanage. At the table across from this millionaire sat old George. Mr. Page said to us, "That man is a marvel of the grace of God. He has been my trusted mail carrier for eight years. I have trusted him with thousands of dollars. I have never lost one penny in all these years. I would trust him with all that I have."

> *"Selfishness is always unreasonable."*
>
> *Finis Dake*

Anyone could ask old George if he knew whether he was saved or not and he would soon tell you. He would tell you in no uncertain terms that if you were saved you would know it. What a pity that thousands of church members are uncertain as to their relationship to God. Multitudes think they are saved when they are not. It will pay everyone to do anything necessary in order to be assured of old–fashioned salvation. Let no man think that he cannot know. Neither let any man trust that he is all right if he does not know that he is saved and born again. If one will confess his sins and mean business with God he can soon know that he is saved.

In addition to this salvation account of George Nye, Dake also learned of the healing of Charlie Page's wife. This also left a lasting impression upon Dake as to the power of God to heal when God is approached in the right way. Again and again, throughout his ministry, he would recount this story:

> Charlie Page, a multi–millionaire of Tulsa, Oklahoma prayed for his wife's healing and bargained with God to help the poor, if He would do it. But he didn't get an answer. He went back to God and confessed to trying to bargain with God to get something personal. He then went back to God and promised to help the poor because it was right, not because he wanted his wife healed. She was instantly healed and he gave millions of dollars to the poor throughout many years. Charlie Page was a man who learned that it pays to help others and put the interest of others above his own.

PAULINE REMEMBERS GREAT REVIVALS

Dorothy's sister, Pauline McAfee, also had many fond memories of the revivals the Dakes would hold during these years. She recounted that:

> When we were on the field, the three Dakes and we three McAfees conducted some "glorious" revivals, some lasting up to five weeks. The first part of our services were musical. We all played instruments and sang together, even the two little ones (Finette and Pauline's son Wayne). I can see them now as they held hands and swayed as they sang, "when the *road* is called *the piano* I'll be there!"[72] Then Finis would lecture about the plan of the ages using his big canvas chart. Saving the best for last, Dorothy would bring a stirring evangelistic message which touched the hearts of many unsaved, bringing them to a decision to come forward for the "born again" experience. Our meetings took us to Ohio, Indiana, Illinois and Missouri.

---

[72] *When the Roll is Called up Yonder.* Words and Music by James M. Black.

Dake The Writer

Several of his books were written during his stay at Southwestern. There was *Dispensational Truth,* an extensive study of each age and dispensation, along with their outstanding features; *Romans Expounded* and the *Exposition of First and Second Thessalonians,* which were verse by verse studies of their respective books. There was also *Bible Introduction,* a book explaining how we came to have the Bible in its present form; *Hermeneutics,* a study of the fundamental principles upon which true interpretation of Scripture is based; and finally, *Old Testament Synthesis,* a book–by–book examination of the Old Testament.

Revelation Expounded

Earlier in 1926, Dake had written the manuscript for *Revelation Expounded.* Three years later, in 1929, Dake would send the book to the printers and publish his first major hardbound work. Dake had been very busy writing. Most of these works, however, had been twenty to thirty pages in length. Later, many of these pamphlets or booklets would be incorporated into his monumental work on doctrine and theology titled *God's Plan for Man.*

In the front of the book Dake described *Revelation Expounded* as follows:

> This complete exposition of Revelation and the prophetic parts of Daniel is sane, scriptural, and free from sensational and foolish speculation concerning prophetic events. Literally thousands of questions of vital importance concerning near future and eternal events are fully answered with Scripture.

Dake was, of course, always a literalist and supported all his teaching with at least two or three verses dealing with the subject. In the book *Revelation Expounded,* Dake had collected over 6,000 Scripture references which were used to confirm the truths and prophetic teachings he presented. Yet, in all of this, Dake was proud of the fact that the book was still a simple book. He wrote that *Revelation Expounded* was "a Book for the Classroom and the Home."

As a young man, in the course of his studies, Dake had both heard and read what he called:

. . . a great deal of foolish and sensational speculation among teachers of prophecy. *Revelation Expounded* was written to counteract this sensationalism and to set forth the true teachings of the Bible concerning prophetic events.

In the preface of *Revelation Expounded,* Dake also began to let the world know his stance on understanding Scripture. Dake never liked the word "interpretation"—he believed that the Scriptures were very plain and simple and that they needed no interpretation. He believed that God had spoken and the language used in the pages of the Bible was all the "interpretation" that was needed. Dake said:

Finis and Dorothy Dake

> Let the Scriptures themselves be the final word of authority on any question. If the reader has intelligence enough to understand what is written, he has intelligence enough to believe what is written and that is all that is necessary. . . . we do not need an interpretation of the interpretation!

In the preface to *Revelation Expounded* Dake wrote:

> The author relies on the fundamental principle of Bible interpretation—*that of taking the Bible literally wherein it is at all possible.* When the language of a passage cannot possibly be literal, then it is clear from the passage itself, as well as from other Scriptures, that it is figurative. It must be remembered, however, that all figurative language conveys literal truth.

> As a young man the author was taught many things that were contrary to the plain truths of literal scriptural interpretation. He had to make a decision either to believe that God was intelligent enough to express Himself in human language as men do (and that He did do so) or, that God

gave His revelation in terms different from those used by men, to deliberately confuse them regarding the true meaning of His revelation. This latter idea the author could not conceive of God, so he had to settle upon the fact that God "meant what He said and said what He meant." The Bible is clearly understood when taken in the plain literal sense that the same language would be taken if found in another book.

Dake saw that Bible teachers differed widely in their understanding of the Scriptures, so he decided to follow a new course—taking the Bible to be God's own Word and revelation to men—not interpreting it, but letting the Bible be its own interpreter. He found that when all the passages dealing with a subject were gathered together and harmonized, the meaning of Scripture was clear—without the need for further interpretation. Having decided on his course, he made a covenant with God that he would never teach anything that could not be proven by at least two or three plain Scriptures.

As he studied the Scriptures in order to prove what he had been taught, many times he found just the opposite to be truth. To maintain any degree of honesty with God and His Word, he had to make a decision to teach what the Bible taught—regardless of what others were teaching. He found that much of the teaching on prophecy was unscriptural, as we shall see in the exposition to follow.

> *"Prophecy should be understood as literally as we understand history."*
>
> *Finis Dake*

Revelation Expounded is a verse–by–verse commentary on the book of Revelation. It is 320 pages long and consists of forty–five chapters, covering such subjects as "The Seven Churches," "The Heavenly Tabernacle," "The Two Witnesses," "The Sun–Clothed Woman," "The Beast Out of the Sea," "The Times of the Gentiles," "The Great White Throne Judgment," and "The Eternal Perfect State."

Entire libraries of books have been written dealing with the end–time events recorded in the book of Revelation. Most are filled with arcane interpretations, fad doctrines and sensational claims, causing them to have to be rewritten again and again. This has not been the case with Dake's work on Revelation. In fact, up to the present date, regardless of world changes, the rise and fall of many governments, and the coming and going of men hailed as the Antichrist, the essential truths presented in

Revelation Expounded have not been altered. This in itself testifies to the fact that the book is a safe, sane, and scriptural approach to understanding God's prophetic writings.

REVELATION EXPOUNDED WELL RECEIVED

The first edition of *Revelation Expounded* was well–received and was followed by many letters of commendation from Bible students, laymen, pastors and Christian workers, as well as prominent ministers of many denominations. The book was hailed as: "the best book ever published on prophecy."

One review read: "If one should read it with the idea that his preconceived theories are not to be overturned it would make very uncomfortable reading, for he (Dake) says many things, and proves them by a startling array of proof. The book gives evidence of an amazing amount of highly intelligent work done."

> *"If you will follow the Bible it will pay you great dividends and benefits untold in this life and in the life to come."*
>
> *Finis Dake*

Over the years, the comments and reviews would continue to come in. Even to this day, rarely does a day go by that someone doesn't call the office and comment on the blessing this book continues to bring to those who love God's Word. Not bad for a young man in his mid–twenty's!

STORIES OF THE BIBLE IN VERSE

While Dake was busy with *Revelation Expounded*, Dorothy was also doing some publishing work of her own, in addition to her song writing. Dorothy and her younger sister Pauline,[73] were avid students of the Bible. Their days were filled with studying the Bible and looking for ways to communicate its message, in ways that everyone could understand and thereby draw closer to God.

One method that was very popular in the 1930's was poetry. And in this area Dorothy and Pauline took a backseat to no one. Together they wrote a book of fifty poems and entitled it: *Stories Of The Bible In Verse*.[74]

---

[73] Pauline Dobbins McAfee.

[74] Of the fifty poems that were included in *Stories Of The Bible In Verse*, Dorothy wrote twenty–seven of them.

99

THE SAVIOUR'S VOICE TO ME

There's the cooing of a baby
What a pleasant little sound!
And the voice of children playing;
Happiest music ever found.
'Tis a pleasure just to hear them
In their childish fun and glee—
But the voice that still is sweeter
Is the Saviour's voice to me.

There's the voice of patient Mother—
What a blessing that to hear!
And the gentle voice of Father,
When we're pressed, our lives to cheer.
Trials and struggles would seem worse
Once without them, I'll agree—
But there is a voice that's sweeter,
'Tis the Saviour's voice to me.

There's the voice of some fond lover—
What a gentle soft appeal!
And the comfort from a husband
Or a wife—heartaches to heal.
They are voices that the world
Would not dare without to be—
Yet there's one voice so much sweeter;
'Tis the Saviour's voice to me.

By Dorothy Dobbins Dake

GOD IS MOVING AT SOUTHWESTERN

While the Dakes were involved in music and ministry through teaching and the printed page, this in no way hampered their zeal for a move of God in their lives and in the lives of others. Prayer, fasting, seeking God, living in the Word—these things always result in God's blessings and lives lived in the power of the Holy Spirit.

Dake encouraged his students to believe and accept the Bible just as it was written. He exhorted them to live by faith. On the subject of prayer, he did not allow the common excuses of doubt and unbelief to prevail. In one of his classes he asked his students to list the conditions of answered prayer. He relates the story:

> Once in a classroom each student gave a different condition of what they thought men had to do in order to get answers to prayer. So many conditions were required to get a single prayer answered that it would have been impossible for anyone to get one prayer answered under those circumstances. After they had all given their excuses I said to them this: "Away with such conditions. Away with all these conditions. It is no wonder that God can seldom get to answer prayer for us. We manufacture so many conditions that hinder our faith that God cannot work." I then showed them the all–conclusive conditions of answered prayer that when this is met we can forget all others.

"This holy living is done by the power of God and not of us."

Finis Dake

As the students and faculty of Southwestern were busy with their studies, personal Bible studies and prayer meetings were the order of the day. Even mealtime was a time of the moving of the Spirit. Louise Unruh wrote:

> "I have seen the power of God manifested so many times in that room. Students would come in singing. I have seen them slain in the Spirit and dance in the Spirit. They would forget to eat. There were whole days that students would just pray." [75]

When God is moving there is always a desire to reach out to others. In the heart of every believer is the desire to share his faith with those who do not know Christ. This desire is amplified during times of commitment and consecration to God. This desire was born out of the fact that every student at Southwestern belonged to one of six different prayer groups that met on Friday afternoons to intercede for their particular area of the

---

[75] See *God's Plan For Man*, by Finis J. Dake, (Lawrenceville, Georgia: Dake Bible Sales, Inc. 1949), page 180.

world. In the 1931 yearbook, an article written for *Missionary Day* illustrates the deeply felt needs of the students as they embraced their call to tell the world of Jesus.

> Eternity alone can ever reveal all the good that has been done by the floods of tears that have been shed, the agonizing prayers that have battered their way through the resisting powers of the Evil One to heaven's gate, and to the throne of God. How many have heard that still small voice of God that speaks so distinctly saying, "Go and tell them. I suffered for them too." [76]

A Principle That Brings Controversy

When God's Spirit is moving, controversy often arises. It was during this time, while teaching in Enid at Southwestern, that a controversy arose that brought about a change in direction for the Dakes. From the beginning of his ministry, Dake had always taken the stand that "the Bible means what it says and says what it means." In fact, the principle rule of interpretation for Dake was:

"Have faith in God."

Finis Dake

> Take the Bible literally wherein it is at all possible; if symbolic, figurative or typical language is used, then look for the literal truth it intends to convey.[77]

On the surface it doesn't seem that this kind of policy would be one that would engender any problems. Sadly, as a study of his life has shown, this was not the case. One of the earliest areas of difficulty arose over his literal teaching of the pre–Adamite world and the "sons of God" mentioned in the sixth chapter of Genesis.

---

[76] *Like A Prairie Fire, A History of the Assemblies of God in Oklahoma*, by Bob Burke, Marceline: Missouri, 1994, page 179.

[77] Ibid. page 180.

CHAPTER NINE

DAKE'S TEACHING ON THE PRE–ADAMITE WORLD

SCRIPTURAL PROOF

Dake's teaching of the pre-Adamite world was backed by a wealth of study and biblical evidence. While it is not the focus of this work to give a full discourse concerning this subject,[78] in view of the curiosity and questions that this topic has generated over the years, it seems wise to briefly state Dake's position on this teaching. What follows is a brief overview of Dake's writings which provide some insight into his understanding of the pre–Adamite world.

IN THE BEGINNING

The term "in the beginning" in Genesis 1:1 refers to the original creation of the heavens and the earth, not to the time or work of the six days of Genesis 1:3–2:25. Note the following four facts:

> *"Hundreds of places spoken of in the Bible have been definitely located by geographers and explorers."*
>
> *Finis Dake*

1) While Genesis 1:1 records the original creation of the heavens and the earth, Genesis 1:2 records the original dry land, or earth, made into chaos and flooded through a great catastrophe which destroyed all life on a pre–Adamite earth.

2) The word "was" in Genesis 1:2 is from the verb "to become," not the verb "to be," providing further evidence that the earth became waste and empty since its original creation and habitation "in the beginning."

3) The phrase "without form" in Genesis 1:2 is from the Hebrew *tohuw* (HSN–8414), meaning waste or desolation. It is translated "waste" (Deuteronomy 32:10), "without form" (Genesis 1:2; Jeremiah 4:23), "vain" (Isaiah 45:18; 1 Samuel 12:21), "confusion" (Isaiah 24:10; 34:11;

---

[78] For a full treatment concerning this subject based on the writings of Finis Dake, see the book *Another Time, Another Place, Another Man*, edited by Mark Allison and David Patton, (Lawrenceville, Georgia: Dake Bible Sales, Inc. 1997)

41:29), "empty" (Job 26:7), "vanity" (Isaiah 40:17, 23; 44:9; 59:4), "nothing" (Job 6:18; Isaiah 40:17), and "wilderness" (Job 12:24; Psalm 107:40). It can be seen from these passages what the condition of the earth was in Genesis 1:2. Yet Isaiah 45:18 states that God did not create the earth "in vain," or *tohuw* (HSN–8414). Therefore, the earth was originally perfect, dry land, beautiful, and inhabited, but later became empty, waste, and a ruin because of sin (Deuteronomy 32:4; Ecclesiastes 3:11).

4) The Hebrew for "void" in Genesis 1:2 is *bohuw* (HSN–922), "empty, ruined, void." It is translated "void" (Genesis 1:2; Jeremiah 4:23), and "emptiness" (Isaiah 34:11). The Hebrew phrase, *tohuw wabohuw*, "waste and empty," describes the chaotic condition of the earth at the time that it was cursed and flooded because of the sins of Lucifer and the pre–Adamites. It doesn't refer to the earth as originally created—beautiful, perfect, dry land.

THE EARTH WAS CREATED TO BE INHABITED
The earth was created to be inhabited (Isaiah 45:18), and was inhabited before the flood of Genesis 1:2 and the work of the six days of Adam's time (Genesis 1:3–2:25; Isaiah 14:12-14; Jeremiah 4:23-26; Ezekiel 28:11-17; 2 Peter 3:5-7).

DRY LAND IS CALLED EARTH
The earth is called "dry land" in Genesis 1:10, which means that Genesis 1:1 could read, "In the beginning God created the heaven and dry land." Since it was created dry, it stands to reason that the flooded condition of Genesis 1:2 was a curse, not a creative act. According to Psalm 136:6, the earth was originally "stretched above the waters," not covered by them (for more information, see the note in the *Dake Annotated Reference Bible* for Psalm 136:6). This requires a pre–Adamite race whose sin brought such a curse.

THE EARTH DESTROYED
In Genesis 1:2, the earth is not only flooded with water but covered in total darkness, causing all life on earth to be destroyed. This requires a pre–Adamite world with vegetation, birds, animals, and human beings, as proven in the *Dake Annotated Reference Bible* notes on Jeremiah 4:23–26.

THE EARTH WAS CREATED THEN RESTORED

Genesis 1:2 reveals that the earth, waters, and darkness were already in existence before the work of the six days which began in Genesis 1:3 and continued until the earth was restored to a second habitable state in Genesis 2:25. Thus, it is clear from Genesis 1:1-2 (and related Scriptures) that:

"If the Scriptures are inspired they are also genuine."

Finis Dake

1) In the beginning—the dateless past, not 6,000 years ago—God created the heavens, including the sun, moon, and stars.

2) At the same time God also created the earth or dry land.

3) The heavens and the earth were created by God, a personal and an eternal Being. They were not the result of a cosmic accident.

4) The heavens were created before the earth, as revealed in Job 38:4-7.

5) Both the heavens and the earth were created before the earth was flooded.

6) The earth was created dry land, not wet and flooded (Genesis 1:1, 10; Isaiah 45:18).

7) The waters that flooded the dry land were created in the beginning along with the earth, to cause the dry land to become productive (Job 38:4-30), not to curse the earth as in Genesis 1:2.

8) Light and darkness was also created in the beginning, to help sustain life on the earth (Job 38:4-41).

9) The earth alone was cursed, flooded, and filled with darkness—not the heavens (Genesis 1:2).

We therefore conclude that Genesis 1:1-2 proves a pre–Adamite world that was destroyed in a flood, requiring the making of the present world for God's original purpose for the earth to be realized (Isaiah 45:18).

THE SPIRIT MOVES OVER A FLOODED EARTH

Genesis 1:2 reveals the Spirit of God moving on the flooded earth to restore dry land. This confirms that the pre–Adamite world was destroyed, making it necessary to restore the earth to a second habitable state.

JUDGMENT UPON THE EARTH

In Scripture, every instance in which the sun is obscured in order to cause darkness, the result is not creation, but judgment. The same can be said of the two universal floods (Genesis 6:8–8:22; Exodus 10:21-23; Isaiah 5:30; Jeremiah 4:23-26). Furthermore, all predictions of future darkness depict judgment as well (Matthew 8:12; 24:29-31; Revelation 6:12-17; 8:12; 9:2; 16:10; Isaiah 13:10; Joel 2:30–3:16; Amos 5:18-20). Can we say that Genesis 1:2 is the *only* place in Scripture where darkness and a universal flood are not an act of judgment? If not, then Genesis 1:2 proves that there was a pre–Adamite world which was destroyed by darkness and flood.

ADAM TOLD TO REPLENISH

In Genesis 1:28, The command for Adam to replenish the earth (fill it again, not "plenish" it) proves the earth had been filled before (Genesis 1:28). The same command was given to Noah, after the second universal flood (Genesis 9:1-2). Should we conclude that God meant for Noah to fill the earth for the first time, and not refill it? Substitute the word "fill" (meaning "supply for the first time") in Genesis 9:1; Isaiah 2:6; 23:2; Jeremiah 31:25; Ezekiel 26:2; 27:25, as some do in Genesis 1:28 and see if it makes better sense. Whatever we conclude in the other places where "replenish" is used, we should be consistent and give the same meaning to Genesis 1:28.

"The great hindrance to any blessing of God is that of uncertainty in the mind and heart concerning the will of God."

Finis Dake

SATAN FELL BEFORE THE TIME OF ADAM

The fact that Lucifer had already ruled the earth and become a fallen creature before Adam's time is proof that Adam and his race were not the first ones on earth. We must acknowledge that Satan's fall was before Adam's time, because he was already a fallen creature when he came into Adam's Eden (Genesis 3; 2 Corinthians 11:3). Hence, he must have fallen with a pre–Adamite creation.

SATAN'S KINGDOM ON EARTH

According to Isaiah 14:12-14, Lucifer actually invaded heaven from earth, hoping to defeat God and take His kingdom; but Lucifer himself was defeated and his kingdom cursed. Before his defeat, he had a throne, implying a kingdom and subjects to rule over. His kingdom was under the clouds, under the stars, and under heaven—therefore, on earth. Having weakened the nations over whom he ruled, and wanting to be like God and take His place in heaven, Lucifer led the invasion of heaven. All this had to be before Adam's day, because no such things have occurred since Adam was created.

THE TIME OF SATAN'S FALL

Ezekiel 28:11-17 pictures Lucifer before he fell, as the anointed cherub or protector of the earth, full of wisdom and perfect in beauty, ruling in a garden of Eden (before Adam), created by God and perfect in his ways up to the time of his fall. The passage gives both the reason for his fall and the results. The only time this could have been true of Satan was before the days of Adam, thus proving a pre–Adamite world.

JEREMIAH'S VISION

In Jeremiah 4:23-26 we have a full description of the earth under a total curse, as in Genesis 1:2. It was desolate and empty. The heavens had no light, the hills and mountains were undergoing convulsions, and there was neither man, bird, animal, nor fruitful place; no city was left standing because of God's fierce anger. The only time Jeremiah could have seen the earth "without form and void" was at the same time that Moses saw it thus, as recorded by him in Genesis 1:2. There never has been a time from Adam until now when the earth was in such a state—not even at the time of Noah's flood—and there will never be a time of such a curse in the eternal future. The only time Jeremiah 4:23-26 could be fulfilled was before Adam, because the earth was in that condition when the Spirit began the six days' work of restoring it to a second habitable state (Genesis 1:2-21). Regarding the future, this will never be the condition of the earth again, because at His Second Coming Christ will begin to reign over all nations on earth forever, and of His kingdom there shall be no end (Genesis 8:22; Genesis 9:12; Isaiah 9:6-7; Isaiah 59:21; Daniel 2:44-45; 7:13-14, 18, 27; Zechariah 14; Luke 1:32-33; Revelation 1:6; 5:10; 11:15; 20:4-10; 22:4-5). Even the renovation of heaven and earth at the end of the Millennium will not make the earth desolate as pictured in Genesis 1:2 and Jeremiah 4:23-26. Therefore, Jeremiah 4:23-26 must refer to the same judgment as Genesis 1:2, proving further that a real social system—human beings, birds, fruitful places, cities—existed before Adam.

LUCIFER'S FLOOD

Psalm 104:5-9 speaks of God sending a flood on the earth after its creation, at which time the waters stood above the mountains. Psalm 104:7 identifies this as Lucifer's flood, saying "At Thy rebuke they fled." In the case of Noah's flood, the waters slowly and naturally abated. Furthermore, Psalm 104:9 makes it clear that this flood was at a time when God set a boundary for the waters "that they turn not again to cover the earth," and that is what happened in the six days' work of Genesis 1:3–2:25. Thus, Psalm 104:5-9 refers to the same flood as Genesis 1:2 and proves the existence of a pre–Adamite world which was overthrown by a flood.

> *"God will yet have a universal, perfect, and sinless kingdom in the future from which will be separated all rebels against the eternal plan."*
>
> *Finis Dake*

JESUS AND THE PRE–ADAMITE WORLD

Turning to the New Testament we find that Jesus taught the fall of Satan from heaven in Luke 10:18. When did he fall? Before Adam's time, because he was already a fallen creature when he came into Adam's Eden (Genesis 3). Why did he fall? Because of pride and wanting to exalt his earthly kingdom above God's (Isaiah 14:12-16; Ezekiel 28:11-17). What was the result of his fall? All of Satan's earthly subjects, as well as over one–third of God's own angels fell with him (Revelation 12:3, 7-12); and all nations were totally destroyed, along with vegetation, fish, fowl, and animals (2 Peter 3:5-7). Thus, Luke 10:18 substantiates the teaching of Old Testament passages regarding a pre–Adamite world. Jesus further taught the overthrow of the pre–Adamite world by plainly stating that the world had been overthrown. See Matthew 13:35.

PAUL AND THE PRE–ADAMITE WORLD

Paul also taught the overthrow of the pre–Adamite world (Ephesians 1:4; Hebrews 4:3; 9:26). In Colossians 1:15-18 he made it clear that there are thrones, principalities, and powers in heaven and in earth, visible and invisible. It shouldn't be difficult to believe that Lucifer was given one of these thrones and a kingdom to rule over, before he fell. That his kingdom was on earth in a pre–Adamite period is indicated by the fact that he returned to the earth after his fall and brought about the downfall of the new ruler, Adam. Why all this desire to usurp man's dominion on earth if the earth was not at one time Lucifer's place of rulership? Even his eternal punishment will be in the Lake of Fire under the earth, which further proves his sin was in connection with the earth—and when else could that have been but at the time of a pre–Adamite world?

PETER AND THE PRE–ADAMITE WORLD

Contrasting "the world that then was" with the heavens and the earth "which are now," Peter spoke clearly of a social system overthrown before Adam. (2 Peter 3:5-7).

JOHN AND THE PRE–ADAMITE WORLD

John also referred to the overthrow of the pre–Adamite world, as is clear from Revelation 13:8 [John refers to the "Lamb slain before the foundation of the world." The word "foundation" is a translation of the Greek word *katabole*, which refers to something "cast down," or "overthrown."]

DAKE'S CONCLUSIONS

Thus, it is clear that both the Old Testament and the New Testament give proof of a pre–Adamite world. Scientific findings of prehistoric animals and human beings, the age of the earth, and other facts are consistent with the biblical revelation of a pre–Adamite social system. There are many questions which cannot be answered apart from a belief in the pre–Adamite age. How did Lucifer become the Devil and the prince of demons? When did he weaken the nations, ascend into heaven to exalt his throne above the stars, and fall from heaven as in Isaiah 14:12-14? How did demons originate, for what purpose, and when? What caused the calamity of Genesis 1:2; Jeremiah 4:23-26; Psalm 104:6-9; and 2 Peter 3:5-6? Why was hell prepared for the Devil and his angels as stated in Matthew 25:41, and why was it located beneath the earth (Matthew 12:40; Ephesians 4:7-11)? Why was Adam told to "replenish" the earth and not merely to plenish it? These and other questions go unanswered apart from a belief in the pre–Adamite world.

"The steps in getting benefits from God are simple."

Finis Dake

CHAPTER TEN

DAKE'S TEACHING ON THE SONS OF GOD

DAKE'S UNDERSTANDING

A second part of the controversy at Southwestern had to do with Dake's teachings concerning angels—the "Sons of God" mentioned in the sixth chapter of Genesis. This teaching is commonplace in many churches today, but in the late 1920's, it was viewed as strange indeed. Dake's understanding of this doctrine is as follows:

PROOFS THAT GIANTS WERE THE SONS OF ANGELS

1) The fact that giants have lived on earth is clearly stated in Scripture. The Hebrew *nephil* means "giant" or "tyrant" (Genesis 6:4; Numbers 13:33). The men of Israel were as grasshoppers compared to them (Numbers 13:33). The Hebrew *gibbowr* is also translated "giant," meaning "powerful," "giant," "mighty," or "strong man" (Job 16:14). To say these original words refer to their degree of wickedness instead of bodily size is a mistake.[79]

> "Scripture teaches that angels are very similar to men in that they have bodies, souls, and spirits."
>
> *Finis Dake*

The Anakim were a great and tall people (Deut. 1:28; 2:10-11, 21; 9:2; Joshua 11:21-22; 14:12-14). Anak himself was a giant (Numbers 13:33). If all Anakim were as big, we can be assured other giants were also. The land of Ammon was "a land of giants," for "giants dwelt therein in old time" (Deuteronomy 2:19–20). The Emim were also "great, and many, and tall, as the Anakims" (Deuteronomy 2:10-11). The same was said of the Zamzummim who formerly inhabited the land of Ammon (Deuteronomy 2:19-21). Og, king of Bashan, is described as a giant whose iron bedstead was 13.5 feet long, and six feet wide. This is not a measurement of wickedness, but of a material bed for a giant body measuring nearly 13 feet tall (Deuteronomy 3:11; Joshua 12:4; 13:12). Bashan is called "the land of the giants" (Deuteronomy 3:13).

A "valley of the giants" is mentioned in Joshua 15:8 and 18:16. This is the valley of Rephaim, the name of another branch of the giant races

---

[79] Much of the material in this chapter has been taken from *God's Plan for Man*.

mentioned in Scripture (Genesis 14:5; 15:20; 2 Samuel 5:18, 22; 23:13; 1 Chronicles 11:15; 14:9; Isaiah 17:5). The Rephaim were well–known giants, but unfortunately, instead of retaining their proper name in Scripture, the translators of the King James Bible used the words "dead" (Job 26:5; Psalm 88:10; Proverbs 2:18; 9:18; 21:16; Isaiah 14:8; 26:19); and "deceased" (Isaiah 26:14). It should have been a proper name in all these places, as it is ten times otherwise.

> *"The Word of God should be given first place in our lives, not the senses of the body and soul."*
>
> *Finis Dake*

Rephaim is translated "giant" in Deuteronomy 2:11, 20; 3:11, 13; Joshua 12:4; 13:12; 15:8; 18:16; 2 Samuel 21:16, 18, 20, 22; 1 Chronicles 20:4, 6, 8. The phrase "remnant of the giants" in Deuteronomy 3:11; Joshua 12:4; 13:12 should read "remnant of the Rephaim," because there were many nations of giants other than the Rephaim who filled the whole country trying to contest God's claim on the promised land. They are listed as Kenites, Kenizzites, Kadmonites, Hittites, Perizzites, Rephaims, Amorites, Canaanites, Girgashites, Jebusites, Hivites, Anakims, Emims, Horims, Avims, Zamzummims, Caphtorims, and Nephilims (Genesis 6:4; 14:5-6; 15:19-21; Exodus 3:8, 17; 23:23; Deuteronomy 2:10-12, 20-23; 3:11-13; 7:1; 20:17; Joshua 12:4-8; 13:3; 15:8; 17:15; 18:16). Og was of the remnant of Rephaim, not the remnant of all other giant nations (Deuteronomy 3:11; Joshua 12:4; 13:12).

All of these giant nations came from a union of the "sons of God" (fallen angels) and "daughters of men" after the flood. Beings of great stature, some of them even had six fingers on each hand and six toes on each foot and carried spears weighing from 10 to 25 pounds (2 Samuel 21:16-22; 1 Chronicles 20:4–8). Goliath, whom David slew, wore a coat of armor weighing 196 pounds and was nine feet and nine inches tall (1 Samuel 17:4-6).

The revelation that we have of giants in Scripture gives us a true picture of what the Greeks, in their mythologies, attempted to portray. Mythology is but the outgrowth of traditions, memories, and legends telling of the acts of supernatural fathers and their giant offspring—the perversion and corruption in transmission of actual facts concerning these mighty beings. The fact that giants were partly of supernatural origin made it easy for human beings to regard them as gods.

2) The fact that the Rephaim have no resurrection (Isaiah 26:14) proves the reality of giants and that they were not ordinary men. All or-

dinary men are to be resurrected (John 5:28-29); therefore, giants must be a different class from the descendants of Adam. Isaiah makes it clear that the dead (Hebrew: *Rephaiym*) are now in hell (Isaiah 14:9). Solomon confirms this in Proverbs 2:18; 9:18; 21:16 where the Hebrew word for dead is *Rephaim.*

3) The fact that giants came only from a union of the "sons of God" with the "daughters of men" proves that their fathers were not ordinary men of "Adamite" stock. No such monstrosities have been produced from the union of any ordinary man and woman, regardless of the righteousness of the father or the wickedness of the mother. Many converted men who are "sons of God" (in the sense that they have received an adoption and righteousness through Christ), have been married to unconverted women, and no offspring the size of biblical giants has ever resulted from these unions. If, as some teach, giants were born of such unions both before and after the flood, then why do not such marriages produce that kind of offspring today? Why did this happen in every case then and never today?

4) God's law of reproduction from the beginning has been "every-thing after its own kind." It was not possible then that giants could be produced by men and women of ordinary size (Genesis 1:11-12, 21, 24-25; 8:19). It took a supernatural element, the purpose and power of Satan and his angels, to make human offspring of such proportion. After giants came into being, they then produced others of like size instead of men and women of ordinary stature (Numbers 13:33; 2 Samuel 21:16, 18, 20, 22; 1 Chronicles 20:4-8).

5) Not only is it unscriptural, but it is also unhistorical to teach that giants came from the union of ordinary men and women. The question has been: "where did giants get their start"? Genesis 6:4 makes it clear—from a union of the sons of God and daughters of men. If the sons of God were ordinary men in the same sense that the daugh-ters of men were ordinary women, then we must conclude four things:
(1) Ungodly women have the power to produce such monsters if mar-ried to godly men.
(2) Godly men have the power to produce giants when married to ungodly women.

(3) A mixture of godliness and wickedness produces giants.

(4) Extreme wickedness on the part of either parent will produce giant offspring.

All four conclusions are wrong, however, as proven every day by the ordinary offspring of wicked and godly parents. Thus, the theory that giants came from the marriage of Seth's sons with Cain's daughters is disproved.

6) The sons of God could not have been the sons of Seth or other godly men for the following seven reasons:

(1)There were no men who were godly enough to be saved during the Antediluvian Age except Abel (Genesis 4:4; Hebrews 11:4), Enoch (Genesis 5:21-24; Hebrews 11:5), and Noah (Genesis 6:8; 7:1; Hebrews 11:7). Shall we conclude that these three men were the "sons of God" who married the daughters of Cain and produced races of giants in the earth in the days before the flood (Genesis 6:4)? We have no record of any marriage or offspring of Abel before he was murdered. Regarding Enoch, are we to believe that Methuselah and his other children were giants? Are we to believe that Noah's three sons—Shem, Ham, and Japheth—were giants? If so, where is our authority for this? Had this been true, there would have been nothing on earth after the flood but giants, for by Noah's children the whole earth was replenished (Genesis 10). That would cause another unsolved mystery—how giants became ordinary–sized men again.

(2) The time of the marriages of the sons of God disproves the theory that they were the sons of Seth. Marriages of Seth's sons could not have taken place during the first 325 years. He had only one son of marriageable age up to that time (Genesis 5:1-8) and he (Enos) was not godly (see The Line of Seth). To say that there were no such marriages before Enos contradicts Genesis 6:1-2 which shows that sons of God married daughters of men when they began to be born. Shall we conclude that daughters were not born in the first 325 years? If so, where did Cain, Seth and others get their wives?

Furthermore, such marriages between godly sons and ungodly daughters could not have taken place during the last 600 years before the flood, because Noah was the only son of God by righteousness during this time (Genesis 6:8-9; 7:1; 2 Peter 2:4-5). His sons were preserved in the ark because they were descendants of Adam, not because of their own personal righteousness. The facts listed above limit these marriages to the 731 years between the first 325 years and the last 600 of the Antediluvian Age, whereas sons of God actually married daughters of men throughout the entire 1,656 years of that age. Genesis 6:1-2 makes it clear that this happened "when men began to multiply on the face of the earth."

(3) Genesis 6:4 teaches that there were giants on the earth "in those days" (before the flood), "and also after that" (after those days which were before the flood), as a result of the sons of God marrying the daughters of men. If the sons of God were the sons of Seth, we can account for them "after that" (after the flood), for the line of Seth was continued through Noah. But with the daughters of Cain (supposed by some to be the daughters of men) the story is different. Cain's line perished in the flood, which means there were no daughters of Cain after the flood for sons of God to marry.

> *"Regardless of the failure of men we must accept plain truths of Scripture as being of God."*
>
> *Finis Dake*

(4) The Bible gives us no reason to believe that the statement "the sons of God saw the daughters of men that they were fair" should be limited to Cain's daughters. Thousands of families from the many branches of the race both before and after the flood had daughters also. In the 1,656 years before the flood (which is the period in which Seth and Cain lived), there must have been from 150 million to 500 million people. It is unbelievable that as many as half of these were godly and half ungodly; and we know that they were not limited to two lines—the line of Seth and the line of Cain. Regarding Seth's daughters, we have reason to believe that they were as fair as the daughters of Cain—beautiful enough to attract men as husbands for themselves. The line of Seth alone survived the flood, so we know this is true. Genesis 6:1-2 therefore, cannot be said to refer only to the daughters of Cain; and the term "daughters of men" cannot be limited to the daughters of Cain.

(5) The very expressions "sons of God" and "daughters of men" indicate two different kinds—one the product of God, the other the product of man. Seth was not God, so why call the sons of God the sons of Seth?

(6) It is a matter of record that Seth's children were as ungodly as Cain's. The firstborn of Seth even started idolatry, as proven in the line of Seth.

(7) With the exception of Noah and his family, "all flesh had corrupted his way upon the earth" before the flood (Genesis 6:12), which means the entire race (besides Noah's family) had become a mixture of fallen angels and men, or giants. Only Noah and his family had kept their lineage pure from Adam, which is really why they were saved in the ark. They were the only ones capable of giving the race a new, clean start after the flood. It is said of Noah that he was a "just man and perfect in his generations" (Genesis 6:9). The Hebrew for "perfect" is *tamiym* (HSN–8549), which means "without blemish." It is the technical word for physical perfection, not moral perfection. It is so used of the sacrificial animals of the Old Testament, which had to be of pure stock and without blemish (Exodus 12:5; 29:1; Leviticus 1:3; 3:1-6; 4:3, 23-32; 5:15-18; 6:6; 9:2-3; Ezekiel 43:22-25; 45:18-23), without spot (Numbers 19:2; 28:3-11; 29:17, 26), and undefiled (Psalm 119:1). Used of Noah, this word means that he and his sons were the only descendants of Adam left, and for such purity, they (regardless of their position in personal holiness) were all preserved in the ark.

PROOFS THAT THE SONS OF GOD WERE ANGELS:

Since the "sons of God" mentioned in Genesis 6 cannot be the sons of Seth or the offspring of godly men and ungodly women, they must be fallen angels. This is clear from many scriptures:

1) The expression "sons of God" is found only five times in the Old Testament and every time it is used of angels (Genesis 6:1-4; Job 1:6; 2:1; 38:7). It is indisputable that the passages in Job refer to angels. Daniel 3:25, 28 calls an angel "the son of God." Is it not possible then, that the sons of God of Genesis 6 could be angels?

2) Some translations (the Septuagint, Moffatt, and others) read, "angels of God" in Genesis 6:1-4, which is the only idea that harmonizes with this passage and many others.

3) Josephus says, "many angels of God accompanied with women, and begat sons that proved unjust, and despisers of all that was good, on account of the confidence they had in their own strength . . . these men did what resembled the acts of those whom the Grecians call giants" (Antiquities, Book 1, 3:1). Again he says, "There were till then left the

race of giants, who had bodies so large, and countenances so entirely different from other men, that they were surprising to the sight, and terrible to the hearing. The bones of these men are still shown to this very day" (Antiquities, Book 5, 2:3).

4) The Ante–Nicene Fathers also refer to angels as falling "into impure love of virgins, and were subjugated by the flesh. Of these lovers of virgins, therefore, were begotten those who are called giants" (vol. 2, p. 142; vol. 8, p. 85, 273). Justyn Martyr (A.D. 110–165) says, "But the angels transgressed . . . were captivated by love of women, and begat children" (vol. 2, p. 190). Methodius (A.D. 260–312) says, "the devil was insolent . . . as also those (angels) who were enamored of fleshly charms, and had illicit intercourse with the daughters of men" (vol. 6, p. 370).

5) Both testaments teach that some angels committed sexual sins and lived contrary to nature. Genesis 6:1-4 gives the history of such sin. 2 Peter 2:4-5 says that angels sinned before the flood and were cast down to hell to be reserved until judgment. Peter doesn't reveal the sin as fornication, but Jude 1:6-7 does, saying, "the angels which kept not their first estate, but left their own habitation, He hath reserved in everlasting chains under darkness unto the judgment of the great day. Even as Sodom and Gomorrah, and the cities about them in like manner (as did the angels), giving themselves over to fornication, and going after strange flesh, are set forth for an example, suffering the vengeance of eternal fire." If Sodom, Gomorrah and other cities lived contrary to nature and committed fornication, as the angels did, then it is clear that the sin of angels was fornication. According to Genesis 6, this sexual sin was committed with "daughters of men."

"Angels are real personal beings with spirit bodies."

Finis Dake

6) The one scripture used to teach that angels are sexless (Matthew 22:30) doesn't specifically state that they are. It states that "in the resurrection they neither marry, nor are given in marriage, but are as the angels of God in heaven." The purpose of this verse is to show that resurrected men and women do not marry to keep their kind in existence. In the resurrected state they live forever, but not as sexless beings. The Bible teaches that every person will continue bodily as he was born, throughout eternity. Paul said that everyone will have his own body in the resurrection

(1 Corinthians 15:35-38). Both males and females will be resurrected as such, though their bodies will be changed from mortality to immortality (1 Corinthians 15:35-54). There is nothing in the resurrection to "un–create" men and women. Christ remained a man after His resurrection and so will all other males.

Throughout Scripture, angels are spoken of as men. No female angels are on record. It is logical to say then that the female was created specifically to keep the human race in existence; and that all angels were created male, inasmuch as their kind exists without reproduction. Angels were created in innumerable numbers to start with (Hebrews 12:22), whereas humanity began with one pair, Adam and Eve, who were commanded to repro-duce and make multitudes. That angels have tan-gible spiritual bodies, appear as men, and perform acts surpassing those of the human male is clear from many passages.

> *"In short, if one ac-cepts the authority of the Bible, one must likewise accept the reality of angels."*
>
> *Finis Dake*

When Jude states that some angels "kept not their first estate, but left their own habitation" (Jude 1:6), he makes it understandable how a sexual sin could be accomplished by them. The Greek word for "habitation" is *oiketerion*. It is used only twice in Scripture: of the bodies of men being changed to spiritual bodies (2 Corinthians 5:2), and the angels having a bodily change—or at least a "lowering" of themselves in some way (Jude 1:6–7). Thus, the New Testament helps explain the history of the Old Testament

7) There are two classes of fallen angels—those loose with Satan who will be cast down to earth during the future tribulation (Revelation 12:7-12), and those who are now bound in hell for committing fornication (2 Peter 2:4; Jude 1:6-7). Had the ones in hell not committed the additional sin of fornication, they would still be loose with the others to help Satan in the future. Their confinement proves they committed a sin besides that of original rebellion with Satan. That it was sexual in nature is clear from 2 Peter 2:4 and Jude 1:6-7, which identifies this class of fallen angels as the sons of God of Genesis 6:1-4.

8) In 1 Peter 3:19-20, we see that Christ "went and preached unto the spirits in prison; which sometime were disobedient, when once the

longsuffering of God waited in the days of Noah, while the ark was a preparing." Who are these spirits in prison, if not the confined angels who at one time lived contrary to their nature—in sin with the daughters of men (Genesis 6:1-4)? We read "Who maketh his angels spirits" (Psalm 104:4; Hebrews 1:13-14). If angels are spirits, we conclude that the imprisoned spirits Christ preached to were angels and the sons of God referred to in Genesis 6, especially since they "were disobedient . . . in the days of Noah, while the ark was a preparing." The very purpose of Noah's flood was to destroy the giant offspring of these angels known as the sons of God who "came in unto the daughters of men."

THE PURPOSE OF SATAN IN PRODUCING GIANTS:

It was the purpose of Satan and his fallen angels to corrupt the human race and thereby do away with pure Adamite stock through whom the "seed of the woman" should come. This would avert their own doom and make it possible for Satan and his kingdom to maintain control of the earth indefinitely. It was said to Adam and Eve that the "seed of the woman" would defeat Satan and restore man's dominion (Genesis 3:15). The only way for Satan to avoid this predicted defeat was to corrupt the Adamic line so that the coming of the "seed of the woman" into the world would be made impossible. This he tried to accomplish by sending fallen angels to marry the daughters of men (Genesis 6:1-4), thus producing the giant nations through them.

There are two episodes with fallen angels taught in Genesis 6:4. There were giants in the earth "in those days (before the flood), and also after that (after the flood), when the sons of God (fallen angels) came in unto the daughters of men (any daughters of men—Cain, Seth and others), and they bare children to them (to the angels)." Satan almost succeeded in his plan during the first episode, for "all flesh had corrupted his way upon the earth"; of all the multitudes, Noah and his sons were the only descendants of Adam left to be preserved by the ark (Genesis 6:8-13; 1 Peter 3:19-20). The main object of the flood was to do away with this Satanic corruption, destroy the giants, and preserve the Adam's race, thus guaranteeing of the coming of the "seed of the woman," as God planned.

Being defeated before the flood didn't stop Satan from making a further attempt to prevent the coming of the Redeemer who would be his final downfall. It was now to his advantage that God had promised never to send another universal flood upon the earth. Satan therefore reasoned that he should make a second attempt to do away with the Adamic line. If he came within "eight souls" of doing it before the flood, his opportunities were now even greater with the promise that there would be no such flood.

This is the reason the second group of fallen angels married the daughters of men. Again the unions produced giants whose races occupied the land of promise—where the Seed should be born—in advance of Abraham. Limited by His promise not to destroy the earth by flood again, God had to destroy the giants another way. This explains why He commanded Israel to kill every one of them, even to the last man, woman and child. It also explains why He destroyed all the men, women and children besides Noah and his family, at the time of the flood. It answers the skeptics' question regarding why children were taken away with adults in the flood. God had to end this corruption entirely to fulfill His eternal plan and give the world its Redeemer. The Redeemer has come now, so Satan is reserving his forces for a last stand at the Second Coming of Christ.

"I have constantly made Bible research, to confirm what I have taught."

Finis Dake

Thus, it is clear from Scripture that there were giants in the earth both before and after the flood and that they came from a union of fallen angels and the daughters of men.

CHAPTER ELEVEN

THE BATTLE RAGES AT SOUTHWESTERN

WE DISAGREE

Though some may disagree with Dake's conclusions regarding the topics discussed in the previous chapters, it is difficult to see how anyone could apply the label of "heresy" to Dake's teachings. He did, after all, base his beliefs on Scripture! Certainly some may have opposing points of view, but to fail to see that Dake has made—at the very least—an honest attempt to rightly divide the Scriptures on these topics is beyond reason.

Still, it's difficult to part with preconceived ideas. Some may take a stand against truth out of ignorance. For others, a fear of accepting unfamiliar truths may cause them to miss the simple teachings of the Bible. And then there are those who simply follow the popular ideas and opinions of the day. Dake, who did not fit into any of these categories, was bound to stir up some controversy. And that's exactly what happened.

1928

E. S. Williams is elected general superintendent of the Assemblies of God.

DON'T TEACH THAT DOCTRINE

Things were going well for Dake at Enid. Both he and Dorothy were content and happy in their teaching positions at Southwestern Bible College. Dorothy, with her English and Music classes, and Dake, with his Bible History, Doctrine and Language classes, were having the time of their lives as they served the Lord teaching His Word.

In his teaching, Dake often referred to the foundational chapters of the Bible, and discussions of the pre–Adamite world and the "Sons of God" mentioned in Genesis 6 were familiar topics for his students. Eventually, a few students and area pastors began to take issue with Dake's teaching. Complaints were made at every level against Dake and this teaching. At one point, it was even reported that students prophesied "in tongues" of Dake's downfall.

THE DISTRICT LEADERSHIP GETS INVOLVED

At this time, Glenn Millard was the District Secretary and Treasurer of the Enid, Oklahoma district. The following is a letter written by Millard:

9/6/1930

My Dear Brother Dake,

As there has been quite a lot of complaint and uneasy feelings about the teaching of pre–creation and the sons of God on Gen. 3 being fallen angels it seemed wise to the board to pass a motion that we refrain from this teaching entirely. This does not mean that we are able to say whether it is right or wrong, but it has caused quite a stir, and we do not feel that we have lost so much to not teach it. Some have refused to let their children return should we not do something about it, therefore we have taken this action. Kansas and Texas superintendents feel this is a good move, as they have had objections brought to them. We feel that as we have so much uneasiness about it this summer that it will be better to use notes in the school that does not have anything in them about it. I feel sure this will bring some what of a disappointment to you and maybe some additional work, but if you were here so you could see the situation I feel you would understand it.

Several students are coming to Enid already that may be located before school. I think we have about one hundred applications, so we may have a pretty fair number after all. Mother Bamford is here, and I think Robert and Celin are coming a week or more before school starts. There is quite a move on foot to consolidate the school with Texas, and possible Arkansas. I think we may do something about it at the Council this fall.

Expecting to see you before many weeks, I am...

Your brother in Christ, Glenn Millard,

Secretary–Treasurer

This letter illustrates the degree to which the problem had grown. It is clear that parents were not going to allow their children to attend Southwestern if Dake continued teaching these subjects. The controversy had even crossed state lines to Kansas and Texas, with leadership getting involved. According to the board, all of Dake's teaching notes were to be cleansed of this teaching. In fact, the board passed a motion that Dake "refrain from this teaching entirely."

While Secretary–Treasurer Millard may have had a desire to be the peacemaker in this issue, promoting the unity of the school, it is clear that Dake was going to be tested to the depths of his heart and convictions concerning his understanding of these issues.

An Agreement With The District?

It is unclear what Dake's initial reaction to the above letter was. Dake was always one with a desire to teach biblical truth, yet he was always willing to do his best to get along with everyone. In his personal effects a document was found which seemed to be a pledge on Dake's behalf. This document read as follows:

What I Will And Will Not Do

1. I will not teach my personal belief of the "creation" and "Sons of God" dogmatically as the last authority on the subjects, in this District (Texas and New Mexico) or in any other District.

2. I will not teach them in any of the Assemblies of the District where it will cause any friction whatsoever, for an indefinite period and until such a time as it will be considered safe to speak upon such subjects. Even then, the teaching will present both sides in a mild, un–emphatic way as the opinions of men.

1928

Pentecostal pioneer Charles F. Parham dies at age 56.

3. I will not promise never to speak upon this subject either publicly or privately outside of the District. Whenever it is expedient to speak upon them in teaching Dispensational Truth or any other subject, both sides will be presented in a mild, un–emphatic way.

4. I will sell my Bible notes now as they are and when another edition comes out I will give both sides of the subjects and will word same as to leave no offense.

5. I will not revise my chart, as it is needed in its present form to teach all theories of men on the subjects.

6. I will not renounce the subjects as unscriptural and say "I do not personally believe in them."

7. If ever in being called to teach or take charge of a Bible School in this District or out of this District, I will be subject to the board of direc-

tors of the school as to the matter of teaching on the subjects, and not to a promise made to the Officiary of Texas and New Mexico in the past years that I will never mention the subjects in future life anywhere.

8. I will state to this District Council that I am sorry for the contention I have caused in the District and could I do my work over again I would present the subjects in the form of opinions along with other theories.

It is apparent that Dake was considering changing his stance on the teaching on the Pre–Adamite World and the Sons of God.

THE GIST OF DAKE'S CONSIDERED AGREEMENT WAS THAT:
- he would not teach the subjects dogmatically;
- he would not teach in districts where it was a doctrine of contention;
- he would not promise not to teach on the subjects in other districts;
- he would not revise his chart;
- he would not renounce the subjects as unscriptural;
- he would teach both sides of the subjects when he did teach on them;
- he would sell his current Bible notes with the teaching as is, but in future printings he would present both sides;
- he would be subject to the board of directors in whatever school he would be teaching;
- he would state his sorrow for the contention this teaching has caused.

Whether or not Dake actually delivered the document to the district is unclear. From all accounts it seems he formulated the letter but never mailed it. One thing we do know for certain is that the battle continued to rage on into the next year. In fact, by the next year Dake had made his decision.

DAKE RESIGNS FROM SOUTHWESTERN
Friends, co–laborers and fellow professors were all part of Dake's life at Southwestern. He had joined the fellowship of a new and struggling school and had devoted his life to the teaching of the Word of God. The Assembly of God was Dake's life at this point. It was the church he had been saved in; it was all he knew. It was a heart–wrenching decision that

he had to make. But Dake felt his own conscience must be followed in the teaching of biblical truth. On March 5, 1931, Dake, along with his wife Dorothy, sent in his letter of resignation.

Enid, Oklahoma

March 5, 1931

> *"It was all too evident that what was in the Bible and, what was being taught by religion was at variance, and one could not believe both."*
>
> *Finis Dake*

In view of the fact that many are opposed to a few points of my teaching as to the time of the creation of the earth, i.e., the teaching that is commonly known as the Original Earth theory, and my teaching concerning the Sons of God of Genesis 6, and because I do not desire to teach where there is not full cooperation from those who oppose these points, I hereby offer my resignation from the faculty of Southwestern Bible School, to be effective at the end of this present school year.

Signed: Finis Jennings Dake

For the reasons mentioned above, I also hereby offer my resignation from the faculty of Southwestern Bible School, to be effective at the end of this present school year.

Signed: Dorothy Dobbins Dake

Later in life, Dake would preface his teachings and lectures with this statement:

> We are taking for a textbook the Bible itself. And we are going to believe everything that it says about any particular question. Regardless of what it says, we are going to believe it.

Such a statement seems grand and glorious—until one comes to understand the cost of accepting the Bible above all else—above friends, above peers and above denominations. Indeed, to be true to one's convictions does have its cost. But these costs, as great as they may be, always bring God's blessings in the end.

The District Responds To Dake's Decision

As Dake's decision to resign came to light, numerous responses began to come forth. The district, students, other professors, parents of the students—in fact, the General Council in Springfield even weighed in on the matter. Following is the response of the district.

March 7, 1931

Dear Brethren:

In the meeting of the District board after a general discussion, business was taken up. Below I am mentioning some of the things that will be of importance to you.

> "Challenge every opposing force in the name of Jesus."
>
> Finis Dake

Whereas there is a general financial depression over the country a motion was made and carried to not have the state camp meeting this year, and let the presbyters of the respective sections arrange sectional camp meetings if they see fit, and the brethren of that district so desire.

School matters were discussed at this time. A motion was made and carried to retain Mrs. Annie Bamford for the next school year in the position she now holds in the school. Brother and Sister Finis Dake declined to consider a position in the school for next year. Motions were made and carried to retain Robert McCutchan and Miss Celia Swank.

Whereas there is a general financial depression, and whereas the school is short of funds; a motion was made and carried to close the school about three weeks early. The baccalaureate sermon will be on Sunday, April 12, and the commencement service on April 14. We trust many of our people will plan to attend, also remember us in prayer that God will take us through.

In view of the division among the brethren of the District over the teaching of the creation and the fallen angels, the board unanimously agreed again that it should not be taught in the school, and advised the brethren over the

District to avoid discussion over the matter. We feel we must "keep the unity of the Spirit until we come into the unity of the faith."

The deficiency in the different funds of the District was discussed, and the board decided to appeal to the brethren over the field to adhere to the resolution to send at least half of their tithes to the District Storehouse, and more if they see fit to do so at this time. It will be possible for me as Secretary to fill more calls than in the past and especially as soon as school is out, and possibly this will help some.

> *"All must yield to the name of Jesus."*
>
> Finis Dake

Brethren, one of our ministers, Sister Florence Boucher, is in the hospital, and in a very bad condition. We ask you to join in prayer for her deliverance. They are badly in need of some financial help, and if you will send in an offering, I will gladly see that she gets it. This condition is really critical.

Let me again mention the sectional meeting at McAlester. It begins the night of the 11th, and closes the night of the 13th. Asking you to remember the work of the District in prayer.

Your brother in Christ

Glenn Millard

Secretary–Treasurer

Brother Millard met with the District Board and accepted the Dake's resignations, replacing them with Robert McCutchan and Celia Swank. It was stated that the "teaching of the creation and the fallen angels, ... should not be taught in the school."

Though some may question the disctrict's decision in this matter, their heart was in the right place. It was Brother Millard who stated that it was the desire of the district to: "keep the unity of the Spirit until we come into the unity of the faith."

THE STUDENTS RESPOND TO DAKE'S DECISION

Dake's resignation was made and accepted, but things didn't end on a bad note. The students circulated a petition of support for Dake—which most of the students signed. The petition header read:

April 12, 1931

Enid, Oklahoma

To Whom It May Concern:

We, the undersigned, students of the First Year Class of Southwestern Bible School, do hereby certify that Brother Finis J. Dake has taught nothing concerning creation and the six days of Genesis 1:3–2:4, other than that which is found in the School notes.

THE LEADERSHIP RESPONDS TO DAKE'S DECISION

Not only did the students give Dake their support, the District Superintendent, as well as the District Secretary and the President of Southwestern, all gave Dake a wonderful letter of recommendation. Their letter follows:

Enid, Oklahoma

April 12, 1931

TO WHOM IT MAY CONCERN:

This certifies that Mr. Finis J. Dake for the past two years had been a highly esteemed member of the Faculty of Southwestern Bible School. He has a rare knowledge of the Bible, and knows how to impart this knowledge to his students. We love him as a Brother in the Lord, and commend him to the confidence and the fellowship of God's people wherever he may go.

P. C. Nelson, President

James Hutsell, District Superintendent

Glenn E. Millard, District Secretary

Brother Millard must have felt the loss of the Dakes the greatest. In fact, he seemed to think that if some of the preachers in the district had not caused such a stir, perhaps the Dakes could have stayed on at the school. In a letter dated May 16, 1931, he wrote:

> I certainly regret that some of the preachers made the condition such that you would not stay. I feel we will suffer a lot because of it.

It is also of interest that even the General Superintendent of the Assemblies of God had advice for Dake. Brother E. S. Williams[80] wrote to Dake, addressing what he felt might be the problem with Dake's teaching and offering loving instruction on how he might be better received among the brethren. His letter stated that ministers had spoken to him about Dake's teaching. He wrote:

"Don't limit God or His promises."

Finis Dake

> Your teaching lacks what I would call flexibility. . . . it is possible that you have been inclined to speak with emphasis which makes you to appear dogmatic, this I believe the Lord can help you to correct. . . . it seems this has been felt by brethren in different places to be the outstanding weakness of your teaching. I suggest therefore, dear brother, that if there is weakness in your teaching on the line of being over–emphatic you try to correct that and God is certainly going to bless you.

It is interesting at this point to note also that on March 6, 1965, Brother Williams wrote these words concerning Dake:

> I do not know of any man that is more a master of the contents of the Bible than Finis Dake and I do not know of any place his doctrine is erroneous.

This opposition would not end at Southwestern. In the days to come

---

[80] Williams, E. S. (1885–1981). Pastor, dean, author, and denominational executive. He was elected to the office of General Superintendent of the Assemblies of God in 1929. (*Dictionary of Pentecostal and Charismatic Movements*, published by Zondervan Publishing House, 1988.)

Dake would continually have to face his critics. So, with their decisions made and friendships retained, the Dakes left Southwestern after their first year of ministry there. They left in the favor of the Lord, the students and the leadership. This in itself speaks to the character and Christian commitment of all those concerned.

CHAPTER TWELVE

ZION

BACK TO EVANGELIZING

In the summer of 1931, after leaving Southwestern Bible School, the Dake family returned once again to holding their evangelistic services. They travelled up through the Midwest, preaching at a number of churches on the way. Dake would always teach from his Bible chart, "The Plan of the Ages," and Dorothy would would follow his teaching with an evangelistic sermon. Things were going quite well for this young family. Finette, who was about five years old now, was healthy and full of life, and God was supplying their needs in every way.

A TYPICAL DAKE MEETING

Dake ministered at several hundred churches during his lifetime. It is interesting to take a look at some of his earlier meetings and the way they were conducted in the local churches. The Sheboygan Press of Sheboygan, Wisconsin, ran an advertisement for a Dake meeting in November of 1933. This account gives a good summary of a Dake revival meeting.

1933

Kathryn Kuhlman gains recognition by opening the Denver Revival Tabernacle.

> The revival services being conducted at the Sheboygan Gospel Tabernacle, 916 N. Ninth Street, are drawing fine audiences nightly. These services conducted by the Rev. Finis J. Dake of Zion, Il., will continue this week every night, except Saturday, and Sunday will culminate the series. Mr. Dake is a well known Bible teacher and author.
>
> The meetings begin at 7:15 p.m., at which time the chart studies are taken up, and the studies are directly followed by evangelistic services. The chart used is twenty–eight feet long and five feet wide and has upon it the picture of the Bible from cover to cover. The books of prophecy are made very clear on this chart and once one sees the chart pictures of future events prophesied, it helps greatly in producing a good understanding of the divine plan.

Each evening Rev. Dake answers any Biblical questions rendered. A Bible Question Box is available for you to deposit any Bible question you may have. Some of the questions expounded thus far are: "Where did Cain get his wife?" "Where do we go from this life?" "Is hell everlasting?" "Where is paradise?" "Will Christ reign on this earth?" "Will the world come to an end?" etc.

It is expected that Mrs. Dake will speak in the local Tabernacle tonight following the chart studies. She has been an Evangelist for several years and usually accompanies her husband in revival campaigns. The book of Revelation will be future expounded in the chart studies with a discussion of the battle of Armageddon, the Revelation of Jesus Christ and the Millennium.

Thursday evening, a thorough discussion of the "Baptism of the Holy Spirit" will be taken up. Rev. Dake invites all the local Pastors to help in this discussion and the meeting will be thrown open to suggestions, helps and questions— thus it is expected that a conclusion generally acceptable will be obtained upon this most important subject. Some of the questions already received are: "Is the Baptism of the Holy Spirit for today?" "Is it the same as salvation or sanctification?" "Was the church once for all the recipient of this baptism on the day of Pentecost?" and "How may one receive such an experience?"

Ted Schreffier, violinist and pianist, of Milwaukee, and Rev. Dake, baritone soloist and trombonist, together with local musicians help to make an interesting program nightly. Rev. H. A. Fischer, pastor of the local tabernacle, invites all local pastors, regardless of denomination, to attend these services and especially the Thursday evening service.[81]

A CALL TO PASTOR IN ZION

During their travels, the Dakes had many people coming to their services from miles around. Word of their ministry had travelled to the

---

[81] This article taken from the *Sheboygan Press*. Sheboygan, WI. Wednesday, 11/22/33.

Christian Assembly of God church located at the corner of 27th Street and Eschol in Zion, Illinois. The board and members of this church were very impressed with the Dake ministry, and felt led of God to send out a pastoral call.

Christian Assembly of God, Zion, Illinois

In *The Latter Rain Evangel*,[82] Dake wrote a report about the church and his accepting the call to pastor, as well as a revival they had conducted with Rev. Watson Argue. The report as it appeared in *The Latter Rain* follows:

> It was hard for us to believe at first that God wanted us in Zion, mainly because Mrs. Dake and I were evangelistic in vision and purpose. Evangelism was woven into the warp and woof of our being and from all appearances there was little chance for evangelistic pastors in Zion! But we had accepted an invitation from the Board to visit the Christian Assembly with a view to taking the pastorate and try our best to see possibilities in this very religious town.
>
> When the evening arrived for our decision, we started from

---

[82] *The Latter Rain Evangel*: March 1934, page 14. A special thanks goes out to the Assembly of God archives for a copy of this historic document, as well as other issues used throughout this work.

our room expecting to say no to a further stay in Zion, Before I reached the door, a feeling came over me that maybe we were looking at things in the natural and basing our decision solely upon what we could see. I dropped to my knees and called my wife back. "Let us pray," I said "and be sure that we have God's mind in this matter." Mrs. Dake said later that when she turned and saw me on my knees she was sure that our answer to the Board would be "yes" instead of "no." And so it was. This was in June, 1932.

> "We should back our pastor in prayer and be the kind of members that he can depend upon."
>
> Finis Dake

Our greatest desire from then on was to see a revival among the saints and a harvest of lost souls. We became convinced in a short while that there were many in the town who needed John 3:16 and others who would be blessed by Acts 2:4, even though the place was loaded down with religion.

But our desires did not become realities over night. Discouragement was the weapon used by the devil on some of the other pastors and he used the same on us. But this time discouragement was not defeat, for it drove us to our knees. Not only days of fasting and prayer were announced but at one time three weeks of prayer continued day and night in the church; always there was someone there crying: "Lord, send a revival to Zion!" Some days or nights we were but two in number who could spend the time in prayer. But that was enough, for we find the required amount to be "two or three" gathered in His name.

Shortly after that time we began in faith to call evangelists, organize a Young People's Chorus, Orchestra, String Band, and outline a course of Bible School training for our young workers. Little by little at first, the congregation grew and we could see that we were gradually climbing up the hill to a peak which we viewed through the eye of faith.

I ventured to announce one Sunday morning that I was praying and expecting God to fill every seat in the building. A few said "Amen," while many others looked up in surprise. But once again God answered prayer. It is not unusual now in our revivals for the building to be packed out with extra chairs in the aisles and sometimes an over-flow crowd in the basement auditorium. This was especially true in the four weeks' campaign conducted here during the month of January by Evangelist and Mrs. Watson Argue, when even week night crowds often filled the auditorium to capacity. During that time we purchased an amplifier so that overflow crowds might hear the sermon through a loud speaker in the basement. It looks now as if we shall have to add to our present building. Already money is coming in for this purpose.

Our Sunday School, which had grown from its average of 85 when we came here to about 200, received special benefit from the recent Argue campaign, and broke previous records in attendance. The Evangelists took special interest in that department and it increased in numbers until there were 325 in Sunday School the last week of their revival effort in Zion. The church in general was also blessed by their ministry. On some occasions the long altars were practically lined across the front with sin–burdened people seeking Christ. During the campaign 24 were baptized in water and 36 new names were added to the Assembly roll. We shall long remember the ministry of our Brother and his wife in Zion.

– Finis J. Dake, Pastor, Christian Assembly of God

Christian Assembly was founded in 1908, sharing the Shiloh Tabernacle[83] with Grace Missionary Church, a splinter group from Christian Catholic Church, of John Alexander Dowie[84] fame. In the earlier stages of its history, John G. Lake[85] preached at Christian Assembly

---

[83] Shiloh Tabernacle was the building where the congregation of John Alexander Dowie met. It was a large white building that seated nearly 8,000 people.

[84] Dowie, John Alexander. (1847–1907) Pastor from Australia who came to America in 1888. Founded the *Christian Catholic Apostolic Church* in Illinois. In 1901 he founded Zion City. Was known for his healing ministry.

[85] Lake, John G. (1870–1935) A missionary, pastor and mighty man of God used in the healing ministry. A disciple of Dowie and a leader in Zion.

and the periodical *The Bridegroom's Messenger*[86] tells of great services during this time in which God moved with great signs and wonders.

Later, property was secured at the corner of 27th Street and Eschol in Zion, and Christian Assembly built its own building and relocated there. While Christian Assembly had some wonderful services and accomplished much for God's kingdom, it had never been able to capture the glory that Dowie had brought to Zion. This would indeed turn out to be a life–changing experience for Dake, as he faced the reality of an encounter with one of the greatest moves of God in the recent history of the Church.

To understand Dake's ministry in Zion, we must first know a little more about John Alexander Dowie.

---

[86] *The Bridegroom's Messenger,* founded by G. B. Cashwell, of Atlanta Georgia, in 1907. It was a periodical designed to spread the Pentecostal message as widely as possible with its mixture of sermons, editorials and reader testimonies from across the Southeast and even the country by those who had experienced the manifestation of tongues. Many great church leaders were featured in its pages.

CHAPTER THIRTEEN

JOHN ALEXANDER DOWIE AND THE CITY HE BUILT

JOHN ALEXANDER DOWIE

While the life of John Alexander Dowie is not the subject of this work, in view of his ministry's effect upon Dake, we must know something of this man and the city he founded.

David Allen, author of *The Unfailing Stream*[87] writes the following:

In April of 1872 the tiny Congregational chapel at Alma, South Australia, welcomed its new pastor, twnty–five year old John Alexander Dowie. He only stayed a few months and none of the congregation could possibly have guessed that he was to become, in the words of Barry Chant, "one of the most outstanding and controversial leaders of the late C19th."

> *"The secret of power with God is to believe His Word and conform to it to the letter."*
>
> *Finis Dake*

Dowie was of Scottish parentage and his parents, like many of their compatriots, had sought a new life in the expanding, bustling colony of Australia. However, feeling a call to the ministry, John returned to his native Edinburgh to study Divinity there. It was after this period of study that he accepted the call to Alma, South Australia. However, it was in his next pastorate that he came to the attention of the public at large.

While pastoring in Newtown, a suburb of Sydney, having conducted over forty funerals as a result of an epidemic then sweeping the city, he was challenged by the question, "If God healed people in 75 AD, why not in 1875 AD?" Then, after studying the Scriptures on the matter of divine healing, he began to pray for the sick. From that

---

[87] *The Unfailing Stream*, by David Allen. Sovereign World Ltd., Tonbridge, Kent: England, Page 99.

time on there were no more deaths from the sickness in his ever–growing congregation.

There were many outstanding miracles at Melbourne. Dowie moved there in the early 1880's. Lucy Parker blinded in one eye by cancer and now expecting a child, but not expected to survive childbirth—had the sight of the eye restored when Dowie laid hands on her. She later gave birth to a healthy baby. A 16–year–old youth, laid up by tuberculosis, arose from his hospital bed. What makes the cases so remarkable is that both patients had been long under expert medical supervision and that both were completely and instantaneously restored by the simple expedient of the prayer of faith.

There were many hundreds healed, however, and also many thousands who experienced the supreme miracle of the new birth. Dowie never neglected the proclamation of the Good News. And, as the work in Australia expanded, he felt that the time had come to transfer operations to America. First from Evanston, Illinois, and later from "Zion City"—the name of the community he set up on the shores of Lake Michigan in 1900—Dowie propagated/ practiced divine healing.

The Zion City community grew to approximately six thousand persons and though Dowie was somewhat old–fashioned and negative in his notion of what constituted holiness—he was almost fanatically opposed to tobacco and alcohol—in other ways he was what might be called "progressive." Many women engaged in full–time evangelistic work and blacks and whites mixed and worked freely and easily together. Many of those who were associated with Dowie later became founder–members of the Assemblies of God and other emerging Pentecostal churches and groups.

Sadly, Dowie's ministry ended in controversy. He had many critics throughout his ministry. They, like Edward Irving's critics half a century earlier, regarded him as a crank, a charlatan and a fanatic. Dowie, though clearly an important forerunner of the Pentecostal Movement, did leave himself wide open to criticism. In 1901 he claimed that he was the prophesied Elijah (Malachi 4:5) commissioned by God to lead and restore a renewed Church that even the Pope would eventually join! On the platform he began to wear robes similar to those of an Old Testament High Priest. He died in obscurity in 1907, his followers having deserted him and his health having been seriously impaired by a massive stroke.

FROM A PERSONAL POINT OF VIEW

In Gordon Lindsay's book, *John Alexander Dowie: A Life Story of Trials, Tragedies and Triumphs,*[88] a summarization of the ministry of Dr. Dowie, as experienced by Anton Darms, gives personal insight into this man's ministry and his unique place in the history of the church.

1907

John Alexander Dowie holds a unique and definite place in the development of apostolic ideals for the Church of the Twentieth Century. His life, mission, and work present a fascinating, romantic object lesson for those interested in progressive Christianity.

"John Alexander Dowie, founder of Zion, Illinois dies"

Single–handedly, as Elijah of old, he denounced the decadent order of the day, and protested mightily against apostasy, both of the Protestant and Catholic divisions of the Church, and heralded a New Day of a thousand years when Jehovah would hold sway over a redeemed earth.

Like a clap of thunder out of a clear sky, John Alexander Dowie started on his world–wide mission of setting forth

[88] *John Alexander Dowie—A Life Story of Trials, Tragedies and Triumphs,* by Gordon Lindsay, published by Christ for the Nations, Dallas, Texas and reprinted in 1986. This is a monumental work on the life of Dowie and anyone wishing further study on this subject should consult this work. You may obtain this book by contacting: Christ for the Nations Books Department, PO Box 769000, Dallas, Texas 75375–9000. The author expresses his sincere thanks and appreciation to Christ For The Nations for the use of this material.

the Word of God, and putting into practice, the ideals and principles of the coming Messianic Kingdom; and thereby succeeded in making "Zion" a household word throughout the whole world.

It has been said that in him were treasured up the rarest gifts and talents ever given to man. As an iconoclast, he denounced evil in high and low places, tore off the mask of unfaithful shepherds behind the pulpit, protested against the shams and the fads of a giddy world, and heralded the death–knell of a dying age.

Sudden and unexpected as was his entry upon the public arena, so sudden and unexpected also was his demise, compelling thousands of devoted followers to whom God's Inspired Word was a sealed book, to acknowledge that his faithful ministry had resulted in making the Bible a new book to them.

Zion, Illinois

By the time Dake arrived in Zion, Dowie had been dead for twenty–five years. However, the influence of his ministry still filled the town. Dake was taken aback by the work of Dowie in Zion. Whenever he spoke of Zion, Dake would also comment: "Zion was a very religious town!"

The city of Zion was founded in 1900.[89] It was intended to be a city of Christian character where men and women from every race were treated equally. It is located halfway between Chicago, Illinois, to the south and Milwaukee, Wisconsin, to the north and borders the shores of Lake Michigan on the east. Dowie employed Burton J. Ashley of Chicago as his city planner. Reports were prepared concerning topography, drainage, water supply, rapid transportation, park land, and parcel size for the development of a city with a projected population of 200,000.

On July 15, 1901, the city was made available for home sites by those who chose to follow Dowie's ministry. It was on August 2, 1901, that the first residence located at 2802 Elizabeth Avenue was built. By winter,

---

[89] Much of the information concerning Zion was gleaned from a website hosted by David Padfield. See: http://www.ourzion.com/history/zion1979.html and http://www.ourzion.com/history/cardhist.html.za for excellent resources on this topic.

there were more homes built and Zion had a population of 2,000. The land, however, was not sold but leased for a period of 1,100 years, and the lease contained numerous restrictions.

Twenty–thousand shade trees were planted along the streets, which all bore biblical names—names like Lydia, Elijah, Elisha, Aaron, Bethel, Carmel and Elizabeth. In the center of town was a 200–acre park where the Temple Site was located. On this site, Dowie built an 8,000–seat sanctuary in just eight weeks. Beside the Temple was built a radio station for the preaching of the Gospel, Radiophone Broadcasting Station WCBD.

"The energy of prayer is even greater than atomic energy."

Finis Dake

Zion had its own hotel called Zion Hotel (Elijah Hospice), which had 350 rooms. It was here that many of the families stayed while their homes were being constructed.

In 1902, over the main entrance of the original structure, a Bell Tower was built containing a 54 inch, half–ton bell which rang every morning and evening at nine o'clock for a minute of silent prayer.

Shiloh House and Cottage, a 25–room, three–story pressed brick, ornamental tile roof home was built at 1300 Shiloh Blvd. by a Swiss architect and was styled after a Swiss chalet for Dr. Dowie in 1903 at a cost of $100,000.00[90]

The first industry established in Zion was the Zion Lace Industries, which was relocated from England. Zion Banking was also established in those early days. The Zion Cookie Factory was also built, sending fig bars around the world.

Also serving the rapidly expanding Zion community were the Zion Department Store, (the largest merchandising establishment in Lake County) the Zion Police Department, the Zion Fire Station, Zion City Hall, Zion Printing and Publishing, dairy, laundry, feed and seed meat markets, bakeries, a golf course, a marina on the waterfront and a candy plant, just to name a few.

ZION, ILLINOIS—1930's

In the 1930's, many of the buildings Dowie had built were still standing and in use in various ways. In fact, for at least a brief time, Wilbur

---

[90] Or about $2,130,437.00 in year 2005 dollars.

Glenn Voliva, Dowie's successor, was still the head of Zion. In the 1930's, the institutions and industries numbered twenty–seven, and did a business of about $4,000,000.00[91] a year.

Zion's educational institutions—from the kindergarten and junior grades through college—were private, with an enrollment of nearly 1,500 pupils. All the major areas of study were included in the curriculum, including manual training, domestic science and gymnasium work. The Bible was the principal textbook. The Department of Music had over 800 students enrolled.

In an attempt to continue the ministry of healing, Zion Home was established. It laid claim to being the largest divine healing home in the world. In 1932, at the time of Dake's arrival, the city population was at about 6,000 and it was recorded that people were in the city from all quarters of the earth.

---

[91] Or about $40,500,000.00 in year 2005 dollars.

CHAPTER FOURTEEN

DAKE PASTORING IN ZION

After accepting the pastorate at Christian Assembly in Zion in June of 1932, life became even busier for the Dake family. Fresh in their walk for the Lord, the possibilities seemed limitless. Pastoring is a very demanding work. Each day the Dakes were ministering to the needs of their congregation, which numbered about 200. There were sick calls to make, elderly shut–ins to visit, church business to attend to, sermons and teachings to prepare for and, in the midst of all this, there was always Dake's constant study of the Bible. For hours on end he would immerse himself in the pages of the Bible, seeking its truth and all the while searching for the fulfillment of the promises of power from God.

Finis, Dorothy & Finette Dake

Christian Assembly was a large church for a Pentecostal church in its day. However, this was Zion and any church which taught the powerful things of God tended to do very well. The church itself was a brick structure with a shingle roof. It had a steeple over the double–door entrance of the church, which was located on the corner of the building. The main sanctuary could accommodate about 500 people and if needed, the basement would allow for seating of an additional 200 people. When the main sanctuary became "packed–out," an amplifying system would take the sermon from the platform to the basement auditorium where the audience would hear the message through a loudspeaker.

HAVE YE RECEIVED THE HOLY GHOST?

In order to emphasize his belief that all believers needed the power of the Holy Ghost to do the work of the Lord, Dake had written a portion of Scripture from Acts 19:2 across the top of the wall just behind the pulpit. In big, bold letters that could clearly be seen anywhere in the building it read: *Have ye received the Holy Ghost since ye believed?*

Indeed, Dake was there to see that Christian Assembly was a church of ministry and nothing less. His heart's cry was for the church to be a body that demonstrated the very presence of Christ in its midst. To drive

The Sanctuary at Christian Assembly

this point home, Dake created a church statement that spoke from the depths of his heart and printed it on just about anything that the church produced. The statement was:

Not a Lyceum.[92]
Not a Lecture Platform.
Not a Moving Picture Theatre.
Not a Center for Socials and Suppers.

But—
A Place to Worship God.
A Place where God is Manifested.
A Place where Jesus Christ is Pre–Eminent.
A Place where the Holy Spirit is Lord.
A Place where the Sick are Healed.
A Place where Souls are Saved from Sin.
A Place where Christianity is Practiced.
A Place where Men are Baptized in the Spirit.
A Place where the Whole Counsel of God is Declared.

---

[92] A gymnasium near Athens where Aristotle taught. Today it refers to a hall for public lectures or discussions. *(See Merriam–Webster Dictionary)*

CHRISTIAN ASSEMBLY REACHES OUT

The church building was only the central hub for Dake and the church ministry. During his stay in Zion, Dake continued to minister at other churches as well. Most meetings would last about two weeks at a time. When he would minister and the distance did not prohibit it, he would always take a number of workers with him from the church.

Christian Assembly was a very active church. In its church bulletin the Dakes listed their service schedule as follows:

Sunday School ....9:30 am
Sunday Morning Worship ....10:45 am
Young People's Service .... 6:30 pm
Evangelistic Service................................. 7:45 pm
Tuesday Public Bible Study..................... 7:45 pm
Thursday Prayer and Praise Service .... 7:45 pm

The Christian Assembly Choir on the move

Each week, workers would go out from the church to participate in street meetings, revival meetings, and personal evangelism. Choir members would travel for miles in their newly purchased 30–person bus, to sing and minister at various churches and camp meetings.

Singing and music flourished at Christian Assembly. Gifted in music, writing and song, Dorothy Dake was the driving force behind that part of the work. There were choirs for every age group. There was a 50–member choir group that sang each week in the worship services. They worshiped with shouts of praise and hands lifted high. While robes were not the order of the day in this Pentecostal church, there was a coordination of dress. The ladies would wear dresses of blue with collars and cuffs of the purest white. And what should a choir be named that constantly praised the Lord and worshiped with the fullness of the Spirit? The "Hallelujah Chorus" of course!

In the 1930's, before the advent of television and before radio had caught on in a great way, many in the congregation were musically in-

The Christian Assembly "Hallelujah Chorus"

clined. Dorothy worked with them all. From those with the least talent to the greatest, she taught and trained until they amassed quiet an orchestra. The 30–piece orchestra had French horns, trumpets, saxophones, clari-

The Christian Assembly 30-piece orchestra

nets, guitars, violins, marimbas, xylophones, the piano and organ, tubas and, of course, trombone players, of which Dake himself was happy to be a part.

PUBLISHING THE PRINTED WORD

As Dake was studying the Scriptures and writing down his notes, it was inevitable that he would have his church assist him in his printing ministry. Dake had purchased printing equipment which he used to print tracks, handouts, charts, and booklets of all kinds. The church membership was eager to help Dake in his publishing efforts, and help they did. By the thousands and thousands, Dake's sermons and notes on the Bible began to flow out of Zion in all directions. Dake and the church were so eager to spread the Word of the Lord that all of the materials were sent to anyone requesting them, without charge. It was during this time that much of the material for the *Dake Annotated Reference Bible* and *God's Plan for Man* was collected.

ALWAYS A TEAM MINISTRY

In the same way that Dake and Dorothy shared the daily work of the church, they also participated together in the ministry of the Word. Dorothy once again was ministering side by side with her husband. An advertisement for the church during this time read:

> Christian Assembly: A wide–awake congregation of people who believe the entire Bible and receive the experiences taught therein; a body of believers who are growing daily in number and spiritual blessings.

> Pastor Dake has charge of all regular services, except Sunday night. Being a capable Bible teacher, he conducts a profitable Bible study each Tuesday evening, using a large 28–foot art colored chart known as: "The Bible on Canvas" designed by himself.

> Mrs. Dorothy Dake, who has had nearly ten years of experience as a successful evangelist, delivers the regular Sunday night evangelistic sermon. She is talented musically and in the past ten years has organized many musical groups in the Assembly. She is director of the Orchestra, Young Peoples Chorus, Rhythm Band and the String Band, and arranges programs of music for the services.

In addition to print advertising Dake also ventured into the most modern forms of advertising of his day. Not television or satellite, but a church on wheels!

On the side of the church it read:
Our troubles are Moral and Spiritual, not economic.
We face SPIRITUAL REVIVAL or RUIN.
Come Where the WHOLE Truth is Declared.
SEE THE BIBLE ON CANVAS TUES. EVENINGS

Special Singing—Orchestra—String band
Biblical Chart Lectures
Inspiring Preaching
Young People's Chorus

And on the chimney it read:
Jesus Saves, Heals, and Baptizes.

The Christian Assembly Church on Wheels

AN UNUSUAL BIBLE MARATHON

Of the many ministries with which the Christian Assembly was involved, perhaps the most interesting were their Bible Marathons. Bible Marathons were conducted in various ways. On some occasions the church would meet and simply read the Scriptures hour after hour until the entire Bible was read in completion. During this time, they would hook up the church loud speakers and broadcast the readings out over the entire community. This would usually last a minimum of 50 hours non-stop, with Scriptures being read around the clock. With the King James Bible being divided into 66 books, 1,189 chapters, and 31,101 verses, made up of 783,133 words and 3,566,480 letters, it is easy to see how it would take some time to read it straight through.[93] Still a more valuable use of one's time could not be found!

In 1935, with no television and little radio, many in the community were delighted to come to the church and just sit and listen to the Bible being read. During this time, the church would be filled with the presence of God and a warm feeling of peace and contentment.

> *"The Word of God should have first place in our lives, instead of our senses."*
>
> *Finis Dake*

On other occasions the Bible Marathon would take the form of questions and answers. Teams were formed and the contests were lively and educational, as the members of Christian Assembly would answer question after question from the Word of God. At other times, the Bible Marathon would consist of members of the church quoting the Bible. The team with the most accurate quotes would be declared the winner. And, of course, Dake always required chapter and verse for every quote given.

By this time in his life, Dake was acquiring a reputation. With his God–given gift, which allowed him the ability to quote literally thousands of verses of Scripture, he was becoming known as "The Walking Bible." However, there were always those who did not believe. The world has many skeptics, but believers are often in short supply.[94]

Dake, however, loved a challenge. It is told that while in Zion, Dake was challenged concerning his gift. Seeking a way to confirm the gift of God in his life, while at the same time using his gift in a way that would bring God the most glory, Dake met the challenge of the skeptics. Lester Sumrall[95] in his book *Pioneers of Faith* tells of this event:

---

[93] *God's Plan For Man*, by Finis J. Dake, Lawrenceville, Georgia: Dake Bible Sales, Inc. 1949, page 14.

[94] ...Nevertheless when the Son of man cometh, shall he find faith on the earth? Luke 18:8 (KJV)

[95] Sumrall, Lester (1913–1996) Missionary, pastor and broadcaster. Born in New Orleans, Louisiana. Began preaching at the age of seventeen, just three weeks after being miraculously cured of tuberculosis. Ordained by the Assemblies of God. Travelled in missionary ministry with famed evangelist Howard Carter. Founded LeSea Broadcasting company in South Bend, Indiana, with both radio and television networks. Founded World Harvest Bible College and authored more than 100 books. A very close friend of Rev. Dake, whom he had to minister at his church many times over the years. (*Dictionary of Pentecostal and Charismatic Movements*, published by Zondervan Publishing House, 1988.)

> He (Dake) was challenged once by a local preacher on whether or not he could quote the New Testament verbatim. Dake agreed to sit behind a glass window in a large department store and do this, providing the local radio station would put his entire quotation on the air. The station agreed, and Dake quoted the New Testament from Matthew to Revelation without opening a Bible. He gave the number of each verse and indicated chapter changes![96]

The news of Dake sitting behind a microphone, in a storefront window reciting the New Testament, travelled far and wide. Numerous newspaper clippings for years afterward continued to speak of Dake of "Bible Marathon" fame. More and more, Dake would be called "The Walking Bible." Dake's fame brought glory to God as he found many new opportunities to minister in churches throughout the Great Lakes area. Many believers and sinners came to hear the man that could quote the Bible. As a result of the preaching of the Word of God, many believed on Christ and were born again.

PASTOR DAKE HAS A FAMILY

While pastoring in Zion Dake, of course, was a family man—with his beloved Dorothy and his precious Finette, who was at this time around seven years of age. Thinking back, he remembered a very embarrassing moment that Finette brought to the Dake family.

It seems Finette wanted something to eat other than what her parents were allowing her to have. All children love sweets and, as good parents, the Dakes would see to it that Finette ate a well–balanced meal.

One day, Finette looked into the cupboard and didn't see anything that would satisfy her taste, nothing that she really liked to eat. So, she went out and began to tell the neighbors that she was hungry and there was nothing in the house to eat!

Upon hearing this, the neighbors and church members got things going. Soon boxes of food, filled with all kinds of wonderful things to eat, began showing up on the Dake's doorstep.

---

[96] *Pioneers of Faith*, by Dr. Lester Sumrall. Harrison House, Tulsa: Oklahoma, Page 71.

Dake and Dorothy had an embarrassing time, telling their friends that they weren't out of food, it was just that Finette wanted something sweet to eat.

MISSION MINDED

Dake always understood that the mission of Christ applied to all peoples in all lands. The church also embraced this understanding of reaching everyone they could reach, not only in Zion, but around the world. The tracks and booklets being printed would help, but in a personal and financial way Dake and Christian Assembly were reaching out.

A report in 1934 stated that two missionaries were entirely supported by the church. Miss Swarztrauber, who served in Palestine, and Miss Asucherman, who ministered in the Canary Islands, were grateful to have been sent out from this missions–minded congregation. In addition, other missionaries were supported from time to time. For the year 1933, missionary offerings averaged $40.00[97] per week. This same report stated that Dake had even bigger plans for increasing their mission support in the years that were to follow. With this kind of spirit of giving, it is no surprise that the Assembly of God headquarters reported that Christian Assembly was number fourteen in the nation in their mission giving.

"The Dakes were very down to earth, friendly people who mixed with their people and loved and encouraged them."

*Rachel Hyllberg
Member of
Christian Assembly*

PASTOR DAKE PRAYS FOR THE SICK IN HIS CONGREGATION

With all the ministry that was taking place, it should not be forgotten that Dake was a man who loved people. Most of all, he wanted to see people receive all that God had made available to them. And too, Dake's compassion for the sick and the hurting was deeply felt and taken very seriously. One of the members of Christian Assembly gives this testimony of the love and care Dake showed their child during a time of great sickness in his life.

"Pastor Dake would come to Mom and Pop McNair's house periodically during the week. He would pick up Paul, who

---

[97] Or about $541.00 per week in year 2005 dollars.

had been diagnosed with appendicitis, and pray for him. Pastor Dake would hold Paul in his arms and rock him in a chair and pray that God would heal him. On one occasion, Pastor Dake pulled off his coat and hung it on the chair and said: "Now Sister McNair, we have got to go to work," and then he prayed that evening until 1:00 a.m. into the morning. He prayed until Paul was healed! God healed Paul. To this day he has never had another attack of appendicitis and he never had to have surgery.[98]

> *"The plan of God for man includes both the means and the ends, prayer and its answer, the labor and its fruit."*
>
> *Finis Dake*

In addition to praying for the sick at his church, Dake would often pray for the sick at the meetings he would hold at other churches. And on some occasions, he, along with the pastor or deacons of those churches, would visit and pray for those who were sick in the congregations. On one such occasion, he and a deacon paid a visit to one such person. Dake tells the story:

In Detroit, Michigan several years ago, a deacon of a certain church took me to see a man to pray for him. He was paralyzed on one side and he had not walked for eight months. I spoke to him about his faith. The very first words as I recall were: "I believe in healing alright, but I cannot seem to have faith for my own healing." I got up and walked over to the bed and said: "Don't say that again. That is not true. You can have faith. You must have faith if you expect to get healed."[99] I then quoted Mark 11:22-24[100] and emphasized the truth of the passage this way:

---

[98] Audio tape testimony of Elsie McNair, who lived in Zion and was a member of Christian Assembly. The tape was recorded live 7/4/94.

[99] James 1:5-8.

[100] Mark 11:22-24. And Jesus answering saith unto them, Have faith in God. For verily I say unto you, That whosoever shall say unto this mountain, Be thou removed, and be thou cast into the sea; and shall not doubt in his heart, but shall believe that those things which he saith shall come to pass; he shall have whatsoever he saith. Therefore I say unto you, What things soever ye desire, when ye pray, believe that ye receive them, and ye shall have them.

"Believe you have got it and you shall have it." This was my way of expressing verse twenty–four. I said that over several times[101] and got him to promise to believe God, that God will heal him, when we pray.[102] While I was praying the paralyzed man said these very words: "If I have got it what am I laying here for?" With that he jumped out of bed and shouted all over the place! I said: "Now the thing for you to do, is stay up until bed time and then get up tomorrow morning perfectly normal and forget that you ever had paralysis." God miraculously healed that man! Met his faith.[103]

God was confirming the Word that Dake quoted and preached with answers to prayer. Miracles were taking place. However, Dake's heart began to cry out for more than the occasional miracle or healing. Indeed, the city of Zion and the legacy of Alexander Dowie were beginning to bring great changes to this young minister's heart and life.

---

[101] Romans 10:17.

[102] Mark 11:24 …What things soever ye desire, when ye pray, believe that ye receive *them*, and ye shall have *them*.

[103] Mark 9:23.

CHAPTER FIFTEEN

DOROTHY DAKE IS QUITE A PREACHER

AN ASSET IN EVERY WAY

It is said that behind every good man is a better woman! It is not the intent of the author to come to a conclusion on this matter, but in Dake's case . . . Dorothy Dake was an asset in every way, including the preaching ministry.

While helping her husband in his pastoral responsibilities, she was busy with her music ministry. It was in Zion that she wrote and published the song, *Like A Rose*.[104] In addition to her songs, *The Shiloh Scroll* was busy publishing her sermons as well. At Christian Assembly, it was the normal schedule for Dorothy to do the preaching on Sunday nights. These sermons were being transcribed by the journalism students at Shiloh. Below are excerpts from two of Dorothy's Sunday night sermons carried by *The Shiloh Scroll*.

> *"When men sin it is not the will of God."*
>
> Finis Dake

SERMON 1—LAZY BONES

While reading my Bible I have noticed that it is possible for man to get from God anything he needs or wants, from the casting of a mountain into the sea, down to the daily supply of his bread. I see but three things that would keep him from this: SIN, UNBELIEF or LAZY BONES.

Sin

When dealing with sin, we cannot be what my brothers used to call "chicken–hearted." We must deal harshly. To wound that monster in the head is our first duty and until he is out of our lives we cannot expect that God is obligated to us in any way.

---

[104] See the Appendix for a sampling of the many songs Dorothy wrote during her ministry: *The Potter's Masterpiece,* published in 1929 and *Like A Rose*, published in 1935, by Dorothy Dake.

Israel prospered when there was no sin in her camp; she failed when there was. Before the mighty Jericho she was strong but before Ai she was weak. Under proper circumstances the three thousand who went up to smite Ai would have been abundantly sufficient for the task. But with an Achan, a wedge of gold, a Babylonish garment and two hundred shekels of silver in the camp, Israel had no power to stand, and her representatives in the battle took to their heels when only thirty–six men of their company were smitten.

Did Joshua handle the situation with gloves on? Indeed not. He dealt harshly and firmly with sin, taking Achan with his coveted belongings and his tent, his sons, his daughters and even his oxen and sheep to the valley of Achor where all Israel stoned them. "And they raised over him a great heap of stones . . . So the Lord turned from the fierceness of his anger" (Joshua 7:26). May God help us to stone sin to death in our lives without delay.

Unbelief

For the disease of unbelief God has given us a sure remedy—the Bible. Steady, constant, systematic reading of God's Word, without fail day in and day out brings its reward. Rather silently and sometimes unnoticed its great work of healing the mind of the poisons of doubt and wavering is carried on and little by little the treatments work. Faith increases and doubt decreases. But some claim they are too busy to read daily; others are (shall I say it?)—too lazy. Then let them suffer until they have learned that they cannot cheat God and prosper.

Lazy Bones

This brings me down to the third hindering force standing between men and their coveted blessings—lazy bones. To have a pressing need is one thing; to have a persistent desire to get that pressing need supplied God's way is another thing and means hard work for "the old man." His notions about rest and plenty to eat will have to be crucified. The man whose belly frame is composed of lazy bones and "whose belly is his God" may expect nothing more than a long list of unanswered prayers at the close of his Christian walk.

Prayer is work and hard work at that! But it is the avenue which leads to the most of what we need and want. If persistent, systematic praying alone does not bring desired results, then we have one more avenue to try and that is fasting. These together are a strongman's job and no lazy bones will ever try them. But he who does, shows God that he is in for business, not being too lazy to pray or too self–centered to deny himself the pleasure of food. God sees the sacrifice, knows why he who petitions is hungry and so rewards openly that which is requested in secret.

> "The Word alone can give you the basis for answered prayer."
>
> *Finis Dake*

In passing, let me insist that your best praying is not done on the platform, in the public, or even at family worship where others are listening. These all have their places and are profitable, but one's most sincere praying is done alone—with God.

Jacob put even his family, the children and wives he loved, across the brook—but he was left alone to wrestle with God. The future was too uncertain, the strain of meeting Esau too great, and so instead of retiring to toss to and fro on the cot with his worries, he fought the matter out with God. Christian travelers, fight your troubles through in prayer alone. You and God together can master each situation confronting you.

As to fasting, do not forget that Nineveh, who faced destruction in forty days, was not left without her reward when all her citizens, their herds and their flocks, were denied food and water through a fast proclaimed by the king. When hunger pangs struck the children and animals, the mooing, the bleating and the crying ascended to heaven. God knew what it meant.

The kind of praying I am trying to describe was well pictured by Jesus in His parable of the unjust judge. (Luke 18) Please notice first that the odds were against the poor widow who wished to be avenged. Her judge was unjust. Thank God, ours is not. Hers regarded not man. The mistreatment of a widow woman did not strike a chord of sympathy in his heart. Let us suppose that a neighbor through carelessness was responsible for the killing of her cow—her only source of help and support for her children. Let us say that the neighbor denied the deed and refused to pay for the cow. Did this situation make its impression on the judge's mind? Not at all. The troubles of a widow were not his troubles. But praise God! Our judge can be "touched with the feeling of our infirmities"

He who listened to the widow's case feared not God. His conscience was seared and he had passed the place where he suffered, inward rebuke at robbing a widow or taking an orphan's bread. Taking here facts into consideration, our little friend had not a chance—and yet, she got what she went after.

I see her as morning after morning she ties on her bonnet and fastens her apron about her waist, replying to the questions of her young children: "Back to the judge I go, this time to be avenged."

I see the unjust judge morning after morning as he takes his chair to be ready for business, and each time the little widow is there. Somehow she gets her word in and presents her case. The second and maybe the third week he sees her daily trudging up the road with her troubles to repeat. Occasionally she is a little late and he thinks simply he'll go through one day without the annoyance she causes him. No, she has not given up. There she comes again down the road. The judge knows her story by heart and is getting a little tired of hearing it rehearsed. His hope, that she of her own accord will ever quit coming, has vanished and so the widow is avenged—not because she is a friend of the judge, but because there isn't a lazy bone in her body.

What the parable indicates the widow received was not through friendship or justice, but through importunity. How much more might we receive who have established friendship with the God of all justice, if we are the fortunate possessors of the rare jewel—importunity.

The man of Luke 11 whose hungry, traveling friend stopped at his house about midnight only to find the cupboard bare, knew that the odds were against him to start with. His neighbor was in bed, lights were out, the hour was unreasonable, the children of the household were asleep and should not be aroused at midnight. But the need was pressing. He knocked and called and called

> *"Prayer is a simple transaction of everyday business between God and man."*
>
> *Finis Dake*

and knocked. Yes, at last he was getting an answer, but such an answer: "I cannot rise and give thee." But the needy host had come for bread and bread he would get or else stand out in the dark and talk about his needs the rest of the night. The quickest way to peace and rest, for his neighbor and children, was not to lie in bed, but to get up, light the candle and hand the petitioner three loaves through the window.

Hear the closing remarks of Jesus in this parable: "Though he will not rise and give him, because he is his FRIEND, yet because of his IMPORTUNITY he will rise and give him AS MANY AS HE NEEDETH.

"And I say unto you, Ask, and it shall be given you; seek, and ye shall find; knock and it shall be opened unto you."

LORD, GIVE US THE SPIRIT OF IMPORTUNITY!

SERMON 2 – LABORERS

The Christ of Galilee did not go about performing His work with official dignity. He actually worked until He was not only tired, but physically exhausted. There were times when He could go no further without stopping to rest by the side of a well. Now and again, He was unable

159

to keep awake on a sea journey. A borrowed pillow He was glad to get and His sleep was deep even in the face of stormy weather, because He had dropped in His tracks through fatigue.

When Christ said "Come unto me all ye that labor . . . and I will give you rest" (Mt. 11:28), He knew from personal experience what longings the hard worker has for at least occasional relief from his heavy burdens and many duties. He did not say as many quote: "Come unto me all ye that are weary . . . and I will give you rest." Some folks are born tired and others get weary of well–doing before they are half started.

Today the Lord is looking for real laborers, hard workers, men that will earn their living by the sweat of their brow whether they be preachers or otherwise. I use the word "preachers" reluctantly, for I believe God is overstocked with material thus branded. He needs men and women of the laboring type who are not afraid to soil their cuffs and collars, and who shun not the shoe with turned up toe. God needs ditch–diggers who will dig on their knees and fill those ditches with sweat and tears.

I used to begrudge the fact that the public demanded so much of my time. I thought that time should be divided and about half of it be my own. But as I studied the life of Christ I found my reasoning unfounded. If I am a CO–LABORER with Him, then I must try at least to keep step with Him and that means that I shall often be tired because of a full day's work.

Let us recall only one small portion of the wonderful and complete record we have of His life and see Christ as He left Judea, departing again into Galilee and going through Samaria.

We are always so anxious to turn to the verse in St. John 4 where the woman left her water pot to tell all her city friends that she had found the Christ, that we very often do not see the dear Master with His swollen feet sitting on the well. But He was there, friends, and that with a body no stronger than yours or mine, as regarding its need of rest. This journey had been a little longer than usual, or maybe He wasn't sufficiently refreshed before He started.

The disciples went to the city for eats. He might have gone along to respond to whatever need there might have been there, but this time He was too tired. With a sigh that is akin to a groan, He likely dropped to sitting posture on the side of Jacob's well and buried His head in His hands while He cautioned His disciples to proceed without Him to the town.

"We should get busy for God and use every opportunity we get to be a witness for Jesus, either in public or in private."

Finis Dake

But Christ was a worker. Tired or rested, He never let an opportunity pass to labor for the Father. The woman of Samaria came and after her the crowds gathered. Modern preachers would have dismissed the congregation in view of the fact that they themselves hadn't had dinner yet and were tired out from previous services.

The primary concern of our Lord was His field of labor. How slow He was on this occasion to reach for the bread and meat. His followers saw the far off look in His eyes, and knowing how hungry and faint He was beforehand, prayed Him to come to Himself and taste the good food they had brought.

Something had replaced that desire for meat—an unexpected opportunity to labor on. "My meat," said He, "is to do the will of him that sent me, and to finish his work." Some preachers have a career, but Christ had a work. He stayed with it many hours over time each day, without extra pay. Working through meal time and rest time was a common practice with Him—His work came first.

The immensity of the field overwhelmed Him as it often does us, but He did not take that as an excuse to stop. He gave His full time and full strength, praying when He didn't preach, and thereby accomplished many times more than the most of us who go at our gospel work as if we were holding down part–time jobs. At one time He sent out seventy (Luke 10:1), two by two, directed to thirty–five different cities and places where He Himself expected to come to labor. How would you feel with seventy other persons out at one time, doing preliminary work prior to your arrival? Could you exchange the few duties you have for work on a scale as large as that?

> "To believe on Christ as the Scripture has said is the greatest work of God men can do."
>
> Finis Dake

All of us at times have wished that we were twins or triplets so that we could better attend to our pastoral charges. Dare I say that if we would actually set our lives apart to accomplish things for God and seek His face for a special endowment or anointing for service that we should face the possibility of carrying on the work, not only of twins, but of as many as seventy other persons? I think I dare, for all of us can recall meetings where one anointed to do the works of Christ accomplished more in two or three hours than any fifty or a hundred other workers pounding away at the pulpit desk at the close of a prayerless day.

Moses accomplished great things as a full–time worker for God and when his duties were divided among the elders, it took no less than seventy of them to fill his place. If the work you do for God was divided among the brethren, how many of us would it take to fill your place? Lord, help us not to make a side issue of our great profession—the ministry.

When Jesus sent the seventy out, He said "The harvest truly is great, but the laborers are few; pray ye therefore the Lord of harvest, that he would send forth laborers into his harvest." Notice that He did not say "pray for preachers to be called," but "for laborers to be sent forth." Harvesting, whether it be grain or souls, is labor and cannot be done by those who nurse dainty, white hands.

Let us roll up our sleeves, pick up our tools and WORK for Christ. Do not play at the job or look for an easy place. There is a lot of harvesting to be done, too much for the few of us who are swinging the sickle. Therefore PRAY! If you are too lazy to go, or can't go, pray for a brawny, tough–skinned old worker to be thrust forth in your place.

Those who are afraid of work should stay home. God wants harvest hands and if you seek success on the field, that's what He'll make out of you. Your daily labor will make you tired, but your garners will be full and running over. Praise God! Let us swing the sickle until Jesus comes!

> "Let us LABOR for the Master,
> From the dawn till setting sun.
> Let us talk of all His wondrous love and care;
> Then when all of life is over,
> And our WORK on earth is done—
> When the roll is called up yonder,
> I'll be there."

By Dorothy Dobbins Dake

Chapter Sixteen

Dake Builds Another Bible School

God Wants Me To Do More Than Preach

It would seem that for Dake, pastoring a church—with its many duties and responsibilities—would be more than enough ministry to fulfil the call of God upon his heart. But Dake always had more of the teacher in him than the pastor! Though he experienced joy in his pastoral duties and loved ministering to God's people, deep within his heart was the yearning and calling to teach the Word of God and make it as simple for others as God had made it to him.

> *"I have promised God that I would never teach one thing that I could not prove by Scripture."*
>
> *Finis Dake*

In 1934, Dake sought God through prayer and fasting—and the more he sought God the more powerful the vision of a new Bible school became. Finally, he and Dorothy made a decision: they would begin a brand new Bible school as soon as possible. But where was a Bible school to be located in the town built by the late Alexander Dowie? It must be a school dedicated to God where great things were expected from Him. It must be a school where faith was at its heart. It must be a school that would be fitting to the call of Christ and to the memory of the founder of Zion. Of course, the answer was clear—what better place to locate the new school than in the very home and properties of the late Alexander Dowie himself!

This was certainly a very ambitious undertaking for a preacher with no money or means to acquire such expensive property, but nothing was too big for Dake's God. Indeed, Dake always had a strong faith in God. Dake believed very strongly the Scripture: "Ah Lord GOD! behold, thou hast made the heaven and the earth by thy great power and stretched out arm, and there is nothing too hard for thee," Jeremiah 32:17. Years later, he would attach this note to this passage of Scripture in his *Dake Reference Annotated Bible.*

> If men could only believe this and trust God for His many blessings, there would be untold benefits coming to them which they now go without because of unbelief and ignorance of His will. If nothing is too hard for Him, and He has promised men all their needs and lawful wants in life—here and hereafter—then there is no excuse for lack of supply.

Now Dake's faith was going to be tested once again. Like David, he *"slew both the lion and the bear"*[105] by serving as the principal of "Texico Bible Institute" and the dean of "Southwestern Bible School." Now he would begin an even greater adventure. He would build Shiloh Bible Institute for God's glory.

THE HOUSE THAT DOWIE BUILT

Shiloh House and Cottage was built by the founder of Zion, John Alexander Dowie, in 1902. It was his home and no expense was spared in its construction, which cost more than $100,000.00.[106] The Swiss-styled edifice stood proudly on a five–acre tract, having twenty–five rooms on three floors. There were six bathrooms, which were beautifully finished in Grecian marble. The closets were cedar and the floors were all hardwood. The walls of the house were eighteen inches thick and there were two fireproof steel vaults located in the building. The basement housed a number of enclosed fruit cellars.

> *"The Bible is in truth the very Word of God in human language, and it should be understood on the same basis that we do other books in human language."*
>
> *Finis Dake*

The roof of the house was constructed of ornamental tile and was built to symbolize the Holy Spirit emanating from Zion City. Surrounding the property were more than fifty fruit trees, all pointing to the beauty of God's creation. Truly, Shiloh House, located on 1300 Shiloh Blvd., was a sight to behold. In its day, Shiloh House was one of the most unusual houses in the entire state. Some even called it bizarre. There was always a lot of talk about the house—even a rumor of an underground secret passageway connecting the house with the stables. These, of course, proved to be untrue.

After Dowie's death in 1907, things went downhill for Zion and the ministry he had built. The city of Zion and the Dowie holdings were thrown into bankruptcy, including Shiloh House. For a few years, Shiloh House was owned by Dowie's successor and the overseer of the Christian Catholic Church, Wilbur Glen Voliva. But this ownership soon came to

---

[105] 1 Samuel 17:36—Thy servant slew both the lion and the bear: and this uncircumcised Philistine shall be as one of them, seeing he hath defied the armies of the living God. (KJV)

[106] Or about $2,130,437.00 in year 2005 dollars.

an end when Shiloh House and Cottage, along with the stables, were sold by the government at a Federal Receiver's sale to a Mrs. Emma G. Gring of Newport, Pennsylvania.

Mrs. Gring's family maintained possession of the property until 1932 when Mrs. Dowie and her son, an Episcopal minister, returned and purchased their old dwelling place on contract from the late Theodore Goldsmith. They were ousted nine months later when they failed to make their payment. In 1934, Lillian Evans SeRine bought Shiloh from the Theodore Goldsmith estate.

Christian Assembly Buys Dowie's Mansion

It was in March of 1935 that Christian Assembly committed to buy Shiloh House from Mrs. Lillian Evans SeRine of Waukegan. Dake's dream to turn the Dowie mansion into a Bible school would be finally

A School Banquet

realized. Christian Assembly was allowed to buy the Dowie estate for a mere $7,000.00[107] which was to be paid in full on September 1, 1935. At this time Christian Assembly did not have that kind of money, but with the people giving and working and with a small note from the bank, they would raise the full amount by the deadline. The purchase included Shiloh House and Cottage (which also served as Dowie's stables), located just across the street about a half block down from Sheridan Road.

From the very beginning, the members of Christian Assembly were firmly in support of Dake's vision of a Bible school. The board of trustees voted to support the new school to the fullest extent, even designating all

---

[107] Or about $96,635.00 in year 2005 dollars.

monies above the actual operating expenses of the church to be given to the school.

The District Council of the Assemblies of God in Illinois voiced their support for the project with an official endorsement of the school, making it available for support from all its churches in the state and throughout the midwest.

Dake and the members of Christian Assembly were to remodel the buildings themselves. Shiloh House would be used for a Bible school, which would include student classes, the women's dormitory and an assembly hall. In the basement, there would be room for the school laundry, the printing shop and the woodworking department. Shiloh Cottage would be used as a men's dormitory, complete with the kitchen and a large dining hall. If all went well, Shiloh Bible Institute would welcome over 100 students and open for its first day of school on Monday, September 30, 1935.

None of this was done without a deep and devoted dependency on the Lord. A prayer was included in *The Latter Rain Evangel*[108] which provides some insight into the heart of Dake and those who were depending on God to meet every need for this new work.

> God grant that from these consecrated halls there will go forth a great host of young men and women of high Christian standards who will shine forth as luminaries in the habitations of darkness and cruelty; and that from them may emanate Gospel rays that will transform communities and lives.

---

[108] *The Latter Rain Evangel*: July 1935, page 17. A Special thanks goes out to the Assembly of God archives for a copy of this historic document, as well as other issues used throughout this work.

CHAPTER SEVENTEEN

SHILOH BIBLE INSTITUTE

A DESCRIPTION OF SHILOH

Shiloh Bible Institute was birthed in Dake's heart through much prayer, fasting and seeking God, and was an outgrowth of his desire to teach the Bible, plain and simple. In Dake's day, for the most part, one man could teach one congregation at a time. But by training Christian workers the simplicity of and literal truth of the Bible, Dake would multiply his ministry many times over, through the lives of those the school would influence and train for the work of the kingdom.

But what kind of school would Shiloh Bible Institute be? How would it operate? Who would work with Dake in helping to train the many young people who would come? What was day to day life like at the school? What subjects were taught? Who would do the teaching? What rules or conduct would the students follow? How would the school be financed? These questions and many more need to be answered. For in knowing about the school we, in fact, learn a lot about Dake's heart and his ministry.

To best answer these questions a look at the school catalog is in order. Therefore, allowing it to speak for itself, the First Annual Shiloh Bible Institute Catalog of 1935 is included in the pages that follow.

Students at Shiloh Bible Institute

First Annual Catalog

Of

Shiloh Bible Institute

(Pentecostal)

In

The old home of Dr. John Alexander Dowie

Zion, IL

1935– 1936

Shiloh House

Shiloh Cottage

Beautiful Shiloh House and Cottage—once the elaborate home of the founder of Zion City, who blazed the trail with a divine healing ministry before the recent outpouring of Pentecost.

Old acquaintances of Dr. Dowie say these two buildings of Swiss architecture were erected at a cost of around $100,000.00.[109] Today they are the home and property of Shiloh Bible Institute.

Shiloh House has four floors of large rooms, marble baths, cedar storage room, hardwood floors, fire–proof steel vaults, fancy tile roof and other features of luxury. Walls of both structures are eighteen inches thick.

Shiloh Cottage, once Dr. Dowie's stable, is equipped with spacious stalls and carriage room, which will be made into dining room and kitchen. Above this will be three floors of dormitory rooms. It is expected that Shiloh House and Cottage together will accommodate from 150 to 200 students.

On the lots belonging to these buildings there are more than fifty fruit trees which will prove an added blessing to the school.

BOARD OF TRUSTEES

(Official Board of the Christian Assembly, Zion)

J. A. Spicer, Zion, IL	A. D. Swarztrauber, Zion, IL
John Erickson, Waukegan, IL	K. J. Boyer, Lab Villa, IL
Julius Johansen, Winthrop Harbor, IL	

EXECUTIVE BOARD

The above named Trustees and Finis J. Dake, Supervisor.

ADVISORY BOARD

Rev. Arthur Bell, District Supt. of Illinois, Belleville, IL
Rev. R. L. Scharnick, Dist. Supt. of Wisconsin, Oshkosh, WI
Rev. Paul B. Peterson, Pres., European Mission, Chicago, IL
Rev. Neils P. Thomsen, Pastor, The Stone Church, Chicago, IL
Rev. Hugh M. Cadwalder, Pastor, Full Gospel Church, Chicago, IL

---

[109] Or about $2,130,437.00 in year 2005 dollars.

FACULTY

Finis J. Dake,

School Supervisor

Pastor, The Christian Assembly, Zion, Illinois.

Author of "Revelation Expounded," many courses of Bible study and designer of detailed chart (The Bible on Canvas) used by teachers.

Former Principal, Texico Bible School. Dean of men and Bible teacher two years in Southwestern Bible School. Studied one year in Glad Tidings Bible School, San Francisco, and three years in Central Bible Institute, graduating 1925.

Subjects: Dispensational Truth, Prophecy I and II, Epistles I and II, Bible Introduction, Hermeneutics, Christian Work, Greek.

Theodore A. Kessel

Ordained minister and President, Illinois State Young People's Work.

Studied in Southern Illinois Normal University and in the University of Indiana. Holds a teacher's certificate and for the past nine years has taught in the public schools of Illinois.

Subjects: Old and New Testament Studies, History of Missions, Religions of the Mission Fields, Church History, Music I, English I, II, and III.

173

Mrs. Dorothy Dake

In charge of women students

Local church evangelist and Director of Chorus, Orchestra and Rhythm Band.
Taught two years in Southwestern Bible School. Studied singing and speaking voice with Switzer School of Music and Expression in Dallas, Texas; voice technique with Robert Ellis Jones, M. B. Sherwood School of Music; instrumental music, advanced theory and conduction with Rein Dyksterhuis, graduate Brussels's Conservatory, Belgium, Professor of Music, Phillips University: public speaking with Annabel Sayles, A. B., B. O., Phillips University in Enid, Oklahoma.

Subjects: Public Speaking, Homiletics, Bible Atlas, Music II and III, Training of School Orchestra and Chorus.

Otis R. Keener

In charge of men students

Pastor Bethel Temple, Chicago; Sectional Presbyter of Illinois Council.

14 years experience as pastor, evangelist, and bible teacher through the midwest.

Subjects: Doctrine I and II, Typology, Christian Evidences, Parliamentary Law, Cultism, Personal Evangelism.

Fred Schott, B. S.,

University of Illinois

Former teacher of architecture in Chicago Y.M.C.A. night schools. Twenty–five years experience as architectural draftsman. A number of years Chief Draftsman under Cook County architect.

Studied Music under University of Illinois and Dr. Thos Mendsen of Western Conservatory and Metropolitan Opera.

Subjects: Vocal Technique, Sign Painting, Plan Reading and Drafting.

Cecil Liddle

Teacher of Instruments (private lessons)

Assistant Chorister

Choral training under George Schumann, B. M., Cottey College.

Studied harmony under Otto Graham, B. S. and played in a band under his supervision.

Received special training, one year in a Saxophone Sextet which won second place in a national contest.

175

Mrs. Dorothy Archibald

Teacher of Piano (private lessons)

Studied harmony under Otto Graham, B. S., Missouri State Teachers' College; piano six years under Rowena Skilbeck Hess, B. M., American Conservatory of Music.

Charles T. Hart, Chef

Served as Mess Sergeant in the World War; Two years experience catering at a State Teachers' College; Chef three years at Southwestern Bible School; one year at Texico Bible School, etc. Has operated boarding houses, restaurants and lunch rooms.

Being well–informed in dietetics and having had a wide range of experience, Mr. Hart is equipped above the average person of his profession to take full charge of the Institute's cooking and buying. Well–balanced meals of wholesome food, simply prepared and served regularly help to preserve and promote the health of the student. With this foremost in mind he will manage the school cuisine.

LOCATION

Being midway between Chicago and Milwaukee, two great centers of industry in the midwest, with some eight million people within a radius of fifty to seventy–five miles, makes Zion a most suitable place for a Bible School.

With a little more than an hour's driving one may reach either of these major cities. The North Shore Electric Line, the fastest electric road in America, and the Northwestern Railroad both go through Zion and connect it to Chicago and Milwaukee with hourly service.

Though the town itself is not large, there are cities of good size very near which can be reached promptly by bus or otherwise. Waukegan, Ill. with its 35,000 inhabitants lies six miles South. Adjoining that is North Chicago with about 9,000. To the North of Zion eight miles is Kenosha, Wis. with a population of 52,000 and only ten miles further is Racine with 67,000 inhabitants. These and other nearby places are open fields for gospel work.

Located between Zion and Chicago are many aristocratic sections (Wilmette, Winnetka, etc.) where students of other Bible Schools in times past have found sufficient work in the summer to make possible their return to school in the fall.

The town is situated in a great agricultural area where vegctables and fruit abound. This makes possible the serving of excellent foods at the low rate herein stated.

Spots of historical interest are nearby—Fort Sheridan, the Great Lakes Naval Training Station and Fort Dearborn. The shore line of mighty Lake Michigan is but a little more than a mile away. Field's Museum, Alder's Planetarium and the "Shedd Aquarium" in Chicago all hold special attractions for students.

For the foregoing reasons and for the very fact that Zion was founded by one whose original thought was to make it a training ground for missionaries and workers who should go into all the world with the gospel, it is more than evident that this is an ideal location for a Pentecostal Training School.

Some sixty or seventy persons have already gone from the Zion Assembly into active Christian work as missionaries or preachers and it is believed that God will use this place as a starting point for many others as long as Jesus tarries.

Shiloh Institute itself is located near the business district and yet only about four blocks from the Christian Assembly, which will be the church home of those attending school.

Nearby parks and trees provide places for recreation and inspiration for study and meditation. In cold months the various small lakes afford healthful recreation in ice skating.

Altogether the location of Shiloh Bible Institute meets every requirement for the welfare and happiness of a student body.

REQUIREMENTS FOR ADMISSION

Unless special permission is otherwise granted, it is required that all who enter training be at least sixteen years of age. That they be of sound health is also expected, due to the intensive study necessary.

Applicants must be sincere Christians of good standing. They are to manifest a teachable spirit and possess a purpose of heart and mind to study the Word of God with a view to becoming more useful in His service.

Because adjusting themselves to the life of a school dormitory plays an important part in the development and training of students, it is required that all who are not married or who do not receive special permission to do otherwise, take up board and room in the Institute buildings.

Because expenses connected with operating the school are to be kept as low as possible in order to give students the advantage of unusually low rates, those who enroll will be expected to work as much as one hour a day in the performance of whatever duties are assigned.

Since rules are necessary where many congregate to study and live, reasonable regulations have therefore been adopted which will protect the rights and happiness of all concerned. Cheerful compliance with these is expected and it is understood that application for admission obligates one to meet this requirement.

SOCIAL REGULATIONS

Courtesy is always in order but intimacy is frankly discouraged. The spirit of friendliness and comradeship will be welcomed, but because of the Christian character of the institution, undue familiarity between sexes will not be permitted.

SCHOOL CALENDAR 1935–1936

Registration Day .... Sept. 30, 1935
Beginning of First Semester.................... Oct. 1, 1935
Thanksgiving Vacation........................... Nov. 28 to Dec. 2
Christmas Vacation .... Dec. 21 to Dec. 30
Beginning of Second Semester............... Jan. 15, 1936
Commencement Exercises...................... May 7 and 8, 1936

DAILY SCHEDULE

6:00	Rising bell.
6:30 to 7:00	Private devotions.
7:00 to 7:30	Breakfast.
7:30 to 8:15	Household duties.
8:15 to 9:00	Chapel Service.
9:00 to 10:20	Recitation periods.
10:20 to 10:40	Recreation.
10:40 to 12:00	Recitation periods.
12:00 to 12:30	Prayer for Missions.
12:30 to 1:15	Dinner.
1:15 to 2:00	Recreation.
2:00 to 4:00	Study hours.
4:00 to 5:30	Household duties and recreation.
5:30 to 6:00	Supper.
6:00 to 7:00	Recreation.
7:00 to 7:30	Prayer.
7:30 to 9:45	Study period.
10:00	Lights out.

COURSE OF STUDY

Shiloh Bible Institute offers a three year course of study providing a sufficient amount of biblical and non–biblical subjects to train and equip one for any phase of Christian work.

Each year is divided into two semesters for convenience in grading and recording of credits. Subjects are begun at the opening of the first semester and continued throughout the school year.

It is recommended that all students begin with the first year's work as outlined below and carry the entire course through as given. However, in cases of necessity, persons can arrange for special courses of study requiring only one or two years' work by conferring with the supervisor.

First Year Subjects	Hours weekly
Dispensational Truth	5
Old Testament Studies	4
New Testament Studies	3
Bible Atlas	1
Typology	1
Personal Evangelism	1
English I	2
Music I	2

Second Year Subjects	Hours weekly
Epistles I	3
Prophecy I	3
Doctrine I	2
Bible Introduction	1
Homiletics	1
Cultism	1
Church History	1
Parliamentary Law	1
Christian Evidences	1
English II	2
Music II	1

Third Year Subjects	Hours weekly
Epistles II	3
Prophecy II	3
Doctrine II	2
Hermeneutics	1
Public Speaking	2
History of Missions	2
Religions of the World	1
Christian Work	1
Music III	1
Greek	1
English III	2

(Hours subject to change)

Dispensational Truth

A comprehensive study of creative ages, the seven dispensations and their outstanding features, the eternal future, kingdom of heaven parables, Matthew 25:25 the kingdom of heaven and the kingdom of God, Jews, the Church, times of the Gentiles, the tribulation, rapture, coming of Christ, resurrections, spirit world, underworld, judgments, covenants, Satan, the Anglo–Saxon theory, etc.

Old and New Testament Studies

Covers the whole Bible book by book. The contents of chapters, lives of main characters, histories, main subjects, the unity, plan and construction of the entire Bible are dealt with so as to furnish a background for second and third year studies.

Typology

A study of the "word pictures" of the Old Testament comes under this heading. The Tabernacle, priesthood, offerings and feasts are thoroughly covered in Typology, without which much of the Bible is not clearly understood.

Bible Introduction

To explain how we got our Bible in its present form and to trace its translation from earliest times to our present day is the purpose of Bible Introduction. It deals with the genuineness and authenticity of the Bible and is designed to equip the student to meet modern attacks on our Bible and to prove beyond doubt that it is the very Word of God.

Hermeneutics

The true science of interpretation of Scripture. One who fully masters the principles, rules and methods of biblical interpretation places himself in a better position to understand or explain any biblical passage.

Doctrine I and II

A complete study of God, Christ and the Holy Spirit, Man, Sin, Salvation and other fundamental doctrines of the Bible.

Prophecy I and II

All prophetical books of the Bible are taken up in detail. Prophecy I

181

covers all the prophecies given before the exile: Isaiah, Jeremiah, Hosea, Joel, Amos, Obadiah, Jonah, Micah, Nahum, Habakkuk and Zephaniah. Prophecy II covers all the prophecies given after the exile: Ezekiel, Haggai, Zechariah, Malachi, Daniel and Revelation.

Epistles I and II
A detailed study of General, Pastoral and Pauline Epistles. The courses in Epistles I covers I and II Thessalonians, I and II Corinthians, Philippians, Colossians, Philemon, I, II and III John and Jude. Epistles II covers Romans, Galatians, Hebrews, Ephesians, I and II Timothy, Titus, James, I and II Peter.

Homiletics
Preparation, construction and delivery of sermons are dealt with in this course. Texts and suggestions as to how to enlarge upon them are taken up fully.

Bible Atlas
A study of the history, geography and topography of Bible lands is covered in Bible Atlas, which course is quite essential to a complete understanding of much of the Bible.

Church History
A thorough study of the history of the Church throughout this age, and is intended to enable the student to understand more fully the fulfillment of God's plan.

History of Missions
With a view to showing the student how successful mission work may be carried on today, missionary work throughout this age is thoughtfully considered in classes pertaining to this subject .

Cultism
A study of the major false religions of today and a course to be valued by anyone intending to do extensive Christian work.

Religions of Mission Fields
False religions to be found on mission fields are studied in this course,

which with the course in Cultism will give the student a comprehensive view of the religions of the world.

Christian Evidences
Students learn why Christianity is the true religion and the only way of Salvation.

Christian Work
Instructions for conducting cottage meetings, daily Vacation Bible Schools, Sunday Schools, local church Bible classes, Young People's work, evangelistic, pastoral, street, jail, slum, visitation and other kinds of Christian work are combined under the general heading: Christian Work.

Personal Evangelism
Designed to equip the student for dealing scripturally with all classes of people in an attempt to lead them to Christ.

English I, II and III
English I is a grammar course for those who need such foundation studies. English II includes brief studies in journalism with instructions and practice in preparation of reports suitable for newspaper use in addition to oral and written composition. English III is a thorough course in Business English.

Public Speaking
Acquaints the student with the possibilities of his speaking voice and to give him an understanding of practical rules which will improve his talent along that line. A very thorough course dealing with pitch, inflections, modulations as to volume, articulation, gestures, facial expressions, breathing, drills intended to free the voice and readings is given.

Music I, II and III
Music I is a study of rudiments and sight singing with choral practice from time to time. Music II and III include choral practice, a brief study of hymnology and suggestions for conducting choirs and orchestras.

Parliamentary Law
Every Christian worker should know how to preside over and participate

in church business meetings. In order that parliamentary procedure may be understood a course in Parliamentary Law is provided.

Greek
To equip the student for free use of his Greek lexicon and Greek concordance and to make possible his reading the New Testament in its original language is the aim of this course.

ELECTIVE COURSES

Vocal Technique
Individual and class instructions are given in this thorough course of voice placement. Groups of eight or ten may study together at reduced prices.

Sign Painting, Plan Reading, Drafting
Studies designed to increase the Christian worker's usefulness along the lines of drafting, sketching, blackboard drawing, sign painting, chart–making and the reading of building plans make this a practical and complete course. Persons interested are requested to bring drafting tools and supplies.

Instrumental Music
Capable instructors have been provided by the school management so that students desiring to specialize in playing the piano or any other instrument, may have the advantage of private lessons at low cost.

SPECIAL LECTURES

Ministers and missionaries of matured experience who have been blessed with outstanding success on the field often visit the Chicago area. Suggestions from them are of benefit to prospective Christian workers and so arrangements for special lectures by these leaders will be made from time to time.

PRACTICAL EVANGELISM

Students will not be left to imagine what they would do if placed in charge of some branch of gospel work. Each will be required to do his share of practical evangelism.

The Christian Assembly bus which holds about thirty persons will be available for use in this work. With the many large towns spaced but a few miles apart along this north shore of Lake Michigan, unlimited opportunity awaits the student.

Jails, factories, hospitals and shops, are plentiful in these manufacturing centers, so that students may do practical Christian work in places where they feel especially called. Successful street work has already been established in nearby cities and large crowds gather to hear the Gospel. This will be continued as long as the weather permits.

It can be said of upper Illinois and much of the Wisconsin area near Zion that they are yet practically untouched with the Pentecostal message. It is hoped that students with the aid of faculty members will see established churches in the greater part of this virgin territory as a result of their labors.

FINANCES

Registration

All students will be charged a registration fee of twenty dollars ($20.00) per year, payable on Registration Day at the beginning of the school year.

Board and Room

The low price of four dollars ($4.00) per week will be charged for board and room. This includes light and heat.

Breakage and Library Fees

Payment of a breakage fee of three dollars ($3.00) and a library fee of one dollar ($1.00) for the year will be required on Registration Day also.

SPECIAL DISCOUNT FOR CASH IN ADVANCE

A special discount of fifteen percent will be allowed all students who pay cash in advance for the following:

Registration.......................................$ 20.00
Board and Room, 32 weeks...............128.00
Breakage fee...3.00
Library fee...1.00
....$152.00
Less 15 percent for cash......................22.80
....$129.20

(There will be no rebates on Registration, breakage or library fees).

Laundry

Students who prefer to do their own laundry may have that privilege by paying fifty cents (.50) a month for use of the school laundry equipment.

Special Music

For all private lessons a charge of fifty cents (.50) each will be made. Students who begin such courses must be prepared to continue lessons at least one semester.

Persons who enroll in classes of Vocal Technique made up of eight or ten students, will pay twenty–five cents (.25) each per lesson. This course must also be continued a full semester.

Sign Painting, Plan Reading, Drafting

A very reasonable charge will be made for entrance into this class, according to the number who enroll.

Books and Supplies

It is estimated that eight dollars ($8.00) or nine dollars ($9.00) will cover the cost of books and supplies. A good serviceable Bible may be brought by the student or purchased on arrival.

Tuition

Boarding students will not be charged tuition. Day students (persons who live or work outside the school and attend classes during the day) will pay tuition monthly in advance at the rate of fifty cent (.50) per week.

Certificates and Diplomas

Students who have not been more than three weeks late at the beginning of the first semester and who have satisfactorily completed the first or second year course of study will be issued certificates.

At the end of the third year, diplomas will be granted to those who have satisfactorily completed the full three years' course. A grade of seventy–five percent (75%) will be considered the lowest passing mark in any one subject.

Student's Outfit

3 sheets for single bed
1 pair blankets
2 or 3 comforters
2 pillow cases
1 pillow
face and bath towels
3 napkins
1 napkin ring
1 laundry bag (washable material)
1 washable bed spread to be purchased on arrival so as to match color scheme of room.

Uniforms

Women students are required to wear dark blue dresses of good length, long sleeves, collar of same material and red silk ties. Neatness of appearance must be kept in mind when making uniforms. Selection of materials will be left up to the student. Part wool may be advisable for persons unaccustomed to Lake Shore climate. Women are also requested to bring a dark blue beret, and in addition to dark dresses, one white uniform for closing day exercises.

Dark suits for men are preferred. All students must have shoe heels equipped with rubber taps.

Additional Information

Persons desiring information not given herein or applicants whose cases demand individual consideration are invited to correspond with the school by addressing: Finis J. Dake, Supervisor, Shiloh Bible Institute, Zion, Illinois.

SPECIAL NOTICE

The entire three year course of subjects offered by Shiloh Bible Institute will be taught the opening year of the school. Students ready for second and third year work may enroll for classes to begin October 1st, 1935.

Shiloh Bible Institute Band

Things Must Be Done In Order

In addition to the school catalog, the rules and regulations of Shiloh Bible Institute will also give us an idea of what was expected of the students in their day–to–day life at the school, as well as what was expected when they ventured out in public. In fact, students were even told when they could take their Saturday bath! Things certainly have changed!

"If one does not seem to have faith, let him praise God, just as much as if he felt that he did have faith and he will find that faith will grow."

Finis Dake

Included in the Rules and Regulations below, you will notice the name *Hallie Dake* listed as the housekeeper. Hallie Dake was the wife of Arthur Dake, who was Dake's older brother by about eight years. Arthur had recently died of appendicitis and Hallie had come to live with the Dakes, along with her sixteen year–old daughter, Rhada. Rhada, who loved the Lord very much, graduated from Shiloh Bible Institute in April of 1938. A number of years later she would marry a Church of God minister named Ariel Yorkman, at which time both she and her mother would move out of the Dake home.

RULES AND REGULATIONS

- A student's graduation from Shiloh Bible Institute depends upon his observing rules and regulations of the Institute, as well as actual grades from class work.

- A student may be detained from graduation whose class work is satisfactory but whose deportment is deficient. Warning is hereby given of this fact.

- A system of demerits has been worked out by the faculty and record books will be in the possession of all faculty members, C. T. Hart, Chef, and Mrs. Hallie Dake, housekeeper.

- Name of persons found breaking rules or regulations will be entered with notation of offence. This record will be kept and considered in connection with graduation.

- The entire daily schedule must be observed strictly. Prayer periods must find students in prayer, study periods must find them sitting in chairs around tables studying, not talking, laughing or lying on beds. Ten o'clock must find them with lights out.

- Students being excused from classes for good reason must have written permission from the Supervisor to present to the teachers of such classes.

- Before appearing late for classes, chapel or meals, demerit may be avoided by calling at the office for excuse if student can present good reason for such tardiness.

- There will be no sleeping or lying on beds during study periods. Persons so physically weak as to require an afternoon nap may appear at the office for written excuse the day this is absolutely necessary and adjustment for afternoon rest or retiring early will be made if the case is worthy. Written excuse will be given.

- Let no two persons at any time lie on one bed or cot.

- Demerit will be given if any student is caught visiting any dormitory or teacher's room during a study or prayer period.

- All students, married or single, must return from town in time for study or prayer periods unless properly excused. This applies to Friday and Saturday as well as other days.

- At no time may single students go out of Zion to town without permission.

- No student may take a bath during a study period or prayer period or after 10 o'clock at night. Recreation periods and Saturday afternoons are sufficient for that. If not, consult those in authority.

- At all study periods, afternoons and nights, doors of all dormitories and rooms must be thrown wide open so that faculty members may walk through halls at intervals to enforce order. There must be no walking around except necessary trips to bathrooms and positively no laughing or talking. If necessary to inquire of another student the assignment or ask a question having to do with lessons, let this be done quickly and with whispering voice only.

- No person may miss a single meal without written excuse unless engaged in a spirit of prayer at a devotional service. In such case the student shall be permitted to pray on if he desires. However, he shall not be permitted to go to kitchen or dining room late for eats. He must wait until the next regular meal. Excuse to persons desiring to fast will be freely given.

- No food at any time may be taken from the school store room, kitchen or dining room without written permission. Every tray delivered to sick students must receive the daily O.K. of office through written slip.

- Waste of food and returning of unused butter on side of plate is an offence worthy of demerit.

- Kitchen workers or dining room crew will receive demerit for being late to their assignment. They must report at 6:30 a.m., 12:00 p.m., and 5:00 p.m. No student may come late and then stand in the kitchen and eat while others work. No student may eat in the kitchen at any time without written permission from office.

> *"Strong faith is the kind that refuses to be defeated."*
>
> *Finis Dake*

- Demerit will be given any person seen in the kitchen any time day or night, except when on strict duty or given a special permission from those in authority.

- Students shall not take it upon themselves to eat extra desserts and delicacies not directly given to them by Mr. Hart.

- Demerit will be given any student marching out of dining room ahead of any faculty member or guest.

- No cooking may be done by students whatsoever at any time. Do not ask cook or teachers for such privilege. If special food is necessary for the sick, bring the matter to the office.

- Girls are required not to come to dining room with sleeves less than elbow length. This requirement positively must be met.

- Extra demerit will be given any girl seen or caught in nightclothes or pajamas outside of her own private room or bathroom. Any vulgarity of dress in this Bible school will be severely dealt with. Girls not equipped with wrappers that reach to the ankles and cover all the night clothes, must take care to keep behind closed doors.

- Boys, likewise, are required to keep out of halls unless decently clad. No boy is allowed above the first floor of Shiloh House. If necessary to see Mr. Kessel, get permission from those in authority on the first floor.

- Let no girl ever cross over to the boys' dormitory. When necessary to see Mr. Keener, arrange to do so when he is downstairs or in this building, except special permission is given by Mrs. Dake.

- Keep rooms tidy at all times. Clean them every morning and make beds promptly. Don't throw clothes around bathrooms or on beds and chairs. This is subject to demerit.

- Laundry room must be cleaned daily by the users. When you have finished your washing, clean and dry all tubs, starch pans, spoons, etc. Do not leave the laundry room until papers are picked up and all equipment is cleaned and dried. Return clothes basket promptly after you have put clothes on line and return clothes pins promptly after clothes are taken down.

- All students must attend church services somewhere, morning and night on Sundays, including Sunday School and Young People's service, unless written excuse is applied for and received at the office. This means every Sunday of the school year.

- Persons visiting over the weekends must have written permission to leave the school. Students must make satisfactory arrangements for their work assignments to be met before applying for permission at the office.

- Students showing disrespect or making light remarks to faculty members, C. T. Hart, Mrs. Hart or Mrs. Hallie Dake, when being observed or corrected will receive demerit for such offence.

- Until 9:30 p.m. each night all students must keep fully clad in street clothes so that at any time faculty members finding it necessary to consult students will not suffer embarrassment.

CHAPTER EIGHTEEN

THE SHILOH SCROLL

A SCHOOL PAPER

Most schools and colleges develop a school paper to communicate to the student body and the public some of the special events and activities of the school. Shiloh Bible Institute also had its school paper, produced by the school's journalism students. On November 15, 1935, the first edition of *The Shiloh Scroll* was published. In *The Shiloh Scroll* we find out much about Dake, the life of the student body, and the ministry and outreach endeavours of the school. The following are some interesting items from *The Shiloh Scroll*.

> *"Faith has no relationship with feelings or the evidence of the senses."*
>
> *Finis Dake*

SHILOH SCROLL – NOVEMBER 15, 1935

Shiloh Bible Institute – For years the elaborate home of Dr. John Alexander Dowie stood vacant and neglected. Many people passed these beautiful buildings daily regretting that they were idle and not in use for God. It is due to the God–given decision and burden for a Bible school of our Supervisor, Brother Dake, and his good associates and co–workers that prayer and efforts began to be put forth to acquire this property. About March 1, 1935, the Lord moved in answer to prayer and this property was acquired.

New Term Begins – The buildings are almost filled to present capacity with happy consecrated young people seeking a deeper knowledge of the Word of God. It is more than gratifying to hear the frequent floods of prayer and praise that come from the hearts of the student band and many times each day.

From the Editor – No step has been taken, nothing has been done in the editing of the paper that has not been preceded by prayer. We have asked for God's blessing and guidance and He has given it to us.

Missionary Prayer Band Organized – Being desirous of increasing and deepening their missionary vision, the student body has systematically organized into a student missionary prayer band. In order that every country might be represented in this prayer band, the following plan is being carried out. A missionary president and secretary were elected. Then the student body was organized into five groups, which represent the following countries: Europe, Asia, Africa, Australia and the Islands of the Sea, and South and Central Americas, Mexico and the American Indians. Each day from 12:00 to 12:30 these groups meet together to intercede for lost souls on the mission fields; and to lift up to God the missionaries who have sacrificed all for the cause of Christ. On Monday the first group has charge of the service: on Tuesday the second group and so on up until Friday.

Chapel – If you will permit me, I shall take you to the chapel services which are held each morning. The students are in charge of these services. God has blessed in a marvelous way. During these services the school is sometimes favored with special musical and vocal numbers and occasionally a special speaker. God has blessed Shiloh Bible Institute with many talented young people who have consecrated their talents to the Lord to be used for His service. The student in charge delivers a short message or gives three Scripture readings as the Lord leads; this is followed by a season of prayer, after which we pass to our classes.

Prayer – Each class is opened with a chorus and prayer. It would be a difficult task to state the most interesting subjects as some students prefer Prophecy and Epistles, whereas Doctrine and Church History appeal to others. Nevertheless, God blesses us as we study together and reveals to us His hidden treasures.

Prayer is the key that unlocks heaven, it is fellowship with the Unseen and Most Holy One. Prayer is the highest part of the work entrusted to us; therefore, it should be the Christian's first duty to be performed. Our faculty has set aside "prayer periods" throughout the day, which are observed by the students.

The Spirit Moves – One of the most precious times so far this year occurred during our Typology class one morning about two weeks ago. As we were discussing Joseph and his family in relation to Christ and His family, Brother Keener, our teacher, received an anointing of the Spirit. Everyone was moved and received a wonderful blessing. Our next class period was suspended so that the Lord might have His way. Many were refilled for the first time in several years. We praise the Lord that although we have our plans for classes if God desires to change them we are willing.

SHILOH SCROLL – DECEMBER 1, 1935

Food Donations – We receive so many letters asking if we are accepting food donations. Yes, we are more than glad for every one of them. If you have any fruits or vegetables canned that you wish to donate to the school it will be greatly appreciated. We will be glad to receive it.

Courses – *Dispensational Truth,* perhaps, our most valuable course, is a study of the plan of the entire Bible. Many Bible questions have been cleared up and during the year we hope that the Book will become much more simple to us than it has previously been.

> "One can know that he is right, not by what any man says, but by the Bible."
>
> Finis Dake

In *Old and New Testament Studies* each book is taken individually. The contents of the book is studied in its relation to the other books of the Bible. Under the heading of *Typology* comes types of the Old Testament and their fulfillment in the New. Types are merely word pictures which we find very interesting.

Another valuable course which will be very useful in the future is *Personal Evangelism.* We can know the Word of God, and yet not be able to use it in winning souls for our Master. This subject is beneficial for each of us since we can all have a part in personal work, regardless of what field we enter.

With these studies one can easily see we are busy people at Shiloh Bible Institute, preparing ourselves for whatever the Lord sees fit to call us.

SHILOH SCROLL – DECEMBER 15, 1935

Social At Shiloh – Socials come but once a month here at the school so obviously it is a great day for many who are thus minded, however a good time for all is planned.

It was on Monday, November 25th, that the students and the young people of the church had their first social in the school, although shortly after the opening of school, the students and young people had an outing at Brother Boyer's farm.

The Program for the social was in the hands of a committee who planned the games and entertainment. After several games had been played we all enjoyed a number of special features from different students.

Refreshments were served at the close of the evening. Each person was given the name of a partner with whom he was to eat.

> *"The fact is that the United States is not once mentioned in prophecy anywhere."*
>
> *Finis Dake*

The usual bed time for the students is 10 o'clock, but due to the special occasion the curfew was prolonged until eleven at which time a group of happy young people returned to their homes and rooms.

The Menu – The menu consisted of the following: assorted canapés, orangeade, mashed potatoes, giblet gravy, chicken a la king, fresh turnips, pickles, stuffed olives, celery, lettuce with French dressing, fruit jello, pumpkin pie with whipped cream, coffee, and mixed nuts.

Brother Dake Teaches Prophecy – If anyone has any doubts as to the authenticity of the Bible they need only to attend our Prophecy class. We feel very fortunate in having Brother Dake as instructor as he is an authority on prophecy.

Women's Hair – In studying Corinthians the other day we got into quite a discussion as to how long "long hair" should be. The affirmative side assured us that it meant one should never cut it at all. However, there is an old saying: "A man convinced against his will is a man who is unconvinced still."

Gratitude – We are very grateful to all our dear friends for your cooperation during the subscription campaign. To date it has resulted in 510 paid subscriptions from many states and foreign countries. We certainly do appreciate the way you responded in sending your subscriptions. May the Lord bless our paper to you is our prayer and aim of one and all of us here at Shiloh Bible Institute. And still the subscriptions are coming in. Again we say "Thank you and may you have a most Joyous Christmas as well as a Happy New Year."

Shiloh Scroll – January 1, 1936

Prayer Campaign – More praying has been done since Mrs. Dake's campaign. You undoubtedly would like to know about this campaign. Well, let me tell you about it. It is called the "Back to Your Knees Campaign." This does not mean just breathing a prayer every now and then, but just as the title suggests, to spend time in prayer, down on your knees.

We are beginning to reap the results of this campaign for God never forsakes those who call upon Him.

Meal Time at S.B.I. – Meal time at Shiloh Bible Institute is welcomed by everyone, faculty and students alike. Breakfast is served at seven o'clock, dinner at twelve–thirty, and supper at six.

The waitresses and dishwashers eat half an hour early so that they can serve the others. Three girls and four boys make up the "kitchen crew" as it is commonly known around school. The members of this crew are taken from the student body and they remain on duty for one week. Upon entering the dining room everyone stands behind his chair, and some chorus or song is sung after which the blessing is asked by a teacher or student.

Everybody then sits down to a most tempting meal prepared by our excellent chef, Mr. Hart.

Either a faculty member or upper classman acts as head and the rules of good etiquette must be observed.

After the meal is over a bell is tapped, another chorus is sung, and all leave the dining hall.

Shiloh Scroll – January 15, 1936

Study Period at S.B.I. – In the last issue of the paper I told you about the meals at S. B. I. This time I shall give you a different phase of life in a dormitory. One thing that is very necessary if we are to learn anything at all is study.

Each room is furnished with a long study table and chairs, and this is where the students spend the two study periods that must be observed each school day: one from two to four in the afternoon: the other from seven–thirty until nine–thirty in the evening.

Although there should be no noise in the rooms, one walking through the halls might hear some, which only goes to prove that students are still human, but like all other Christians are striving toward perfection. However our aim is to "Study to show ourselves approved unto God."

Shiloh Scroll – February 1, 1936

Recreation at S.B.I. – Recreation periods at Shiloh Bible Institute find the students engaged in various activities in which they can rest themselves both physically and mentally.

For an hour after dinner and supper we have a recreation period and, also, for those not engaged in some duty there is a period between four and five–thirty o'clock. We have a twenty–minute recess period in the morning when every student is required to go outdoors for fresh air.

"Without the book of Revelation the canon of Scripture would be incomplete."

Finis Dake

Some students take walks, while others engage in snowball fights: some go to town on specified days, and still others remain at the school practicing their music lessons. Many times a group will gather around the piano and play and sing together.

On special days, although not every week or even two weeks we find a great deal of pleasure in going ice skating.

Recreation, especially in school is very necessary, for as the old saying goes. "All work and no joy makes Jack a dull boy."

Subscribe For *The Shiloh Scroll* – To meet our many expenses we need 100 more subscriptions and the paper will pay for itself the first year. Isn't that a record? Come on, help us! Send in a subscription for a friend.

We have a large number of copies of every issue except the first and will assure you that you will get every one of the back numbers. Come on! Subscribe now!! Fifty cents per year in the U.S.A.

Shiloh Scroll – February 15, 1936

Church Home of S.B.I. – The church home of the students who are attending Shiloh Bible Institute is the Christian Assembly in Zion, where Finis Dake, our supervisor, is pastor.

Sunday morning finds the students getting ready for Sunday School. Some of them teach and others quite often substitute. After this service we attend the regular morning worship at which time Brother Dake speaks, that is, if anyone does. Sometimes the Lord so wonderfully blesses us that he doesn't even get to preach.

In young people's meeting Sunday evening various members of the student body take charge, and then Mrs. Dake, the church evangelist, always brings the message at the evangelistic service which follows.

Those who play instruments are members of the orchestra and the rest belong to the chorus. Many have rendered special musical numbers from time to time. We enjoy these organizations as well, as the regular church services.

We feel very fortunate to have such a fine church to attend while preparing for the work of the Lord, and we can truthfully say it is our church home since the people of the assembly have so heartily welcomed us and made us feel as if we had always attended church there.

SHILOH SCROLL – MARCH 1, 1936

God's Sunshine at S.B.I. – Zion, like other towns all over the country, has been hit by the extremely cold weather and severe snow storms. Although it was twenty–six below zero part of the time and for several days around fifteen below, it was indeed a beautiful sight to see so much snow and so many high drifts.

It is the first winter some of our students have ever spent in the north, and they really seemed to enjoy it more than those who have always lived in this part of the country.

However, while it was snowing, and blustering weather outside we thought of so much for which we could be thankful just as many of our readers undoubtedly did. We praised God that we had plenty of food, a warm place to stay, plenty of clothes and most of all for Jesus to whom we could go in all times of distress and need.

"I reasoned that there must be something vitally wrong with the religious world and with the thinking of men who could read the same plain statements in Scripture and differ so widely as to the common meaning of common words."

Finis Dake

A Time Of Blessing – Friday morning, March 3rd, was a most blessed time for the student body. At the close of the chapel service a young man stood to testify and thank the Lord for His goodness to him. The power of the Lord fell, and all our classes for the morning were suspended. In fact, there were some of the students who prayed right through the dinner hour.

The Lord wonderfully baptized this same young man, who stood to testify, with the Holy Spirit. Every person present received a real touch from heaven. It is at these times we long for heaven and to see our Master face to face.

Household Duties – As was stated in the catalog, in order to give students as cheap a rate as possible it would be required that they work for one hour a day.

Various duties are assigned to individuals from time to time. It does not always take a full hour however, to do them. In fact, it very seldom takes that long.

Keeping Shiloh House clean is one of our duties. Each girl has a separate room to keep clean or other duty to perform. She is to keep it as she would like her own home to be kept.

Just as the girls must keep Shiloh House clean the boys must take care of Shiloh Cottage where the dining rooms and kitchen are located. They must keep them swept and ready for inspection at any time.

The assignments are for two week periods with the exception of kitchen and dining room duties which last for only one week.

We generally find the students happy while they are at work and if they are not, they try to take as their motto, "Grin and bear it."

Shiloh Scroll – April 1, 1936

SHILOH SCROLL – APRIL 15, 1936

Bible Charts – A large chart *"The Bible on Canvas"* is a valuable asset to congregations and groups of persons studying the Bible. A complete outline of the Bible from beginning to end is divided into 14 main periods and given in picture form. The books of Revelation and Daniel are pictured in detail. From one of these charts one may get a bird's eye view of God's plan for man in the past, present and future. These charts may be had in three sizes:

"I am entirely free from all sensational speculation, man's interpretations, church traditions, spiritualizing tendencies, fanciful imaginations, all reading 'between the lines' and finding, hidden meanings to the Bible."

Finis Dake

1. A durable waterproof linen chart, two by six feet – $5.00.

2. A lecture chart on linen as above, four by sixteen feet – $22.50.

3. A paper chart in two colors, nine inches by thirty three inches, suitable for home study, for only 25 cents.

Tracts – Rev. F. J. Dake has many splendid tracts which he sells at a very small price. His tract on *Can a Lost Man be saved? Can a Saved Man be Lost?,* is one that everyone should read, for it gives sound scriptural arguments for this much debated question. This is a six page tract and sells for 25c per 100: $3.00 per 1,000, postpaid.

The tracts *Women preachers,*[110] *Religious Emotionalism*[111] and *What Must I Do to be Saved?* sell for 25c per 100; $2.00 per 1,000, postpaid.

SHILOH SCROLL – MAY 1, 1936

Missions – Some sixty or seventy persons have already gone from the Zion Assembly into active Christian work as missionaries or preachers and it is believed that God will use this place as a starting point for many others as long as Jesus tarries.

Prayer Conference – Zion, Illinois, June 7–July 5 Prayer conference for the purpose of seeking God for a worldwide outpouring of His Spirit, conducted daily at 6: 30 a.m.

---

[110] See the Appendix for this tract.
[111] See the Appendix for this tract.

Bible School courses for adults consisting of: *Foundation Studies of Scripture, Doctrine, Old Testament Studies,* and *Homiletics;* taught by Finis J. Dake, Supervisor, O. R. Keener, Theo A. Kessel, and Dorothy Dake, all of the Shiloh Bible Institute faculty. These classes will meet daily except Saturday and Sunday at 9 a. m. Persons expecting credit for this work must enroll before June 1st.

Morning services, for those not attending Bible School, in the large tent across the street from the Bible School buildings, at 10 a.m. …Afternoon and night preaching services at 2:30 and 7:30 p.m.

Promise Boxes – "Through the Bible by Promises." To our many departments here at the Institute, a woodworking department has been added. One of their first products is a brand new SCROLL PROMISE BOX. It is designed on the plan and style of a small cedar chest with the promises printed on a scroll within that is turned by dial control. It is a very beautiful little box and contains 450 promises from the Bible. These promises have been selected and are applicable to Christians today. It has a beautiful lid, finished like the box and completing the cedar chest design effect, removable with a small open-ing to show a star when a promise is ready to be read.

Promise Box

The scroll on which the promises are printed is 21 feet long. As said above, it contains 450 promises, or 7,250 words, or more than twice as much as an ordinary promise box. It cannot wear out.

This is the most outstanding thing of its kind ever made. It's ready for distribution. Price, $1.15, postpaid.

Shiloh Scroll – October 1, 1936

Holy Spirit Fullness – We are having some interesting class discus-sions and chapel talks from Brother Dake on the fullness of God and workings of the Spirit in New Testament times which have made us all desirous of more power in our lives. We believe that the students of today, wherever they may be, are the evangelists, pastors, teachers and preachers of tomorrow and as such we pray that God may send us forth equipped to bring blessing in the power of the gospel.

Shiloh Scroll – October 15, 1936

Studies – Our studies are becoming a part of us, and we feel that we are beginning to get a new insight in the Word of God. As yet we have had no examinations, but our powers of thinking are being enlivened and stirred. During our first session of class in Dispensational Truth, Mr. Dake took us through his entire chart. Some of the students have never seen a chart which is as detailed as this one, and were quite uncertain as to their bearings; however, with persistent teaching, the students are beginning to comprehend the pictured *Plan of the Ages.*

"I wish I had about 40/11 hours to get into the subject of God with you. I would point out some things you've never heard before – because I read it in a book called the Bible!"

Finis Dake

A Day's Visit at Shiloh – Should you decide to spend a day at Shiloh you would be awakened at six a.m. by the ringing of a bell, perhaps wondering why a bell so early in the morning, especially when you think you have just fallen asleep. This is the rising bell so no more sleep for this day. At six–thirty everyone must be ready for prayer which lasts till seven o'clock. We always begin our day with private devotions. We need God's guidance and help throughout the day. Just because we are in Bible School does not mean we are exempt from trials and temptations. We need the Lord to help us bear our burdens and give us power to overcome the trials and temptations which are sure to cross our pathway in our Christian walk. About this time we realize we are a bit hungry and in a few minutes the bell calls us for breakfast. Our rooms are cleaned and dusted and also the beds are made after we return from breakfast.

Now it is eight–fifteen and another bell is ringing which reminds us it is time for chapel. Our lessons for the day are put aside as we worship the Lord together in song and prayer. Each morning either a faculty member or one of the students has charge of the chapel. Occasionally we have visiting missionaries and preachers speak at the chapel and noon missionary services. They always receive a warm welcome from the students and faculty.

Classes begin at nine o'clock and continue till ten–thirty at which time we have a short recreation period. During this period everyone goes out to enjoy a few minutes of sunshine and fresh air. The familiar sound of the bell calls us back to our respective classrooms where classes are resumed till twelve o'clock. Each class is opened with prayer.

The missionary prayer band which includes all students meets from twelve till twelve–thirty to pray for the mission fields and missionaries. We know the missionaries have many challenges to meet on the foreign fields and they do appreciate the prayers of God's children in the homeland.

The twelve–thirty bell means it is time for us to go to the dining hall where the waitresses are already waiting, ready to serve dinner. The time between dinner and study period is spent in recreation.

A period of quiet reigns from two until four o'clock, for everyone is sitting at their study table busy with their lessons for the following day. This quietness is interrupted by the ringing of the bell which means study period is over for this afternoon.

The various household duties which are assigned to the students each week are faithfully performed between four and five o'clock.

"Who is that group of people," will probably be the next question asked? Those are only the students marching to the dining hall, for it is now five–thirty and their supper which has been prepared by our chef, Mr. Hart, is awaiting them.

The time after supper is spent in recreation until prayer period. Seven to seven–thirty o'clock finds every student on his knees in prayer.

The study bell rings at seven–thirty. Every student is again busy studying from seven–thirty till nine–thirty.

The last bell you will hear rings at ten o'clock. This means all lights must be out and everyone in bed for soon we will be awakened by the rising bell which means the beginning of a new day.

Shiloh Scroll – May 1, 1937

Jail Services – Every evening three or four of the boys have gone to the city hall and witnessed to the men who come there for a night's lodging. The crowd varies from one to a dozen or more but always, in spite of weather and other activities, someone goes and tells these men of the Saviour who can save them and change their hearts and lives. At times this service grows tiresome and seems not worthwhile but then, when it has been the most discouraging, perhaps, the Lord blesses and the boys come home shouting because one of these men has given his heart to the Lord.

The boys go every evening after supper and sing and testify to the men. Then one of then gives a very brief message from the Bible and they pass out tracts and deal individually with the men. They get very valuable experience in personal evangelism as they deal with these men. Among the transients who come to the jail for shelter from the cold they find many types of men and meet up with all the argument and excuses that are common in dealing with the unsaved. It takes the wisdom, power, and love of God to touch the hearts of these men, but, Praise God! they have been touched and during the year about as many of these men have been saved as there were in the two Student Revivals.

Our Missionary Program – The missionary program at Shiloh Bible Institute is carried on by our organized Student's Missionary Council. This council is composed of a president, a secretary, and five representatives or group leaders, one from each of our five groups: Asia, Africa, Europe, North America and Islands of the Sea, and Latin America. The programs, special speakers, and business are all carried on by this council.

We have daily missionary meetings from 12:00 to 12:30 p.m. which are in charge of the above named groups. Monday, European group; Tuesday, Asia group; Wednesday, African group; Thursday, Latin American group; Friday, North America and Islands of the sea group. At these meetings we pray for the missionaries.

Every Friday afternoon from 2:00 to 3:00 is set aside for group meetings, at which time the groups meet separately and spend an hour of prayer for the missionaries.

CHAPTER NINETEEN

THE HALLS REMEMBER DAKE

ONE OF DAKES MOST LOVED STUDENTS

It has been said that the greatness of a man is measured by those who he trains to take his place after he is gone. If this rule of measurement is used concerning Dake, then we would have to conclude that Dake truly was a great man. For many are the names of those faithful ministers and believers who continue to love, study and teach their Bible in the plain and simple way that Dake taught them.

> *"Brother Dake's strength lay in his God–given knowledge and amazing power of recall of the Scriptures."*
>
> *John G. Hall*

One of Dake's greatest students and beloved friend was a man by the name of John G. Hall.[112] Rev. Hall was a graduate of Shiloh Bible Institute and for the three years while he was at Zion, he and Dake became very close friends. Rev. Hall has some wonderful accounts of the time he spent with Dake during his Bible school years. In addition, Louise Hall, John's wife who also attended Shiloh Bible Institute, adds to the story.

JOHN G. HALL REMEMBERS

Two remarkable men had great influence on my life, first when I was an eager young student, and later as a minister of the gospel. These men were my heroes and role models. One was Dr. P. C. Nelson, a man of towering intellect and spiritual insight. According to an article in the Readers Digest, he knew and spoke 13 languages, and was listed as one of the seven smartest men in the world.

Dr. Nelson founded Southwestern Bible Institute, now Southwestern Assemblies of God University. He was assisted in those pioneering years by the second man whose influence greatly shaped my life—Brother Finis J. Dake.

---

[112] Rev. John G. Hall, of Newcastle, Oklahoma, is a gifted and anointed preacher who ministers from his own dispensational chart and has written several books on prophecy and the plan of God. His books include: *God's Dispensational and Prophetic Plan*, 202 pages, ©1994; *Prophecy Marches On*, 246 pages, ©1994; and a full color dispensational chart entitled *God's Dispensational and Prophetic Plan*.

These two spiritual and intellectual giants had much in common, particularly their strong desire and determination to teach and train young people for the Pentecostal ministry. Each of their ministries was unique, and they complemented each other. Whereas Dr. Nelson's knowledge of the original Bible languages gave him certain perspectives, Brother Dake's strength lay in his God–given knowledge and amazing power of recall of the Scriptures. Under the power of the Holy Spirit he was able to quote Scriptures he could hardly remember reading.

"One time Brother Dake felt led of the Lord to personally go on an extended fast, which lasted 40 days and nights."

John G. Hall

It was after Brother Dake and his family moved to Zion, Illinois from Enid, Oklahoma, and opened Shiloh Bible Institute that I became acquainted with him. I had come to Zion on the advice of the pastor of my home church, Rev. C. C. McAfee, who knew of Brother Dake's ability to teach the Scriptures. And so it was that Brother and Sister Dake became my beloved pastors and respected teachers while I was a student at Shiloh for three years. He remained a precious and valued friend to my wife and me for as long as he lived. His insights and Spirit–guided understanding of the Word of God still affords instruction to us and to many through his writings.

Brother Dake was a man gifted in many areas. One of the most outstanding and unusual was his ability to recall and quote long chapters of Bible. He not only quoted passages in public, but I have personally heard him quote chapter after chapter of the Bible while walking the floor in the prayer room waiting upon God. He received this gift at the time God baptized him in the Holy Spirit.

As a youthful student of the Bible, and especially of Bible prophecy, I recognized this man of God as someone from whom I could learn much. He taught not only by precept but also by example. It was through his example that I learned to appreciate the value and effectiveness of fasting and praying. On one occasion several of us fasted and prayed with Brother Dake for three days and nights. We neither ate nor drank anything during that time of waiting upon God to be led of Him.

Once we lay on our faces on the floor before God for eleven hours, without once getting up for any reason. God was molding our lives and preparing us under Brother Dake's leadership for years of ministry ahead.

One time Brother Dake felt led of the Lord to personally go on an extended fast, which lasted 40 days and nights. He locked himself in a room to be alone with God until he felt a release from the fast. He did drink some liquid, and during the latter days of the fast his wife took him some bread out of her concern for his physical well–being. When I saw Brother Dake after that experience, I could have wept for what it had cost him physically. His features were gaunt, and his suit coat hung dangling about his now boney shoulders. But his eyes were clear and his spirit strong, and God used him as a man "mighty in the Scriptures."

We gradually became good friends even while we were in a teacher/student relationship. For my part, I knew I was privileged to be taught by this man of God! But only learned that he was held in high regard as a teacher and expositor by many others, including some top leaders of the Assemblies of God.

When we had our home in Springfield, Missouri, it was often our privilege to entertain some of the outstanding leaders who lived in or came to Springfield in connection with the Assemblies of God headquarters there. One evening the guests at our table included Aaron A. Wilson, Howard Carter of Great Britain, Foreign Missions Director Noel Perkin, and Ernest S. Williams, retired General Superintendent of the Assemblies of God. In our conversation about the work and experiences in the ministry, the name of Finis Dake came up. Brother Williams, who was often the quietest among us, chose his words carefully. He said firmly and without hesitation, "There was no finer teacher than Finis Dake, but he was ahead of his time." My heart answered, "Amen!"

In these early days in Zion, Pentecostal churches, ministers, and schools were generally scorned by the community. In fact, Pentecost was despised, openly ridiculed and criticized, particularly by the one local church which virtually controlled the city of Zion. Their bold opposition to the Full Gospel was magnified by the secular press, which willingly joined in the clamor against the work of God, and often distorted the facts or fabricated stories to keep the rumors and innuendo going. It did sell papers!

> "Brother Dake had courage and staying power in the face of opposition and false accusation."
>
> John G. Hall

Actually, my introduction to the opposition we faced came within days of my arrival in Zion. Brother Dake took me to the area of the opposing church and showed me two highly visible signs the church had erected. One, pointing toward Grace Missionary Church, read "GOAT HOUSE." The other, pointing directly toward Christian Assembly where Brother Dake pastored, read "MONKEY HOUSE." And just remember Wilbur Glenn Voliva, the pastor of the church, just lived two doors up the street from the Dakes.

Brother Dake, who was bold in the Lord and not intimidated in the least by his detractors, tore down the MONKEY HOUSE sign. But the church soon restored it. So I knew from the beginning that Brother Dake had courage and staying power in the face of opposition and false accusation.

Another time he and I were standing outside the Bible Institute when a paper boy came by. Brother Dake obtained a paper and read a headline proclaiming that he had been in Chicago the day before, and that he had been seen doing certain things, going certain places, etc. He laughed as he showed me the story, for both he and I knew it was a pure concoction by some reporter. We had been together at the Institute during the entire day in question, and he had not set foot out of Zion, let alone gone to Chicago.

He became accustomed to such spurious reports and took them as part of the persecution about which Jesus said, "Blessed are ye, when men shall revile you, and persecute you, and shall say all manner of evil against you falsely, for my sake. Rejoice . . . for great is your reward in heaven" (Matthew 5:11-12).

Sometimes in the fervor and blessing of the altar services in the church, there was loud prayer and rejoicing (although not noisier than the cheers of fans at a ball game, or the response of youth at a rock concert). Nevertheless, one night a policeman came in to attempt to interfere with a brother praying at the altar. He laid his hand on the back of the brother and told him to be quiet. About that time, Brother Dake, who was a large man of commanding stature, strode over to the policeman, turned him around and escorted him to the door. There he invited the policeman to leave and promised, "If I ever need you, I'll call you." And that was the end of that.

Brother Dake's knowledge of the Scriptures, both divinely imparted and through his disciplined study of the Bible, led him to settle on a single principle of interpretation. In his own words, that principle is that of "literalizing rather than spiritualizing." Dake always said, ". . . Take the Bible literally wherein it is at all possible; if symbolic, figurative, or typical language is used, then look for the literal truth it intends to convey."

He began the notes, which culminated in his *Annotated Reference Bible*, while still a young man, not trained in the biblical languages of Greek and Hebrew. However, he later saw the need to study those languages. So he eventually became well–versed in the original languages of the Bible. Added to his Spirit–imparted knowledge of the English version of the Bible, the understanding of the original texts, greatly enhanced the value and accuracy of his complete *Annotated Reference Bible*, published in 1963.

The *Annotated Reference Bible* is his lasting legacy to students of the Word of God. Brother Dake has gone to glory, and we who were privileged to personally know this humble and gifted man of God will also pass on. But through the *Annotated Reference Bible* his influence will live on to bless other generations who will also "search the Scriptures" in order to "rightly divide." – *John G. Hall*

LOUISE HALL REMEMBERS

I was 18 years old when I arrived in Zion, Illinois. It was a joy to attend the Assembly of God church where Rev. and Mrs. Finis Dake were pastors. Since Rev. Dake was also the president of Shiloh Bible Institute, the church attracted the students, as well as many local young people.

"Not only was Sister Dake a powerful preacher of the Word, but she was also one of the favorite teachers in the Bible Institute."

Louise Hall

There was a revival spirit in the church at all times. Brother Dake preached on Sunday mornings and Sister Dake preached every Sunday evening. Her emphasis was on faith and divine healing, a message I had never heard. I was hungry for God, and her ministry really met my need. I drank in every word and it was a great blessing to me.

She would sometimes tell humorous things while preaching, and we would laugh with her. But then at times she would weep and the congregation would be moved by her sincere love and concern for people. Her ministry had more influence on my life than that of any other person in those crucial years.

The Sunday evening meetings always closed with great altar services. It was not unusual for people to pray till two o'clock in the morning. The altars were filled—some getting saved, some being healed, others being filled with the Spirit. It was wonderful!

Even the young people didn't think about going somewhere to eat after church, but rather looked forward to the good times of prayer and waiting on God at the altar.

One night I was so tired I decided to go home from church early. But when I got home, just two or three blocks from the church, the conviction was so strong concerning the coming of the Lord that I returned to the church and joined those praying around the altar. The Dakes' ministry emphasized the coming of the Lord in such a vivid way that we lived in the light of His soon return and truly expected it at any time.

Not only was Sister Dake a powerful preacher of the Word, but she was also one of the favorite teachers in the Bible Institute. As a pastor's wife she was "tops" at directing Christmas plays that blessed the whole church. Most of all, she was a woman of integrity and prayer.

During my stay in Zion, I met and married one of the students of the Bible Institute. The memories we share of the church in Zion are precious and still uplifting and encouraging to this day.

Some time after we left Zion and entered the ministry, our little daughter Donna became ill and was at the point of death. Doctors gave us no hope for her recovery. In desperation we called the Dakes and asked them to pray, for we knew they would touch the throne of God in her behalf. My husband also prayed all night one night for her recovery. God answered prayer and miraculously healed our daughter, for which we shall always be grateful.

Although these precious soldiers of the Cross have gone to their reward, their ministry is not forgotten. Their influence lives on and their works do follow them.
– *Louise Hall*

CHAPTER TWENTY

LESTER SUMRALL REMEMBERS DAKE

THE FRIENDSHIP BEGINS

The late Dr. Lester Sumrall of South Bend, Indiana, was a close friend of Finis Dake. Throughout both of their lifetimes they maintained their relationship both in ministry and in friendship. This friendship started in the mid–1930's. In Dr. Sumrall's Book *Pioneers of Faith,* he gives an insightful account of some of his memories of Dake while in Zion.[113]

DAKE WAS ONE OF MY BEST FRIENDS

Dr. Finis Dake was one of the best friends I have ever known. I met him when he was president of the Shiloh Bible Institute in Zion, Illinois. Dake had secured the premises of John Alexander Dowie's home and carriage house for the Bible college. He used the giant stables where Dowie kept his horses and carriages for the dining area and kitchen and used the magnificent old home for classrooms and offices. Dake loved that spot.

> *"I can see him now, me looking over his shoulder, books stacked at least two feet high on every side of him."*
>
> *Lester Sumrall*

When you met him, you saw a man whose eyes were red, and you would wonder, "Why are his eyes so red?" He would timidly say, "Well, I haven't been to bed in two days. I have been working on annotating the Bible."

I can see him now, me looking over his shoulder, books stacked at least two feet high on every side of him, working away late at night writing his giant Bible that is now sold all over the face of the earth. He had a very large body, not fat, not heavy, but strong. He was a big man.

---

[113] See Dr. Sumrall's book, *Pioneers of Faith*, Harrison House, Tulsa, Oklahoma, Page 67. This is an excellent book, which gives Dr. Sumrall's personal accounts of the lives and ministries of the men and women who led the twentieth–century outpouring of the Holy Spirit.

SUMRALL SLEEPS IN DOWIE'S BEDROOM

He said to me when I was first there, "Lester, I am going to do you a great favor. I have had the ladies prepare Dr. Dowie's private bedroom for your stay. You will actually sleep in the bed where he slept. I have never let anyone sleep in that bed. You will be the first to do so since Dowie died."

Dake loved that place more than any other place he lived in his entire life.

> *". . . he began to quote verbatim the entire book of Revelation from memory."*
>
> *Lester Sumrall*

He took me to the basement and showed me an enormous concrete vault as large as a bedroom that Dowie had built before there were any banks in the city of Zion which he founded. On the walls were shelves: one for $1.00 bills, another for $5.00 bills, another for $10.00 bills, and so forth. The coins were stored in wash tubs. In those days, you could buy practically anything with a penny. Dowie was almost like King Midas in the fairy tale, surrounded with "gold." Dowie had a lot of money, but he lost the reality of God's calling on his life.

I lectured to Dake's students for several days, having just returned from Germany and Russia where I had seen the gruesome Nazi and Communist regimes destroying humanity. The students were especially interested in prophecy. He also pastored a church in the city, and I spoke there several nights. We were together constantly on this visit.

Later in life he told me it had taken 100,000 hours to write the notes for his Bible. I saw the office where he worked. He taught in the Bible school by day, and after dinner each night, he would work on his Bible, often working all night long.

DAKE WAS A PIONEER IN THE WORD

He was a different kind of pioneer, a pioneer in the Word of God. He learned Greek and Hebrew by staying up all night. He could tell you the true meaning of every word in the Bible and give you the opinions of various scholars.

When we opened our church in South Bend in 1967, Dr. Dake was one of the first spiritual pioneers to teach in our Bible seminars. He came at least once a year to teach our people.

One night at my church in South Bend, to everyone's amazement, he began to quote verbatim the entire book of Revelation from memory. With the congregation following line by line, we were amazed as he went straight through the entire book. At one point he smiled at the people and said, "Would you also like the punctuation?"

I recognized him for the mighty giant he was mentally and spiritually. He will long be remembered as a man of the Book.

CHAPTER TWENTY–ONE

CRISIS IN ZION

WHAT IS THE BAPTISM IN THE SPIRIT

While Dake pastored Christian Assembly and presided over Shiloh Bible Institute, much was accomplished for the cause of Christ. However, Dake felt he was never able to recapture the glory that Dowie had brought to Zion. This city would indeed turn out to be a life–changing experience for Dake, as he faced the reality of an encounter with one of the greatest moves of God in the recent history of the church.

> *"No man can approach God except through Jesus Christ."*
>
> *Finis Dake*

For the rest of Dake's ministry he would often talk of his crisis which took place while in Zion. Zion literally changed Dake's theology in a number of areas, but none quite so dramatically as his understanding of the baptism in the Holy Spirit.

A CLASSIC DEFINITION

Dake had come into Zion believing in a classic understanding of the baptism in the Holy Spirit. In the book, *"Bible Doctrines: A Pentecostal Perspective,"* Pentecostal authors William W. Menzies and Stanley M. Horton, define the classic understanding of the Baptism in the Holy Spirit in this way:

> All believers are entitled to and should ardently expect and earnestly seek the promise of the Father, the baptism in the Holy Ghost and fire . . . This was the normal experience of all in the early Christian church. With it comes the enduement of power for life and service, the bestowment of the gifts and their uses in the work of the ministry (Luke 24:49; Acts 1:4, 8; 1 Corinthians 12:1-31).
>
> This experience is distinct from and subsequent to the experience of the new birth (Acts 8:12-17; 10:44-46; 11:14-15; 15:7-9). With the baptism in the Holy Ghost come such experiences as an overflowing fullness of the Spirit (John 7:37-39); Acts 4:8), a deepened reverence for God

(Acts 2:43; Hebrews 12:28), an intensified consecration to God and dedication to His work (Acts 2:42), and a more active love for Christ, for His word and for the lost (Mark 16:20).[114]

This definition of the baptism in the Holy Ghost is biblical and well–defined. However, as is often the case, the definition and the experience as practiced are sometimes very far apart. Even in these early years of the Pentecostal experience, the definition in practice had become condensed, toned down and virtually accepted to mean something far less than the classical definition demanded. For Dake, as well as many other Pentecostals, the baptism in the Holy Ghost primarily was an experience received after the new birth and was simply accompanied by the initial evidence of speaking with other tongues as the Spirit of God gave the utterance. For the most part, this practicing definition is accurate as far as it goes. However, Dake was to learn that his understanding of this wonderful experience was far short of what was needed in order to do the work and ministry of Christ.

CONFRONTED WITH DOWIE'S LEGACY

As Dake went about his everyday duties in Zion as pastor, he talked with many people who had been affected by Dowie's ministry. He learned of the power of God that was manifested in Dowie's life. He became more and more interested in the power of God as he studied Dowie's life. He even collected many old photographs of Dowie and the events which took place during his ministry in Zion. Some of the photographs were used by Gordon Lindsay in the writing of his biography on the life of Alexander Dowie.[115]

Beginning in 1935, Dake became deeply burdened over his inability to do the works of ministry that Alexander Dowie had done. After all, was he not baptized in the Holy Ghost? Had he not spoken with tongues and continued speaking in tongues, even to that day? Had he not received the fullness of the Holy Spirit? Yet when he compared his ministry to Dowie's, he fell far short. Alexander Dowie, while praying for the sick

---

[114] *Bible Doctrines: A Pentecostal Perspective*, by William W. Menzies and Stanley M. Horton. Login Press, Springfield, Missouri, 1993, Page 122.

[115] *John Alexander Dowie—A Life Story Of Trials Tragedies And Triumphs*, by Gordon Lindsay, published by Christ for the Nations, Dallas, Texas and reprinted in 1986.

with great success, did not accept the experience of speaking in tongues.

For Dowie there were miracles in abundance. It was reported that Dowie prayed "for as many as 70,000 people each year, with thousands of the most astounding and remarkable miracles taking place."[116]

The *Voice of Healing* magazine reported the following:

> "The divine healing miracles that the Lord performed under the ministry of Dr. Dowie ranged from instantaneous cures of every disease and malady from simple broken bones to cancer and gun shot wounds to insanity. One of the most prominent and publicized miracles was the healing of Miss Amanda Hicks of Clinton, Kentucky. She was instantly healed of terminal cancer in the final stage. Miss Hicks was the president of a denominational church college and the cousin of President Abraham Lincoln. Her church authorities summarily dismissed her from her position in their denial and protest against modern day divine healing miracles."[117]

During this time all that Dake could seem to think about was the fact that Dowie had seen the lame walk, the cripple restored, the mute speak, the deaf hear, blind eyes opened, limbs lengthened—some up to six inches long—and literally all manner of healings take place. He was told by eye witnesses that Dowie:

> . . . could take a gallon of alcohol and pull a cancer right out of someone's body and put it in the alcohol right while he prayed.

He had seen the pictures of braces, crutches, built–up shoes and other trophies of the Devil hanging on the walls of the Tabernacle Dowie pastored.

This is not to say that Dake did not see God perform the miraculous. He did, as has already been stated in earlier chapters. And throughout his life he would see God answer prayers. Even during his tenure as a teacher and

---

[116] Sandford, Frank. *Tongues of Fire*. Magazine date: 3/1/1897.
[117] *Voice of Healing*. Gordon Lindsay, editor. Dallas, Texas: 1949 May edition.

administrator at Shiloh Bible Institute he had seen God answer prayer.

On one occasion, just three days before graduation, a student came down with chicken pox. This was a very serious matter in those days and there was talk of sending all the students home without graduating! Dake, however, gathered all the students into the chapel and read to them the 91st Psalm. He then told them they were all going to pray. They did pray, and they believed God. No one else came down with chicken pox and they had their graduation. Afraid he might catch chicken pox, one student *did* leave. He caught chicken pox while at home! So Dake had seen the hand of God again and again.

> "God has created in the world an abundance of everything that man needs, and there is enough for all."
>
> Finis Dake

Yet the degree to which the miraculous had been displayed in Dowie's life had not been displayed in his, and it was that for which he hungered.

THEY WANTED ME TO DO WHAT DOWIE DID

Years later commenting on this season of his life, Dake preached a message telling of his crisis during this time. He said:

> I went to that city preaching the baptism in the Holy Spirit. They thought that was wonderful that somebody in modern times had a baptism in the Holy Spirit. The man that had started that city who had done all those wonderful miracles in the name of Jesus Christ, did not claim such a baptism, did not claim such a wonderful thing. And yet, he did all those things without the baptism in the Holy Spirit. Now I come in to that city preaching a greater power, a greater experience, a greater blessing than Dr. Dowie had had. They were looking for greater things. They had a right to. They expected me to have what the apostles had, what Jesus Christ had. Because I was telling them that God was pouring out His Spirit in modern times like in apostolic days. I was telling them that we had the baptism in the Holy Spirit. No wonder they expected us to duplicate the works of Christ. They had a right to.
>
> They began to call me out into all kinds homes to pray for the crippled, the maimed, the lame, the blind, the deaf, the

dumb, twisted bodies, and deformed limbs until I almost pulled the hair out of my head in defeat. They expected me to get the job done. To heal those people because I had the baptism in the Holy Spirit.

I TRIED AND FAILED

I went at it with all my heart.[118] On some occasions I stayed in a home two and three days at a time fasting and praying. Still the work wasn't done. God did do some wonderful things. In other cases I never saw results at all.

I've always been at least half–honest. And I expect most folks are. I was determined to show my concern for those people I could not help by getting honest with God. They were looking to me for help. Depending on me to bring deliverance. And I was so helpless to help them.

I saw that what I had was not as much as what the apostles had. I saw that what I had was far short of what I was reading about in the New Testament. I not only prayed for those cases, but I had a church full of people that claimed to have the baptism in the Holy Ghost. So that made us doubly able and they should have expected more out of myself and that crowd who claimed such blessings in our lives.

The whole crowd of us, we prayed for certain cases day in and day out, every service regularly, week in and week out, month in and month out, and *still* certain cases could not be helped. What were we to do? Were we to give up the ghost and get discouraged? No, I thought, I would use common sense and search the Bible and find out what was wrong.

A SEARCH FOR SOMETHING MORE

I have always had sense enough to know that if I had an automobile and it went dead on me, that something had to be wrong with it. I could put my foot on the accelera-

---

[118] When Dake tells of his whole–hearted seeking of God, he humbly leaves out the fact of his long fasting during this time. Rev. John G. Hall tells of at least one 40 day fast Dake fasted during this season of his life. Truly he was seeking God with great intensity.

tor and have it full of gas and everything else, and if it would not work then something must be wrong. What would I do in regard to the automobile that does not work? Would I just sit there and say, "Bless God, this thing works, I know it will run?" Well, of course not! I have learned that there are some men called mechanics, and that if I don't know anything about it, somebody else does. I know where to get it fixed. It can be towed in or someone can come out and fix it. I applied that same common sense to religion.

> *"Pride, willfulness, and rebellion against what 'is written' are the causes of the Bible being hard to understand."*
>
> *Finis Dake*

I put this proposition before my church: Let's gather together and find out what the Bible teaches. Let's find out what is wrong. Let's find out why this prayer business doesn't work. This baptism in the Holy Ghost isn't as powerful as we read about in the New Testament, or else we don't have it or something else is wrong! Let's find out what is wrong.

I didn't think that was too far off. I thought it was a good idea and the church did as well. We gathered together and we read the Bible through night after night until we finished the New Testament. We brought our pencils and our papers and we wrote down everything we found that we are not practicing and everything we find that we do not experience or that isn't normal in our Christian experience. We found out a lot.

IS JUST SPEAKING WITH TONGUES THE BAPTISM IN THE HOLY GHOST?

Before this I thought I had everything the New Testament had taught. Because I had received the baptism in the Holy Ghost some eighteen years ago, I thought I had it all just because I talked in tongues one time. But do you know, when we read that New Testament through just one time, and I honestly put down everything I found that I was not doing or which I did not have in experience. I had 165 things—different things that I had never seen in Christian experience in any local Christian church or in one individual life, including my own.

I couldn't believe it. I couldn't believe that with my eyes I could read the Bible through one time and that I had never seen those things. It almost made backsliders out of all of us to find out so many things that we were not doing.

I never will forget that the first night when I really learned the secret of it all. We got as far as Matthew, Chapter 10, and I read this in verse one: ". . . he had called unto him his twelve disciples, he gave them power against unclean spirits, to cast them out, and to heal all manner of sickness and all manner of disease." I read a little bit further in verse eight: "Heal the sick, cleanse the lepers, raise the dead, cast out devils: freely ye have received, freely give."

That hit me between the eyes! I stopped suddenly and I said, "I think we have found the answer the very first night. Do you know why we cannot freely give out? Because we have not freely received!"

JUST THE FACTS

I asked them a question. I talked about some of those cases we were praying for: a blind woman over on Emmaus Avenue, a crippled woman on Elizabeth Avenue and another crippled woman over on Elim Avenue. I pointed out these three cases and I asked, "Do you think we would hold out on these three cases if we had freely received something to give them? Do you think we would be going through this embarrassment week in and week out if we had power to heal them?"

I reasoned a bit more. I said, "Prior to the disciples receiving the power from Jesus to heal they could not heal a broken leg on a gnat a minute before. But here, just that quickly, He gave them power against unclean spirits to cast them out and power to heal all manner of sickness or disease without exception. They were told to freely give out what they had freely received."

DAKE YOU ARE WRONG

We were reasoning along these lines for a few minutes and a Pentecostal preacher jumped up in the back of the church and said: "Brother Dake!" I said, "What is wrong?" He said, "I got the baptism in the Holy Ghost." I said to him, "I never said you did not have the Baptism in the Holy Spirit."

I said, "Brother, as I have said, we have all these people in our church with all these needs. Now, tomorrow you and I will pay a call on these folks and you can pray for them. You can restore sight to the blind, give power to the lame to walk and raise up those who are bed fast. I have already seen what I can do. This whole church has seen what I can do, now let's see what you can do!"

"I present authoritative Bible answers to Bible questions without coloring or personal theories."

Finis Dake

This brother said, "I can't do anything to help those folks." He said, "I have the power but I don't know how to use it." I then told him, "You have the power and don't know how to use it, and we don't have the power, so we can't use it. It looks like to me we are both in the same boat!

"Why don't we all find our way to the altar tonight and pray. This brother can pray for the knowledge to use the power he has and we can pray for God to give us the power we do not have." To make a long story short, we all got up from the altar at 2:00 a.m. in the morning.

WHAT I HAVE NEED OF IS GOD

We left the church that night and walked down the street on our way home and the brother said to me, "You've got a future in this organization if you will just use a little sense and not get carried away with this kind of thinking." I told him, "Future or no future, in this or any other organization, as long as I get the power I am wanting, all I have need of is God!" At that we parted and we both went on about our business.

So it was in Zion that Dake came to understand the baptism in the Holy Ghost to be something more than what he had. He was faced with the reality that he could not do what Dowie had done. More than that, he could not do what the disciples of Christ in the New Testament had done. Dake reasoned:

> This man did not claim a baptism in the Holy Spirit as I do, yet he could do all these wonderful things. I, on the other hand, claim a baptism in the Holy Spirit and am unable to do these things. I must be missing something.

Throughout the rest of his ministry Dake would never again lay claim to the baptism in the Holy Ghost. Dake was still Full Gospel and Charismatic as defined by modern Christians. He spoke in tongues and continued to do so. But he never claimed to have the Spirit without measure, as Jesus did, ever again. For how could he claim an unlimited supply of the Spirit, when he was faced with the reality that he was in fact limited?

So for Dake just what was the baptism in the Holy Ghost? The baptism in the Spirit was received after the New Birth. It was accompanied by the manifestation of tongues. He said:

> *"Not one Bible question has been asked in all these years but what I have been able to give two or more Scriptures to prove the answers."*
>
> *Finis Dake*

> We conclude from a study of the Bible and history that no one has ever received, or ever will receive the real baptism in the Spirit without the initial evidence of speaking in other tongues as the Spirit gives utterance.

So tongues were included in the baptism in the Spirit. But Dake's definition went further:

> It is the immersion or burial of the believer in the Spirit at which time he receives the Spirit in his life "without measure" and not just "by measure" as men received before Pentecost. It is the full anointing of the Spirit that Christ received and demonstrated on earth.[119]

---

[119] See: Isaiah 11:1-2; 42:1-7; 61:1-2; Matthew 11:4-6; 12:18; Luke 4:16-21; John 3:34; 14:12; Acts 10:38.

It is the Spirit coming in, upon, filling, overwhelming, infusing, anointing, and enduing with full and complete power to do the works of God among men, and not just a measure, as in Old Testament days. It is the Spirit taking full possession of the believer to live, speak, and work through him in the same degree that was manifested through Christ and the apostles. It is the fulness of what men had in part before Pentecost. It is more than a mere "filling." It is a baptism as well as a filling of the Spirit.

For a better understanding of this empowerment, the next chapter gives a full description of Dake's view of the baptism in the Holy Spirit, including the evidences that are present when one is filled with the Spirit without measure.

CHAPTER TWENTY–TWO

THE BAPTISM IN THE HOLY SPIRIT

NOTE FROM THE AUTHOR:

This chapter is taken directly from Dake's writings on the subject of the Holy Spirit. It is presented here in order to provide a more complete insight into Dake's understanding of the Spirit baptism.

A MISUNDERSTOOD SUBJECT

The baptism in the Holy Spirit is one of the most misunderstood subjects in the Bible. It has also caused a great deal of division within Christianity as a whole, and for that reason every sincere person should search the Scriptures for themselves, with an open mind and receptive spirit. I invite your unbiased attention to the following facts found in Scripture, which clearly state the whole truth about the baptism in the Holy Spirit:

> *"The fact is that men are depraved and fallen creatures and out of harmony with God."*
>
> *Finis Dake*

1. The Fact of a Spirit Baptism

The fact of a Spirit baptism in Scripture is very clear. John the Baptist said to his followers concerning Christ, "He shall baptize you with the Holy Ghost and with fire" (Mt. 3:11; Mk. 1:8; Lk. 3:16; Jn. 1:31-34). Jesus said to His disciples just before Pentecost, "Ye shall be baptized with the Holy Ghost not many days hence" (Acts 1:4-8). See also Mt. 20:20-23; Acts 2:33, 38-39; 8:11-22; 9:17; 10:44-48; 11:14-18; 15:7-11; 19:1-7; Gal. 3:14).

2. The Spirit Baptism is for All Believers

1. John the Baptist said that it was for all believers: "I indeed baptize you with water unto repentance; but he [Christ] shall baptize you with the Holy Ghost, and with fire" (Mt. 3:11; Jn. 1:31-34).

2. Jesus promised the Holy Spirit to all men who were children of God: "How much more shall your heavenly Father give the Holy Spirit to them that ask him" (Lk. 11:13). The Spirit that Jesus promised was not to be for the world (the unsaved), but only for men who were saved and were not of the world (Jn. 14:16-17; 17:14).

Jesus promised that "If any man thirst, let him come unto me and drink. He that believeth on me . . . out of his belly shall flow rivers of living water . . . this spake he of the Spirit, which they that believe on him should receive: for the Holy Ghost was not yet given; because that Jesus was not yet glorified" (Jn. 7:37-39).

3. Peter promised at Pentecost that the same baptism would be given to all who would become Christians. He said, "Repent, and be baptized . . . and ye shall receive the gift of the Holy Ghost. For the promise is unto you, and to your children, and to all that are afar off, even as many as the Lord our God shall call" (Acts 2:38-39). He promised further that the same baptism would be given to all men who want it in the latter days. He said of the experience at Pentecost that "This is that which was spoken by the prophet Joel and it [this same prophecy of the Spirit baptism upon all men] shall come to pass in the last days, saith God, I will pour out of my Spirit upon all flesh: and your sons and your daughters, shall prophesy." When was this to be fulfilled? "In the last days" of this age when God will "shew wonders in heaven above, and signs in the earth beneath" (Acts 2:16-21). Thus, a fulfillment of Joel's prophecy of the Spirit baptism upon all men happened at Pentecost and it will happen again in the last days during the Great Tribulation. It has been promised to every generation between those two points of time even upon "as many as the Lord shall call." Peter further promised that the same Spirit they had received at Pentecost should descend upon "them that obey" God (Acts 5:32).

"One must be willing to accept the Bible as God's Word."

Finis Dake

3. Various Terms Used of the Spirit Baptism

Being baptized in the Spirit is called a "baptism" (Mt. 20:20-23; Heb. 6:2), the "promise of my Father and the enduement of power from on high" (Lk. 24:49; Acts 1:4-8; 2:33; Gal. 3:14), the "Spirit without measure" (Jn. 3:34), "rivers of living water flowing out of the innermost being" (Jn. 7:37-39), the "gift of the Holy Ghost" (Acts 2:38-39; 5:32; 8:19-20; 10:44-48; 11:14-18; 15:7-11; Jn. 7:37-39; Lk. 11:13), the "full anointing of the Holy Ghost and power" (Acts 10:38; Isa. 11:2; 42:1-7; 61:1-2; Lk. 4:16-21; 1 Jn. 2:27), and the "fulness of God in the life of a believer" (Eph. 3:19; Rom. 15:29; Jn. 1:16; 7:37-39; Eph. 5:18).

4. Jesus Was the First to Receive the Spirit Baptism

Jesus was baptized in the Spirit after coming up out of the river Jordan (Mt. 3:16; Mk. 1:10; Lk. 3:21-22; Jn. 1:31-34). That this was a "baptism" is clear from the fact He said to the sons of Zebedee, "Are ye able to be baptized with the baptism I am baptized with . . . Ye shall . . . be baptized with the baptism I am baptized with" (Mt. 20:20-23).

5. The Spirit Baptism Not Given Before Pentecost

Men in general were not baptized in the Spirit until the day of Pentecost and until Jesus was glorified. This is clearly stated in Jn. 7:37-39: "He that believeth on me, as the Scripture hath said, out of his belly shall flow rivers of living water. (But this spake he of the Spirit, which they that believe on him should receive: for the Holy Ghost was not yet given; because that Jesus was not glorified)."

Jesus said to the disciples ten days before Pentecost, "Ye shall be baptized with the Holy Ghost not many days hence" (Acts 1:5). Peter on Pentecost confirmed the fact that on this day the Spirit baptism was given for the first time because Jesus had been glorified. He said, "Therefore being by the right hand of God exalted, and having received of the Father the promise of the Holy Ghost, he hath shed forth this, which ye now see and hear" (Acts 2:33).

It is clear that if "The Holy Ghost was not yet given, because that Jesus was not glorified" the baptism in the Holy Ghost was never given to men in Old Testament days. If this be true, then no experience of any man before Pentecost can he taken as the baptism in the Spirit.

6. What the Spirit Baptism is Not

It is not any one of the many experiences of the Old Testament saints, or of the disciples before Pentecost, listed in point VII above. It, therefore, could not be a mere filling of the Spirit, one of the nine gifts of the Spirit, some fruit of the Spirit, the new birth, sanctification, justification, or some phase of salvation that many today claim is the Spirit baptism. For if men had all these blessings before Pentecost, then it is scripturally settled that they are not the Spirit baptism, which was not given until that time.

7. The Words "Baptize" and "Baptism" Defined

The Greek word for "baptize" is *baptidzo*, from *bapto*, meaning "to dip, plunge, immerse, or cover wholly with the element used in baptism."

It has the same meaning as the word "dip" in Lk. 16:24; Jn. 13:26; Rev. 19:13. Only two times is *baptidzo* translated "wash" and in these cases it means to be wholly wet and not merely sprinkled (Mk. 7:4; Lk. 11:38).

The words "dip" and "immerse" mean "to bury, douse, duck, immerge, plunge, sink, and submerge." Since the Greek word *baptidzo*, translated "baptize" 60 times, means "to dip or immerse" it is clear that baptism is by burial into the element used in baptism. In fact, baptism is spoken of as a burial in Rom. 6:4 and Col. 2:12.

8. There are Seven Baptisms in Scripture

Paul taught the "doctrine of baptisms" (Heb. 6:2). There are five different elements people have been baptized or immersed into. The seven baptisms and the five different elements used in baptism are as follows:

"The old theory that the tribulation will be worldwide is not stated in one Scripture."

Finis Dake

1. The baptism "unto Moses in the cloud and in the sea" (1 Cor. 10:2). This refers to the crossing of the Red Sea when Israel was hid from Pharaoh in the sea on both sides and the cloud in front and back and all over them to protect them from the Egyptians. They were completely covered by the clouds and went through the sea. This was a true baptism in the cloud and in the sea. Cloud and water are the elements used in this baptism.

2. John's baptism in water (Mt. 3; Lk. 3; Acts 1:5; 19:3-4). This was immersion in water (Mt. 3:16; Mk. 1:10).

3. Christ's baptism in water (Jn. 3:22-23; 4:1-2). These last two baptisms were not continued, because they were in the name of the Father only and not in the name of the Father, and of the Son, and of the Holy Ghost, as Jesus authorized in Mt. 28:18-20. Both John and Jesus did work in the name of the Father only (Jn. 5:30-36; 5:43; 10:25; 17:1-6). Paul rebaptized the disciples of John thus proving that baptism in the Father's name only was not recognized after Christ died (Acts 19:1-7).

4. Baptism of suffering (Lk. 12:50). This was a baptism that Christ was yet to be baptized with after He spoke of it in this passage. It refers to His sufferings and the element He was to be baptized into speaks of the overwhelming agonies that He was to go through in taking the sins and sicknesses of the race (Isa. 52:14; 53:1-12; Mt. 8:17; Lk. 22:44; 1 Pet. 2:24).

5. Baptism "into Christ" and into His body, the Church (Rom. 6:4; 1

Cor. 12:13; Gal. 3:27; Eph. 4:5; Col. 2:12). These Scriptures have been taken to refer to water baptism, but not one of them mentions water as the element the believer is baptized into. If they referred to water baptism it would read "buried with him by baptism into water," but they plainly say "baptism into Christ," "baptized into one body," and "baptized into Christ." In Col. 2:12, Paul says men are saved by being "buried with him in baptism, wherein also ye are risen with Him through faith of the operation of God" and not through water administered by man. Whatever baptism this passage refers to, it is one by "the operation of God" and not through the operation of man. It, therefore, could not possibly refer to water baptism by man.

6. Christian water baptism (Mt. 28:19; Mk. 16:15; Acts 2:38, 41; 8:12-16, 36-38; 9:18; 10:44-48; 16:15, 33; 18:8; 19:1-5; 22:16; 1 Cor. 1:13-17; 1 Peter 3:21). These 15 passages are all the Scriptures teaching water baptism. The element used is water and the administrator is man. Candidates are supposed to be already saved and disciples of Christ (Mt. 28:19). Water baptism testifies outwardly of an inward work and is merely a "figure" (1 Peter 3:21) and a "witness" of the change previously made in the life of a candidate through faith in the death, burial, and resurrection of Jesus Christ (1 Jn. 5:6-10).

7. Baptism in the Holy Spirit (Mt. 3:11-16; 20:20-23; Lk. 24:49; Jn. 1:31-34; 3:34; 7:37-39; 14:12-17; Acts 1:4-8; 2:1-4, 33, 38-39; 5:32; 8:14-22; 9:17; 10:38, 44-48; 11:14-18; 19:1-7; Rom. 15:29; Gal. 3:1-3, 14; Eph. 3:19; 2 Tim. 1:7; Heb. 6:2; Isa. 11:2; 28:9-11; 42:1-7; 61:1; Joel 2:28-29; Hab. 1:5).

9. Three Baptisms for Believers

There are three baptisms for believers in Christ. They are the last three of the seven mentioned above. The first four are not for Christians today for they have been done away with, for reasons we have stated above. Note the following facts concerning the three baptisms:

1. *The Agents, Elements, and Candidates.* The three agents who administer the three baptisms are: the Holy Spirit, Jesus Christ, and the minister. The three elements are: Christ, the Holy Spirit, and water. The candidates in all three baptisms are: the believers of the Gospel.

The Holy Spirit is the agent that baptizes the believer "into Christ" and "into one body," the Church, which is the body of Christ: "For by one Spirit [the agent] are we all [believers] baptized into one body [the element], whether we be Jews or Gentiles" (1 Cor. 12:13). This is called being baptized "into Christ," not into water or into the Holy Spirit, and refers to the saving of the soul by the Spirit and the Word of God and of making one a member of Christ and His body, the Church (Rom. 6:4; Gal. 3:27; Col. 2:12).

> *"When men limit God, they naturally limit His blessings to themselves."*
>
> *Finis Dake*

Christ is the agent that baptizes the believer into the Holy Spirit. John the Baptist said, "He [Christ, the agent] shall baptize you [believers] with the Holy Ghost" (the element, Mt. 3:11; Jn. 1:31-34).

Ministers are the agents who baptize believers into water (Mt. 28:19). This kind of baptism is solely a work of man, and not of God.

2. Scriptural Order of the Three Baptisms. The Holy Spirit baptism can take place both before and after water baptism, but always after baptism into Christ and His body, the Church. It is only for saved men (Lk. 11:13; Jn. 7:37-39; 14:17; Acts 2:38-39; 5:32) It can be received whether one is baptized in water or not, as proven in the cases of Paul and the Gentiles (Acts 9:17-18; 10:44-48; 11:14-18; 15:7-11). Others received this baptism after baptism in water (Mt. 3:16; Acts. 1:4-8; 2:1-4; 8:12-25; 19:1-7). It is, therefore, proper to baptize one in water before or after he is baptized in the Spirit, but never before he is baptized into Christ and is a member of the body of Christ by the new birth.

3. The Purpose of the Three Baptisms. The purpose of the baptism into Christ and into the body of Christ is to save the soul. It is the only baptism essential to salvation. The purpose of baptism into water is to witness to the reality of salvation and is essential only to obedience and to testimony after one is truly saved.

The sole purpose of the Spirit baptism is to endue men fully with power to do the works of Christ, and even greater works than He did (Jn. 14:12; Lk. 24:49; Acts 1:4-8); to carry on the work that Jesus began "both to do and to teach" (Acts 1:1-2, 4-8; Mt. 28:20); to confirm the Word of God among men (Mk. 16:15-20; Heb. 2:3-4); to give men the Spirit of God without measure and in all fulness (Jn. 7:37-39; 14:12; Rom. 15:29; Eph. 3:19); to anoint men fully to preach the Gospel to the poor, to heal the broken–hearted, to preach deliverance to the captives, and the recovering of sight to the blind, to set at liberty them that are bruised, to preach the acceptable year of the Lord (Isa. 61:1-2; Lk. 4:16-21); to cast out devils, to heal all manner of sickness and all manner of disease among the people, and to take God's salvation to the ends of the earth (Mt. 10:7-8; 11:2-6; 12:17-21; Mk. 16:15-20; Jn. 14:12; Acts 1:8); and the blessings enjoyed by men in Old Testament times who had the Holy Spirit only by measure (2 Cor. 3:6-11; Heb. 8:6; Jn. 14:12; Rom. 15:29; 1 Cor. 1:7; 2:4-5; 4:18-21; 2 Cor. 10:3-11; Eph. 3:19; 6:10-18; 1 Thess. 1:5; Heb. 2:3-4; Mk. 16:15-20; Acts 1:4-8).

10. What the Baptism of the Spirit Really Is

It is the immersion or burial of the believer in the Spirit at which time he receives the Spirit into his life "without measure" and not just "by measure" as men received before Pentecost. It is the full anointing of the Spirit that Christ received and demonstrated on earth (Isa. 11:1-2; 42:1-7; 61:1-2; Mt. 11:4-6; 12:18; Lk. 4:16-21; Jn. 3:34; 14:12; Acts 10:38).

It is the Spirit coming in, upon, filling, overwhelming, infusing, anointing, and enduing with full and complete power to do the works of God among men, and not just a measure, as in Old Testament days. It is the Spirit taking full possession of the believer to live, speak, and work through him in the same degree that was manifested through Christ and the apostles. It is the fulness of what men had in part before Pentecost. It is more than a mere "filling." It is a baptism as well as a filling of the Spirit.

"Power and radiance come from a change of heart and from Christ's living in you."

Finis Dake

11. A "Filling" and a "Baptism" Illustrated

The difference between a "filling" and a "baptism" in the Spirit, or the Spirit "by measure" and "without measure" may be illustrated by a glass and a pitcher of water. To the extent water is poured into a glass it is filled. A person can fill a glass by pouring different measures into it at different times, or he can fill it at one pouring. He can keep pouring until the glass is full and running over and still it is not baptized. It is only full and running over. But if a person takes the glass and immerses or buries it in the fulness of water it is both filled and baptized. This explains how the disciples were all "filled" (Acts 2:4) as well as "baptized" in the Spirit at Pentecost (Acts 1:4-5). A filling always accompanies a baptism, but a baptism does not accompany a mere filling.

A person so "filled" and "baptized" must keep that way, for the minute he gets out of the "fulness" of the Holy Spirit and lives in self, or lives as he lived before, he is not baptized in the Spirit any more than the glass would be baptized in water if taken out of the water. Like the glass, it is possible to get un–baptized and still retain a "measure" or be more or less "filled" with the Spirit as before being baptized in the fulness of God. Christ kept himself baptized in the Spirit by prayer and daily yielding to God for more virtue and power to bless all who came to Him (Mt. 14:23; Lk. 5:16; 6:12; 9:18). The disciples also lived in prayer and received new infillings and anointings from time to time (Acts 4:21; 6:4). They gave themselves continually to the ministry of the Word and prayer (Acts 6:2-4).

12. Biblical Evidences of the Spirit Baptism

Includes power to:

1. *Have rivers of living water flowing out of the innermost being* (Jn. 7:37-39). This expresses the idea of the Spirit without measure (Jn. 3:34) and is certainly different from the "well of water" of Jn. 4:14, which can be measured. This is the same fulness of God mentioned in Rom. 15:29; Eph. 3:19; Lk. 24:49; Acts 1:8.

2. *Do the works of Christ and even greater works than He did* (Jn. 14:12-15). This plainly expresses the degree of power the baptism in the Spirit will bring to every believer. It is both scriptural and logical to conclude that the Spirit baptism which Jesus received will produce the same results today, if and when one receives it. If one is not able to do the works of Christ, he does not have the same full anointing of the Spirit that Jesus had. He is simply coming short of the fulfillment of the full baptism in the Spirit, which is rightfully his through Christ.

The law of nature and the law of mechanics prove that two persons or machines of equal power can do exactly the same things to the same degree. The stronger of two persons or machines will be able to do more than a weaker one; each can do exactly according to the degree of power possessed. It is likewise true in the spiritual realm (Mt. 12:23-30). To the extent one is endued with power from God he will be able to do the works of God, as in the case of Elijah, Elisha, and others who had different measures of the Spirit. Christ received the Spirit "without measure" (Jn. 3:34) and was unlimited in His power to destroy the works of the Devil. So will it be with anyone who receives the same baptism in the same fulness with which Christ received it. He made no failure. Some men claim he failed in Mk. 6:5, but the claim is only an excuse for their lack of power. Even here He healed everyone for whom he prayed. The rest would not come to Him to be healed. So our failures cannot be blamed on Christ, but rather on our failure to seek God until the full enduement of power is manifest. It only proves men today have not yet received in fulness what Christ had.

3. *Destroy the works of Satan* (1 Jn. 3:8). This Scripture refers to the life of Christ in "healing all that were oppressed of the devil" (Acts 10:38). A similar power is to be the experience of every believer who receives the true Spirit baptism (Jn. 14:12; 1 Jn. 4:4).

4. *Bind and loose anything* (Mt. 16:19). Some argue that this promise was to Peter only, but Mt. 18:15-20 promises the same power to each believer. If we are going to limit this promise to Peter simply because it was addressed to him, then we should be consistent and limit Mk. 11:21-24 to Peter; limit Mk. 9:23 to the father of the lunatic boy; limit Mt. 28:16-20 to the apostles, and limit all other commissions and promises to the persons directly addressed. We end up with a Bible that is out of date and irrelevant for us today. On the other hand, if it is true, then all of it is true and applicable for us today. We must believe that all the promises are "yea and Amen" to all believers (2 Cor. 1:20). If there is anything that needs to be bound or loosed concerning sickness, sin, bad habits, or any other work of the Devil in anyone, it is in the power of one who has the anointing of Christ to do it (Jn. 14:12; 20:22; Mt. 8:1-9; 9:1-8). Believers are to do anything Christ did, on the same basis as He, and by the same Spirit. He did nothing of Himself and neither can any man. He did everything by the authority of God and by the Holy Ghost. When God authorizes any man and gives him the same Spirit and power He gave His Son, that man can do what God authorizes him to do, for God is still sovereign (Rom. 9:11-24).

> *"Obey the Word of God to the letter, regardless of how foolish it may appear."*
>
> *Finis Dake*

5. *Control the elements and do all kinds of miracles.* Did Christ do these things? If so, then the works that He did we may do also (Jn. 14:12; Lk. 24:49; Acts 1:4-8; 1 Cor. 12:1-11; 2 Tim. 2:21; Heb. 2:3-4).

6. *Exercise all the gifts of the Spirit* (1 Cor. 12:1-11). Is it possible for one person to have all nine gifts of the Spirit? The answer depends upon whether Christ had all of them or not. He did have them all, for He

had the Spirit "without measure" (Jn. 3:34). If he had every gift, then any believer may have all of them. In fact, a believer must have all of them if he is to do the works of Christ, and even greater works than He did. Paul told the Corinthians (1:7) that they should not come behind in any gift. He prayed for the Ephesians (3:19) to be filled with all the fulness of God. Paul said that he had the fulness of God (Rom. 15:29). Paul said Timothy could do the works he did, so he also must have had all the gifts (1 Cor. 16:10). Any vessel of God can be prepared to do "every good work" (2 Tim. 2:19-21; 2 Cor. 10:4-6; Eph. 6:10-18).

7. *Be used in imparting spiritual gifts to others.* Christ imparted great power to the disciples before Pentecost (Mt. 10:1-20; Lk. 10:1-20). Paul imparted spiritual gifts to others (Rom. 1:11; 1 Tim. 4:14; 2 Tim. 1:6). This power will be in every believer when he receives the fulness of God to do what Christ, Paul, and others did.

8. *Be used in imparting the Holy Spirit to others.* Not only were spiritual gifts imparted by men who had the fulness of God, but the Spirit came upon men when hands were laid on them (Acts 8:14-22; 9:17; 19:1-7). The doctrine of laying on of hands is mentioned in other Scriptures (Heb. 6:2; Mk. 16:17–18; Acts 5:12; 11:30; 13:3; 14:3; 19:11; 28:8; Ex. 29:10-15; Lev. 4:15; 8:14-22; 16:21; 24:14; Dt. 34:9; Gen. 49:14). Jesus used this method in blessing others (Mt. 8:3, 15; 9:18; 19:15; Mk. 6:2, 5; Lk. 4:40; 13:13).

9. *Execute judgment.* This judgment is not that of giving rewards, but of punishment for rebels as practiced by Peter (Acts 5:1-12), Paul (Acts 13:6-12; 1 Cor. 4:18-21), and by the Church (1 Cor. 5 and 6; Mt. 18:15-19).

10. *Cast out demons.* This is one of the signs of the Gospel that will follow "them that believe" (Mk. 16:15-20). Such signs did follow Christ and the disciples, both before and after Pentecost (Mt. 4:23-24; 10:1-8; Lk. 10:1-20; Acts 5:16; 6:8; 8:7; 11:21; 16:18; 19:12), and will follow today when men receive power over demonic forces. If men had power over demons before Pentecost, without the baptism in the Spirit, certainly they will have this power when baptized in the Spirit in all fulness.

11. *Be immune from poisons and have power over wild beasts.* Jesus and the disciples had this power before Pentecost (Mk. 1:13; Lk. 10:19). It is promised to all believers (Mk. 16:17-18; Lk. 10:19). Old Testament saints even had it without the Spirit baptism (Ps. 91), so naturally this power will be included in the fulness of power that comes with the Spirit baptism.

The Greek word for "take up" serpents in Mk. 16:18 is *airo*, translated elsewhere to "take away" sins (Jn. 1:29; 1 Jn. 3:5), "taketh away" or cut off branches (Jn. 15:2), "put away" sinners out of the church (1 Cor. 5:13), "take ye away" or remove a stone (Jn. 11:39), "take away" or destroy a nation (Jn. 11:48), "put away" sin (Eph. 4:31), "took it out of the way" or abolished the law (Col. 2:14-17), "away with" or kill (Lk. 23:18; Acts 21:36; 22:22), and of the removal or destruction of other things. This indicates that snakes are not to be used in a religious side–show any more than the fornicator at Corinth. The truth is that believers can be immune from snake bites or poisons should they happen to be poisoned or bit by a snake. Snakes should be destroyed just as Paul set the example in Acts 28:3-6 and as Jesus gives power to do, according to the promise in Lk. 10:19 and Ps. 91:13.

> *"Step ahead of the crowd and be an example to others and never stumble over anyone."*
>
> *Finis Dake*

12. *Cleanse lepers.* Christ did this (Mt. 8:1-34; Lk. 17:12-14), and like power will be given to anyone who receives the same Spirit baptism that Christ had. Men before Pentecost had this power (Mt. 10:1-8; Ex. 4:6-8, 30; Num. 12; 2 Ki. 5), so men who claim to have the Spirit baptism should be able to do at least what men could do who never experienced such baptism.

13. *Raise the dead.* Christ and the apostles did this after being baptized in the Spirit (Mt. 9:25; Jn. 11; Acts 9:40; 20:9-10). Old Testament saints without the Spirit baptism raised the dead (1 Ki. 17:17-24; 2 Ki. 4:18-37). Jesus gave this much power to the disciples before Pentecost (Mt. 10:7-8), so naturally He will give power to do this when He gives the Spirit baptism, or the fulness of God.

14. *Get an answer for everything prayed for in faith according to the promises of God.* Many promises say we can have "what ye will," "anything," "whatsoever," "What things soever ye desire," and if we believe without a doubt "it shall be done" (Ps. 34:10; 84:11; 91:1-12; Mt. 5:6; 7:7-11; 9:28-29; 17:20; 18:15-18; 21:22; Mk. 9:23; 11:22-24; Jn. 7:37-39; 8:31-36; 12:25-26; 15:7, 16; 16:23-26; Lk. 11:1-13; 18:1-8; 24:49; Acts 1:4-8; 2:38-39; 5:32; 1 Cor. 12:1-11; Heb. 11:6; Jas. 1:4-8; 4:6-10; 1 Jn. 3:18-24; 5:14-15).

There is no limitation or qualification to these promises concerning any good and lawful thing for which one may ask. Every limitation on them is human, and not divine. All one must do is to meet the conditions contained in the promises in order to receive full benefits. They state in no uncertain terms what God will do, if men will only believe without wavering. If one does not have the promises fulfilled in him, if he is constantly wavering and living in unbelief, and if prayers are not answered, it is certain that he is not Spirit baptized in all the fulness of God. Christ received answers to all His prayers (Jn. 11:41-42). He had power in the Spirit and by the gifts to bring about His answers for everything He asked of God. He could receive help for Himself and for others, and this is bound to be the case with anyone who has the power to do what Christ did (Jn. 14:12).

> *"All that is needed is to find chapter and verse in the Bible itself, which plainly states the doctrine, or answers the question. Then believe it just as it is written."*
>
> *Finis Dake*

15. *Heal everyone prayed for.* This much power was given to disciples before they were baptized in the Spirit at Pentecost (Mt. 10:1-8; Lk. 9:1-6; 10:1-20; Mk. 6:7-13). If they had such power before they were baptized in the Spirit, surely they had as much after receiving the Spirit in all fulness. It is recorded twenty times that Christ healed everyone He prayed for. There is not one record of His failing to heal anyone He undertook to heal (Acts 10:38). The disciples after Pentecost healed all that were prayed for (Acts 2:43; 5:12-16; 6:8; 8:6-7; 19:11-12; 28:1-10). When men today receive the fulness of God as did Christ and the apostles, they will also have this power, for such is promised by Jesus (Jn. 14:12-15; Mk. 16:17-18).

We do not have the space to answer all the arguments of unbelief, but the case of Trophimus (2 Tim. 4:20), Paul's thorn in the flesh (2 Cor. 12:7), and Timothy's stomach (1 Tim. 5:23) are stock excuses which unbelievers use to prove that God ceased doing miracles in the early church, that the apostles failed to heal everyone, that the Spirit baptism is not for all believers today, and that it is not always God's will to heal.

The Bible does not say that Trophimus had a disease and that Paul failed to heal him. The word for "sick" in the Greek in 2 Tim. 4:20 is *astheneo*, meaning "weak, feeble, tired or worn out, or strength–less." It is used in numbers of places of weakness where no disease is involved (Rom. 4:19; 8:3; 14:1-2; 1 Cor. 8:7-12; 2 Cor. 11:29). Substitute "disease" for "weak" in these passages and see how ridiculous it is. If we did this we would have a diseased or sick faith, a sick law, and a sick conscience, but no sick or diseased Paul, for he said in 2 Cor. 11:29, "I am not weak". So this would do away with his thorn in the flesh as being some disease and that excuse of unbelief would be no more. Trophimus evidently was worn out in body and had a physical breakdown over too much work, as was the case of Epaphroditus in Phil. 2:25-30. He naturally would need to stay at Miletus and regain his strength.

Paul's thorn in the flesh is plainly stated to be "a messenger [Gr. angel] of Satan" (2 Cor. 12:7). This was not a disease but a real angel who followed Paul and caused him to go through all the sufferings that are listed in 2 Cor. 11:23-29. This thorn was the same as the giants who were thorns in the sides of Israel in Num. 13:33; Josh. 23:13; Judg. 2:3; 8:7. As to Timothy, nothing is known of the cause of his trouble other than water that Paul himself mentions. It could be that Timothy had been drinking stagnant water between rainy seasons when the cistern water would not be good to use. Even certain sections of this country have such bad water that visitors depend on bottled drinks constantly to enjoy a drink at all.

To say the least, men of religion should be ashamed to contend for false doctrines on the excuse of any such cases. If all the apostles failed God, and not one of them ever had power or healed one person, the fact remains, and it will face us in the day of judgment, that Jesus promised full power in the Spirit baptism to do the works that He did and even greater works (Jn. 14:12-15).

16. *Have sound health.* It is certainly clear that every believer who can do the works of Christ by the Spirit baptism will have power to obtain victory over sickness and disease in his own life. This fact is particularly true in light of the fact that Christ died to heal all sickness and disease (Mt. 8:16-17; Isa. 53; 1 Pet. 2:24). Receiving answers to prayers, as promised in point 14 above, would bring sound health even if healing was not provided in the atonement of Christ. God promised that "all things are possible to him that believeth" (Mk. 9:23; 11:22-24).

Old Testament saints had power, both to heal others and to be in sound health themselves. Abraham and Moses healed whole nations by prayer and not one person remained feeble in all the tribes of Israel (Gen. 20:7, 17; Ps. 105:20; 107:37; Ex. 15:26). David was healed of all his diseases (Ps. 103:1-4). Abraham and Sarah were both renewed in youth and had Isaac when they were past the age to have children (Rom. 4:16-21). Others did mighty works of God by faith (Heb. 11). In Ps. 91 and Isa. 58 we have God's secrets of both healing and health, and even immunity from sickness. If such provision was made in the Old Covenant, then surely a better provision is made in the New Covenant which is based upon better promises (Heb. 8:6; 2 Cor. 3:6-15).

17. *Speak in new languages.* It is on record that when men were baptized in the Spirit they "began to speak with other tongues, as the Spirit gave them utterance" (Acts 2:1-11, 33; 8:12-22; 10:44-48; 19:1-7). Compare Acts 9:17 with 1 Cor. 14:18 and Isa. 28:9-11 with 1 Cor. 14:21-22. This speaking in tongues was in fulfillment of prophecies and promises of Isaiah (Isa. 28:9-11) and Jesus (Mk. 16:17; Jn. 15:26; 16:13-15). For other Scriptures on speaking in other languages by the Holy Spirit, see 1 Cor. 12, 13, and 14.

An honest investigation of the passages dealing with speaking in tongues will reveal a number of purposes and benefits of this spiritual exercise, such as God speaking to men by the Spirit, giving refreshing and rest (Isa. 28:9-11); a sign to unbelievers (1 Cor. 14:21-22); one of the signs of the Gospel to follow all believers (Mk. 16:15-20); an aid in prayer and worship (Rom. 8:26; 1 Cor. 14:2, 14-18); speaking mysteries unto God and not to man (1 Cor. 14:2); personal edification to the speaker (1 Cor. 14:4, 17); edification to others when interpreted (1 Cor. 14:5, 23-28); a gift of the Spirit set in the Church for the edification of the body of Christ (1 Cor. 12:7-11, 28-31); and a source of knowledge and doctrine (Isa. 28:9-11).

18. *Exercise unlimited authority in all the fulness of God.* The main point we should recognize concerning the Spirit baptism is that it is the fulness of God in the life of a believer, and that such is just as attainable today as it was in the early church.

13. Unlimited Authority Exercised by Ordinary Believers

Many believers today think that biblical characters in both Testaments were special people, and that we cannot receive the same experiences and spiritual blessings that are recorded of them. Heroes of the Bible were great simply because they believed God and this was counted to them for righteousness (Rom. 3:21-22, 26-31; 4:1-25; 9:11, 30-33; 11:5-6; Heb. 11:1-40). These, and other Scriptures, plainly state that what men of old received from God was through grace without works, and that it is the duty of every person to "walk in the steps" of that faith and grace (Rom. 4:12; Heb. 12:1).

God's grace is full and rich to all who will believe, "for there is no difference" (Acts 15:9; Rom. 3:22; 10:12) and "there is no respect of persons with God" (Rom. 2:11; Eph. 6:9; Col. 3:25; Acts 10:38). All things are freely given by grace through faith, and God will bless any man or woman who will give themselves to conform to the means of grace and set themselves apart to seek God and do His whole will. All have the same promises and if all will draw nigh to God He will draw nigh to them (Jas. 4:6-10). Jesus said, "If any man serve me, him will my Father honour" (Jn. 12:26). Again, "He that believeth on me . . . they that believe on him . . . them that believe" and like terms are used in Scripture to prove each person can have from God what Christ, the apostles, and Old Testament saints had.

In conclusion, we emphasize once again that anyone who has the Spirit only by measure is not filled with all the fulness of God. Let us not be satisfied with what the Old Testament saints had, who were never baptized in the Spirit. Also, let us not be satisfied with present experiences, concluding that we are truly baptized in the Spirit in all fulness just because we have been born again, sanctified, justified, saved from sin and have the witness of the Spirit, or even a great filling or some anointing of the Spirit. Let us not be content even if we are filled to the point of having some gift of the Spirit, such as healing, tongues, miracles, faith, or whatever it might be. Let us not be satisfied until we are all filled with all the fulness of God and are fully able to do what Christ did and what He promised each believer (Jn. 7:37-39; 14:12).

"From the very beginning of my ministry, I have permitted anyone to ask any question or demand plain Scriptures to prove any statements made by me in the teachings of the Holy Bible."

Finis Dake

The Spirit baptism was given solely to endue men with power to confirm the Gospel by signs and wonders, so that multitudes of men could be attracted to the truth and be saved (Heb 4:2; Rom 15:18-19, 29). This was the program of Christ and the apostles (Mt 4:25; 9:8, 33, 36; 12:15; 15:20; 19:2; Acts 4:4, 32; 5:4, 16).

CHAPTER TWENTY–THREE

DAKE LEAVES ZION

THINGS WERE GOING GREAT

In Zion, things were going great as God's blessings were being poured out daily. Christian Assembly was flourishing and the church was involved in both its own local church work as well as its support of Shiloh Bible Institute.

For a new school, Shiloh Bible Institute was doing very well. It had a faculty who were well–qualified and had a deep desire to preach the simple Word of God, bathed in the power of the Holy Spirit. Its bills were being paid and students were coming from far and wide. Ministry was going forth on a daily basis.

Finis, Dorothy and Finette

Dorothy and eight year–old Finette were in good health and happily working in both the church and the Bible school. As for Dake himself, he was carrying on his work as pastor of Christian Assembly, running the school as its supervisor and teaching classes, filling his life with study and biblical research. In his spiritual life, he was both seeking and searching for a greater move of God. His days involved fasting and prayer and living in God's Word.

It is at times such as these, when the kingdom is advancing and the work of the Lord is being done, that the Devil lets loose with his greatest attacks. This was the case for Dake.

VIOLATION OF THE MANN ACT

On February 9, 1937, Finis Jennings Dake was sentenced to six months in jail, after reluctantly pleading guilty to violation of the Mann Act.

It seems that Dake had transported a sixteen year–old girl across state lines. Dake swore that nothing wrong had occurred, and his lawyer called the incident "an unfortunate mistake."

Years later, he told Lester Sumrall[120] that he had passed this girl hitch-hiking along the side of the road in winter time. He gave her a ride and talked to her about Shiloh Bible Institute. He said she was a runaway, belligerent toward her parents and toward school. He said:

> Now, I knew better than to pick up a girl hitchhiker, although I was twice her age. But I didn't act on my better judgment. I took her with me, feeling sorry for her, and thinking I could turn her life around.
>
> As soon as I let her out of my car, however, she called her parents in Illinois and laughed in their faces. She told them a real handsome man with a beautiful face gave her free transportation all the way to St. Louis. When they got my name, they immediately took out a warrant.

EVERYONE STOOD BY DAKE

While many years have passed and little is known about the specific events of this tragic situation, there are a number of observations that can be made.

Zion, Illinois, was more or less a border town, situated only about three and a half miles from the Wisconsin state line. In the course of everyday life, many residents of Zion crossed the border every day. And, in fact, Dake was assisting a pioneer church there getting its roots. Earl Hoyt remembers:

> I went with him a number of times to a large room above a tavern in uptown Kenosha, where we sang and I played my sax and Brother Dake would speak to those who came out.[121]

Under the pastorate of James Davidson, the Kenosha Assembly of God moved into its new location on Roosevelt Road in 1935. So Dake was travelling back and forth from Zion to Kenosha on a regular basis in his assistance to this church. While we in no way lessen the seriousness of the Mann Act, which involved transportation of minors across state

---

[120] *Pioneers of Faith*, by Lester Sumrall, Harrison House, Tulsa, Oklahoma, Page 71.
[121] Hoyt, Earl. Personal letter on file.

lines, for those living in and around this area, crossing the state line was a common everyday occurrence.

Dorothy stood by Dake. She believed his account that nothing had happened. She was steadfast in her defense of her husband. She stated that the girl in question was in fact a hitchhiker and that she herself had met the girl. She said that Dake was taking her to East St. Louis in order that the girl would have a home and where Dake's sister, Mrs. Daisy Smith, found work for her as a domestic. Dorothy said that those opposed to Dake and his teachings had learned of this incident and had pressed the charges. It is also worth noting that Dake and Dorothy were married for sixty–two years prior to their homegoing in 1987. Indeed, Dorothy stood by her man.

1935

Evangelist Billy Sunday dies.

The staff and students of Shiloh Bible Institute also stood by Dake during this incident. In fact, during Dake's absence from the church while serving time, Rev. Theodore Kessel—an instructor at Shiloh—assisted Dorothy in the day–to–day activities of the pastoral work at Christian Assembly. Rev. Kessel later went on to be Secretary of the Illinois District from 1942–1948.

The members of Christian Assembly supported Dake. In one church service over 300 members rose in support of their pastor. In fact, the day of his trial the courtroom was crowded with more than 100 of the members from Christian Assembly who were there to lift up and encourage him. One of the members of Christian Assembly said:

> The church people really prayed for and stuck by the Dakes and dearly loved them through it all.[122]

To this day Christian Assembly still has kind words to say about Dake. For their church history states Dake:

> . . . left behind a great legacy in the form of his *Annotated Reference Bible* and the Great Lakes Bible Institute.[123]

Government prosecutors themselves admitted that their investigations of the girl showed no evidence that she was, in their modest terms

---

[122] Hyllberg, Mrs. Rachel. Personal letter on file.
[123] www.christianaog.com/historic/building.htm

of the day, "ruined." According to records of the event, this gave some substance to Dake's story.

Dake's attorney, Eugene Sullivan, told the court that Dake had made an unfortunate mistake, but added that no improper relations took place during the trip. He added that "there is no actual moral offense committed here."

As for the girl, she herself said that nothing happened. She even wrote her father when she arrived in East St. Louis, telling him not to worry about her "because I have got religion." Government agents had said the girl was under the spell of the minister and believed he would bring her into the church, but she said that she accompanied him voluntarily, that he never forced her to do anything and that nothing happened. It is also worth noting that till her dying day she never changed her story. She insisted nothing happened.

WHAT ABOUT DAKE?

Dake denied the charges, saying he didn't transport the girl for immoral purposes. He just wanted to help her find work.

He maintained that nothing happened. However, to get this thing behind him and to spare his family and the ministry the shame of an embarrassing trial, he pleaded guilty and threw himself on the mercy of the court.

In a farewell sermon to Christian Assembly, where the building was packed to capacity and with people standing in the aisles, Dake talked about this whole ordeal:

> I have learned a lesson, I have had a little sense knocked into my head. I am disgusted with the devil. If the devil had a tail and I could get hold of it . . . I'd grab it and wrap it around a tree.

But Dake said that in spite of it all, "I am the happiest man this side of Heaven." In the farewell service Dake played his slide trombone and then his beloved Dorothy addressed the congregation and promised to carry on in her husband's absence. Dorothy closed the service with the singing of the hymn, *Thy will Be Done.*

The Spirit of God was mightily upon this service and at the close of the meeting the Dake's had an altar call and twenty people came forward and accepted Christ!

MILWAUKEE HOUSE OF CORRECTIONS

Dake entered the Milwaukee House of Corrections on Monday, February 15, 1937. He was to serve six months. Because of his good behavior he only served five months and was released on Friday, July 16, 1937.

When he left the institution he said he left without bitterness. He said that confinement "galled" him, but he could not be bitter and still be a Christian. He had used the time to write and study the Bible. He said he was going home and wanted no reception and no fanfare.

HIS FIRST SUNDAY BACK

On his first Sunday back to Christian Assembly, on July 18th, when he arrived in the building, the people enthusiastically welcomed him with open arms. They all began to sing a hymn and at this point, Dake threw up his arms and said, "Now friends, let's just forget our sorrows and the past, I feel God and I know that He's here."

Amid a chorus of "halleluiahs," he declared "I'm not going to preach a sermon, I am just going to make a few remarks." He then talked and warned the people against human weakness and urged them to forget the past. The church was full and at the conclusion of the meeting many of those came forward to hug and shake the hand of their pastor.

"We must be enlightened as to the true source of our troubles and turn to God for help."

Finis Dake

HIS SMILE RETURNS

As Dake would soon end his stay in Zion he ended it on a very high note. Finette who was now almost 11 years old had brought much joy to the Dake family, but now a new arrival would come. On Wednesday, June 15, 1938, Dorothy and Dake welcomed into the world their second child—Rhoda Annabeth Dake. Annabeth was born in Shiloh House and would bring a smile back into the heart of the Dake family. Changes were taking place and Dake was moving with the change.

Even though Dake had much support in Zion, he felt as though it was best for him to now leave. It was a very difficult decision but God's church and the school must come first. Because of what had happened he and his family needed a new start in some other place, and the school and church needed new leadership.

Christian Assembly would continue to reach out in its ministry to Zion for many years to come. Shiloh Bible Institute would continue, but it too would face changes. The school later became know as the "Great Lakes Bible Institute." It was placed under the control of the Illinois District of the Assemblies of God. The Great Lakes Bible Institute eventually combined with Central Bible Institute in Springfield, Missouri.

SUMMING IT UP

Lester Sumrall makes an important observation:[124] "God brought good out of what the devil meant for evil."

In jail, Dake had time to work on his writing and his Bible annotations. And just as Howard Carter had received the basic revelation and outline on the gifts of the Holy Spirit in jail, and as the classic Christian book, Pilgrim's Progress, came out of John Bunyon's time spent in prison, so too Dake would redeem the time.

"You can be a conqueror in the very things wherein you have suffered defeat."

Finis Dake

Most of us want blessing without suffering, but if there had not been a cross, there would have been no resurrection.

It is interesting to note that no matter how people judge these events in Zion, Dake himself never let it hamper his ministry. For as we shall see, he and Dorothy went on to even greater ministry. They continued to write and publish books culminating in the *Dake Annotated Reference Bible.* Daily, for the rest of their lives, they would spend themselves for the cause of Christ. As we look at the remainder of Dake's ministry, it becomes increasingly evident that he lived a life of faithfulness and devotion to God and his kingdom.

---

[124] *Pioneers of Faith*, by Lester Sumrall, Harrison House, Tulsa, Oklahoma, Page 72.

CHAPTER TWENTY–FOUR

ST. PAUL AND BRISTOL

ST. PAUL, VIRGINIA

It was in the first week of August, 1938, that the Dakes left Zion. From there, they drove just over 600 miles east to St. Paul, Virginia. Dorothy's sister Pauline and her husband Caleb McAfee were pastoring an Assembly of God church in St. Paul at this time. The Dakes stayed with the McAfee's in their bungalow parsonage for a few months. Later, they were able to move out when a doctor's home became available for rent. During this time they rested and refocused their sight on new ministry and new direction, as they sought God's will for their continued ministry.

> *"When one is nothing from the standpoint of the Bible he is somebody, and when he is somebody he is nothing."*
>
> *Finis Dake*

St. Paul was a beautiful part of Virginia, nestled in the Blue Ridge mountain range. Dorothy's sister Pauline remembers, ". . . the summers were cool and the winters were a little rough, but oh so beautiful with the snow on the mountains."

The Dakes were truly enjoying themselves in this beautiful part of the country, and the fellowship of Dorothy's loving sister and family were just what they needed at this time of direction change in their life.

A PASTOR AND A BUSINESSMAN

While in St. Paul, God opened up a door of ministry at a Full Gospel church. The people were so impressed with Dake that they asked him to stay and pastor. Dake agreed, and so for a little less than a year, Dake lived in St. Paul with the McAfee's and pastored this Full Gospel church, which was located nine miles away in Banner, Virginia.

The church was small and not able to pay Dake a full–time salary. To earn a living, the Dakes invested $75.00[125] in printing equipment, rented a basement in a store and started a newspaper business. Dake himself was the printer, and Dorothy was the general editor and writer of the society news. The newspaper was very successful and within just a few months it became a tri–county paper.

---

[125] Or about $965.00 in year 2005 dollars.

DAKE GOES ON THE RADIO

In addition to Dake's pastoral ministry, it was here in Virginia that he started his first radio ministry. On Sundays and Wednesdays, Dake was preaching at the Full Gospel church. Throughout the week he and Dorothy were running the newspaper business. And on Saturdays, he was teaching the Bible on the local radio station.

"I have promised God that I would not change nor attempt to change what the Scripture plainly says."

Finis Dake

Still, both Dake and Dorothy knew that this would not be their home for long. Deep in their hearts they believed that God was going to open other doors of ministry—doors that would allow them to do something powerful and very big for the kingdom of God.

IT TURNED OUT TO BE A GREAT INVESTMENT

After only a few months, a wonderful blessing came their way. A local businessman wanted to buy their new, but thriving, newspaper. After prayer, they felt it was the will of God to sell the paper and move on. For a newspaper business they had only started less than a year before—and had opened with an initial investment of only $75.00—they were happy to sell out for $1,500.00.[126] Quite a sum of money in 1939!

BRISTOL, TENNESSEE

Drawn southward, they moved to a town about sixty miles away. The town was Bristol, Tennessee. In Bristol, they located a house on 824 Kentucky Avenue that was for sale for $2,100.00.[127] For the $500.00[128] down payment they used part of the $1,500.00 they had received from the sale of the newspaper business. After paying some bills, they had just enough to make the down payment, and for what they lacked a yearly mortgage was secured. Their house payment would be $200.00[129] per year.

FINIS JENNINGS DAKE, JR.

It was also in Bristol that, for a third time, Dorothy became pregnant. Dake and Dorothy loved their two little girls—Finette (12 years old) and

---

[126] Or about $19,681.00 in year 2005 dollars.
[127] Or about $27,554.00 in year 2005 dollars.
[128] Or about $6,560.00 in year 2005 dollars.
[129] Or about $2,624.00 in year 2005 dollars.

Annabeth (16 months). No ultrasound was available in 1939, but for some time the Dakes had been convinced that their third child would be a boy.

As the time for her delivery came closer, Dorothy called her sister Pauline in St. Paul to come be with her. She was planning to have her baby at home and wanted Pauline to assist in the delivery. As it turned out, Pauline arrived at the Dake home only about thirty minutes before the baby was born. And

824 Kentucky Avenue

as was anticipated, Dorothy had a boy. Pauline said:

> . . . there was no mistaking it, the baby was a boy. He was all boy, the spitting image of his Dad—blonde hair, blue eyes, big hands and feet and broad shoulders.

And what should such a baby boy be named who was the spitting image of his Dad? Why, Finis Jennings Dake, Jr. of course! How could they have named him anything else?

ANNABETH'S GRAND PERFORMANCE

Dorothy's sister Pauline remembers this day and the fact that so much joy and love filled the Dake home. In this midst of this special day, Annabeth gave a "grand performance." Pauline remembers:

> Annabeth, at this time, was of course just a baby herself. Finis had told her that today a baby was coming and they were gong to put it in the basket that sat by the bed. All morning long Annabeth walked around saying, "baby, baby." When she first heard Finis, Jr. cry she began clapping her hands, and grabbing the people in the room around the neck saying, "baby, baby." She was thrilled to have a new brother, as were the rest of the family.

So on Tuesday, October 17, 1939, Finis Dake, Jr. was born in the front room of the house on 824 Kentucky Avenue, Bristol, Tennessee. He was nine pounds and twenty–two inches at birth.

AND YET ANOTHER CHILD IS BORN

During their time in Bristol at 824 Kentucky Avenue, the Dakes, along with their three children, would continue to travel and hold meetings—mostly in the Virginia, West Virginia and Tennessee areas. As Dake's popularity began to rise, his meetings included revivals, conferences and camp meetings. After all, people were always eager to hear the man who was known as *The Walking Bible.*

"All honest physicians admit that they cannot heal, they can only assist nature."

Finis Dake

In July of 1940, the Dakes had travelled to Clarksburg, West Virginia, about 150 miles away from their home in Bristol. They had just begun a revival where souls were being saved and the Word was going forth. By this time Dorothy had again become pregnant with what would be their fourth child.

PROBLEMS WITH THE PREGNANCY

The pregnancy was not without problems. Dorothy began to experience pain and bleeding. As quickly as he could, Dake took his wife to St. Mary's hospital in Clarksburg. At the hospital, an emergency caesarian operation to stop the hemorrhaging was performed. Dorothy's life was saved, and their child was born. It was Tuesday, July 9, 1940.

They named their new arrival Steven Arthur Dake. He was premature however, only weighing four pounds. Sadly, at just six hours old, tiny little Steven Arthur Dake died. Dake and Dorothy's hearts were broken. The loss of their fourth child was a blow that would last a lifetime. Sister Pauline, who was also by their side at this time, said:

> The Dakes were very saddened and their loss was great, but Dorothy's life was spared and they were grateful. At this time Dake got on his knees by her beside in the hospital and told her it would be her last pregnancy.

A MISSED FUNERAL AND A MISSED CHILD

On Wednesday, July 10, Dake and his three children—Finette, Annabeth, and Finis, Jr.—along with a few other close family members, gathered at the cemetery for a touching graveside funeral service.

Dorothy was not able to attend the funeral, for she would remain in the hospital for two more weeks. Later, when she returned home to Bristol,

Tennessee, she was bedridden for an additional week. She would heal and her body would mend. She would even return to the ministry by her husband's side. But she would never again have another child, and she would always carry a love in her heart for little Steven Arthur Dake.

CHAPTER TWENTY–FIVE

CHURCH OF GOD PREACHER

SAXTON, PENNSYLVANIA

In 1942, after two years as travelling evangelists, the Dakes left Bristol and moved 430 miles north, to the very small town of Saxton, Pennsylvania. They did not sell their house however, but rented it out to earn some much–needed extra income.

While in Saxton, Dake pastored the Church of God (Cleveland, Tennessee) for about one year. The members of the Saxton Church of God had purchased a store building by the side of the railroad tracks and were remodeling it.

WASHINGTON, PENNSYLVANIA

After pastoring the Church of God in Saxton until about 1943, once again the Dake family moved. This move took them 140 miles west to the town of Washington, Pennsylvania. Washington was much bigger than Saxton, but still considered a small town.

Here the Northeastern District of the Church of God appointed Dake as Pastor of the Church of God. To assist him, Dorothy Dake was officially set in office as the Assistant Pastor.

> *"The devil's long–range program is to keep men from getting power with God over him and his works."*
>
> *Finis Dake*

It was only just a few months after this that Dake was also recognized by the Church of God as an evangelist. On September 5, 1944, Dake was issued an Evangelist Certificate (#5396) by the State Overseer of Pennsylvania, Glyndon Logsdon. It was also signed by the General Overseer, John C. Jernigan.

Indeed, Dake and the Church of God were working well together. While in Washington, both Dake and Dorothy would be very busy preaching the Word of God and ministering to God's people.

SANTA CLAUS

Finis Dake, Jr., who was five years old at the time, remembers that it was in December of 1944 that he and his sister Annabeth, now about six years old, first saw Santa Claus. Dake, having grown up without a father in the home and in very humble circumstances, never really celebrated

Christmas as a child with gift–giving. But after this event, he really got into Christmas celebration with his children, even to the point of dressing up like Santa! In fact, every Christmas from then on, for as long as the children could remember, Dake continued to dress as Santa Claus at Christmas time.

It was Dorothy's desire to give her children a really nice Christmas, but it was a difficult thing to do on a pastor's salary. In past Christmases, to help with purchasing Christmas gifts, Dorothy made donuts and sold them door to door. God blessed her efforts and the money she earned was enough to provide many nice gifts for the children. Dorothy wrote a short story about this event.

> ### ALL *I* WANT FOR CHRISTMAS IS *NOT* MY TWO FRONT TEETH
> Even Kriss Kringle knows better than that!
>
> Mama Stouffer–Dobbins' only marriage vow for me to take—for her—was:
>
> "Promise me, Dorothy, that when you get married you will not teach your children that there is a Santa Claus!"
>
> In all honesty, and without any "Here Comes the Bride" music, I said:
>
> "I WILL . . . not."
>
> I promised and fulfilled my vow. But it didn't work. As soon as my children were old enough to understand sound reasoning—and could go with their young cousin to the business area of the small mountain town we lived in—it happened.
>
> It was the Christmas Season and they came home glowing with interest and enthusiasm over something. I recalled my vow and cautioned them again:
>
> "Now, children you *know* that there is *no* Santa Claus." They said, "We know better—we already saw him in town!"
>
> Whatever Kriss Kringle did to them that day has lingered a little through the years—and that without causing the damage Mama thought it would. My sweet Mama died

and went to heaven before I could get down to the bottom of this thing—her pet peeve in life.

Mama had to live up North awhile and became acquainted with various Europeans who knew all about Kriss Kringle and the December 6 date on which he was supposed to arrive with lots of goodies for the kids—a date many days before the very solemn commemoration of the birth of Christ with simple feasting, prayer and singing.

> *"It is the purpose of the devil to convince men to live in doubt and unbelief concerning the promises of God."*
>
> *Finis Dake*

Mama was German/English, half–'n–half, and maybe it was the German in her that was resenting Kriss Kringle being allowed to come on her Lord's birthday here in America, for in Germany he was scheduled for December 6. Mama called him *Old Nick* which, to her, meant the devil. In this she needed some enlightenment which, at the time, I could not give.

DAKE IS A BUSY PREACHER

In June of 1945, Dorothy Dake began teaching at the Summer Bible School in nearby Somerset, Pennsylvania. She taught English, Church History, Elocution and Homiletics. For this class she wrote a secular book. The book was titled, *Oral and Written Composition.* The book was a "how to" manual, and Dorothy described it as putting "one's thoughts into words that are clear, orderly and connected."

Dake was becoming a very popular preacher in the Church of God and was in much demand, not only in Pennsylvania but in other states as well. In July of 1946, he traveled to preach the Camp Meeting and State Convention of the Church of God in Flat River, Missouri. In the Church of God state magazine called *The Missouri Tidings*, an advertisement for the meeting read:

> . . . he quotes hundreds of Scriptures from all parts of the Bible in proving the truths he presents and in answering off–hand the many Bible questions dropped in the question box each night. He does not use his own Bible in

public but invites you to use yours, so that you can see for yourself that what he says is written in plain English in your own Bible.

Not only was Dake preaching in the States, but he also made a trip to Canada. Beginning July 20, 1947, Dake preached a camp meeting for the Church of God in Ontario, Canada. The advertisement for this camp meeting stated that Dake would teach from his chart for two hours every day and be available to *answer all Bible questions!*

By this time, Dake had proved himself with the Church of God and on March 26, 1948, Dake received his Ordination (#5396). This ordination was signed by the State Overseer of Pennsylvania, Glyndon Logsdon, and the General Overseer, John C. Jernigan.

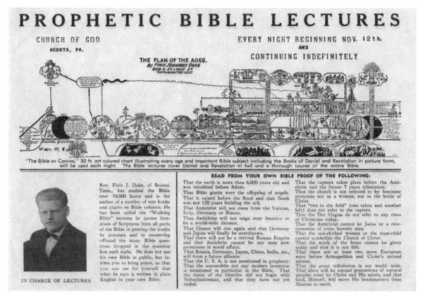

Advertisement for Dake's lecture

JOHN MILLER IS HEALED

While Dake always kept his nose to the scriptural grindstone, so to speak, studying the Bible for hours on end, he was still seeking God daily for the anointing to do the works of Christ. It was during his time in Washington that an incredible miracle took place.

A man by the name of John Miller had broken his back. The doctors had done what they could for him and had placed him in a cast so that his back could mend. He was in quite a bit of pain and the cast would have to remain on for several months. During this entire time he would be confined to his bed.

The family called for Dake to come and pray for the man. Dake, sensitive to the man's condition and having compassion on him, prepared himself with prayer and fasting prior to visiting the man at his home. When Dake arrived at the home he was ready. His faith was active and God's anointing was upon him.

In a simple prayer, Dake prayed for the man's healing. In a matter of moments, God's power came on the man and he was healed. All pain left him and on that same day he removed his cast. The next day, John Miller went to work and resumed his normal activities. For many years to come the people of Washington would speak of the John Miller miracle, giving God all the glory.

FINETTE'S GRADUATION

In 1945, things in America where quite different than they are today. World War II was coming to an end as German Field Marshal Alfred Jodl signed and unconditional surrendered on May 7. The Japanese would later surrender on August 15, just after the dropping of the atomic bomb on Hiroshima and Nagasaki. America's sons and daughters would be coming home and there was a lot to be thankful for. During these days, Christianity was at an all–time high. Prayers had been answered and America's heart was focused on God. Finette, now seventeen years old, was graduating from high school. This was a happy day for the Dake family and attending Finette's graduation ceremony was a real joy. It was, in fact, more of a worship service than a graduation.

As one reads the graduation program, it reads more like a church service. It included prayers, music, Scripture, a sermon, and every song was a Christian hymn. Contrasted with modern public school graduations throughout America, it would almost seem that Washington High School was a Christian School. Yet it was not—it was simply that the public school system at that time had not shut God out of their program. A graduation program of this nature surely needs a closer look.

Baccalaureate Service
Washington High School
Sunday, May 27, 1945 at 7:45 P. M.

Prelude – Excerpt from Finale, New World Symphony.......Dvorak
   The Band

Processional – All Hail the Power of Jesus Name…..………Holden
   The Band and Chorus

Invocation………………………………...…………..Dr. John S. Allison

Music – Lift Thine Eyes………………...…………..…….Mendelssohn
   Senior Chorus

Hymn – Praise For Peace……………..……………….Congregation

   Father in Heaven, in Thy love abounding,
   Hear these Thy children thro' the world resounding,
   Loud in Thy praises thanks for peace abiding,
   Ever abiding.

   Filled be our hearts with peace beyond comparing,
   Peace in Thy world, joy to all heart's despairing,
   Firm is our trust in Thee for peace enduring,
   Ever enduring.

   God of our Fathers strengthen every nation,
   In Thy great peace where only is salvation,
   So may the world its future spread before Thee,
   Thus to adore Thee.

Scripture…………………………..……….Major Hedley A. Burrell

Music – The Lord's Prayer……………………...……….Malotte
   Senior Trio

Prayer..Major Hedley A. Burrell

Music – He Shall Feed His Flock..............................Handel
  Girl's Ensemble

Sermon..Dr. John S. Allison

Hymn – Beneath the Cross of Jesus........................Congregation

> Beneath the cross of Jesus,
> I fain would take my stand
> The shadow of a mighty Rock
> With–in a weary land;
> A home with–in a wilderness,
> A rest upon the way,
> From the burning of the noontide heat,
> And the burden of the day.
>
> I take, O cross, thy shadow
> For my abiding place;
> I ask no other sunshine than,
> The sunshine of His face;
> Content to let the world go by,
> To know no gain nor loss,
> My sinful self my only shame,
> My glory all the cross.

Benediction.......................................Dr. John S. Allison

Recessional – Coronation March............................Meyerbecr
  Band

DAKE, I CHALLENGE YOU

Throughout Dake's ministry he faced challenges from those who did not believe in a literal interpretation of the Bible. In the early part of 1946, such a challenge confronted Dake.

A Seventh Day Adventist minister by the name of H. R. Veach became quite upset at Dake after listening to him on the radio. He could contain himself no longer and spent the money to take out a large ad in the local paper challenging Dake to an open debate. The ad read:

An Open Letter

Waynesboro, Pa.

March 9, 1946

Attention: Mr. F. J. Dake of Washington, Pa.

Before thousands of people, and hundreds upon hundreds of audiences, I have repeatedly challenged folk, preachers, teachers or, laymen, to bring Bible proof, a *thus saith the Lord,* for certain practices, that are followed in the Christian churches. But, never have I challenged anyone to debate. I have never felt that two men fighting over the Scriptures, or caviling in verbal combat over the Holy Inspired Word of God, is conducive to the salvation of lost souls. In fact, I have seen some such occasions in which I was compelled to believe that many souls were hurt, and some were utterly lost over the contention of debate.

> *"For thirty years I have thrown my meetings open for free and open discussion, and have invited anyone to give Scripture to contradict anything taught by me."*
>
> *Finis Dake*

However, your ungentlemanly, indecent, and utterly unchristian methods of advertising are so misleading and false, and of such a degraded nature; that I am compelled against my better judgment, to meet you in debate. You claim to be in the holy work of God and the salvation of souls. And yet, you have used advertising methods that no one has ever known any ordinary business man or politician to stoop to. Therefore, in the outright defense of the Truth and my own name, reputation and character, as well as the organization I represent, I, H. R. Veach, hereby state that I will meet you, F. J. Dake, in open debate upon the reasonable premise, the details of which have been handed to you through your Local Minster Friend who is involved with you.

H. R. Veach,

The Veach Bible Chautauqua

Mr. Veach was very serious about this debate. In fact, he was so serious that he offered money to entice Dake into debating him. In a letter delivered to Dake he wrote:

Statement One: I am going to make seven propositions to you and this offer will hold good for any layman or preacher alike.

1. I will give $1,000 to anyone who will give me scripture showing that the 7th day Sabbath of the 4th commandment was done away and that Christians are not obligated to keep Saturday as the Sabbath.

"If I do not have plain Scripture to support what I teach, then I do not discuss a question as being a Bible subject."

Finis Dake

2. I will give another $1,000 to anyone who will give me scripture showing that there has been a change made in the ten commandments Old Testament and that they have been done away and that all of them are not part of the New Testament (especially that the 4th commandment is not a part of the New Testament and that Christians are not obligated to keep it).

3. I will give a third $1,000 to anyone who will give me scripture showing that the early Christians worshipped or gathered together in a religious meeting on any other day except the 7th day or the Jewish Sabbath.

4. I will give a fourth $1,000 to anyone who will give me Scripture showing that the apostles did not command Christians to keep the 4th commandment of the 7th day Sabbath.

5. I will give a fifth $1,000 to anyone who will give me Scripture and history showing that the Lord's day of Rev. 1:10 is not the 7th day Sabbath which is to be observed by Christians.

6. I will give a sixth $1,000 to anyone who will give me Scripture showing that I am not obligated to keep the 4th commandment of the 7th days as the Sabbath.

7. I will give a seventh $1,000 to anyone who will give me Scripture showing from history that the Catholic Church did not change the Sabbath from the 7th day to the 1st day of the week.

Signed: H. R. Veach

Statement Two: I will debate with Rev. Finis Jennings Dake for six or more nights on the following subjects (two hours each night of thirty minutes each speech):

1. Two nights on the Sabbath.

2. One or more nights on hell and the state of the dead.

3. Three nights on prophecy.

It is first understood that Rev. Finis Jennings Dake will take the opposite side of what I have been teaching in Waynesboro, Pa., and attempt to prove that:

- Christians are not obligated to keep the 7th day as the Sabbath.

- The Catholic Church did not change the Sabbath from the 7th day to the first day of the week.

- The 4th commandment and the 7th day Sabbath is not part of the New Testament.

- That the Pope of Rome is not the Antichrist.

- Hell is eternal and the unsaved will spend eternity in literal hell and will never be annihilated.

- The souls of the dead are conscious between death and resurrection.

- The earth will be inhabited during the Millennium.

And that most everything I have been teaching on prophecy is unscriptural; the exact list of my unscriptural claims to be worked out between Rev. Dake and myself before the debate begins.

Signed: H. R. Veach

P.S. The above money to be deposited in the First National Bank or the Citizen's National Bank or the Citizen's National Bank of Waynesboro, Pa., to be given to Rev. Dake upon sufficient Bible and historical proof; such proof to be fairly and honestly decided by three unprejudiced judges composed of the best and most reputable citizens of Waynesboro, Pa. Awards will be given only upon the grounds of plain scriptural and historical proof as decided by the judges by a two–thirds majority vote.

Signed: H. R. Veach

> *"Let the plain language of Scripture settle every point of difference and confirm what you believe."*
>
> *Finis Dake*

DAKE ACCEPTS THE CHALLENGE

Dake, not being one to back down from a biblical debate of any kind, decided he would take Mr. Veach up on his offer. On two different occasions, Dake traveled from Washington to Waynesboro, Pennsylvania, to meet with Mr. Veach to work out the details of the purposed debate. Both times Mr. Veach refused to meet with him.

Dake had been challenged publicly. He had attempted to agree to a debate. Yet Mr. Veach was nowhere to be found. What was Dake to do?

Coming from the "show me" state of Missouri, Dake decided if he could not debate Mr. Veach, he would simply have to show his responses in another forum. He would schedule a meeting in the local Church of God in the same town that Rev. Veach was holding his meetings. For advertising, he too chose the local newspaper. He would use the interest that had been stirred up by Mr. Veach to attract people to come and hear the Word of God. The following is his response and invitation as was printed in the local paper.

MR. VEACH REFUSES TO MEET REV. DAKE IN A PUBLIC DISCUSSION. COME HEAR REV. DAKE REFUTE THE FOLLOWING STATEMENTS!

Church of God
14 North Church St.
Waynesboro, Pennsylvania

Seventh Day Adventist teach the following false doctrines:

1. That all the New Testament that was not written before Christ died is not in force, and that nothing given by the apostles after the cross is part of this covenant. This would mean that not one verse of the New Testament from Matthew to Revelation is for us today, for it was all written after the death of Christ.

2. That Saturday is the Christian Sabbath and that all who keep Sunday have the mark of the beast of Rev. 13:16-18. This would mean that all who have ever kept Sunday are doomed to hell, as proved in Rev. 14:9-12; 15:2; 20:4. Why does Mr. Veach want Sunday–keepers from our churches to join the Seventh Day Advent church here, if they are to be damned in hell?

3. That the Pope of Rome is the Antichrist; that all churches outside of Adventists are Babylon and "anti–Christ" and are apostate religions; that the Devil is "pagan–Rome," the Catholic Church is "papal–Rome," and protestant America is the "false–prophet" of Rev.13 and all will be cast into the Lake of Fire and will be burned up in about "five minutes."

4. That Adventists are the 144,000 "sealed ones" of Rev. 7 and 14, but the Bible calls the 144,000 a purely Jewish company of all the tribes of the children of Israel (Rev. 7:1-8).

5. That hell is not eternal and all the wicked will be annihilated in about "five minutes"; that the dead are dormant in the graves between death and resurrection and even while they are being judged; and that Satan is our "sin–bearer" who will be annihilated with our sins upon him.

6. That the earth is the "bottomless pit" and that it will be desolate during a thousand years for the purpose of giving Satan plenty of time to sit on a log and reflect on his wickedness "until he is led out to his execution" and annihilated with the sins of the saints upon him.

7. That all animals, even the clean animals of the law of Moses, are unfit for food due to the fact of their diseased condition.

8. That the U.S.A. will become "the great persecuting power of Christians" of the future, and that we will lose our religious freedom in America and be controlled by Catholics.

9. That the Sabbath was changed by the Catholic Church and by Constantine in 321 A.D.

These and many other false doctrines are being now taught by Mr. Veach and all Seventh Day Adventists according to their own literature. Mr. Veach has boastingly bragged of $7,000 offered to any minister or layman who can give him Scripture to disprove that Christians are not obligated to keep Saturday as the Sabbath. I arrived from Washington, Pennsylvania, Tuesday afternoon and, went to his service in the Armory to accept his proposition and he refused to meet in public discussion. He refused to put the money in the hands of a disinterested committee to give to me if I gave Scripture that would disprove his claims.

We regret that we do not have a larger building to accommodate the crowds, but you are invited to come and bring your Bibles and read with your own eyes and hear with your own ears that the teachings of Mr. Veach are unbiblical. Rev. R. E. Nuzum, Pastor of the Church of God, 14 North Church Street, has opened his church for the lectures. Services will be held Saturday and Sunday nights at 7:45 and at the Pentecostal Church at Greencastle, Pennsylvania, on Sunday afternoon at 2:30.

So the debate between Mr. Veach and Dake never took place. But it was not because Dake didn't try to make it happen—he did. However, because of the advertising in the local paper and the great interest that was aroused, the meetings were packed with both believers and sinners who were finding their way to God. All in all, God's kingdom was advanced.

BACK TO BRISTOL

In 1946, the Dakes received a letter from their previous neighbors in Bristol, Tennessee. Their neighbors, who lived just across the street from them at 900 Kentucky Avenue, had died. The letter came from their children, who were asking the Dakes if they were interested in buying their parents home, which included two lots.

"Conform your ideas to the Bible."

Finis Dake

For a while now, Dake and Dorothy had been feeling a need to get away for a time of seeking God, free from the responsibilities that pastoring demanded. Their hearts were crying out for a season of prayer and fasting. So when this letter came, Dorothy and Dake took it as direction from the Lord to return to Bristol.

THE HOUSE NEEDS REPAIR

Dorothy was a real prayer warrior. While Dake prayed often as well, Dorothy would pray for longer periods of time. For some time now, she had been praying several hours a day. It was finally decided that they would resign their church in Washington, move back to Bristol, and purchase the house on 900 Kentucky Avenue. There Dake would continue to travel and evangelize while Dorothy would focus as much time as she could on prayer and seeking God.

When they returned to Bristol in the fall of 1946, they found that the house needed much repair. Dake had always been a natural at carpentry. After all, his Dad was quite successful in carpentry before his death and Dake had spent a lot of time remodeling Dowie's home in Zion. It was only reasonable, given their limited financial resources, that Dake himself would do the repairs and make the necessary updates to their new home.

The house was large. It had three rooms in a row on the left side, then a hallway in the middle and down the entire length of the house, and then three rooms in a row on the right side of the house. They felt that this house would provide more than enough room for their family. Indeed it did, for later Dake turned it into apartments and rented them out. This provided some much–needed additional income for the Dake family as he traveled the country preaching the Gospel.

After the repair work was done and they were settled in their new home, Dake concentrated more on evangelistic work and Dorothy settled in for a season of prayer. Dorothy and Dake were intent on having God move in their lives in an even greater way. They desired all the gifts of the Spirit to be operational in their lives.

Of course, Dorothy was a mom and a wife and not all of her prayer time was about "spiritual" things. She also had a desire. Dorothy wanted a new house for her family—one that she and Dake did not have to fix up and remodel. So some of her praying was also spent asking God for a new house.

Dorothy was one to pray on her knees. And the hard wooden floor sure got cold—not to mention very hard on the knees. With this, she decided to make something she called "Prayer Pillows." This was a simple pillow about eight inches high which had lots of padding that made praying much easier on her knees.

DAKE LOVES HIS CHURCH

With the house completed and Dorothy content with having a place to seek God, Dake continued his ministry, preaching in the Church of God.

At this time, Dake was quite fond of the Church of God. He found within the church a group of people that were open to his teaching and really had a heart for God. Because of this, he invited his brother–in–law, Caleb McAfee, Pauline's husband, to the Church of God Convention being held that year in Tennessee. The McAfee's really enjoyed their fellowship at the convention. Pauline would later write:

> I didn't know there were so many "Church of God" folks. The auditorium it was held in seated 10,000 and Jr. and I never did get a seat for the night services—all seats were taken by six–thirty. The fellowship during these days was glorious.

After prayer and a great deal of soul–searching, the McAfee's felt it the will of God at this time to join Dake in the Church of God. Thanks to

Dake, their involvement with the Church of God would continue for the next thirteen years. Yes, Dake was really sold on the Church of God.

Not Another Bible School

In 1948, as Dake continued his evangelistic work, he also preached several more camp meetings—one in Pennsylvania and another in Minot, North Dakota. At the North Dakota meeting, Dorothy and all three children were able to attend. Dake taught from his chart and prayed for the sick where many received a touch from the Lord.

It was during this time period that Finette remembered seeing the gift of God at work in her father's life.

Finette was sitting on the front row of the church when, at the end of a service, a man rose up with a Bible question for her Dad. As the service had been dismissed, the two walked toward the back of the church. Dake was talking about this and that, and it seemed as though he was rambling.

Then it happened! All of a sudden, scripture after scripture began to flow from her Dad's mouth. He answered the Bible question and quoted numbers of passages in support of the answer he gave. Even though Finette was only fifteen years of age, she realized what she had just seen. The person of the Holy Spirit had come upon her Dad and given him the answer to the man's question! From that day forward, she knew that her Dad's knowledge and ability in the Scriptures was not just the result of a very good memory, but truly a gift of God.

In February of 1948, Dake received a letter from a Church of God official in Canada. In this letter, Rev. Arnold E. Erickson, who had heard Dake preach, offered him the opportunity to come to Canada and help in the building of a new Bible school. Rev. Erickson gave Dake the opportunity to be the new school's superintendent for the school year starting in September, 1949.

Dake had enjoyed his years running Texico Bible School, as well as his time spent as the dean at Southwestern Bible School and the founding and supervising of Shiloh Bible Institute in Zion. But now it seemed that God had other plans for him. He didn't quite know how or when, but for some time he had wanted to put all of his teaching notes in book form—maybe even one day to create a commentary on the entire Bible. So, for now, he would say "no" to the new school—not knowing the "when, how or where" of it all, yet knowing that God had something more in store for him—something big!

CHAPTER TWENTY–SIX

ATLANTA

A LIFE–CHANGING MEETING

As Dake traveled during 1947 and 1948, his teaching ministry continued to take him all over the United States. While preaching in the Atlanta area, a great change in his ministry would take place.

1947

Dake was holding a meeting at the Church of God in Riverside, Georgia, about 22 miles west of downtown Atlanta. While he was there, he also scheduled a meeting with the Hemphill Church of God (now Mt. Paran) in Atlanta.

Evangelist Smith Wigglesworth dies.

When he returned to the Hemphill Church of God for the meeting, Pastor Phillips, the church's pastor at the time, had a radio program on WGST–AM Radio. During the meeting with Dake, he shared his radio spot with him in order to advertise the meeting. And, of course, while on the radio, Dake would take live call–in Bible questions—answering them right on the spot. In his own words, Dake said:

> One meeting in particular I was holding in Atlanta, Georgia, I was answering Bible questions on the radio just as fast as people would phone them in. I would answer them right back and give them the Scripture too.

His answers—complete with Scripture quotations and references—caused quite a bit of excitement among the radio audience.

A FAITHFUL BROTHER LISTENS IN

Listening in the radio audience was a man named Lee Watson, a charter member of Hemphill Church of God. Mr. Watson was amazed at Dake's gifts and abilities, and began to give Dake a bit of free advertising as he told numbers of his friends. In addition to his friends, Mr. Watson also told his employer about this man on the radio who could answer any Bible question asked of him.

Mr. Watson worked for Carroll Baking Company, Inc., the operators of the Dutch Oven Bakeries. The owner was a man by the name of Mr. W. E. Carroll, called "Bill" by his friends. Mr. Watson encouraged Bill

Carroll to tune in and listen to the program. In past conversations with Bill, he knew of his interest in religious matters and his quest to find the truth. Until this point, he had never found anything in religion that had satisfied him, but still considered himself open to the truth if he should find it.

"God gets great pleasure out of men daring to believe that anything is possible."

Finis Dake

The very next morning, Bill Carroll tuned in to the Hemphill Church of God radio program at 9:30 a.m. While he was not comfortable with anyone associated with the "Pentecostal blessing" or "tongues movement," he was amazed as he listened to Dake answer a number of Bible questions, complete with the scriptural quotations, without even opening a Bible! In just a few minutes of listening to Dake on the radio, he decided he must go—even to this Pentecostal church—and hear this amazing man known as *The Walking Bible*. Dake said it like this:

> A certain man in that city the last day I was there, tuned in and heard me on the radio. He said, "I never heard anything like that before in my life. I'm going out there to hear that preacher."

DAKE MEETS MR. CARROLL

It was the last night of the meeting at Hemphill and Dake taught from his chart and then answered Bible questions. During the entire service, in the back of the church, sat Bill Carroll. If Bill Carroll was impressed by the few minutes he had heard Dake on the radio, he was even more impressed now that he had actually seen him in person. He just had to meet this man!

After the service, Lee Watson approached Dake and asked if he would meet his boss, Mr. Carroll. Dake agreed and Lee Watson introduced Dake to Bill Carroll for the first time. Later in life Dake remembered:

> All the people there made quite a to–do about this man. He had never been inside of a Pentecostal church in his life and had never been inside of any kind of church in over thirty–five years. He had been brought up Presbyterian, but did not get what he was looking for there, or from

any other church. So he said, not only of that church, but of any that he had attended from his youth up—he never heard the Bible preached just like it was written.

He was disgusted with religion and Christianity and had never been inside a church for all those years for that reason. He was dabbling in Christian Science, New Thought, Unity, and every fooled, damnable religion under the sun. He had stacks and stacks of books on all those "tom fool" religions.

YOU OUGHT TO BE BEFORE THE WORLD

As Dake and Carroll talked Mr. Carroll said:

". . . you ought to be before the world with that knowledge of the Bible you have." Carroll continued, "If you come with me I've got a proposition to offer you, I'll get you before the world!"

Dake could hardly believe what he was hearing. Thinking about Mr. Carroll's words to him at this time, Dake said:

Well that was something I had never heard of before. Dorothy and I had been praying for years for God to open up someway to get the truths of the Gospel out just like it was in the Bible. And . . . to get my books printed. I've written numbers of books in my lifetime, but about half of them I've never had money enough to publish.

So, at the first meeting, it seemed as though Mr. Carroll would be a divine instrument of God.

Dake, however, was not one to just jump at any business opportunity or ministry change without prayer and seeking God. Dake continued his recollections:

At any rate, I didn't know what to think. He said, "I'll get you on radio stations all over this country and the city auditoriums, if you will come and go with me." Well, that sounded good. I did not know what to think about it. He wanted me to quit right now and come with him. I didn't know the man. He was a sinner, a smoker, a rebel against God as far as I could see. I wasn't going to hook up with a man like that! So I said, "We will pray for you. I can't right now, but maybe in a few months."

Mr. Carroll was not the kind of man to take "no" for an answer or want to wait a long time until things could be worked out. He asked Dake if he could hear a series of his lectures on the Bible, all the way through. Dake saw nothing wrong with Mr. Carroll coming to his services, while he prayed about things, so he said that he would let him know the next time he would be ministering in the area.

> *"All carnality is not sin."*
>
> *Finis Dake*

DAKE RETURNS

Well as it turned out, Dake was in Marietta, about 18 miles from Atlanta, for a series of lectures just a few weeks later. He informed Mr. Carroll by letter. Mr. Carroll was a busy man, however, and was out of town. He did not arrive back in town until the day the meeting was to begin. Even so, the first night Dake started the meeting, he looked out over the vast audience and saw Mr. Carroll seated in the auditorium.

At the conclusion of the meeting, Mr. Carroll approached Dake and asked him to come home with him. Dake had other accommodations, but nothing would satisfy Mr. Carroll but for Dake to come home with him—and stay in his home for the entire meeting.

Dake remembered this night very well. He gives his recollections as follows:

> I no more than got into the car until he took out a long black cigar—almost made you sick at the looks of it, much less the smell. And he said, "Well, what about smoking?" I said, "We'll talk about that when we get home."

> Well, when we got to his home, the first thing he said when we got settled was, "What about smoking?" I gave him all I had about smoking. He said, "Well, I see your point. That means, if we go together, I'll have to give up smoking." I said, "That's what it means."

For the entire meeting, Dake stayed in Mr. Carroll's home. And, true to his word, Mr. Carroll attended every service Dake held in Marietta. At the conclusion of the series of meetings, Dake was setting out to take a three week trip to preach in a number of different churches. As it turned out, however, he would not be traveling alone.

Mr. Carroll Accepts Christ

Dake said:

> For the next three weeks he followed me all around the country to every meeting. For a week at a time he would come and stay with me and attend the lectures. That man, during those three weeks of lectures, asked me literally thousands of questions. From morning until night we did nothing other than talk Bible. It seemed he had more questions than the Queen of Sheba ever dared to have!
>
> He asked questions until he became throughly convinced that the Bible was the Word of God, and that the Bible had the answer to every problem of life, and that the Bible did answer every desire of his heart. That man turned to God with a whole heart! He gave up his sins and his tobacco. He confessed every sin before God, both he and his wife. It was then that I decided I could go to work for him.

Mr. Carroll's salvation was the greatest event of his life, but it did not end there. As he listened to Dake's teaching his faith grew greater and greater! Dake said of him:

> I don't know any preacher or believer around the country that believes God as much as that man does. He is throughly sold on getting the Gospel out to the world. Divine healing and miracles and gifts of the Spirit, and all the full Gospel as we all know it. That man believes in it all. That man has a faith in God that few people have had.

The Pentecostal Doubter Is Filled With The Spirit

Believes in it all? He sure did. Even to his own amazement, he began to believe in the Holy Ghost baptism. Dake said:

It wasn't long after until the Lord woke him up in the middle of the night. In an instant, He gave him the baptism in the Spirit. He spoke in tongues for hours! Mr. Carroll said, "If I had gotten that from somebody I might have thought something peculiar about it." But God gave it to him from heaven—a Presbyterian! He went back in to the Presbyterian church and he has been having a time trying to get them to believe the Bible and to believe in all these wonderful experiences.

Mr. Carroll backed Dake with his financial resources. He began to help Dake in the publishing of his books. One of the first things Mr. Carroll wanted was for Dake to write a Bible correspondence course. He wanted all those honest–hearted seekers across the land to have access to the truths of the Bible in a simplistic form, just as Dake had given it to him.

Upon hearing this, Dake was quite amused—this was exactly what he and Dorothy had been praying for. Dake recalled:

The first thing he wanted me to do was to write a Bible course. He said, "For fifteen years, I've had a dream of a man who would come along, that could write the truth about God's Word—the Bible." He said, "I think you might just be the answer to my prayers." I thought to myself, that he might just be the answer to my prayers as well!

DAKE MOVES TO ATLANTA

Dake was thrilled to finally have the opportunity to begin publishing his teachings on the Bible in a big way. As it turned out, in 1948, Dake himself moved into Mr. Carroll's home. There he began writing. From early morning until late in the night, for eight months, he wrote what he called, *God's Plan for Man.*

As he worked on *God's Plan for Man*, Mr. Carroll could see that Dake missed and needed his family. So, after much discussion and prayer, Dake decided to move his family to Atlanta. They would attend the Hemphill Church of God of course, but where would they live?

Not a problem—there was plenty of room in Mr. Carroll's neighborhood, so he suggested they build a house right behind his on 2232 Belvedere Avenue. In fact, the backyards of the Carrolls and the Dakes adjoined one another. It was a very nice house indeed—a ranch with twelve rooms and three baths. The Dakes felt as though they had moved into a mansion!

2232 Belvedere Ave.

Now Dorothy would have another one of her prayers answered. She had the new house built just like she wanted it—and to think it had never been lived in before! So, in June of 1948, Dake sold both of their houses in Bristol and moved to Atlanta. Yes, God was truly blessing the Dakes and yet there was still so much more to come.

GOODBYE MOTHER

In the midst of all the blessings coming into Dake's life, sorrow was about to grip his heart. On July 19, 1948, he received word from Los Angeles, where his mother was living at the time, that she had gone home to be with the Lord.

His heart was heavy, as memories of his mother's care for him as a child swept through his mind. He remembered her caring for him and his brothers and sisters by herself, after the death of his father, when he was only ten years of age. He remembered her sickness and frailty during his childhood. She had lived a hard life. She was seventy–eight years old. Now she was gone.

Dake made the long trip to the funeral. He had a few words to say, but he would not preach the funeral sermon. For in this service, Dake was part of the family who had suffered the loss.

Dake's mother's memorial

Only God Satisfies

Upon returning to Atlanta after the funeral, Dake and Dorothy were more determined than ever to be channels for God's power. With all the blessings that were being poured out in their lives, both Dake and Dorothy were hungry for a greater move of God in their lives. The house was nice, just what they wanted. It was wonderful not having to be so concerned with finances. The family was healthy and Finette was happily in college. Yet the Dakes still felt a hunger for God that even a big new house could not fill. Dake said:

> *"A number of years I became greatly awakened for the modern church that God was not doing for modern believers what I read in the New Testament."*
>
> *Finis Dake*

God had blessed us with a nice home and still we were not satisfied. I thought to my wife and myself that if we ever got a nice home we would be satisfied. I always had to buy these old worn–out houses and remodel them. I've spent more money fixing up old houses and tearing down and rebuilding old chimneys, and I got so tired of it, that I said, "Oh God, if we just had a new home we would be satisfied."

God provided a wonderful home for us. A nice ranch house, twelve rooms, three baths and everything. But that new home didn't satisfy. Dorothy wanted a Hammond organ in the home. We got that and that didn't satisfy either. We wanted this and we wanted that and we got it, and that didn't satisfy. The more we wanted and the more we got, the more miserable we became. Nothing satisfies but God. After we got that beautiful home and everything fixed up just like we wanted, I came home one day and I heard Dorothy praying "Jesus this doesn't satisfy. I wanted all this, but it is not what I want." You can get everything in life you want, but if you miss God you've missed it all! Only God satisfies!

CHAPTER TWENTY–SEVEN

GOD'S PLAN FOR MAN

A MAMMOTH TASK

The writing of *God's Plan for Man* was a mammoth task. Over the years Dake had kept all of his notes and, for the most part, *God's Plan for Man* would follow the syllabus outline that he had originally developed for his classes at Shiloh Bible Institute. In fact, Dake's book *Dispensational Truth* was really the skeleton outline for *God's Plan for Man*. It would take eight months—June 1948 through about February of 1949—before Dake would complete the course.

1948

Israel becomes a nation once again after almost 2,000 years.

Originally, *God's Plan for Man* consisted of twenty–six booklets. Each booklet consisting of two lessons and a supplement. The booklets were forty pages long. Dake described it as:

> A complete Bible course, literally answering every question you could possibly ask about any subject.

A BREAKDOWN OF THE LESSONS

The four main divisions of the course and lesson subjects:

Part I: The Origin of All Things – Lessons 1–8 consisting of: The Holy Scriptures; How to Interpret the Bible; The Truth About God; The Original Creations of God; Satan and the Spirit–World; Rebellion and Overthrow of the First Social System; The Story of Re–Creation.

Part II: God's Historical Dealings with Man – Lessons 9–18 consisting of: The Dispensation of Innocence; Providence: God's Plan for the Needs of Man; The Dispensation of Conscience; Why God's Plan for the Needs of Man is Not Realized; The Dispensation of Human Government; Divine Healing and Divine Health; The Dispensation of Promise; Asking and Receiving from God; The Dispensation of Law; The Old Testament Church.

Part III: God's Present Dealings with Man – Lessons 19–36 consisting of: The Dispensation of Grace; The New Testament Program for the Modern Church; The Truth About Jesus Christ; A Christian's Power of Attorney; The Bible Doctrine of Sin; How to Get Rid of Sin and Sickness; The Deity of the Holy Spirit; The Gifts and Fruit of the Holy Spirit; The Doctrine of the Trinity; Faith–How to Attain to All the Known Needs of Life; The New Testament Church; The Truth About the Baptism in the Holy Spirit; The Kingdom of Heaven & the Kingdom of God & the Parables; The Old and New Covenants; The Bible Doctrine of Salvation; The Truth About Sanctification and Justification; The Truth About Eternal Security; Fifteen Great Covenants of Scripture and British–Israelism.

"The Bible is God's inspired revelation of the origin and destiny of all things."

Finis Dake

Part IV: God's Future Dealings with Man – Lessons 37–52 consisting of: Where are the Dead?; The Seven Judgments of Scripture; The Book of Daniel; Daniel's Seventieth Week and the Tribulation; A Gist of the Book of Revelation; Heaven and the Resurrections; The Rapture of the Church; Exposition of Matthew 24 and 25—The Ten Virgins; Sun–Clothed Woman; Man–child; Dragon; Beast; False Prophet; The Beasts out of the Sea and Earth; The Beast With Seven Heads and Ten Horns; The Ten Horns and the Beast Itself; The Marriage Supper; Second Advent; Armageddon; The Dispensation of Divine Government; The New Heaven and the New Earth; The Bride of Christ.

Dake himself describes *God's Plan for Man* as a:

> . . . a complete study of the entire Bible from Genesis to Revelation. Dealing with all the ages and dispensations and their outstanding features and happenings, as well as all major subjects of the entire Word of God. The course is really designed to make the Bible a very simple book to understand for all people.

BIBLE RESEARCH FOUNDATION

In order to write, print and publish the Bible course, *God's Plan for Man,* Mr. Carroll and Dake formed a non–profit corporation. It was called the Bible Research Foundation, Inc., and was established in 1948. Mr. Carroll was the president, Dake was the vice–president and Dorothy would serve as the secretary. The legal address for Bible Research Foundation, Inc. was Post Office Box 4446, Atlanta, Georgia, U.S.A.

The Bible Research Foundation would be in charge of printing and publishing all of Dake's books. Mr. Carroll and Bible Research Foundation would jointly hold the copyrights. Later however, Dake would acquire full copyright in his own name. For now, however, it was jointly held.

When Dake's twelve–room house with a basement was built, he had in mind that he would be publishing his books there for a time. In the basement of his house he set up a printing press, a cutting machine, a stapler and a manual typewriter. It was there that he would ship out his orders for *God's Plan for Man* in it's 26–booklet format.

MAKING GOD'S PLAN FOR MAN AVAILABLE

When *God's Plan for Man* was finished, Dake began to offer it to the public. Wanting to get the book out to as many people as possible, he developed several ways that people could purchase the course.

He sent out letters and offered the course one book at a time for $1.00 each, postpaid. He gave people the choice of choosing any number of the twenty–six books at this price.

He also made the whole course available and allowed people to make monthly payments of $2.00 down and $2.00 a month for twelve months, making a total of $26.00 for the whole course.

Then, of course, the whole course could be paid for at once. The cash price was $20.00 for all twenty–six books. With this payment method he would also include a small four–color Bible chart, *The Plan of the Ages,* just like the one he taught from, and *Revelation Expounded.*

ADVERTISING GOD'S PLAN FOR MAN

Many companies send out sales flyers or advertising brochures to gain sales for their products. Most of the time these are only one page, perhaps even postcards. Not with Dake! His letter advertising *God's Plan for Man* was four typewritten pages long! In addition, Dake wanted to catch people's attention on the very first line. It was bold, pointed and began:

Dear Friend:
"YOU ARE GOING TO HELL!"
If I were to make such a rash statement to you, I would not
only be displaying manners of the worst kind, but would be

285

taking great liberties with the truth, and making a prophecy which I could not possibly substantiate or prove in any way. Furthermore, your reaction would justifiably be one of personal slander, crude impertinence, and possibly would call for vindication or reprisal on your part!

> *"To believe and to have faith is to act on the Word."*
>
> *Finis Dake*

Certainly, I have not the slightest intention or inclination to make such a damaging, insulting remark to you, regardless of what your reaction might be! However, I can't help wondering what your reaction would be if I told you that "JESUS CHRIST HIMSELF WENT TO HELL!"

Would you be shocked? Would you cry out indignantly, "It's a blasphemous LIE!" Chances are you would do just that! But, would your reply be the same if I pointed out (and PROVED) that your own BIBLE is my authority for this statement! Yes, it is written in the Bible that Jesus Christ Himself went to Hell!

How shamefully LITTLE the average man knows of what the Bible teaches! Even in the pulpit, less than ONE–FOURTH of the Bible's countless truths are ever mentioned or clarified. But now, thanks to the tireless efforts, the divinely inspired life's work of the Reverend Finis J. Dake, the mystery, the misrepresentations, the false face has been lifted from God's Holy Word. At long last, your Bible can be seen and understood in all its divine simplicity and power as you read and study *God's Plan for Man,* written by Reverend Dake.

God's Plan for Man Produces Faith

Dake had always wanted to see miracles in the lives of those to whom he ministered. And as *God's Plan for Man* began to go out to the people, that is just what began to happen. Dake said:

> We have many unsolicited testimonies from actual letters in our files showing what these books are doing for others. Not

only are men getting a thorough knowledge of the Bible, but they are also getting many answers to prayer. Faith miracles are being wrought almost daily in the lives of ordinary men and women of which the following are but a few:

- God healed me of kidney and bladder trouble that I had nearly all my life.

- After twenty–five years of suffering with stomach trouble I have been healed.

- God has healed me of deafness. I can now hear good as anyone without my hearing aid.

- I have been saved and healed of heart trouble since I did what you told us to do.

- God has healed me of arthritis and delivered me from my bad habits.

- Through your books I have been healed of a skin disease after 10 years of suffering and which three noted skin specialists failed to cure by many expensive treatments.

- I have been healed of sugar diabetes through reading your books.

- My husband was healed of cancer through your Bible studies.

- I was healed of cancer through your Bible studies.

- I was healed of blindness through your teaching. I am 90 years of age and yet I can read without glasses.

It was not just healing miracles that began to happen—as wonderful as those are—but business, financial, and personal problems began to be resolved as well. At long last, Dake was beginning to see, in a small way, the results of the teaching ministry that he and Dorothy had been praying for. Dake said:

> . . . through *God's Plan for Man* all the promises of God and the simple Bible teachings that were given to help men

in all phases of human living are made simple and easy to understand. So simply that anyone can reap their benefits by faith in Jesus Christ and His Gospel.

God's Plan for Man was the meat of Dake's teachings. It represented the heart of his teaching and the essence of everything he wanted people to know and learn. More than that, it also represented what he wanted people to believe and thereby receive from God—all their needs being met. Dake wrote in *God's Plan for Man:*

> . . . all believers are told to "Ask and ye shall receive, that your joy may be full" (Jn. 14:12-15; 15:7, 16; 16:23-26). So, you see, the Lord WANTS you to be blessed and to be prosperous. He WANTS you to be successful and happy and healthy. He WANTS you to be a leader among men; and you have only to set your life in order to enjoy the fulfillment of God's promises!

With all of his heart Dake believed that *God's Plan for Man* could be the key that would open the door to a new and glorious life for God's people. Not just when they die and go to heaven, but now, here on this earth.

BELIEVE IT OR NOT

Dake did not shy away from controversy either. He knew what the Bible said and that gave him confidence to boldly state his positions. In talking about *God's Plan for Man,* Dake boldly proclaimed:

"I made the decision, as we all must do, whether to believe what the Bible taught, or what man said."

Finis Dake

Every controversial Bible subject known to man is covered and thoroughly clarified in one or more of these 26 Bible books. You cannot name one important thing in the Bible, cover to cover, that is not discussed, simplified, and made more clear in *God's Plan for Man.*

As we have seen earlier, some accused Dake of being dogmatic. Well, in the writing of *God's Plan for Man,* those who had this attitude about

Dake would indeed have more ammunition. For without a second thought for how people might respond, he once again boldly proclaimed the Word of God and then, as a matter of fact, would say: "Believe it or not"!

These "believe it or nots," were bold statements, but Dake had many Scriptures to prove his points. Here is a brief listing of just a few of them:

Believe it or not . . .
Jesus Christ Himself went to hell!
Men with natural bodies have actually gone to heaven!
Christ was crucified on Wednesday instead of Friday!
There is no end of the world taught in Scripture!
There are animals in heaven like we have on earth!
Adam was not the first worldwide ruler of the earth!
Angels will be judged by human beings!
The bride of Christ is not the church!
The Roman Empire will never be revived!
The time will come when man cannot commit suicide!
Methuselah was not the oldest man that ever lived!
Saints will not spend eternity in heaven!
The Holy Spirit has a personal body, soul, and spirit!
The Devil now has access to heaven!
Men will some day see God in bodily form!
Giants twice lived on the earth 15 to 30 feet tall!
Many of you who read these words may continue to live in your natural bodies right here on earth . . . FOREVER!

These statements, and many more, Dake made in promoting *God's Plan for Man*. The response of many was "shocking," "unbelievable," "controversial," and "impossible." Yet when one took the course, they found that Dake had the exact Scripture references to prove the truth of every one of those statements.

Dake was so sure that people would be blessed by *God's Plan for Man* that he offered a money–back guarantee. He wrote:

We guarantee satisfaction and that the books are what we claim they are or your money will be cheerfully refunded. You are to be the sole judge.

And so in early 1949, *God's Plan for Man* was completed and began going out to the Body of Christ. For Dake, this was one of the happiest times of his life. He was fulfilling the call of God on his life and God's Word was going forth.

CHAPTER TWENTY–EIGHT

DAKE ON THE RADIO AGAIN

WE WON'T BEG FOR MONEY

When Mr. Carroll first met Dake, he promised to put him on the radio. With the printing of the Bible course *God's Plan for Man,* both Mr. Carroll and Dake felt the time was right. Dorothy fully supported Dake in

Finis J. Dake

Dake on the radio

this new outreach opportunity, but had a single reservation. She had heard other ministers beg for money on the radio. To her, this represented a doubting of God's ability to supply their needs. She had prayed about the methods some ministries used to raise money and told Dake that God had spoken the word "gadgetry" to her. She would agree to support this ministry, but would have no part of begging for money over the air. With that, Dake and Mr. Carroll agreed. They decided to offer Dake's Bible course to listeners and his books for sale at very reasonable prices. After those receipts were used to pay for radio time, any money still needed would be paid by Mr. Carroll himself.

In the early summer of 1948, Dake went on the radio. His program was heard Monday through Friday, twice a day. His program was heard once in the morning on WGST–AM at 7:45 a.m. and then in the afternoon at 1:00 p.m. on WCON–FM. Some time later he also appeared on WTJH–AM and WEAS–AM, with a morning program only.

Imagine listening to the radio in those days. On WCON–FM you could listen to Bing Crosby, Milton Berle, Groucho Marx, Ingrid Bergman and Abbott and Costello. Then, along side of these radio giants was Dake. The station advertised him as: "*FINIS J. DAKE*—Known as *The Walking Bible,* invites listeners to submit Bible queries by courtesy of the Dutch Oven Bakeries."

This was a great beginning for Dake's radio ministry which would extend for the next thirteen years. Mr. Carroll was proud to be sponsoring Dake on the radio. In 1954 he wrote a general endorsement of Dake's radio program.

Carroll Baking Company, Inc.
720 Stewart Ave. SW
Atlanta, Georgia

To Whom It May Concern:

Having had a man so used of God around me for several years, enjoying the freedom of open discussion and the unlimited privilege of having biblical questions answered for me, and the privilege of reading and examining the rich material found in his many writings, where he was close by to explain the many intriguing new truths found therein, truths which seem to have been lost to our present and several past generations of Bible scholars—this indeed has been a rare privilege and I thank my God for having sent Finis J. Dake my way.

Truly, I would class Finis J. Dake the most able writer on Bible subjects living today. One has only to examine his many books together with thousands of Scripture references in each of his works to realize surely, here is a man that God is using for these troubled days.

My appreciation for his wonderful gift of writing and lecturing can best be attested to by stating that he has been sponsored twice daily over the radio and in many personal appearances by my company for the past four years.

We have received thousands of grateful letters attesting to the lasting benefits this man is bringing to a lost and confused world. I personally consider Finis J. Dake worthy of any honors the Christian world could bestow on him.

Gratefully yours,

CARROLL BAKING COMPANY, INC.

W. E. Carroll, President

Not only was Mr. Carroll proudly endorsing Dake, but in 1955 the radio station on which he was being aired also gave their endorsement:

WGST
Forsyth Building
P. O. Box 674
Walnut 8441
Atla.ta, Ga.

To Whom It May Concern:

As manager of WGST, it has been my privilege for the past five years to have listened to the broadcasts of Finis J. Dake on this station. I also had the pleasure of reading many of his fine writings on the Bible, as well as supervising the large volume of mail which his program has brought from the interested listeners in his Bible interpretations and his writings.

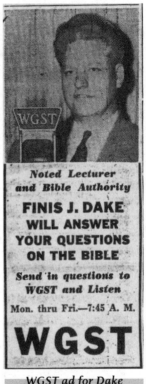

Noted Lecturer and Bible Authority

FINIS J. DAKE WILL ANSWER YOUR QUESTIONS ON THE BIBLE

Send in questions to WGST and Listen

Mon. thru Fri.—7:45 A. M.

WGST

WGST ad for Dake

I consider him to be one of the finest authorities on the Bible alive today as attested by his scripts for broadcasts and his many books. Consistently, Reverend Dake has received a volume of mail as high or higher than any feature on this station.

Any honors that might be bestowed on him would be more than richly deserved.

Sincerely,

RADIO STATION WGST

John Fulton, General Manager

Of course, many thousands of letters came in from listeners during the thirteen–year history of Dake's radio program in Atlanta. Most were Bible questions and praises for the program, but he would also receive letters from those who disagreed. Over the years, the program proved to be a blessing to the body of Christ and an instrument for bringing *God's Plan for Man* to thousands of homes.

As Dake's listening audience grew, his ministry began to grow as well. As this expansion began to take place, Mr. Carroll saw the need for a larger ministry headquarters. So, in December of 1952, Mr. Carroll purchased a building on 669 West Peachtree Street, in downtown Atlanta, right behind the historic *Fox Theater.* In that building, Dake opened a bookstore, a reading room, a lecture hall and consulting offices.

MR. CARROLL SPEAKS

At the time of the writing of this book, many are skeptical of those who invest heavily in the lives of ministers. One might rightly ask for the reason and motivation behind Mr. Carroll's generosity. Of course, only God knows the intentions of the hearts of men, but it seems that, in this case, things were just what they appeared to be. Mr. Carroll wanted to spread the truth that he had found to as many people as possible, using his own resources if need be.

> *"'Providence' is the most comprehensive word in the language of theology."*
>
> *Finis Dake*

In 1952, Mr. Carroll wrote a small article entitled *Someone Cares About You.* In this article it was easy to see the change that had taken place in his own life and the desire that he had for that same change to take place in the lives of others.

SOMEONE CARES ABOUT YOU

Many have been the times when most of us were besieged with fears and anxiety, and in a measure, overcome with what seemed to be *"the futility of life."* At such times we have turned in every direction for worldly help and assistance, only to find that all such efforts failed us or were in vain. . . . In times of stress and urgency many of us have sought God. Because there was no other place to turn we sought Him earnestly. He has heard us and banished such fears and anxieties from us. His deliverance has been complete.

Most of us are daily reminded of the great and inspired truths of the Holy Bible and the teachings of Jesus Christ. These truths and teachings are without equal; they are without parallel in all history of mankind.

In these days of trying times, everyone hungers for a solution to the conflicts among men and nations which affect all the peoples of the earth; we would all like to see an end to dissension and strife. In these efforts, more people are seeking more knowledge of the Holy Bible and the teachings of Jesus Christ.

We of the Dutch Oven Bakeries feel that we have helped to add a small bit to your spiritual knowledge, through the sponsorship of the great and inspirational teachings of the Holy Bible. These messages have been brought to you for the past four years over radio station WGST by one of the outstanding Bible students of all times, Rev. Finis J. Dake. We feel that you who have heard and will continue to hear Reverend Dake, will reap many benefits from it.

Sincerely,

W. E. CARROLL, President,
Carroll Baking Company

CHAPTER TWENTY–NINE

NEW TESTAMENT CHURCH

A TIME OF FASTING AND PRAYER

The Bible Research Foundation on 669 West Peachtree Street, Atlanta, was Dake's ministry headquarters. The year was 1954, and Dake would occasionally hold lectures in the lecture hall and invite the public to attend. At the time Dake began these lectures he had no thought of starting another church. In fact, the lectures were held at 3:30 p.m. on Sunday afternoon, so as not to interfere with other church services.

Some of the folks who attended these lectures had a hunger for God just as Dake had. No matter what part of the ministry Dake was involved in: writing, pastoring, evangelism, or just his routine day–to–day activities, he was always seeking God for a move of His Spirit. He longed to see New Testament experiences lived out in the lives of men and women. With this hunger deep within his heart, he lead a nightly prayer meeting which lasted for over one year. At this prayer meeting—as in Bristol and in Zion—he would pray for hours on end, seeking God for an outpouring of the Holy Spirit. He wanted to see all the gifts of the Spirit in operation. For Dake and a small group of dedicated believers, prayer and fasting was the order of the day.

"Man's part is to ask and simply believe and refuse to doubt after prayer."

Finis Dake

WE NEED A CHURCH

Those who were attending the lectures and the prayer meeting began to talk to Dake about the need for a church. A church where sound doctrine was taught in the simple and literal way Dake was doing it. Out of these Sunday afternoon lectures a church was birthed.

At first it was a very informal setting and they simply called themselves the *Atlanta Bible Church,* a name which was used off and on throughout the years. It wasn't long, however, before they saw the need to officially incorporate as a church and change the name of their fellowship. In September of 1955, the church was renamed *New Testament Church, Inc.* The church incorporation cover letter, signed by the chairman and the secretary, read as follows:

New Testament Church, Inc.
Meeting of Incorporators
Atlanta, Georgia
September 1955

At a meeting of the incorporators of this corporation held at the offices thereof at 669 West Peachtree St., NE, Atlanta, Georgia, the following were present, to wit: J. Howard Fry, Jr., J. Paul Durbin, Jr., B. E. Tipton, Finis J. Dake, being all of the incorporators.

Mr. Dake presided over the meeting and Mr. Fry acted as secretary thereof.

Mr. Dake stated that pursuant to instructions of the congregation and the board of deacons of New Testament Church, he and the other incorporators had engaged counsel and procured a charter for New Testament Church, Inc., which charter has been granted by Fulton Superior Court on September 14, 1955.

The charter was duly examined by all present and upon motion by Mr. Dake and seconded by Mr. Fry the same was accepted as granted.

Mr. Dake stated that a Constitution and By–Laws for the government of the corporation had been prepared and which he wishes to present to the incorporators for their consideration and approval. The same was duly examined by the incorporators and upon motion by Mr. Fry and seconded by Mr. Tipton, the same were adopted as the Constitution and By–Laws of this corporation.

Mr. Dake stated that it would be in order for the corporation to open a bank account for the deposit of its funds, also bank account for the deposit of the Sunday School funds and the Mission Fund, and presented a resolution, copy of which is attached hereto, providing for the opening of the bank accounts with the First National Bank of Atlanta.

There being no further business the meeting adjourned.

CONSTITUTION AND BYLAWS

And with that meeting, the New Testament Church was born. The constitution and bylaws are too lengthy to reproduce here in their entirety, but they do contain important sections that continue to show Dake's love for Scripture and desire to walk righteously along its narrow path.

For example, what would be the churches doctrine? Their rule of faith and conduct? The preamble of the constitution states:

> *"A businessman needs God in his business in order to have guaranteed success."*
>
> *Finis Dake*

Resolved, that we recognize ourselves as New Testament believers and as a part of the New Testament Church, that we adopt the entire New Testament and related Scriptures of the Old Testament as the rule of our faith and conduct, and that we give expression to our faith and recognize and promote scriptural methods of worship, unity, fellowship, work and business for God, as Christ and the Apostles would do if they were yet alive as God's representatives on earth.

More specifically, the church's *Statement of Fundamental Truths* would be larger than could ever be printed!

ARTICLE IV, STATEMENT OF FUNDAMENTAL TRUTHS

We accept the teachings of the entire Bible as expounded in *God's Plan for Man,* published by the Bible Research Foundation, Inc., 669 West Peachtree St., Atlanta, Georgia.

How would people become members of the church?

ARTICLE V, MEMBERSHIP

Any person born of the Spirit (John 3:3-5) and who is living a consistent Christian life, and who will agree to believe and obey the whole Bible, may become an active member of the church by presenting his or her name to the board. Upon approval of the board the name shall be presented to the membership of the church for final approval, whereupon the name shall then be inscribed upon the church roster.

Big Changes Take Place

With the establishment of this new church, a big change would take place. First, Dake would officially be leaving the Church of God. He had loved this church and had been accepted by its members and ministry. But in order to reach all people he felt he needed to step beyond denominational barriers. So, on September 25, 1955, Dake received his new ordination granted by the New Testament Church, Inc.

"True understanding and faith comes by hearing the Word of God."

Finis Dake

There was another change that would affect Dorothy deeply. Over the years, Dake had always preached the Sunday morning services and Dorothy would preach the Sunday night services. No more! There was a conflict with Mr. Carroll. He had accepted all of Dake's teachings on the Bible but one. He did not believe that women should preach! The three of them struggled with this issue for a while, but there was no common ground that could be found. Of course, Dake was standing by the Word of God and his wife Dorothy on this one, but to keep the peace and to keep the Gospel going forth without hindrance, Dorothy decided to step back. She would concentrate on helping Dake with the writing and other work of the ministry, playing the piano in the church, but for the sake of the kingdom she would not preach.

New Testament Church

As the Bible Research Foundation, Dake had held his lectures on Sunday afternoons at 3:30 p.m., but now, as the New Testament Church, the service schedule would have to change. There would be Sunday School at 9:45 a.m., Morning Worship at 11:00 p.m., Evening Worship at 7:00 p.m., and a midweek service on Wednesdays at 7:30 p.m.

The worship style at New Testament Church was traditional, for the most part. The singing was classic hymn books. There was no choir, and everyone just sang from their seats. The music was provided by Finette on the piano, who was now home from Lee College, and Dorothy, who would fill in when needed. On occasion, Dake and Dorothy would sing a duet. The other three members of the family would join in too—a trio consisting of all three children, Finette, Annabeth, and Finis, Jr. would sing special songs. Dake played his trombone very little. It seemed that at this stage of his life, his musical days were now gone.

There were very few special speakers at New Testament Church. It seemed the people always wanted to hear Dake. Through the years, Dake performed a few marriages, a few funerals and some baptisms in water, but for the most part the church was more of a teaching ministry than anything else. When you look back at the sermons Dake ministered to his congregation during these years, they are in fact the lessons you find in *God's Plan For Man*. Dake preached on sermon subjects like: The Doctrine of the Trinity; Infidels Tasting Eternal Punishment; How We Got The Bible; and The Antichrist. The Sunday School curriculum was none other than the lessons found in *God's Plan for Man*.

Church attendance averaged about 100 people. Of course, during special events or special lectures by Dake, the attendance would be up. It must be remembered that during this stage of his life Dake was concentrating on writing his Bible notes. The sermons he preached were, for the most part, the result of his studies. For those who are reading and studying the Bible, the Dake notes are interesting, inspirational and informative. But for the average person coming to church, it may be a little unexpected to hear a four–part series of Sunday morning sermons on *Biblical Proof That the Beast out of the Abyss is The Prince of Grecia*. Then too, Dorothy, who had always preached on subjects that attracted the crowds—like faith, healing, and living the overcoming lifestyle—was no longer ministering.

During Dake's pastorate at New Testament Church, the church only paid half of his salary. Mr. Carroll paid the other half. It seemed that both the church and Mr. Carroll knew that it was best to keep Dake teaching and writing. This was his gift from God and everyone was working to see that Dake had as much time as possible to do just that. His name even spoke of the relationship he had with the members of the church. They did not call him Pastor Dake, but simply Reverend Dake.

THE DAKES CELEBRATE THEIR LOVE

Throughout their lifetime together, Dorothy and Finis truly loved each other. In the good times they laughed and played together. In the difficult times they cried together. They were always there for each other.

During Dake's study in the Word of God, he came to a change of heart about an issue which had been with them since the day they were married. It had to do with wearing wedding rings. In the early days of Pentecost when the Dake's were married, most Pentecostal people frowned on the wearing of rings, even wedding bands.

The more Dake studied the Scriptures on this issue, the more he became convinced that there was no sin in a married couple wearing wedding bands as a symbol or token of their marriage vows. So with that, Dake went to the local Sears and Roebuck department store and bought a set of wedding rings. Dorothy, of course, was in full agreement and was thrilled to show her love and commitment to her husband by the wearing of her wedding band.

Dorothy's gifts and talents were many. But poems and writing were some of her favorite ways of expressing her feelings. On June 15, 1957, she wrote the following poem to her dear husband.

> *"God loves each one and deals with each one personally according to his faith."*
>
> *Finis Dake*

MY "FINIS"

At the end of an anxious and youthful search,
A quest of the heart for its Love,
I came to the dawn of a sunlit day
Finding YOU. What a day, my Dove!
('Twas a search with "eureka" its "finis.")

We've feathered a nest—had young—we two;
We've seen a wee fledgling try a wing.
We've shed a tear; we've said a prayer
Together we've learned HOW to sing.
(Because my search led to this "finis.")
And now, in the gloaming when love is mature
yet sparked by some fireflies of dream,
I catch from your eyes the fulfillment of wish
Looking deep in the clear, bluish gleam!
(That's my further reward for such "finis.")

We sit in a garden, in–breathing its blooms,
That are fragrant with memories long past,
Then, finally our kiss betokens our vow
To a love while Eternities last.
(In this there can be no "finis.")

By Dorothy Dobbins Dake

THE DREAM IS BORN

After Dake completed *God's Plan for Man,* he also wrote *Bible Truths Unmasked* and produced a second edition of *Revelation Expounded.* He was continually writing and making Bible notes.

Once in a service at New Testament Church, a lady by the name of Alice Cannon saw his Bible notes. She asked what they were. He explained his dream to create a sort of Bible commentary. She was excited and encouraged him to go to work fulltime doing just that.

Dake had thought of doing this for a long time now, and had been collecting Bible notes in his looseleaf notebook, but somehow the encouragement that lady gave him got him started. So it was that in 1955, he seriously began working on his Bible notes, which would one day come to be known as *Dake's Annotated Reference Bible.*

CHAPTER THIRTY

DAKE AND HIS BIBLE NOTES

THE BIGGEST TASK YET

Writing a Bible course such as *God's Plan for Man* was one thing. Writing a book such as *Revelation Expounded* was another. But then writing notes for every book, chapter and almost every verse of the Bible, would be a task for which Dake felt sure he would need some help. Some big help.

I'LL NEED SOME HELP

Right away, Dake decided to approach the big publishing companies with his proposed project. He originally planned to name the Bible the *Dake Emphasized Reference Commentary Bible.*
He could see it clearly. He would take care of the study and the draft writing, letting a staff of editors correct his spelling and check his references. Printing departments would print the Annotated Bible on the best of Bible paper. The finest leather would be chosen. Big Bible publishers would market and offer his work to the public. His work would go out to all the world. This was Dake's dream.

1954

United Methodists grant full ordination to women.

THEY ALL SAID NO

However, Dake was an unknown and most of the Bible publishers he approached with his project were simply not interested. Over the next several years the rejections would come in.

On February 6, 1956, Thomas Nelson and Son Publishers said "no":

> We regret to inform you that although the proposed book has a great deal of merit we are not in a position to consider it at the present time. As you are aware—this would be a very expensive publication to produce.

On February 14, 1956, The Macmillan Company said "no":

> We have carefully considered your request for our editorial review of your entire work, and we have conferred

with the members of our Editorial Council in regard to the possibility of our publication of the work. Unfortunately, in view of the present requirements of our publishing program, it is necessary in this instance to discourage the submission of your work.

On April 2, 1958, the A. J. Holman Company said "no":

I find it quite interesting and of undoubted great value. I am sorry to say that we would not be interested in publishing your Bible.

On April 16, 1958, the Cambridge University Press said "no":

I am obliged to you for sending me the sample books from the Dake Emphasized Reference Commentary Bible. This is indeed an interesting work. I regret, however, that we could not undertake publication as it would not be within our province.

On April 22, 1958, Harper and Brothers said "no":

I have examined your Emphasized Reference Commentary Bible with care and a great deal of interest. It is extremely thorough, and most carefully done. At this time we are not seeking to enlarge our Bible Department, and I doubt whether, if we were, we would be a good publisher for a Bible based on dispensational doctrine.

On April 24, 1958, the John C. Winston Company said "no":

The project is such an interesting one, as well as an impressive one, that we wish we could avail ourselves of the opportunity of publishing it. It's very nature, however, makes it impossible for us to consider it because of the immensity of the typesetting work.

On May 7, 1958, Moody Press said "no":

Our editorial committee has been working along faithfully on the evaluation of your material and find it good.

Meanwhile, our sales promotion group has come in with a report questioning our ability to sell a Bible of this kind in adequate quantities unless it could be put out in thin paper with a leather binding. This would probably require a complete new typesetting, which we would estimate to run in the neighborhood of $75,000, and thus far we do not feel that we ought to proceed with the project.

On May 13, 1958, World Publishing Company said "no":

After very careful consideration and much as we appreciate your offer, our production and editorial departments have decided that the publishing of the Dake Reference Commentary Bible would not fit into our publishing program.

Even with all the bad news, Dake was continuing to work on his Bible annotations. He believed it was of God and that when the time came to publish, the way would be made. He just needed to make a few adjustments, that's all!

The other options had failed and it was decided that rather than having a large company publish the Bible, Bible Research Foundation would do it. Rather than having a staff of editors work on the Bible, Finette and Annabeth would type them all out. Finis, Jr. would be away at college and seminary, but would still lend a hand proofreading from time to time. Church members would paste them up. Dorothy would proof and edit his often–too–lengthy notes. Rather than getting it done right away, however, it would take him and his dedicated family from 1955 to 1961 to complete the New Testament, and until 1963 to finally publish the entire Bible. It might be a little slower and a little more difficult, but it would get done!

> *"The human faith in union with the divine will make all things possible to the believer."*
>
> *Finis Dake*

DAKE NEVER GAVE UP

As the years progressed, Dake worked on his Bible. The research and the note–making for the new Bible went on endlessly, almost day and night. Still, he had not given up on getting a larger Bible publisher to take his Bible. Then, in 1960, a break came. Zondervan Publishing House in Grand Rapids, Michigan, decided to look seriously at his project.

He sent as much of his manuscript as he had completed to Michigan, which included portions of the New Testament, Daniel, Psalms and Proverbs. At Zondervan, two scholars were assigned to look over the work, Dr. Herbert Lockyer,[130] and Dr. Wilbur Smith.[131] For a period of three weeks, these men of God studied the Dake Bible and made comments for the Zondervan editorial board to consider.

"I never give one opinion of man on any question, not even my own."

Finis Dake

Later he and Dorothy went to Michigan to discuss his project with the editorial committee at Zondervan. When he came back from that meeting, he gave the following report to the New Testament Church congregation on Sunday, October 2, 1960. Dake said:

> Now I know some of you have been already asking about the result of our trip to Michigan. We have good news, nothing bad. But, we didn't expect to have anything bad when we went.

Concern Over A Few Notes

The publishers at Zondervan had been concerned over several of the notes in the New Testament. They enlisted several critics to briefly look over the text. Dake told his congregation:

> We just took those letters of the two critics—the one critic that criticized the other critic . . . and I first asked them, "are you willing to accept everything that Dr. Lockyer agreed with me on?" (That's the one in England.) And they said, "Yes, we are willing to go along with you on every one of those points." I said, "well, there are just four or five points between us now."

> So, we took up each item—one by one. And, they never requested us to take out any doctrine at all, only change

---

[130] Dr. Herbert Lockyer (1886–1984) was a writer and respected theologian who lived in London, England.

[131] Wilbur Morehead Smith (1894–1977) was a Presbyterian and had taught at Moody Bible Institute. At this time he was a highly acclaimed professor at Fuller Theological Seminary.

the wording here or there. For example, they wanted "disciples" where I had "ministers" in one place. Well, that was all right. We are disciples. That was all right. They are disciples. We just changed some wording here and there.

We went through everything, including the doctrine of the man–child. That was the main thing that they had never heard before. They thought, according to the critics, that it would be robbing the Christian world from a wonderful doctrine. But I showed them where that could not possibly be a true doctrine, and let them turn to the Scriptures and everything. I quoted every Scripture that I had them turn to. They just read right along with us. So they questioned that one a little further. They wanted further time to study it.

All the rest of the small problems just worked out perfectly. And so we had that session from nine to twelve on Wednesday. And everything was alright except that one thing. So they agreed to have a meeting the next day. At the end of this first day, one of the Zondervan boys met me in the washroom as we went out to dinner, just getting ready to go out to dinner. He said, "Brother Dake, you amaze me. I have never heard of anything like that before. "

THE PROBLEMS HAVE BEEN RESOLVED

The next day we gathered from ten to twelve. When we got there the next morning, we thought we would have to go thoroughly into the subject of the man–child and perhaps other questions. But everything was settled with them. They said, "We have the 'go' signal. Everything is all right." I said, "You don't want to discuss the man–child any further?" "No, we will go along with you on that too."

I don't know whether they believed everything or not, but they were willing to go along with it, because we had Scripture for it. They were just open to everything it seemed that the Bible said.

And not only those doctrines, but other doctrines came up. Naturally, they would. Like one of them brought up the question of the bride of Christ. "That's the church, isn't it?" "No," I said. "It is not the church—it couldn't be the church." "Why, we have got books here in the publishing house on that subject!" I said, "I can't help what kind of books you have. It is definitely wrong."

"He must accept what the Bible says, not what men interpret it to say."

Finis Dake

I said, "Will you turn to Revelation 21:9-10?" One of the men turned to that passage and said, "My, I have never seen that before, in all my reading of the Bible." That was the way it was in so many things. Everything is all right from that standpoint.

DAKE WAS IMPRESSED WITH ZONDERVAN

I have to be so grateful for men like we met the other day. Heads of big concerns like that who publish hundreds of books. Humble enough to accept the Bible just like it is. That is to be really praised. I don't suppose there would be another publisher in the country that would be just as open to the Bible as those boys are.

I have been teaching you about "the works that I do shall he do also"—the signs following believers. All I had to do was just let them read Mark 16 . . . that's what it says . . . ok, that's all. If it says that, then that is what it means. I wish we could get everybody open to the Bible like that. Don't you? Everybody to believe what the Bible says.

But it seems like the majority of people, even the church members, that they don't know anything about the Bible in the average church. They know more about it than everybody else. They know what is right and wrong and they are not open to the truth like they ought to be. One thing that I would like to get in every one of our lives is the openness to the Bible. Those men believe in divine healing, they believe in gifts of the spirit, they believe in healing in the atonement, they believe in all those things; it is surprising how far you do get faith in certain doctrines in certain circles.

You Look Scholarly

Well, now we are to get the final sheets to them this next week. They even want a picture of me to go on it. I don't know what they want to do with that! They said, "You look scholarly. We want the people to have a picture of you!" We will get that all to them next week and then it will be up to them. We tried to get them to assure us to have it all out by Christmas, but we will just have to wait and see if they can work it in with all the other. We will get it as soon as possible. I have no assurance one way or the other.

I am going to make this little interesting note about Sister Dake. The second day, when we got ready to leave, they said, "We think a whole lot more of you now since we met your wife. She was very helpful in various suggestions and so on." I guess that's all. All right, that is the report.

Not Happy, Just Content

But, you know, I thought I would be shouting happy, but I am not. I really am not. It just left a good feeling. Trust it be the will of God. It really is the only feeling we have to go on. We prayed that on our end, they took it that it would be the will of God. So we have to accept it as the will of God. So you keep on praying the Lord will work out every detail concerning the marketing of the Bible.

Suppose we all stand and just thank the Lord for it. Shall we? You prayed about it and it worked out that way. Now Lord God, we do return thanks to you and give you the praise from our hearts for the way you have opened the hearts of those men to receive truth. We thank you for the way things have gone. We just trust that everything will be done after the counsel of your own will. Thank you for working out all these problems which we thought in some cases were insurmountable, but you are wonderful. Your Word gives light and truth to all men. Thank you for it. Amen.

ANOTHER PROJECT TOO

In addition to agreeing to print and publish the *Dake Annotated Reference Bible—New Testament*, the management of Zondervan also had an idea for another book. They wanted a King James Version concordance with other versions included as well. Dake explained it:

The first Dake Bible

They are wanting me now to make a complete concordance for them with King James Version and the different versions—the different renderings together—and combine them into one. I don't know if we will ever get that done or not. We will get the Bible out first.

So, in 1961 the first 10,000 copies of the *Dake Annotated Reference Bible—New Testament* edition were printed. So successful was this first edition that in May of 1961 a second 10,000 copies were printed.

CHAPTER THIRTY–ONE

DAKE BIBLE SALES

A PARTNERSHIP IS FORMED

With the printing of the new Bible, the Dakes felt the need to set things in order within the family. Until this time, all copyrights and all the promotion of the Bible had been held through the Bible Research Foundation and Mr. Carroll. With the completion of the Bible—primarily by Dake and his own personal family—it only seemed right that a new company should be formed to handle the sales and distribution of the Bible.

> *"My work is simple and scriptural."*
>
> *Finis Dake*

So, on January 13, 1961, a partnership to sell the *Dake Annotated Reference Bible* was established. The partners consisted of: Finis Dake, Dorothy Dake, Finette Dake Kennedy, Annabeth Dake Germaine and Finis Dake, Jr., who was away at Taylor University at this time. Each partner held one vote in the partnership. Together they would finish the entire Bible, handling all the typing, proofreading, editing and, later in the process, the printing and promoting the sale of the Bible.

As with most new businesses, Dake Bible Sales would start small—very small! The Dakes would remove all of their living room furniture in the house at 2232 Belvedere Avenue, using this space and the basement area in which to operate Dake Bible Sales. Each day they would use their own cars to make trips to the post office. Dake would continue to be the writer and Dorothy would run and manage the company. For now, the personal phone line would also be used as the business phone.

WHERE IS MR. CARROLL?

It is interesting to note that Mr. Carroll was not included in this new arrangement. This is as it should be, of course, and no ill will was present with the forming of this new company.

Over the years Mr. Carroll had done everything he could to promote Dake's ministry. In the beginning there were a lot of big ideas and Mr. Carroll had made a lot of big promises. Not all of those promises came to fulfillment, however. It seems that within Mr. Carroll's family there were some restraints placed on him—some restraints not of his choosing. These restraints did not allow him to use as much of his family's resources as he would have liked in the promotion of Dake's ministry. However, Mr. Carroll and Dake remained the closest of friends and continued to work together on the Bible Research Foundation at New Testament Church.

> *Faith laughs at impossibilities and cries, "It is done."*
>
> *Finis Dake*

For almost fifteen years, Mr. Carroll had been a primary backer of almost everything Dake wanted to do. While Dorothy and Mr. Carroll had had their differences on the subject of women preachers, they had settled things in Christian love, neither holding it against the other. Mr. Carroll could not have been more pleased to see the success of the Dakes in this dream of a lifetime coming true.

THE OLD TESTAMENT IS FINALLY COMPLETED

It was toward the end of 1962 that Dake and the family finally completed the Old Testament notes. By now, Zondervan Publishing had been printing the New Testament for almost two years. Dake felt that, with the completion of the Old Testament notes, Zondervan would be happy to print the entire Bible. However, that was not the case.

It seemed that the editorial staff had reviewed the Bible notes once again. As before, some of the same questions came up, as well as a few new ones. Again the Dakes went to Michigan for a meeting.

YOU HAVE GOT TO CHANGE THESE NOTES

Dake expressed his thoughts about that meeting:

> The people that were under contract to publish the Bible thought I was far away from truth. They had to decide whether this was biblical or not . . . [They] decided that we had better leave out certain doctrines. They wanted me to leave out all on the Baptism in the Holy Spirit and everything on the gifts of the Spirit.
>
> They wanted me to do away with divine healing and that God had a body—that He was even seen with the natural eye—that He even will be seen with the natural eye, that the pre–Adamite world is a fallacy.

They had so many fallacies that I just had to sit and scratch my head and wonder what in the world is going on here. Is that what the public really believes about the Bible? Here I've been believing all these years that God could possibly mean what he said... instead of what didn't say.

They told me, "you've got so many new things in this book, we are afraid to tackle it. It will not be accepted by the Christian world." I said, "I have chapter and verse for everything I say." They said, "we know you have." But their answer was the same—without changes they could not publish my Bible. So I just had to reject all that.

An Unexpected Blessing

God's grace prevailed. At that the end of this meeting it was decided that Zondervan would not publish the complete Bible. The editorial staff had wanted a number of changes to be made in the Bible notes. Dake argued that those notes reflected his literal approach to understanding the Scriptures and that if he yielded to their changes, the Dake Bible really would not be a Dake Bible! The committee at Zondervan was understanding and compassionate toward Dake, but they too would not yield.

As a goodwill gesture on the part of Zondervan, they decided they would print 10,000 copies of the entire Bible—both Old and New Testaments, complete as Dake wanted it. However, it would not bear their company name. On the title page of the Bible it would list the publisher as "Dake Bible Sales, Inc." As far as payment was concerned, Dake would be allowed to pay Zondervan for the printing as he sold the Bibles, paying $1,000.00 a month until paid in full. And to help them sell the Bibles, they were given a listing of Christian bookstores in America. In response to Zondervan's generous offer, Dake responded: "That's okay with me—that's what I wanted in the first place, "

To say that Dake and Dorothy were pleased is an understatement for how they really felt. They were overjoyed and elated, for once again they had seen the hand of God working on their behalf.

From this time on, the *Dake Annotated Reference Bible* would be published by Dake Bible Sales. And when it came time to publish the second printing of 10,000 Bibles, Dake was on his own. However, he came up with the money! He risked everything, but he did it. He said:

After I published the first 10,000 Bibles, I had to mortgage my home for $20,000.00 in order to pay for the paper on the second printing. I borrowed money here and there for the rest of it—and I was in business.

Dake Describes His Bible

To get his Bible out to the public, Dake began to do many things, one of which was advertising in print media. He began to describe his Bible as a "Compact One–Volume Library."

A Word Of Caution About A Great Bible

Truly, there is nothing quite like the *Dake Annotated Reference Bible.* When one surveys its contents it is overwhelming. People may agree or disagree with all the notes it contains, but most walk away with the knowledge that God must have inspired this man. Certainly, without God's divine touch upon Dake's life, he could have never accomplished such a task.

Early Ad for the Dake Bible

That being said, the notes and annotations need to be kept in their proper perspective. They are notes of a man, not the Word of God. Dake himself emphasized this again and again throughout his ministry. He would say: "Only the text is inspired, not the notes!" In a sermon he expressed his thoughts:

> Here is one thing I might warn you against. Do not depend upon marginal references and footnotes and notes of men or even references. Only the text is divinely inspired. All these other things, such as summaries of chapters, footnotes, headings in the Bible, notes and suggestions for helps of various kinds . . . they are all man–made. Sometimes they help and sometimes they don't help. So the thing for

you to depend upon is the very text itself. Only the text is divinely inspired and it only is the Word of God!

RECOMMENDATIONS START TO COME IN

As Dake's completed Bible began to go out to various outlets, it was well received. *The Wesleyan Methodist* wrote one of the first reviews.

This is a large book, surprising to open, the pages seem cluttered until you notice that the middle two columns feature the Bible text (King James) and the two outer columns provide the amazing array of Bible helps. At the first the scholar or seminary student might disdain the book, but looking at it further he will not dismiss its helps so quickly. It is an ideal book for the pastor, the serious Bible student and Bible class teacher.

The book wastes no time in printing trivia. It includes notes most valuable to Bible study—meaning of Greek verbs, historical references, related Scriptures and references, and detailed outlines.

The prophetic slant of the book is staunchly premillennial. Its theological slant is Armenian.

It must suffice to say that I know of no other Bible study book like this. After all other comments are read on the passage, you can still consult this reference work with much profit. It's a lot of book for a little money.

– George E.

The *Baptist Standard* in Dallas, Texas, weighed in on the Dake's Bible as well.

A most helpful book which combines a commentary, dictionary, concordance, lexicon, and encyclopedia within its pages. Not only will this book be helpful to the pastor, but Sunday School teachers will find it a welcome addition to their libraries.

Charles Gresham of *Standard Publishing Foundation* wrote:

> *Dake's Annotated Reference Bible* is a remarkable and comprehensive study tool, which provides adjacent to the actual biblical text, cross references, sermon outlines, notes, original language studies, and doctrines, Bible customs, etc.
>
> In this reviewer's opinion, this volume is unique in its field. It combines the values of a Bible Dictionary, New Greek Testament Lexicon, and a cross reference Bible. For the local Bibleschool some interpretations particularly in Revelation and Daniel, may be subject to differences of opinion. I would highly recommend this exhaustive evangelical work.

"If we are going to believe in the Bible at all, then let us believe it in its entirety."

Finis Dake

It is interesting to note that while Dake cherished the reviews and recommendations he received from the larger Bible companies—and there are far too many to include here—he was also most pleased to know that his Bible was blessing the "everyday" Bible reader. As a cherished possession, Dake kept in his files one of his best–loved recommendations.

> Dear Sir,
>
> I'm a fifth grader who is studying to write business letters in English at World Harvest Christian Academy. I have purchased a DAKE Bible and read it every day. I thank you for writing it. I've learned so much from it. Please send me more information about the DAKE Bible and write me back. Thank You.
>
> Sincerely,
>
> Matt Reed

In addition to his print advertising, Dake also wanted to introduce his Bible to Christian bookstores across the nation. For this, he chose the yearly Christian Booksellers Association. In 1963, the CBA convention was being held in Washington D.C. Dake decided he would make the 640–mile trip to Washington. Accompanying him would be Dorothy and his son, Finis, Jr. Finis, Jr. was now at Dallas Theological Seminary, but since CBA was held in the summer, he would be able to help. This would be their first trip to a CBA convention, but not their last. Over the years, members of Dake Bible Sales would make many such trips.

NEW TITLES IN DAKE BIBLE SALES BOOTH 616

GOD'S PLAN FOR MAN—"The Key to the World's Storehouse of Wisdom." Acknowledged source of sermon material by ministers of many denominations. Had widespread distribution in loose leaf form for about 20 years. Now in book form—a compact, comprehensive study of God's Plan from eternity past to eternity future. Author: Dake **$12.50**

REVELATION EXPOUNDED—"Eternal Mysteries Simplified." A most thorough treatment of Bible PROPHECY. In 45 chapters it gives a complete exposition of the book of Revelation and the prophetical parts of Daniel and other books. Sane, sensible, convincing and absolutely free of sensational speculation. Author: same as above title **$4.95**

Dake's Annotated Reference Bible — Today's time-saver for today's busy people. Unique 4-column arrangement with 2 of King James text and 2 of notes by Finis J. Dake. Finger-tip fact-finder on any Bible question. What is needed from about 20 other books—in the one handy volume.

▶ *A half-million cross-references throughout 35,000 notes!*

| Regular edition $21.50 | Deluxe edition $29.50 | New Testament $7.95 |

Dake Bible Sales, Inc.   Station A   Box 11110   Atlanta, Ga. 30310   Tel. 404 755-0317

CBA Booth Advertisement

So, in 1963, Dake was off and running with his Bible in hand. He was charging the Devil's kingdom with the truth of God's Word. It was a small company, new and fledgling, but filled with hope and optimism, and a faith that God would always provide for the spreading of His Word. The foundation was laid and Dake's work was clearly cut out for him. He had his vision and his dreams, and together with God's will for his life, he must not allow himself to fail!

Goodbye Mr. Carroll

In 1963, things were going well for the Dakes and Dake Bible Sales. However, things were not going well for Mr. Carroll. An unknown financial problem surfaced during this time.

Financial Problems

It seems that Mr. Carroll's accountant had been dipping into the funds.

A discrepancy of around $300,000.00[132] was discovered. This brought about drastic consequences for Mr. Carroll and his business, Carroll Baking Company. He found himself with no options left but to sell the company.

With the sale of the company, the sponsorship of the radio program by the Dutch Oven Bakeries would no longer be possible. So in 1963, Dake aired his last radio program and ended his fifteen years of radio ministry in Atlanta.

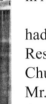

In addition, Mr. Carroll's accountant had also been keeping the books for Bible Research Foundation and the New Testament Church. Money was missing there as well. Mr. Carroll reluctantly faced the reality that he would no longer be able to help the church with one–half of Dake's salary. And sadly, he would have to sell the very building the church was meeting in on 669 West Peachtree Street.

For whatever reason, Mr. Carroll did not prosecute, but made the decision to leave Atlanta and move to Florida. Over the years

Selling the Dake Bible

however, he would remain a close friend of the Dakes and they would always be thankful for God bringing them together for the fifteen years that they shared in ministry.

New Testament Church Moves

The New Testament Church building was sold to "The Abby" restaurant, which is still located in Atlanta to this day, but not in the same location. Several years later "The Abby" would sell to "BellSouth."

New Testament Church Moves Without Dake

Even though the church building was sold, the New Testament Church would not shut down. It would simply move south, to a new location at 452 Springside Drive, which was about nine miles away. However, Dake would not move with it. With the success of Dake Bible Sales, Dake felt he needed to devote more of his time to his publishing company. Dake

---

[132] Or about $1,832,406.00 in year 2005 dollars.

did not move with New Testament Church and Rev. William Talmadge Smallwood became its new pastor.

Dake began to attend Faith Memorial Assembly of God in Atlanta, which was pastored by Ralph Byrd at the time. Dake would no longer be a pastor, however, the leadership at Faith Memorial would not let a talent such as Finis J. Dake go unused.

For years, when he was in town and not out on a meeting, he would teach the adult Sunday School class. Also ministering on Sunday nights for several years at Pastor Mayo's Assembly of God church, Dake would be quite busy for some time to come.

CHAPTER THIRTY-TWO

THE ACCIDENT

NO CHURCH, NO MR. CARROLL

Dake was now starting a new chapter in his life. He was no longer a pastor and was not confined by pastoral duties. Mr. Carroll was no longer part of the decision–making, nor was he there to assist Dake. He had completed his Bible notes, and was now printing the *Dake Annotated Reference Bible* on his own, through Dake Bible Sales. Now, Dake would give full concentration on getting his Bible out to the world.

ZONDERVAN EXPANDED CONCORDANCE

When Dake agreed with Zondervan for the publishing of his 1961 edition of the *Dake Annotated Reference Bible*, he also agreed to do a special project for them. Zondervan wanted a King James Version concordance that also incorporated seven other versions throughout the book. Zondervan had been so impressed with Dake's knowledge of the Scriptures that they felt he was the only person who could complete such a task.

The book was an unusual concordance. It was to include all the words from the *Authorized King James Version* together with key words from the following modern translations: *The Amplified Bible,*[133] *The Berkeley Version of the Bible,*[134] *The New Testament in Modern English* by J. B. Phillips,[135] *The Revised Standard Version,*[136] *The New English Bible,*[137] *The English Revised,*[138] and the new words from the

[133] Zondervan Publishing House. *The Amplified New Testament.* Copyright 1954 and 1958 by the Lockman Foundation. *The Amplified Bible.* Old Testament, Copyright 1962, 1964 and 1965 by Zondervan Publishing House.

[134] Zondervan Publishing House. *The Holy Bible, The Berkeley Version in Modern English* by Gerrit Verkuyl. Copyright 1959 by Zondervan Publishing House.

[135] The Macmillan Company. *The New Testament in Modern English.* Copyright 1958, 1959, 1960 by J. B. Phillips.

[136] *The Revised Standard Version of the Bible.* Copyright 1952 by The Division of Christian Education, National Council of Churches of Christ in the United States of America.

[137] Oxford University Press and Cambridge University Press. *The New English Bible: New Testament.* Copyright 1961 by The Delegates of the Oxford University Press and The Syndics of the Cambridge University Press.

[138] Thomas Nelson. *The English Revised* also called the *American Standard Version.* Copyright 1901 by Thomas Nelson.

New Scofield Reference Bible.[139] It would take years to complete.

It was in the first part of February, 1963, that Zondervan gave Dake the go–ahead on the project. Dake, who would be paid by the hour, felt that he could dedicate 25 hours a week to this concordance. Each month he would add up his hours and submit them to Zondervan for payment.

> *"All man's needs are met by the Bible."*
>
> *Finis Dake*

The concordance was a very long project. In reality, he worked as hard on the concordance as he had worked on his Bible. Each day he would head into his office to work on the concordance, wearing a white shirt with no tie. He cared very little about his clothes, and even when he did wear a suit and tie, the tie was usually over twenty years old! But his five years of effort paid off. In 1967, Dake completed his work.

Zondervan chose Dr. Charles W. Conn[140] to write the forward to what was finally named: *The Zondervan Expanded Concordance.*

FOREWORD

One of the blessings of our day is the great interest in modern speech translations of the Bible. There is probably a greater wealth of modern translations today than at any time in Christian history. The availability of these translations, however, has created some confusion in the mind of the Bible student, especially in an effort to remember just which translation gives a particularly helpful rendition of some specific passage. The *Zondervan Expanded Concordance* will, therefore, render a great and much–needed service to the Bible student. Its need is so obvious that I have long wished for such a concordance. It goes without saying then that I am delighted that Zondervan has issued such a work. The work is clearly arranged, which in itself is a significant achievement.

---

[139] Oxford University Press. *The New Scofield Reference Bible.* Copyright 1967 by Oxford University Press, Inc.

[140] Charles William Conn. Born in Atlanta, Georgia, in 1920. Author, editor, educator, serving as general overseer of the Church of God, Cleveland, Tennessee, as well as president of Lee College.

I commend Zondervan for the vision of bringing out this work, and I commend the concordance to all serious students of God's Word.

DR. CHARLES W. CONN
General Overseer, Church of God

HEADED TO PREACH A CAMP MEETING

It was a morning in the first week of July, 1964. At this time, Dake was 62 and Dorothy was 61. In the morning they had risen from bed, dressed, and eaten their breakfast. They got in their car and started out on the 63 mile trip toward Gainesville, Georgia. Dake was to be the morning teacher in a camp meeting service there.

They were making this trip in a 1961 full–sized Cadillac, which Mr. Carroll had driven for about a year and then given to the Dakes. Their last vehicle had been a 1948 Mercury and before that a 1939 Chevrolet. This Cadillac was one of the nicest automobiles they had ever owned.

It was a rainy morning and, as usual, Dake was doing the driving. Dorothy had a license, but had not made a practice of driving since 1948. She simply did not like the styling of the newer model cars. She complained that with the automobiles' new wide styling, she just could not seem to keep them pointed in the right direction!

They had driven about 38 miles from their home on 2232 Belvedere Avenue. They were traveling on highway 317 with only about 25 miles to go before reaching their destination in Gainesville.

"I have found this out—that it pays to trust God."

Finis Dake

AND THEN IT HAPPENED

It was at this point in their trip that an accident took place. Dake collided with a pickup truck that was being driven by an elderly man. In the hospital, a few days later, the man died.

Dake's Cadillac was a total loss. Both Dorothy and Dake were injured. They were both taken to the South Fulton Hospital on Cleveland Avenue, in East Point, Georgia, which was about 4 miles away from their home on 2232 Belvedere Avenue.

At the hospital, it was discovered that Dake was badly bruised and had suffered a crushed and shattered kneecap on his right leg, as well as loosing several teeth. The kneecap was so badly damaged that Dake underwent surgery to remove it. He was then placed in a cast, which completely immobilized his leg for the next five weeks. He would be allowed to go home in about three weeks, at the end of July.

DAKE AND DOROTHY HOSPITALIZED

While in the hospital Dake wrote in a letter:

> Daughter Finette is typing this for me from the hospital. Mrs. Dake and I are both coming along as well as could be expected. She, of course, will have a longer stay here than I. It is expected that my cast will come off in another two weeks. I am already able to sit up some and my eyes are gradually regaining strength. I am hoping that before many days I will be able to sit up long enough to resume a little work now and again.

Dorothy's condition was much worse than Dake's. She had lost several of her front teeth, which would require dental surgery. In the accident, she had been thrown from the car and suffered a broken pelvis and hip socket. The cartilage in her hip had been destroyed. During her stay of almost six weeks in the hospital, she was in traction most of the time. It would be the middle of August before she would return home.

"Every kind of sin, pain, sickness, failure, and need was fully met by Christ on the cross."

Finis Dake

Dorothy suffered terribly from her hip injury. There was a possibility of hip replacement surgery, which may have relieved some of her pain. However, since her stay in the hospital at the loss of her fourth child Steven Arthur, where she almost bled to death, she was not comfortable with having surgery.

BACK HOME, BUT STILL RECOVERING

After returning home—Dake at the end of July and Dorothy the third week in August—both Dake and Dorothy were confined to bed. On Monday, September 7, 1964 Dorothy wrote in a letter:

> You have probably heard that the both of us were in a wreck two months ago. I spent nearly six weeks in the

hospital, most of it in traction for broken pelvis and hip socket. Finis spent three or four weeks there with leg in cast, after a crushed knee cap was removed.

I still face dental surgery because of front teeth knocked out. We lie at home now, in bed side by side, and he is able to be up some on crutches. I can only sit on the side of the bed at intervals. (This is only the second letter I have typed.) I will be X–rayed in another week to see if the socket is strong enough by then to hold up under my weight.

By November of 1964, both of the Dakes had greatly improved, however, some of the injuries that had been sustained would be with them for a quite a while. Dake would walk with the aid of crutches for several months. Dorothy, however, would sit in a wheel chair for the rest of her life. She could walk with the aid of crutches, but with no cartilage in her hip, the pain was excruciating, and arthritis had set in.

Four Months Later

On November 7, 1964, Dorothy closed a letter with a report of their present physical condition. She wrote:

We are, indeed, fortunate to be alive, the driver of the other car (a truck) having died in a few days. And, of course, we are thankful to the Lord, and we also say "thanks" to our many friends who continually remember us in prayer.

We are both up from the bed but I get around a lot more slowly than Finis does. He now hobbles about without crutches and also spends much of the day at the desk. I hadn't looked forward to arthritis taking hold of my previously bedfast joints, so pain was a surprise and disappointment to me, when I arose to try out my crutches a month ago. I recalled the doctor telling me I would be pretty crippled up and very stiff for about six months, but somehow the message didn't soak in until I took to the crutches.

However, there are many praying with me and I do believe that I see little changes for the better now and again. The

Lord can shorten that predicted six month period for me and I want you to pray that He will.

THE SPIRIT IS WILLING THE FLESH IS WEAK

The Dakes were both strong in spirit and determined not to let the physical problems they had incurred in the accident stop their ministry. Eventually, Dake went back to work at Dake Bible Sales and by September of 1965 he was back full-time, and he resumed his traveling ministry which would continue for years to come. Dorothy also, in spite of her pain, continued her work running Dake Bible Sales, spending most of her time behind her desk sitting in her wheel chair.

> *"The way to get power to heal self and others is by believing in Christ according to the Gospel."*
>
> *Finis Dake*

During their recuperation, and indeed over the difficult years that would follow, they always left open the possibility of a complete healing for Dorothy, brought about by a miracle from God. In 1971 Dorothy wrote:

> I myself am crutch–bound in the office and go out only rarely, and then by wheelchair whenever my husband is here to take me out for the recreation of a cafeteria meal and a roll through the dime store of an area mall (to see what the ladies are finding "new" to buy these days).
>
> Finis, Sr. and I were in an auto wreck nearly seven years ago which resulted in this handicap, but I tell the children we can thank the Lord it was my legs instead of my head, for this leaves me to do a great deal of the marketing so needed at present. I work a full day, with others in the office (at age nearly sixty–eight) and thank the Lord for being so good to me.
>
> Healing is not something outside the realm of possibility, I know, and I have not ruled out the possibility of a miracle for myself, sometime. It can easily happen when "faith as a grain of mustard seed" is present.

CHAPTER THIRTY–THREE

THE SEVENTIES

DAKE GETS A NEW HOME

It was in 1971 that Dake moved the locations of both his home and Dake Bible Sales. He had found forty acres for sale in the town of Lawrenceville, located about forty miles to the north of his present home in Atlanta. The property was located on 764 Martins Chapel Road.

The property was for sale for $30,000.00.[141] He believed that he could sell his present home on 2232 Belvedere Avenue and pay cash for the land. That took care of the land, but where would he live? A 100 year-old house was located on the property; needless to say, it wasn't in very good condition.

Dake decided that he would tear down the old house and build a new one. In fact, not only would he build a new home, he would also build Dake Bible Sales and combine the two. As it would eventually work out, the facility would mostly house Dake Bible Sales, with living quarters in the end of the building for Dake and Dorothy.

THE FAMILY LENDS A HELPING HAND

Annabeth and her husband, David Germaine, would play a very important part in helping Dake with his new building project. Annabeth remembers that she and her dad pulled every nail out of every board of the old house and completely disassembled it. Some of the materials that were salvaged would be used in the construction of Dake Bible Sales. On the weekends, David and other family members would lend a helping hand.

> *"God is the true source of help."*
>
> *Finis Dake*

Together, they dug by hand the footing of the building and poured the foundation. With the aid of Dake's nephew, Brice Durbin, they erected the framing and did most of the carpentry work. Of course, they were able to do all of the painting as well. The tasks they were not able to do themselves had to be hired out.

As the old building was being torn down and the new one erected, they needed a place to live. They brought out a forty–foot trailer and lived in it during the construction.

---

[141] Or about $142,717.00 in year 2005 dollars.

FINALLY FINISHED

It took a while, but the building was finally completed. Dake had managed to pay for it as it was built. Dorothy was always opposed to borrowing money, so no loan was secured on the property. However, the help of a small loan that was available to them on their life insurance policy was needed to finish the building.

In 1972 the Dakes moved both Dake Bible Sales and their home to its new location in Lawrenceville.

THE SEVENTY'S A TIME OF MINISTRY

For Dake and his Dake Bible Sales company, the 1970's was a time of growth and travel. He and Dorothy would attend the Lawrenceville Church of God. Dake himself would teach the adult Sunday School class for most of the seventies.

"If God has promised something, then it is already His will or He would not have made the promise."

Finis Dake

When Dake wasn't in the office helping Dorothy run Dake Bible Sales, he was on the road. From coast to coast he would travel, teaching from meeting to meeting and spending a good portion of his time promoting his Bible.

DAKE PREACHES FOR ANYBODY ANYWHERE

Even in his seventies—being born in 1902—and officially in his retirement years, Dake continued his preaching and teaching ministry. He ministered in churches, auditoriums, colleges, convention centers, camp meetings, tent meetings and literally anywhere an open door was available.

As he had done all of his life, he preached in the Assembly of God, Baptist, Foursquare, Methodist, Church of God, Presbyterian and just about every denomination one could think of. Throughout his lifetime Dake's ministry was truly inter–denominational.

In addition to the many ministry opportunities Dake fulfilled in the seventies, there are several that stand out and are worth mentioning here.

SEVERAL HIGHLIGHTS

Dake loved Israel and, having been there several times, he enjoyed talking about the land where Jesus walked. On one occasion he led a tour group to the Holy Land, working with the Ford Philpot Evangelistic Association.

In 1973 he ministered at Melodyland Christian Center in Anaheim, California with Pastor Ralph Wilkerson, as part of their *Word At Work* week. There he ministered along side of Corrie Ten Boom, Dr. J. Rodman Williams, David Du Plesis, Dick Mills, Dave Hunt, Larry Christenson, and Ralph Wilkerson.

He also ministered at the 1973 World Convention in New York, which was sponsored by the Full Gospel Businessmen's Fellowship International. Here he ministered with many of his ministry friends, men and women of faith such as: Demos Shakarian, Rex Humbard, Oral Roberts and Kathryn Kuhlman.

In 1974 he conducted a School of Evangelism meeting with Lester Sumrall in South Bend, Indiana. In fact, beginning in 1967 and through-out the seventies, Dake was a regular guest speaker at South Bend on an annual basis.

Of course, he would also attend the annual CBA conventions. Here people of all faiths would crowd around the Dake booth to speak to and hear the man known as "The Walking Bible."

THE PTL CLUB

A highpoint of his ministry came in the mid–seventies. Christian television in America was beginning to take hold. A young man in Charlotte, North Carolina, was taking the Christian world by storm. Jim Bakker had managed to build one of the most popular vacation destinations in America—second only to Disney World!

Bakker's flagship television program was called the PTL Club.[142] It was in April of 1976 that Dake appeared on the PTL program. This is one of the few pieces of video footage that exist of Dake ministering the Word of God and displaying his wonderful "gift of Scriptures" in action.

Needless to say, Dake was an instant hit as he quoted Scripture after Scripture, answering the many Bible questions that were called in. In total, Dake would appear on PTL three times. In October, he would return to teach a week–long Bible Seminar.

---

[142] The PTL Club was located in Fort Mill, South Carolina. It was very successful in televangelism during the seventies and eighties. PTL stood for "Praise The Lord" and "People That Love." Jim Bakker and his wife, Tammy Faye, used the program to develop a Pentecostal–oriented resort, theme park, shopping mall, cable network, and entertainment center called Heritage USA. By the mid–eighties it drew more than five million visitors a year.

DOROTHY IS STILL WRITING

While Dake was busy with his traveling ministry, Dorothy was not idle. Dorothy—still confined to her wheelchair—was running Dake Bible Sales. She enjoyed her work and did not let her disability slow her down. She also found time to do more writing.

When one is confined to their home and wheelchair–bound, you have a lot of time to think. Time to think and ponder God's Word. During her quiet times with the Lord she would write down her thoughts. One such writing was called: Meditation—alone with your thoughts.

MEDITATION—ALONE WITH YOUR THOUGHTS

By Dorothy Dobbins Dake

Psalm 19:14—Let the words of my mouth, and the meditation of my heart, be acceptable in thy sight, O LORD, my strength, and my redeemer.

To be alone with your thoughts is not to be despised or rejected. But you must learn to be the master of those thoughts; do not let them master you.

Sift the memories as they come through to you and permit only the high, the lofty, and the inspiring ones to linger in your mind or even cross the threshold of your heart.

Sweep every corner of your soul clean before you make exit from the room where meditation has swayed you by her influence for one shortened hour. And, should meditation sway you sometime in the hammock of her garden, then be sure that nothing remains but the fragrance of sweet flowers as a result of your quiet thought.

Meditation is a book. You may open it and close it as you will. Take advantage of the opportunity on a day which the world describes as gray and dull. Open your book and let its pages first solemnize your emotions.

Then, while your face is sober and maybe while a tear is tracing its course downward, look at the pages again which record that heartache and see if you have memorized the lessons of that chapter.

And then, turn promptly to another chapter with dog–eared pages where happy experiences are written. Rejoice over them; let the laughter of gladness ripple freely. Forget not to give thanks for them and then, close the book for the day.

Open it again tomorrow and proceed in the same manner. Take two such chapters daily—the bitter and the sweet. They will cause the fruit of character to ripen within your soul.

"Do not try to make the Bible conform to your ideas. Always reconcile your ideas to the Bible."

Finis Dake

Meditation is a cup, refilled for those who care to sip its contents. Some refuse and therefore the finer traits of manhood and womanhood are missing.

The cups of meditation are not always as bitter as the cups of actual experience. At least we need not drink them to the dregs as in real life. A few sips from the top regularly taken, can cure us of faults we possess. Remembering past sowings and reapings can curb us in the future.

Hast thou had sorrow? Then perhaps it was God's rod. Pass under it like a child and be sure that afterward you recall the lesson as often as the whipping. Remembering the sad happenings of life too often or too long at a time is not profitable, but a little each day should do the work of a medicine, helping to throw off the poisons of present temptation.

Prescribe only so much for yourself, like a faithful doctor, that you may obtain the good there from, and when that amount is taken, brush your tears away and thank God for His love. Whom He loves, He chastens.

Hast thou had joy altogether? Then you have been especially favored by the Almighty. You are fortunate above the average. Heaven is usually reached partly down a thorny path. But, if you have never suffered, and grief wrapped in her gray–tones of mourning attire has never rapped at your door, then you have reason for praise without ceasing.

Keep watch that pride does not seize the throne of your thinking and cause you to blame the blighted. The common sort of humanity usually passes through flames of affliction to hills of accomplishment. Keep yourself humble and thankful and pray for those who know so little of the coveted path you travel.

> "I'm not going to talk about preachers. They are good fellows. I like them."
>
> Finis Dake

Meditation is a teacher. Let her instruct you in righteousness. Let her show you the failures of the past from time to time and point out to you the beautiful possibility of improvement. This is the quickest way to maturity and the fastest route to the kind of perfection required of us in this life.

And so, make meditation your daily hidden manna.

A Surprise Visit

It was also in the late seventies that Dake received a surprise visit. Evangelist Billy Graham had been to India to hold a crusade and conference for ministers. On his way back from this meeting he stopped in at Dake Bible Sales. He wanted to meet this man of the Word that people simply called "Dake."

They had a wonderful meeting as they talked about the Bible. They rejoiced in what both ministers had been able to accomplish through their respective ministries. With a type of prayer, the visit came to an end.

Dake's Days Are Numbered

In 1978 Dake would hold one of his last public meetings, preaching at the Congregational Holiness Church Camp Meeting in Union Grove, Georgia. As he and the family would soon discover, Dake had a disease that would take him from this world.

CHAPTER THIRTY–FOUR

THE MAN OF THE WORD GOES HOME

In the late Seventies, as Dake was enjoying his ministry across the United States and his work at Dake Bible Sales, things began to change for him in the area of his health. Until this time, except for the accident in 1964, he had enjoyed good heath. It was in 1977 that he began to notice changes.

As he was teaching Sunday School at the Lawrenceville Church of God, he noticed that from time to time he would begin to slur his words. This was something he had never done before. As a speaker, he was very articulate and definitive in his pronunciation of words.

> *"God's plan is a mutual one for the best and highest good of all creation."*
>
> *Finis Dake*

At first the family thought that maybe he had had a small stroke of some sort. With that, they suggested he see his family doctor, Dr. Thomas Hamilton, which he did. His family doctor sent him to a specialist at North Georgia Neurology.

After a thorough exam, the specialist diagnosed Dake's condition as Parkinson's disease. At this time Dake was seventy–six years of age.

PARKINSON'S DISEASE

The *Merck Manual of Medical Information*[143] gives the following information on Parkinson's Disease:

> Parkinson's Disease is a slowly progressive, degenerative disorder of the nervous system. Parkinson's disease has several distinguishing characteristics: tremor (shaking) when at rest, sluggish initiation of movements, and muscle rigidity. It is the fourth most common neurodegenerative disease of the elderly.
>
> Its symptoms and signs include: Tremors of the hand. The tremor is maximal at rest, diminishes during movement, and is absent during sleep; it is enhanced by emotional

---

[143] *The Merck Manual of Medical Information,* published by Merck Research Laboratories, Whitehouse Station: N.J. 1997, page 315. Also see: http://www.merck.com

tension or fatigue. Usually, the hands, arms, and legs are most affected, in that order. Jaw, tongue, forehead, and eyelids may also be affected, but the voice escapes the tremor.

In many patients, only rigidity occurs; tremor is absent. Rigidity progresses, and movement becomes slow, decreased, and difficult to initiate. Rigidity may contribute to muscular aches and sensations of fatigue. The face becomes mask–like, with mouth open and diminished blinking, which may be confused with depression. The posture becomes stooped. Patients find it difficult to start walking; the gait becomes shuffling with short steps, and the arms are held flexed to the waist and do not swing with the stride. Steps may inadvertently quicken, and the patient may break into a run to keep from falling. The tendency to fall forward or backward when the center of gravity is displaced results from loss of postural reflexes. Speech becomes hypophonic, with a characteristic monotonous, stuttering. Hypokinesia and impaired control of distal musculature results in micrographia and increasing difficulty with activities of daily living. Dementia affects about 50% of patients, and depression is common.

Dake Slows Down

From this time on, Dake really slowed down. He was almost seventy–six at the time and would hold no more public meetings. He would also hand his Sunday School class over to someone else a bit younger.

Still, his life was Dake Bible Sales. Annabeth and her husband Dave, Finette and Finis Jr. and a few other employees were now handling most of the work, but Dake and Dorothy still had their hearts involved in the business, even if their bodies were now indicating that it was time to rest.

Slowed Down But Still Working

With a love that only family members can understand, every day one of the three children would see to it that Dake and Dorothy were dressed and taken to the office.

Once there, from her wheel chair, Dorothy would make a few phone calls and look over the accounts and do a work here and there. Dake may even spend a little time writing and, on occasion, speak with someone by phone—usually while looking out the window and viewing the countryside. But, as the next couple of years came and went, their real involvement in the business would drop steadily. However, they would always want to stay at work until the office closed, just like everyone else.

A Visit From An Old Friend

It was during this time that his old friend, Lester Sumrall, paid him a visit.

> After Dake's retirement to his home in Georgia, I went to visit him several times . . . The last time I visited Dake and his wife, it was very sad . . . She had arthritis, and he had suffered from Parkinson's and could not speak clearly.
>
> As he showed me around the great printing room where thousands of Bibles were continuously being shipped out, tears ran down his face as he reminisced about our friendship . . . .
>
> He smiled and cried and held on to me, this man with the high forehead and a face like a prince. I recognized him for the mighty giant he was mentally and spiritually. He will long be remembered as a man of the Book.[144]

"The secret of knowing truth is to find out what God says and then believe it."

Finis Dake

A Decline In Health

Over the next couple of years, the health of Dake and Dorothy began to decline more rapidly. Dake began to slur his words even more. His hands began to tremble just a bit—but not a great deal—and he walked bent forward, with a shuffle. He had trouble lifting his feet and his muscles became stiff. At the office each day, as well as at their home, lovingly, the children would massage his muscles trying to ease the stiffness that was setting in.

---

[144] *Pioneers of Faith*, by Dr. Lester Sumrall. Harrison House, Tulsa, Oklahoma, Page 72.

THE CHILDREN HELP BEAR THE LOAD

The children cared for their parents, not only at the office, but at their home as well. In fact, during the last five years of their lives, they lived in an apartment that was added on to Dave and Annabeth's house. When their health first began to decline, they installed a doorbell in their apartment beside their bed. With just a tap of the bell, one of the children would quickly be by their side to help in whatever way they were needed.

Annabeth would prepare their supper every day and see to it that they made it to bed. Then, at about 10:00 p.m., Finnette would come over and spend the night with them and then get up early the next morning and prepare their breakfast. After breakfast she, or some of the grandchildren, would take them to the office.

"If you have faith you have the answer."

Finis Dake

At the office all three children would usually be around to keep an eye on them and see to it that they took their medicine. Dake was not accustomed to taking medication however. So the children, as advised by the doctors, had the chore of trying to get him to take his medicine. This usually brought about a bit of tension, to say the least. But it was nothing that lasted, for both the children and Dake knew that it was for the best.

On the weekends the Dakes wanted to stay in their own apartment so, sacrificially, the children took turns caring for them. Annabeth would stay with them one weekend and Finette another. Finis Jr. helped out by bringing meals.

CANCER

Dorothy, whose primary concern had been her hip and the arthritis that came with the accident, seemed to be doing a bit better than Dake in her old age. However, she did face a very real health crisis.

It was around November of 1986 that she began to have internal bleeding. Her family doctor, Dr. Hamilton, who even in 1986 still made house calls, examined her and wanted to do additional testing in the hospital. She was admitted, the tests were run, and the results came back—it was cancer of the bladder.

THE EFFECTUAL PRAYER OF A RIGHTEOUS MAN

On a Monday evening, Dorothy's son–in–law Dave Germaine, who was very close to his mother–in–law, was going to the hospital to visit

Dorothy. On his way, he stopped by a local church that he knew was meeting for prayer. He stopped in and asked for prayer for his mother–in–law. The minister and Dave prayed together for Dorothy's healing.

When he got to the hospital, he told Dorothy of their prayer and that they were believing God for her healing. Dorothy's faith was lifted and she, along with the rest of her family, claimed her healing.

DOROTHY SAYS I'M HEALED

With this, she told her doctor she was healed. Dr. Hamilton was a good man and knew that the Dakes believed in the power of answered prayer. Still, as a good physician, he and the specialist felt another test was in order. This, however, was not something with which Dorothy was comfortable.

Still, the doctor was able to persuade her to stay for some additional tests—with one condition. He himself would have to pay for the test! He agreed and ran the test. Amazingly, the test results came back and there was no sign of cancer of any kind! Dorothy never had any more internal bleeding.

DOROTHY GOES HOME

Dorothy went home and had a wonderful Christmas with her family as they all thanked God for his wonderful works.

Still, Dorothy had other health problems and she was at this time about eighty–three years of age. Although she returned to her work at Dake Bible Sales on a daily basis, her home–going would not be far away.

It was a Thursday in February when Dorothy began to have problems breathing. Annabeth, who was with her on that day, noticed it and became concerned. She called her husband, asking him what she ought to do. Dave told her to call 911. While Annabeth and Dave were speaking, Dorothy went home to be with the Lord.

DAKE'S HEART IS BROKEN

Her beloved husband was by her side, sitting at the foot of the bed. Seeing his Dorothy slip away, his eyes filled with tears as he simply bowed his head and cried. It was Thursday, February 19, 1987.

Even though the family knew Dorothy was now with her Lord in Heaven, everyone was saddened that she was no longer around. But none quite so much as Dake himself. From this time on, he was much more quite than he had ever been. It seemed his mind was always far away. Even with all of his family gathering around him more than ever, he grew more and more lonesome. He was lost without Dorothy by his side. As the days rolled on all he ever talked about was going to Heaven to join her.

> *"Do not fail God, and He will not fail you."*
>
> *Finis Dake*

Even though Dake's broken heart kept on beating, without his Dorothy, his health began to fail quickly. He had developed a fever that would not break and on May 19, 1987, he entered the hospital, which would become a three–week stay. He was simply exhausted, broken–hearted, and just plain tired of living.

About the second week in June, he was released and came home. There the family cared for him, as he slept on an air mattress to help him with the pain. During this time, he was in and out of consciousness. The family would have to feed him through a feeding tube. He complained so much about the tube that the family agreed to have the tube removed.

MORE LOVE SHOWN BY THE CHILDREN

Once again, the love of the children for their Dad was evident. Each of the children would take turns feeding him. Tomato juice, soft foods, and other liquids became his diet—sometimes, he even ate a little ice cream.

As it worked out, Finette was able to stay with their Dad during the day as the other children continued to run the business. They were always just a phone call away however. About two weeks before his home–going, Dake began to talk a little more.

He would tell Finette how he missed their Mom and, when the time came, to let him "go beyond the grave." Finette promised that when the Lord called, she would not intervene.

THE GIFTS OF THE SPIRIT

It is interesting to note that even during these late days of his life he was still thinking about the power of God and the gifts of the spirit. He told Finette that one day: "somebody is just going to reach out there and get them," referring to the Holy Spirit gifts.

Indeed, Heaven began to grow mighty close for Dake. Just a few days before his home–going he told the children that there was a chariot parked outside. He would ask: "Do you see it? There it is right out there."

A Good Day With His Grandchildren

Over the next couple of weeks, Dake would not get any better, rather, he would grow worse. But there were a few light days here and there.

On one Saturday in late June, Dake was fully awake and he asked for the grandchildren. Finette, excited over her Dad's sudden energy, said she would get them at once.

She called the grandchildren and they all gathered around their Papa. For the next two hours they laughed and talked together until Dake became tired. The grandchildren hugged their Papa goodbye and left to let him rest.

Home At Last

With a happy kind of tiredness, Dake closed his eyes to take a nap. He would never open them again. Just a few days later on Tuesday, July 7, 1987, Dake joined his beloved Dorothy and entered into the joys of the Lord. He was eighty–four years of age.

CHAPTER THIRTY–FIVE

CONCLUSION

In 1987, Finis J. Dake went home to be with the Lord, but the Bible and the ministry that he left continue to this day. Dake Bible Sales changed it's name in the early nineties to Dake Publishing, Inc.

With the change of name, however, there was no change in Dake's original vision—to make the Bible plain and simple, and get the Word out to as many as possible. For years to come, Dake Publishing will continue to make a lasting impact on our generation for the cause of Christ.

Indeed, while Dake has gone on to his reward, his writings, *yet speaketh.*[145]

FOR A LIFETIME DAKE ALWAYS WANTED MORE

In closing this book, what thoughts should be left in the minds and hearts of the reader? As I have pondered this question for many days—even years—I am left with a startling conclusion. Dake was a man who did not fully know the gift that he had. I understand that may seem strange, but after studying his writings and his life for more than thirty years, that is my conclusion.

You see, Dake was changed to his very core when, as a classic Pentecostal, he was exposed to the powerful ministry of Alexander Dowie in Zion, Illinois. After the 1930's, his life was never the same. It was then that he developed a hunger for God and His power as he had never had before.

"All things can be ours for the asking if we have faith and doubt not."

Finis Dake

Yet Dake's hunger for a powerful move of God was always offset by his love for the Scriptures, and his drive to spend thousands upon thousands of hours in its pages. While he knew his calling to make plain and simple the Word of God, he also struggled with a desire to fast and pray until all the gifts of the Spirit were manifest in his life. And, for what he thought was a lack of giftedness in his life, he felt condemned.

---

[145] Hebrews 11:4—By faith Abel offered unto God a more excellent sacrifice than Cain, by which he obtained witness that he was righteous, God testifying of his gifts: and by it he being dead yet speaketh.

In the latter part of his life, he shared in the pulpit from the depths of his heart concerning what he thought to be his shortcomings in life:

I HAVE BEEN HUNGRY FOR GOD

From that day until now, 1935, periodically I have been hungry for God, running around here and there, not giving time to prayer and fasting as I should.

I have neglected the most important thing in life and ministry, and that is giving myself continually to the Word of God and prayer. God has dealt with me again and again—on several occasions—and it seems He has almost killed me, trying to drive me into a place of prayer.

It's a place where I will seek his face more and more. Calamity after calamity has come to my life. I'd get cold and indifferent. I'd get hard. I tell you this after many years of experience in God.

I KNOW WHAT IT IS TO BE FILLED WITH THE SPIRIT

I know what it is to be filled with God. I know what it is to have the Holy Spirit speak out of my innermost being and have rivers of living water flow from me. I know what it is to be lost in the Spirit and get in that spiritual realm where everything is heavenly.

In June, a man came to me and said: "I'm going to support you for three months, to do nothing but pray and fast until you get all these things you've been preaching about. You've been wanting to pray. You've been wanting someone to support you while you pray. I'm going to do it. I want you to pray. You've been teaching these things. You've been preaching this baptism in the Spirit—healing for the body and all these wonderful things. Now I want you to get these things!" Well, it means more than that—just telling a fellow to get something from God.

If any one of you will pray through until you get these things I've been teaching about, I'll support you as long as is necessary, just so long as you get these things from God.

We need men and women that will get serious before God and receive these blessings.

I HAVE BEEN TEACHING ALOT OF BIG THINGS

I've been teaching a lot of big and great things. To preach those things and to be told to get those things, that's all right, all well and good. But getting those things, well that's another proposition.

"The believer is unlimited if he will exercise unlimited faith."

Finis Dake

After thirty years or more of preaching the Gospel all over the country, I have had brethren to fight me all over the country, because they don't believe what I taught.

They have classed me as the very Devil himself. Attempted to throw me out of their churches, because they don't believe what I teach. Try to hinder your ministry in every quarter, and talk about you as a false prophet.

I've had that for a good many years now. More brethren have fought me than cooperated with me. I have had argument after argument, arguing that the Bible means exactly what it says.

DOING THE WORKS OF CHRIST

For example, I have been teaching that "he that believeth on me, the works that I do shall he do also, and greater works than these shall he do because I go to my father." I have had many preachers fight me on this by the hour.

I was told that the Scripture must be translated wrong or it must have been only for the early church. I have maintained through the years that:

whether I have it or not . . .
whether any preacher has it or not . . .
that if the Bible declares it . . .
then it is so.

Anyone reading this portion of Dake's sermon, and hearing his words, as they flow from his heart, cannot help but hear the words of an honest man. We hear the words of a man who felt that he never really acquired the "more" that God had for him.

"How much of the Old and New Testament can you quote? I'm not quoting any of the Old Testament. . . . I know John 3:16 and I can brag about that anytime I want to."

Finis Dake

Dake's words remind me of another man's words—a man who felt much the same at the end of his journey. In a letter to Charles Wesley dated January 5, 1763, John Fletcher (1729–1785) wrote:

What I want is the light and mighty power of the Spirit of God. As to my parish, we are just where we were: we look for our Pentecost, but we do not pray sufficiently to obtain it.[146]

DAKE HAD A WONDERFUL GIFT FROM GOD

It is not my intention to dampen the zeal or heart's cry of anyone who seeks God, especially the man whom I have come to love over the years as I have studied his writings.

So even with Dake's confession weighing heavily upon my heart, I would still contend that while he had every right to hunger after God, that he did not fully recognize the value of what God had given him.

While it is true that he never received the gifts of the Spirit to the degree to which he yearned, he did receive a wonderful gift from God—to supernaturally recall Scripture.

A PERSONAL EXPERIENCE

I have made a lifetime of the study of the history of the church and the many powerful men and women that have contributed to its growth and ministry. Yet I have never encountered such a man gifted with the "gift of Scripture" as was Finis Jennings Dake.

Many years ago, I remember visiting the office that Dake once used to prepare for his daily radio programs. I had heard Dake many times as he

---

[146] John Fletcher, vol. 2 of *The Works of the Rev. John Fletcher,* 2 cols. (London: Printed for Thomas Allman), page 513.

answered literally thousands of Bible questions, and in so doing quoting Scripture after Scripture. As I looked through his study and surveyed the books on his shelves, I noticed a set of three–ring binders, about twelve in all. On the spine of these black books was written "Radio Programs," with the number of questions in each book, such as 1– 250, 251–500 and so on.

"The reader will be astonished at some of our claims and will perhaps argue at first that such is not the teaching of the Bible, but if he will be honest and open to what the Scriptures really say, he will be convinced that these truths are plainly written in the Bible and that they are for all believers today."

Finis Dake

As I saw these books, I thought to myself, I have found a great discovery! Here in these books are thousands of Bible questions, with all the Bible answers, that Dake gave while on the radio over the years! I felt as though I had died and gone to Heaven.

So I picked up a book and sat down at Dake's desk, ready to read and learn from the wisdom of the Bible. But I was soon to be disappointed. When I opened the first book to read the questions and learn the Bible answers, I did not find any of the answers. I thought perhaps they were in one of the other books. So I picked up a second book—but there were no Bible answers, only the questions. I picked up a third book—still no Bible answers, just the questions. I went through all twelve of those books and found the same thing. No answers, only the Bible questions!

I thought to myself, "now where could Dake have stored the answers to all these thousands of Bible questions? They have to be here some-where . . ." And then it hit me. I wasn't going to find any answers to all these thousands of Bible questions. Why? Because Dake had never writ-ten them down!

Over the years of his radio ministry he had relied upon the Holy Spirit and the "gift of Scriptures" that God had given him. With this anointing, he would answer any Bible question with at least two or three verses of Scripture, complete with the Scripture reference.

And here I sat, amazed at the ministry of a man who had already gone on to his reward. Sitting in astonishment at how God could use a man in such a mighty way. In fact, I may have felt the same way Dake did, when he first learned of the ministry of Alexander Dowie in Zion, Illinois, back in the 1930's.

DAKE'S MINISTRY LIVES ON

Today, the powerful ministry of Dowie has come and gone, now only to be read about in the annuls of church history. Yet on every continent of this great big world of ours, there is no place you can go that has not been touched by the writings of Finis Dake. Dake has left us with more than wonderful memories, more than miraculous stories of what was . . .

"Don't ask me any-thing that is not a Bible question . . . I'm just a Bible man."

Finis Dake

He has left us with the knowledge of *God's Plan for Man;* He has left us with the *Bible Truths* that have been *Unmasked*; He has left us with *God's Plan of the Ages* that we can all easily see; He has left us with *Eternal Mysteries Simplified;* He has left us with the knowledge of a *Heavenly Host* that surrounds us and watches over us by day and by night; He has left us with hope of *The Rapture and the Second Coming of Christ;* He has left us with the faith that after this life there will be *Another Time, Another Place,* where we will be changed into *Another Man;* He has left us with the Word of God made simple and plain, through the pages of the *Dake Annotated Reference Bible.*

CHAPTER THIRTY–SIX

A LASTING MEMORIAL

On July 23, 1993, the Dake family, wishing to see the writings of their father preserved, made a generous donation of his life's teachings to the *Hal Bernard Dixon, Jr. Pentecostal Research Center* on the campus of Lee College, in Cleveland, Tennessee.

The Library now proudly offers its students, as well as researchers and historians around the world, the opportunity to read and learn of the ministry of Finis J. Dake.

The college officials received the Dake materials in a stately ceremony which reflected their love and appreciation of the ministry of Finis J. Dake. The official program for the acceptance ceremony read as follows:

The Hal Bernard Dixon, Jr.
Pentecostal Research
Center

The Finis Dake
Collection

July 23, 1993

FINIS JENNINGS DAKE

Finis Jennings Dake (1902–1987) has had tremendous influence upon Pentecostals, largely through the wide acceptance of *Dake's Annotated Reference Bible*. First published in 1961 (the Old and New Testaments were published together in 1963), its hallmark was (and is) Dake's commentary on the Scriptures. Not only has the Dake Bible greatly impacted Pentecostals, but it continues to be popular today.

Finis Dake's influence is not limited to his Bible, however. He authored many books and booklets, *including Revelation Expounded* or *Eternal Mysteries Simplified, God's Plan for Man,* and *Foundation Studies of Scripture* or *Dispensational Truth.* He also pastored, taught, and debated.

Since Dake's mark has been in the area of biblical interpretation, let us hear his words on the subject taken from his preface to *Revelation Expounded*: "The author works on the chief fundamental principle of Bible interpretation—THAT OF TAKING THE BIBLE LITERALLY WHEREIN IT IS AT ALL POSSIBLE. When the language of a passage cannot possibly be literal, then it is clear from the passage itself, as well as from other Scriptures, that it is figurative. It must be remembered, however, that all figurative language conveys literal truth." Again: "The author . . . decided to follow a new course of taking the Bible to be God's own Word and Revelation to men, not interpreting it but letting the Bible be its own interpreter. He found that when all passages on a subject were gathered together and harmonized that the Scripture was clear in itself without any further interpretation."

Finis Dake is honored not only for what he has accomplished, but for what continues to be accomplished through the multitudes of Pentecostals he has helped shape and teach. It is with great pleasure that today we open the Finis Dake Collection at the Hal Bernard Dixon, Jr. Pentecostal Research Center.

PROGRAM

Invocation ....David Roebuck
Pentecostal Resource Center

Opening Remarks... Vardaman W. White
Director, Hal Bernard Dixon, Jr. Pentecostal Research Center

Historical Appreciation..................................... Dr. Charles W. Conn
Church of God Historian

Personal Appreciation ....Dr. Steven J. Land
Academic Dean, Church of God School of Theology

Presentations .... Dr. Cecil B. Knight
President, Church of God School of Theology

Benediction ....Dr. Ollie J. Lee
Vice–President and Academic Dean, Lee College

*All are invited to a reception immediately following at the
Church of God School of Theology.*

THE FINIS DAKE COLLECTION

Printed Material

Pamphlets, various titles ....(20)
God's Plan for Man... (72 booklets)
God's Plan for Man... (original typed manuscripts for radio broadcasts)
Foundation Studies of Scriptures or Dispensational Truth...........(1941)
God's Plan for Man.. (one volume, 1949)
Bible Truths Unmasked ....(1950)
The Key to the World's Storehouse of Wisdom ....(1950)
Revelation Expounded...................................... (Second Edition, 1950)
Dake's Annotated Reference Bible...(1963)

Audio Cassette Tape Library

God's Plan for Man..(460 tapes)
Bible Questions and Answers ....(8 tapes)
Full Gospel Businessmen's Convention ....(1977, 4 tapes)

Audio Reel–to–Reel Library

God's Plan for Man... (38 reels)
Special Subjects.. (85 reels)

Video Tapes

The AntiChrist
The Book of Daniel

GRADUATION SERMON

THE SECOND COMING OF CHRIST

The following address was delivered by Finis Dake, one of the graduating students of Central Bible Institute, at the Commencement Exercises in Springfield, Missouri.

FALSE PREDICTIONS

In the past century there have been many days set for the coming of Christ. For example, the Millerites said Christ was coming in 1844, and Mrs. Rowen of the Reformed Adventist Church, in a recent prediction in Los Angeles, said Christ was coming on February 6 of this year. But in spite of these and many other false predictions, God's Word standeth sure. We can say emphatically, He is coming.

OLD TESTAMENT PROOF OF HIS COMING

In the Old Testament the second coming of Christ is mentioned twenty times as often as is His first coming. That is, there are twenty times as many references to His coming as a crowned king to sit upon the throne of David, bringing victory to Jerusalem, and peace upon the earth, as there are to His coming as the meek and lowly Jesus, wounded for our sins, and dying upon Calvary. This is the reason that the Jews, who had been looking for a mighty king, failed to recognize the lowly Nazarene, and still refuse to recognize Him. He did come fulfilling all the redemptive prophecies, and He is coming to fulfill all the kingly prophecies. "Unto them that look for Him shall He appear the second time without sin (apart from sin) unto salvation" (Hebrews 9:28).

> *"The rapture of the Church is also called "the coming of the Lord" but never the second coming of Christ."*
>
> *Finis Dake*

NEW TESTAMENT PROOF OF HIS COMING

In the 260 chapters of the New Testament, His coming is referred to 318 times; that is, one out of every 30 verses of the New Testament is devoted to this glorious theme. The epistles of Paul refer to water baptism only 13 times, while they refer to Christ's second coming more than 50 times. Each time you repeat the Lord's prayer, you are praying for

His coming, "Thy kingdom come" (Matthew 6:10). But can there be a kingdom without a king? The last prayer in the Bible is a great heart–cry for His coming, "Even so, come, Lord Jesus" (Revelation 22:20). The answer rings back from heaven, "Behold, I come quickly; and my reward is with me."

PROMISE OF JESUS

Jesus Himself promised that He would come, saying, "If I go (away to prepare a place for you) I will come again . . ." (John 14:3). What could be plainer? "If I go . . . I will come again . . ." (John 14:3). Did He go away? Acts 1:9 answers, "And when he had spoken these things, while they beheld, he was taken up; and a cloud received him out of their sight" (Acts 1:9). If I go away. Yes, He went away. But listen; ". . . two men stood by them in white apparel; Which also said, Ye men of Galilee, why stand ye gazing up into heaven? this same Jesus which is taken up from you into heaven, shall so come in like manner as ye have seen him go into heaven" (Acts 1:10-11). This same Jesus shall return; not some mystical, invisible spirit, but this same Jesus. A Jesus, who, after His resurrection ate fish and honey with the disciples.

> *"Anything that is based upon human theory is not dependable and is misleading and unscriptural."*
>
> *Finis Dake*

PAUL'S TESTIMONY

Also the apostle Paul bears witness to the same great event, saying, "For the Lord himself shall descend from heaven with a shout, with the voice of the archangel and with the trump of God: and the dead in Christ shall rise first: Then we which are alive and remain shall be caught up together with them in the clouds, to meet the Lord in the air: and so shall we ever be with the Lord" (1 Thessalonians 4:16-17). Such are a few of the definite references to His coming.

HOW IS HE COMING?

But you say, "How is He coming? This event of which you speak, how is it to take place?" There are many theories as to the manner of His return. Some say the coming of the Lord was spiritually fulfilled on the day of Pentecost when He came in the form of the Spirit, comforting the disciples and enduing them with power to preach the Gospel. It is true, a real Person did come on that day, but this Person was not the Lord Jesus Christ, but the Holy Spirit; He of whom Jesus said, ". . . It is expedient for you that I go away: for if I go not away, the Comforter will not come unto you; but if I depart, I will send him unto you" (John 16:7). In this passage, it can be seen very plainly that Christ is not speaking of Himself, but of Another, namely, the Holy Spirit, the third Person of the Godhead. Let us not confuse the office and work of the Spirit with that of the Son. The Spirit has come to the earth to "reprove the world of sin, and of righteousness, and of judgment" (John 16:8), while the Son is at the right hand of the Father, doing His priestly work, just as He was seen by Stephen after Pentecost (Acts 7:55-56).

THEORIES

Others say that the destruction of Jerusalem, 70 A.D., was the coming of the Lord. But an honest study of the Scriptures disproves this, for His coming is to be marked, not by the destruction, but the restoration of Jerusalem. The Jews who have been scattered to the four corners of the earth will again be brought to their own land, where they will be deceived and brought through great tribulation by the Antichrist. Then they will see the Lord coming in the clouds of heaven to deliver them and set up His kingdom on the earth. Still others affirm that the coming of the Lord takes place at conversion. But neither can this be true, for at conversion the sinner comes to the Lord, and not the Lord to the sinner. And yet others maintain that the spreading of the Gospel to all parts of the earth is the coming of the Lord. A moment's reflection on the subject, however, convinces us that this also is a mistaken thought, for His coming is to be sudden, ". . . in the twinkling of an eye . . ." (1 Corinthians 15:52), two will be sleeping in one bed; "the one shall be taken and the other shall be left" (Luke 17:34). Whereas the sending forth of missionaries to evangelize the world has taken centuries and, as all admit, is a slow and tedious process.

HOW IS HE COMING?

The best way to determine this is to search the Scriptures. "And when he had spoken these things, while they beheld, he was taken up; and a cloud received him out of their sight. And while they looked stedfastly toward heaven as he went up, behold, two men stood by them in white apparel; Which also said, Ye men of Galilee, why stand ye gazing up into heaven? This same Jesus, which is taken up from you into heaven, shall so come in like manner as ye have seen him go into heaven" (Acts 1:9-11). The same Jesus, visible! Corporeal! The same resurrected body you have just beheld, with the same pierced hands and feet. "This same Jesus, which is taken up from you into heaven, shall so come in like manner as ye have seen Him go into, heaven" (Acts 1:11).

HE IS COMING IN THE CLOUDS

He went up in a cloud, He will return in like manner; that is, in the clouds of heaven, "Behold, he cometh with clouds; and every eye shall see him, and they also which pierced him: and all the kindreds of the earth shall wail because of him . . ." (Revelation 1:7). Here is a literal statement in God's Word; which cannot be taken in any other way.

HE IS COMING SUDDENLY

"But of that day and hour knoweth no man, no, not the angels of heaven, but my Father only. But as the days of Noe were, so shall also the coming of the Son of man be. For as in the days that were before the flood they were eating and drinking, marrying and giving in marriage, until the day that Noah entered into the ark, and knew not until the flood came, and took them all away; so shall also the coming of the Son of man be" (Matthew 24:36-39). There will not be time to prepare. Then those who are ready to go will be caught up to meet Him in the air, but those who are unprepared will be left behind.

HE WILL COME AS A THIEF IN THE NIGHT

A thief comes to a home at an hour when least expected. The inmates of the home are not notified as to the hour of his arrival. A thief comes with a definite object in view, and when it is accomplished he quickly takes his departure, carrying with him that for which he came. But know this, that if the goodman of the house had known in what watch the thief would come, he would have watched, and would not have suffered his house to be broken up (Matthew 24:43). He does not seek the furniture, nor the carpets. He comes for the gold, the silver, and the precious stones. The richest treasure in the earth today is the redeemed, blood–washed

"The power from God to live clean and holy is ours for the asking."

Finis Dake

and Spirit–filled believers who wait for the coming of Jesus Christ. He is coming for the gold, gold that has been tried in the furnace of affliction; for the silver of atonement which has been wrought out in yielded lives; and for the precious stones which have been digged from the mire of sin and crime, and polished by the Master Himself into glittering diamonds to adorn His crown.[147]

LOVED ONES GONE

That day many homes will be left desolate; for the godly father, mother, husband, wife and child will be caught up to meet the Lord in the air. There will be confusion and despair in many places—loved ones gone. What does it mean? Where can the missing ones be? Then those who are left will begin to remember the words which they had heard for years, heard unheedingly, words which if they had been regarded would have prepared them for that day.

WHEN IS HE COMING?

It is no small wonder that the disciples asked Him the questions, "Tell us when shall these things be? and what shall be the sign of thy coming, and of the end of the world?" (Matthew 24:3). These three questions concern three distinct events: the destruction of Jerusalem and its temple, with the overthrow of Jewish rule, and the dispersion of Israel; the coming of Christ for His saints when they will be caught up to meet Him in the air for the marriage of the Lamb; "the end of the world" (or age), when Satan will be cast into the bottomless pit, and the Lord will begin His reign over the earth as King of kings and Lord of lords.

Can one know the day or hour of His coming? No. "Watch therefore, for ye know neither the day nor the hour wherein the Son of man cometh" (Matthew 25:13). Though we may not know the day or the hour, we are told in that we need not be ignorant of the times or seasons. "But of the times and the seasons, brethren, ye have no need that I write unto you" (1 Thessalonians 5:1).

---

[147] Dake speaks of the coming of the Lord as a *"thief in the night"* in relation to the Rapture. Later in life, he would come to the understanding that the references to the Lord's coming as a *"thief in the night"* were concerning the Second Advent of Christ, just before the Millennium, and not the Rapture of the Church. (See *Dake's Annotated Reference Bible*, Dake Publishing, Inc. Lawrenceville: Georgia, 1963, 1 Thessalonians 5:2 note.)

There have been many signs given us to prove that His coming is near. Let us look at a few to see if the time is not at hand. False Christ's are to appear. "For many shall come in my name, saying, I am Christ; and shall deceive many" (Matthew 24:5). There are over forty people in the world today who claim to be Christ. Among the number may be mentioned: Mr. Swinefurth, Dora Beckman of Minnesota, Mr. Heron of Detroit, MI, who declared himself to be Prince Michael coming to fulfill Daniel 12:1, which states: "And at that time shall Michael stand up, the great prince which standeth for the children of thy people: and there shall be a time of trouble, such as never was since there was a nation even to that same time: and at that time thy people shall be delivered, every one that shall be found written in the book." (Daniel 12:1); and the Bab of Persia, whom so many worshiped as Christ. Many today declare the coming of Mrs. Eddy with her "Science and Health, or the Key to the Scriptures," to be the coming of the Lord. Such are some of the blasphemies of the day and such are some of the fulfillments of this prophecy.

> *"False theories of truth will never set free, for they keep one in a state of constantly questioning the will of God."*
>
> *Finis Dake*

FALSE PROPHETS SHALL RISE AND DECEIVE MANY

This is an age when false prophets and false religions spring up over night, and certainly they do deceive many. Christian Science calls itself Christian, yet denies the deity of Christ and the necessity of the Atonement. Surely they are deceiving many. Spiritualism, the mother of Christian Science, is even less careful to cover its satanic origin and power. Spiritualists claim to call up the dead, yet it is nothing but Satan himself impersonating departed spirits.

"But," you say, "these religions perform many miracles, and therefore must be of God." No. The Devil has power to perform miracles, for did he not cause the magicians' rod to become a serpent? "Then Pharaoh also called the wise men and the sorcerers: now the magicians of Egypt, they also did in like manner with their enchantments. For they cast down every man his rod, and they became serpents: but Aaron's rod swallowed up their rods." (Exodus 7:11-12) He is going to display his power more and more in these last days, for Jesus said: ". . . there shall arise false Christ's, and false prophets, and shall shew great signs and wonders; insomuch that, if it were possible, they shall deceive the very elect" (Matthew 24:24). In the thirteenth chapter of Revelation, we read that in order to deceive the people, the devil will do ". . . great wonders, so that he maketh fire come down from heaven on the earth in the sight of men" (Revelation 13:13). So we see from God's Word that the Devil can and does perform miracles.

LOVE SHALL WAX COLD

"And because iniquity shall abound, the love of many shall wax cold" (Matthew 24:12). Today iniquity and lawlessness abound on every hand. Politics are corrupt; the desire for power and money urges people on. The world is pleasure–mad with feasting, and drinking, dancing, dressing. Yes, iniquity is abounding, and the cup of sin and crime is full to overflowing. Love waxes cold on every hand. Many are falling away from the old faith of the Bible. Everywhere we see the cold forms and ceremonies of apostate creeds. Ministers deny the miracles and the supernatural of the Bible; they declare that only a part of God's sacred Word is reliable and inspired. They not only deny the deity of Christ, but also declare it a sickening shock to refined people to make mention of the blood of Christ. They say, "Let us not have altar calls and weeping for sins, and rejoicing in God for salvation." They no longer believe in these, but do believe in filling the church with concerts, suppers, shows, movies, and pool tables. God help us to tell the truth about this thing. So–called Christian colleges and seminaries teach evolution[148] and modernistic ideas, and so destroy the old–time faith in young hearts that they come out skeptics and infidels, saying: ". . . Where is the promise of his coming?" (2 Peter 3:4). But praise God! There is a people who are not ashamed of God nor of His Word, but who are looking for Christ's coming, looking for the time when: ". . . every knee should bow, of things in heaven, and things in earth, and things under the earth; And that every tongue should confess that Jesus Christ is Lord, to the glory of God the Father" (Philippians 2:10-11).

MANY SHALL RUN TO AND FRO

"But thou, O Daniel, shut up the words, and seal the book, even to the time of the end: many shall run to and fro, and knowledge shall be increased" (Daniel 12:4). Never in the history of the world has it been so easy and common to travel as it is today. Trains speed across the country

---

[148] See *Dake's Annotated Reference Bible*, Dake Publishing, Inc. Lawrenceville: Georgia, 1963, for *"Creation not Evolution"* (Genesis 1:12 note.)

day and night, train after train running within a few minutes of one another; and yet, the depots are always full of thousands of people, running to and fro. Thoroughfares and subways are blocked with automobiles. Aero planes are racing through the sky, carrying their passengers. Thus God's Word, spoken more than 2,500 years ago is fulfilled: ". . . many shall run to and fro . . ." (Daniel 12:4).

KNOWLEDGE SHALL BE INCREASED

"But thou, O Daniel, shut up the words, and seal the book, even to the time of the end: many shall run to and fro, and knowledge shall be increased" (Daniel 12:4). Why did not our forefathers discover all the wonderful things man has discovered in recent years? The, reason is this; that God had set a time for the increase of knowledge; that is, in the last days. During the last two generations we have seen the invention of the steam locomotive, electric trains, trolley cars, and motors, electric lights, the telephone, telegraph, ocean cables, automobiles, airplanes, radio, great coal– and oil–burning steamers, submarines, giant cannon, torpedoes, gasoline–powered, motor–driven farming implements, electric motors that do everything from sweeping floors to lighting whole cities, drawing long trains, and lifting hundreds of tons. Such inventions springing from the minds of two generations! What does it mean? It can mean but one thing; we are in the last days, and He, our Christ, shall soon come again.

> *"I attribute my ability and my gift of knowledge of the Bible, not to my own memory or natural ability, but solely to the anointing and ministry of the Holy Spirit in my life."*
>
> *Finis Dake*

WARS AND RUMORS OF WARS

"And ye shall hear of wars and rumours of wars: see that ye be not troubled: for all these things must come to pass, but the end is not yet" (Matthew 24:6). Since these words were uttered, there have been wars and rumors of wars—from the fall of Jerusalem in 70 A.D. to the warring of the Saxons, of Napoleon Bonaparte, the French Revolution, the American Revolution, down to the late wars our Civil War, the struggle in the Philippines, the Boer War, the Boxer Rebellion, and the World War. There has been one international upheaval after another. Then there have been rumors of wars with Japan, with Mexico, and with many other countries. But Jesus said: "And ye shall hear of wars and rumours of wars: see that ye be not troubled . . ." (Matthew 24:6).

THE CRY OF PEACE AND SAFETY

"But when they shall cry, Peace and safety, sudden destruction cometh upon them, as travail upon a woman with child, and they shall not escape." "For nation shall rise against nation, and kingdom against kingdom, and there shall be famines and pestilences, and earthquakes in divers places." For many years godly men have been teaching that Christ is coming back to earth, but they declared that certain things in prophecy must be fulfilled. There must first be a world war; the Jews must return to Palestine, there must be earthquakes, famines, pestilences, and bloodshed. The declaration that there was to be the greatest war the world had ever known was ridiculed. People cried, "We are too civilized; what did Christ know about our twentieth century? We will decide whether there will be a war or not. No, we will have peace forever." That a world war was possible for a civilized age, they emphatically disbelieved. So the cry of peace and safety sped around the world. But the nations thought the best way to keep peace was to prepare for war, to build up a larger army and navy, so that other nations would be afraid to speak of war. "Then let us build a peace palace," said all the nations, "where the leaders of every government can come together to settle their difficulties without war." So they built at The Hague a Peace Palace costing several millions sterling. Each nation gave costly gifts and donations for its erection. Then they placed in it a marvelous library of 75,000 volumes dealing with the subject of international peace. A body of eminent judges from all nations was brought together as a permanent jury to settle each difficulty of the nations. Thus everything was arranged. There was to be no more war, for the judges would adjust all matters.

The palace was completed, the flags of the nations were floating over it, bands blared forth the national anthems; soldiers marched while crowds cheered. All seemed peace and safety. But the words of the Bible must be fulfilled. There must be a great world war before Christ could come. Like a bolt of lightning out of a clear sky came the cry of war instead of that of peace. Within one month there were thirteen declarations of war. Six out of the great nations were tearing at one another's throats. The German hordes were sweeping through Belgium, longing to reach Paris. People began to realize that the good old Bible was true after all, "For nation shall rise against nation, and kingdom against kingdom." Wider and wider swept the war tornado, until our own United States of America was fighting with the rest.

THERE SHALL BE BLOOD, FIRE AND VAPORS OF SMOKE

Blood? Yes, blood flowed all over the battlefields, till one could see even a deeper dye than that of the poppies. Fire? Fire was shot from the cannon's mouth, towns and villages were aflame, forests blazing, men even fighting one another with sheets of liquid fire. Smoke? The heavens were filled with the smoke of the flames from earth below, from the battlefields, from guns and burning homes. On land man fought with vapor of smoke and poisoned gases; and on sea ships were wrapped in curtains of smoke to hide them from hostile eyes.

> *"The responsibility of conforming to truth is yours."*
>
> *Finis Dake*

THERE SHALL BE FAMINES, PESTILENCES AND EARTHQUAKES

Critics said before the war that there could not be famines, for our storehouses were all full, and every country well supplied. Who among us cannot see the fulfillment of Scripture in the past few years of awful suffering from famines in Armenia, Russia, and other lands, where thousands have died? Pestilences? "We shall never have another world epidemic with our modern medical system," they said. But just think of the plagues of the last generation. Thousands of children were stricken with infantile paralysis; millions of people were killed by influenza, until medical men could not cope with the situation, and caskets could not be made fast enough to bury the dead.

EARTHQUAKES IN DIVERS PLACES

No one wilt dare dispute this sign, for earthquakes have increased over forty percent in the last twenty years. In that time over 300 villages have been destroyed, according to statistics in Washington. Yet we have heard little about them in the daily news. Why? Because Satan wishes to keep the people blind to the fulfillment of the signs of Christ's coming. Recently in Japan there have been 273 quakes in two days; 216 of these were on the day of the great disaster which killed between 300,000 and 500,000 people, and left millions homeless. In many places there are shocks that we know little about. These things should stir us from our indifference to realize that Christ is coming, and coming soon.

Outpouring Of The Holy Spirit

Last, but not least, the greatest sign to me is the outpouring of the Holy Spirit. Previous to 1906, Christians everywhere felt the need of a revival in their own lives and in the life of the Church as a whole. Prayer meetings were held everywhere, until at last God began to pour out His Spirit as He did in apostolic days. People of all denominations were filled with the Holy Spirit and began to speak with other tongues as the Spirit gave them utterance, the sick were healed, the blind were made to see, the deaf to hear, the dumb to speak, and mighty signs and wonders were wrought, and are still being wrought in the name of Jesus Christ. A deeper life and walk in the Spirit, a clearer vision of the whitened harvest fields, and a deeper realization of Christ's coming were the results of this outpouring of God's Spirit. The end has not yet come, for again the church is sending forth the call to pray for a worldwide revival, and the revival is surely coming, for our God is always faithful to our call. But let us heed His Word of warning, "Be ye also ready, for in such an hour as ye think not the Son of man cometh."

> "At any rate we have a very simple book telling us about God, Christ, and the Holy Spirit—a lot of things the average believer has never heard of yet."
>
> *Finis Dake*

For Whom Is He Coming?

Since He is coming, for whom is He coming? He is coming not for some denomination, but for His true saints, the true Church, His Body, His Bride, for those who are washed in the blood and who are walking in all the light God has given them. Thousands and thousands of blood–washed saints from all parts of the world will be caught up to meet the Lord in the air, so shall we ever be with the Lord.

The Rapture Must Be Distinguished From The Revelation

The Rapture is His coming in the air for the saints. He will not literally come to the earth at this time, nor be seen by the inhabitants of the earth. There will be a period of several years, a period of great tribulation between the two events, "Tribulation such as was not since the beginning of the world, to this time, no nor ever shall be." His revelation is His literal coming to earth to set up His millennial kingdom. "Immediately after the tribulation of those days shall the sun be darkened, and the moon shall not give her light and the stars shall fall from heaven, and the powers of the heavens shall be shaken; and then shall appear the sign of the Son of man in heaven, and then shall all the tribes of the earth mourn, and they shall see the Son of man coming in the clouds of heaven with power and great glory."

The saints who will have been caught up to heaven will come back with Him at this time and shall for one thousand years reign upon the earth. At His coming He will deliver Israel from the clutches of the Antichrist, and from the armies of the nations who will then be gathered against Jerusalem to destroy it.

World Not To Be Converted First

We can talk about converting the world and getting it ready for Christ's millennial reign, but the Scripture does not tell us that the world as a whole will be converted before He comes. It will not be until the setting up of His earthly kingdom that all will acknowledge Him as King of kings and Lord of lords. Then "The government shall be upon his shoulder, and his name shall be called Wonderful, Counsellor, the Mighty God, the Everlasting Father, the Prince of Peace."

Genealogies

The James Henry Dake Family

Date	Name	Born In
7/10/1869	James Henry Dake	Miller County, Missouri

James Henry Dake was the son of George W. Dake

Date	Name	Born In
5/16/1870	Mary Ellen (Hicks) Dake	Miller County, Missouri

Mary Ellen Hicks was the daughter of John Knox Polk Hicks

Marriage: James and Mary were married on 6/13/1889.

Their Children Were:

Date	Name	Born In
3/8/1890	George Chester Dake	Miller County, Missouri
8/30/1891	Nancy Emily Dake	Miller County, Missouri
12/5/1892	Daisy Cordell Dake	Miller County, Missouri
9/18/1894	James Arthur Dake	Miller County, Missouri
3/4/1895	William Edmond Dake	Miller County, Missouri
4/18/1898	Joseph Franklin Dake	Fairplay, Missouri
6/30/1900	John Edward Dake	Phoenix, Missouri
10/18/1902	**Finis Jennings Dake**	**Iberia, Missouri**
2/23/1904	Virgil Earnest Dake	Iberia, Missouri
7/4/1906	Stella Eunis Dake	Iberia, Missouri
4/22/1910	Flomarie Etta Dake	Springfield, Missouri

THE NEEL DOBBINS FAMILY

Date	Name	Born In
7/25/1874	Neel Dobbins	Bushnell, Illinois
10/31/1879	Hattie May (Stauffer) Dobbins	Miller County Missouri

Marriage: Neel and Hattie May were married on 6/18/1902.

Their Children were:

Date	Name	Born In
4/10/1903	**Dorothy Virginia Dobbins**	**Joplin, Missouri**
3/5/1906	Pauline Margaret Dobbins	Joplin, Missouri
4/4/1910	Neel William Dobbins	Joplin, Missouri
3/5/1912	Jonathon Joseph Dobbins	Joplin, Missouri

THE FINIS JENNINGS DAKE FAMILY

Date	Name	Born In
10/18/1902	Finis Jennings Dake	Iberia, Missouri
4/10/1903	Dorothy Virginia (Dobbins) Dake	Joplin, Missouri

Marriage: Finis and Dorothy were married on 10/7/1925.

Their Children were:

Date	Name	Born In
8/12/1927	Finette Janelda Dake	Amarillo, Texas
6/15/1938	Rhoda Annabeth Dake	Zion, Illinois
10/17/1939	Finis Jennings Dake, Jr.	Bristol, Tennessee
7/9/1940	Steven Arthur Dake	Clarksburg, West Virginia

DAKE'S TESTIMONY

The True Story Of A Magnificent Gift

I have not always been able to quote as many passages from the Bible or to give scriptural answers to the thousands of questions as I do today. The initial ability came at a definite time of Christian experience while I was yet in my youth.

Until I was seventeen, I wandered in the usual sinful paths, rejecting Christianity and using as my excuse the inconsistent lives of professing Christians. When, at last, I did find a group who lived the life they professed, I realized I was face–to–face with Truth—backed up by Christian example—and must make a decision. To accept Truth would mean a complete surrender of my life to God; to reject it would mean to rebel and go deeper into a life of sin.

Several weeks of struggling with my conscience followed the enlightenment of my mind to the reality of Christianity, and then came my decision. I would serve God the rest of my life and do His will, whatever it may be. I had the usual witness of born–again Christians—the witness of the Spirit with my spirit that I was a child of God, my confessed sins having been forgiven and the blood of Christ cleansing me from all unrighteousness. I was then baptized in water as an outward symbol of an inward work of Christ in my life.

But this did not end it all with me. I was still hungry for God. In fact, I was more hungry for Him now than ever before and for three months after my conversion I cried out for a closer walk with God. I wanted a complete understanding of His will for my life. I wanted to be filled with the Holy Spirit, though I knew nothing of spiritual blessings as promised in the Bible, except the truth that all present day Christians could have the same blessings experienced by early Christians.

With all sins and bad habits renounced and all worldly pleasures rejected I spent hours in prayer and worship seeking God. My soul with all its feelings, emotions and desires became centered upon God and I was occupied in an ever–deepening consecration to Him and His will.

At the end of three months of whole–hearted surrender to God and seeking to be filled with the Holy Spirit, my answer came and I received a great anointing of the Spirit in my life. It happened about two o'clock one morning as I was in prayer. It was in the month of May, 1920.

Suddenly, and without previous warning, there came over my being a cool and rushing wind. It seemed I could hear the fluttering of the wings of a dove settling down upon my body. Then, instantly, there came from the very depths of my innermost being "the rivers of living water" that Jesus promised in John 7:37-39. Torrents of praise and glory began to flow from my lips as I tried to give vent to the unutterable gushings of my soul. I thus received in a measure what the disciples received on the day of Pentecost.

Immediately, I was aware of an ability I did not previously possess. I could now quote Scriptures, hundreds of them, and that without any effort to memorize them. I just quoted "as the Spirit gave utterance" (Acts 2:4) and also noticed a quickening of the Spirit in my mind to know and tell what chapters and books various verses were found in.

I had not yet studied the Scriptures, so how could I memorize them? During the three months I spent seeking God for His will and anointing, I read very little, because I wished to spend every spare moment in prayer. And before my conversion, I cannot recall ever reading as much as one full chapter of the "Book of books." So the ability was a gift to me—the gift of knowledge of the Holy Scriptures—and for this I give God alone all the praise.

From that time—the time of the special anointing of the Holy Spirit when I was a lad of seventeen—until now, I have never had to memorize the many thousands of Bible passages I use in teaching or answering Bible questions. I am just able to quote a verse when I need it, and that I say, by the anointing of the Spirit. And I say again, I humbly give God all the praise and glory for this ability.

After the anointing I began to read and study the Bible, as all other Christians should do, because I thirsted for its pages now that I could quote so many of its verses through the quickening of the Spirit. In my lifetime I have spent over 100,000 hours leafing through its pages and digging into the wealth of its wonderful teachings.

From the very first of my studies, I noticed that the whole Bible became literally simple and clear. It was as if I had known it all my life and understood it as much as I understood my name and address. Knowledge of the Scriptures became a part of my mental and spiritual equipment, just as the divine gift of knowledge became a part of Solomon. Interpretation of the verses was unnecessary. I found that a full knowledge of the scope of truth through daily study, coupled with my ability to quote from any and all parts of the Bible as I yielded to the Spirit, brought about a gratifying result—I could so easily *"rightly divide the word of truth"* (2 Tim. 2:15).

So–called "difficult" passages in prophecy and elsewhere did not seem mystifying to me, for what was not clear in any one particular passage was made clear by other Scriptures on the same subject which would be brought to my mind. My hours of study provided a rich storehouse to draw from as I would yield to the Spirit and enjoy the fulfillment of the promise in John 14:26, which says He will *"bring all things to your remembrance."*

But do not forget that apart from this wealth of material, which is possible to any and all Christians who will devote their time to the study of the Word, I was the privileged recipient of a gift of knowledge of the Scriptures so that the passages, whether I had read them or not, rolled out of my mouth like rivers of living water. This was by divine anointing, and I suppose similar to God's speaking *"by the mouth of all his holy prophets since the world began,"* as in Acts 3:21 and 2 Peter 1:21. Even as a boy, when newly converted, I could always help people finish quoting Scriptures they would forget and even tell them where the passages could be found. This, I repeat, was not from memory.

My wife, who better than any other living person knows the extent of my ability in the field of memory, is often approached by one who says, "What a marvelous memory your husband has." On occasion she has reflected upon her own personal experience with my memory and has replied, "You just send him to town for a spool of thread, and then you'll find out what kind of memory he has."

Let us turn again to my early experiences. Being young and likely to be unaccepted in the ministerial realm from the mere fact that I was young, I decided at the age of eighteen to enroll in a Bible Institute to prepare for the ministry. I soon learned that one must either believe what the Bible alone teaches, or spend his life wrestling with the confusing and varied interpretations of men. The professors did not agree among themselves on some of the basic truths, and a number of them even disagreed with what the Bible itself plainly stated on certain subjects.

Thus, at an early age, I became acquainted with the perplexing array of doctrines set forth by present–day leaders of Christianity. Some of it was in agreement with Scripture, as could be proved when all passages dealing with the subject were brought together and examined. But much of the array turned out to be "hand–me–down" theology of a former generation of preachers, many of whom were great—not *because* of their doctrinal errors—but *in spite* of their doctrinal errors.

Having already had such a contact with God through His Spirit that various Scriptures came to my mind on any biblical subject discussed, I was face–to–face with making another major decision. And, this again, would be a decision for life. I must decide to respect my gift and depend on God and the knowledge of the Word He had given me as a guide to determine what is and is not scriptural truth; or, I must go along with the crowd, winning its applause by accepting all it taught, including the UNCONTESTED and UNCHALLENGED doctrines of former leaders, whom even I admired because of their zeal. But even zeal can be *"not according to knowledge,"* (Romans 10:2) we are told, which is something all of us should take into consideration.

My decision was clean–cut and firm, and was expressed in a promise I made to God—a promise which I have kept for all these years without any regrets. I vowed to my Lord "never to teach one thing in private or in public that I could not prove by the Bible, giving two or three plain Scriptures, as required in 2 Corinthians 13:1," realizing also that *"no prophecy of the Scripture is of any private interpretation"* (to be interpreted by itself or without comparison with other Scriptures, 2 Peter 1:20). I further re-solved not to change or attempt to change what the Scripture plainly says. I reasoned that if the Bible is God's Word in human language, then it means exactly what it says and no teacher, minister or layman has a right to change one word of it. I concluded that any interpretation which is the least bit out of harmony with what is plainly written, must be rejected as the theory of man and not the truth of God.

It was a big decision for a lad, and cost me a few friends now and again—friends who preferred to listen to almost anyone who had gray hair rather than pay attention to the biblical quotings of a youth just emerging from his teens. But my hair is turning gray too now, and yet my decision remains the same—just as clean–cut and firm as ever. The prophecies and promises and admonitions and doctrines of our eternal welfare or degra-dation, as determined by our daily behavior and choice, are there in the Bible the same as they were when I began quoting them years ago. They are in plain language and understandable by anyone who can read and will take time to look up an occasional word in the dictionary.

My early decision has paid off in many ways, one of them being a letter I receive now and again from someone who has written "twenty years late" to say in substance: "I didn't have much use for your teaching years ago, but NOW I find your writings a great help and inspiration in my preaching, etc." Such testimonies or admissions are my rewards for doggedly and persistently carrying out my early vows to believe and teach exactly what the Bible says on any and all subjects it deals with, making it my business to find out what it says and all it says on any point before I present it as Truth.

If I can inspire you, or have inspired you to study God's Word with an open mind, unbiased by unfounded conclusions of yourself or others; if I have influenced you to take Scriptures literally as meaning just what they say and saying just what they mean and if my testimony has made you hungry for God, His Word and His anointing, then I am glad for I have accomplished the purpose I had in mind—that of proving a blessing to your life.

FINIS J. DAKE

WOMEN PREACHERS

By Finis Jennings Dake

The question of women preachers is much discussed everywhere because of the women evangelists who are ministering in various churches. Criticisms which have been made against them are proved false by the following scriptural arguments:

1. In the Gospels, there were several women messengers who proclaimed "good news" (Mt. 28:1-10; Lk. 24:9-11; Jn. 4:28-80; 20:16-18).

2. In Acts 2:14-21, Peter answered the religious people who, after the 120 had been baptized in the Spirit, gathered to mock them for their speaking in tongues, staggerings, prostrations and noises, saying that his companions were not "drunken, as ye suppose, seeing it is but the third hour of the day (9:00 a.m. when they did not yet have time to get drunk on wine); but this is that which was spoken by the prophet Joel; and it shall come to pass in the last days, saith God, I will pour out my Spirit upon all flesh; and your sons *and your daughters shall prophesy*, and your young men shall see visions, and your old men shall dream dreams; and on my servants *and on my handmaidens* I will pour out of my Spirit and they shall prophesy."

The word "prophecy" is clearly defined in 1 Cor. 14:3-4 as "speaking unto men to edification, and exhortation, and comfort." It is further declared that "he that prophesieth edifieth the church." If women were to prophesy in the "last days" they certainly were not to speak to the winds. The following passages will prove to an unbiased mind that prophesying is for the Church—1 Cor. 12:1-31; 14:1-6, 12, 24-26, 29-33.

3. In Acts 21:8-9 we read that Phillip had four daughters that did prophesy. They were evangelists, having a ministry like their father's, which is in accord with Joel 2:28 and Acts 2:17.

4. In Romans 16 we have record of a number of women servants of the Lord who served various churches. In verses 1-2, Phebe is mentioned as being a servant of the church of Cenchrea. In verses 3-5, Priscilla is mentioned as one of Paul's helpers in the Gospel and as having charge of a church along with her husband. Mary, Tryphena, Tryphosa, Persis and Julia (Hebrew and Greek feminine names) are mentioned in verses 6 and 12 as being laborers in the Lord. This chapter proves that their labors

included preaching, for men are also mentioned therein as doing labor for Christ and being helpers of Paul. See verses 3, 9 and 21 where Aquila, Urbane and Timothy were spoken of as laborers. If it can be proved that the labors of the woman did not include preaching, then on the same basis it can be proved that the labors of the men did not include preaching.

5. In Phil. 4:2-3, Euodias and Syntyche are mentioned as being in the ministry and prominent leaders in the Philippian church. Other women laborers are mentioned in the same passage. It is evident that Paul had no criticism to offer against God's use of women in His work.

6. Even the Corinthian women "prophesied" and Paul did not condemn them for it (1 Cor. 11:4-5), so the Scripture "Let your women keep silence in the churches." (1 Cor. 14:34-35) could not refer to legitimate and obedient ministries of women. A close examination of 1 Cor. 14 with 1 Tim. 2:11-15 will reveal the true intent of Paul's writing on the matter. His purpose was to condemn a group of disobedient women who were bringing confusion into public meetings by an excess and abusive use of the gift of speaking in tongues and the gift of teaching. They were "usurping" the authority of the men over them and getting out of their own places of obedience "as also saith the law." Hence came the definite rebuke of such women in the Corinthian assemblies. Both men and women in the Corinthian church were permitted to "prophesy one by one" (1 Cor. 14:24-32) as long as they kept their proper places and caused no confusion. Paul stated that "God is not the author of confusion." Then he adds, "Let your women keep silence in the churches; for it is not permitted unto them to speak; but to be under obedience, as also saith the law." It is here evident that the confusion came from the women who were getting out of their proper places. This is in harmony with 1 Tim. 2:11-15, "I suffer not a woman to teach, nor to usurp authority over the man, but to be in silence." The "law" said to the woman, "He shall rule over thee" (Gen. 3:16), but women have been permitted and called of God to prophesy and do other things man has done when they have proved submissive.

7. In 1 Cor. 12 Paul compares the Church to a human body of which both men and women are members. If both are members of the body of Christ, then both are privileged to receive the gifts of the Spirit for the edifying of the Church.

8. Women were used of God even in Old Testament times as prophetesses (Ex.15:20; Judg. 4:4; 2 Ki. 22:14; 2 Ch. 34:22; Neh. 6:14; Isa. 8:3;

Lk. 1:39-56; 2:36). The Law made provision of women to offer sacrifices, attend feasts and take vows (Dt. 12:11-18).

Women have been used by God in every age and why should it be otherwise? The woman was the first to bring sin into the world and surely she should be among the first to take sin out of the world, which thing is done by the means of preaching the Gospel (1 Cor. 1:18-31). Let it be remembered that it was a woman who was chosen as a means of bringing the Redeemer into the world. It was a woman who carried the first "good news" after the resurrection. A greater part of the missionaries of all denominations on the foreign fields are women. If they can preach to and win souls in other lands why not at home? One of the most convincing arguments in their favor, outside of the Scriptures themselves, is that women are everywhere preaching the Gospel, winning mankind to Christ by the hundreds, and God is daily honoring their ministry.

God uses all who will yield to Him and He takes the weak things of the world to confound the mighty (1 Cor. 1:18-31). In times past He has been known to use a rod (Ex. 4:2, 17); ass (Num. 22:28); ram's horn (Josh. 6:5); ox goad, nail, barley cake, pitchers, jaw bone, millstone (Judg. 3:31; 4:21; 7:13; 7:20; 9:53; 15:15-19); mantle (2 Ki. 2:8); ditches (2 Ki. 3:16); empty vessel (2 Ki. 4:3); cruise of oil, ravens (1 Ki. 17:4, 16); worm, wind, fish, goard (Jonah 1:4 17; 4:6-7); cock (Mk. 14:72); maid (2 Ki. 5) and a host of other things to further His purpose. God made everything and He is still sovereign over all. Let us therefore admit that it lies within His power and privilege to use anything and everything for His own glory and may we pray added blessing upon those who have been chosen by the Lord for special service in these last days!

RELIGIOUS EMOTIONALISM

BY FINIS JENNINGS DAKE

People who are emotional enough to praise God, shout, raise hands in worship, and who hold altar services, pray in unison, fall prostrate, have strange manifestations, speak in tongues and whose meetings are noisy, often are accused of being unscriptural, fanatical and "of the Devil." But just the opposite is true, as proved by the Scriptures which follow. To admit that such things are wrong is to admit the same of the worship of biblical authors and early believers. If such forms of worship in biblical times were prompted by God, then these forms of worship today must also be prompted of Him, and to criticize it would be to criticize God and the Bible. Let the reader consider the following passages, which are only a few of many which deal with the subject.

PRAISING AND SHOUTING

Believers in Old Testament ages were very noisy when it came to praising God and shouting (Lev. 9:24; Josh. 6:20; 1 Sam. 4:5-6; 2 Sam. 6:15; 2 Chr. 15:14; 20:19-23; 1 Ki. 1:40; Ezra 3:10-13). Early Christians were noisy. Modern professors of Christianity would have been shocked at their worship (Lk. 19:37-40; 24:53; Acts 2:4-16, 47; 4:23-31; 8:5-8; 10:44-48; 16:25-26; 19:1-6; 1 Cor. 14:1-32). God's people are commanded to make "joyful" and "loud" noise in worship (Ps. 5:11; 32:11; 66:1; 98:4; 100:1-5; 132:9; Isa. 12:6; Lk. 6:22-23; 1 Pet. 1:8).

If God is the author of all these passages—and if He is pleased with loud shouting and praising—then His opponent, the Devil, must be the author of all criticisms against such worship. The fact that persons who offer such criticisms act like fanatics themselves at a church entertainment or a ball game where clapping, whistling, screaming and even tossing hats are a part of the performance makes one all the more sure of the source of such criticism.

LOUD PRAYING IN UNISON

See Num. 14:1; 25:6; 2 Chr. 15:13-15; Ezra 3:12; Lk. 24:53; Acts 1:14; 4:24-31; 12:12. Praying in tongues and with "groanings which cannot be uttered" is also scriptural (1 Cor. 14:14-15; Rom. 8:26; Gal. 4:19; Eph. 6:18). This is the most quiet world any of us will ever be in.

In Hell there will be unlimited emotionalism—weeping, wailing, praying and gnashing of teeth (Mt. 8:12; 22:13; 24:51; 25:30; Lk. 13:28; 16:19-31). In Heaven, worship will sound like "great thunderings" and "many waters" (Rev. 4:8-11; 5:11-13; 7:9-17; 14:1-5; 19:1-10). It might pay some to attend a noisy church so that they will not feel out of place should they get to heaven.

WEEPING AND CRYING

In biblical times, weeping and crying played a part in the religious experiences of believers (Num. 14:1; 25:6; 1 Sam. 15:11; Ez. 3:13; Jn. 11:35; 20:11; Rom. 12:15; Phil. 3:18; Jas. 4:9).

LEAPING AND DANCING

See 2 Sam. 6:14-16; Ps. 149:3; 150:4; Lk. 6:23; Acts 3:8; 14:10.

CLAPPING AND RAISING HANDS

See 1 Ki. 8:22, 54; Neh. 8:6; Ps. 28:2; 47:1; 63:4; 134:2; 141:2; 2 Tim. 2:8.

SHAKING AND QUAKING

See Dan. 10:7; Ezek. 12:18; Mt. 28:4; Acts 9:6; 16:29; Heb. 12:21.

SPEAKING IN TONGUES

That criticism against speaking in tongues is unwarranted and really has its source in the malice of the Devil is clear from Isa. 28:11-12; Mk. 16:17; Jn. 15:26; 16:13-16; Acts 2:2-11; 10:44-48; 19:1-6; 1 Cor. 12:10, 28-30; 13:1, 8; 14:2-9, 13-14, 18-23, 26-37, 39. Not one Scripture condemns speaking in tongues.

PROSTRATIONS

Scores of prostrations are recorded in Scripture, some as long as from 40 to 390 days, during which time many visions and dreams were seen.

1. Those overpowered by God's presence (Gen. 15:12-17; Dt. 9:18, 25; Ezek. 1:28; 3:23; 4:4-17; 43:3; 44:4; Dan. 8:17; 10:5-19; Mt. 17:6; Acts 2:2-16; 9:4; 10:10; Rev. 1:17; 19:10; 22:8).

2. Voluntary prostrations in worship and prayer (Gen. 17:3, 17; Lev. 9:24; Num. 14:5; 16:4, 22, 45; 20:6; 22:31; Dt. 9:18, 25; Josh. 5:14; 7:6; 1 Ki. 18:39; Lk. 17:16; Rev. 5:8, 14; 7:11; 11:16).

3. Prostrations under burdens of prayer (Josh. 7:10; Mt. 26:39; Mk. 3:11; 5:22; 7:25; 14:35; Lk. 5:12; Jn. 11:32).

If the above–mentioned things are of the Devil, then why do not those who are recognized as serving him openly have such experiences? The Devil never causes his followers to shout, praise God, weep, cry, leap, dance for joy, clap or raise hands, speak in tongues or fall prostrate while in worship and prayer to God. The Devil tries to scare people away from such because he does not want anyone to receive God's blessings.

The early church did all the peculiar things mentioned above, and to on–lookers they even appeared to be drunk. See Lk. 24:53; Acts 2:1-14, 47; 4:24, 31; 9:3-6; 10:10, 44-48; 19:6; 1 Cor. 14:1-34. These things made them "the offscouring of all things," "a spectacle to the world" and "fools for Christ's sake" (1 Cor. 4:9-15; 2 Cor. 4:8-18; 6:4-10).

It is not expected that an unsaved man can understand spiritual things for "the natural man receiveth not the things of the Spirit of God; for they are foolishness to him; neither can he know them because they are spiritually discerned" (1 Cor. 2:14). "They that are after the flesh do mind the things of the flesh; but they that are after the Spirit the things of the Spirit" (Rom. 8:1-8). What is there about a cold, formal church service of a few songs, a prayer or two, and a sermon that the natural man would resent as foolishness? Only that kind of worship previously described is foolishness to man and therefore must be of the Spirit of God.

It would be impossible for a church to have the gifts of the spirit as promised in 1 Cor. 12—gifts intended for every local church—without some manifestations in the services beyond the ordinary, and of a type that would appear foolish to carnally–minded men.

For example, how could one who has received the gift of tongues exercise that gift in a local church without speaking in tongues? How could one who has received the gift of interpretation of tongues exercise it in a church without tongues to interpret?

The same might be asked in regard to any one of the nine gifts of the Spirit. The acid test of any spirit or manifestation by spirit is not whether it pleases natural man, but whether it is biblical, glorifies Christ and confesses that He has come in the flesh, (Jn. 16:13-16; 1 Jn. 4:1-6).

It must be concluded, therefore, that many things might happen in a service where God's Spirit is given full reign. Those who are not living in the Spirit, or who do not know what Scripture plainly teaches in regard to spiritual manifestations, will do wisely to withhold criticisms that they may be clear before the Lord. It would be far better to take the position of an unprejudiced mind in the matter, to search the Scriptures on the subject, and daily seek God for that which the Bible offers.

THE POTTER'S MASTERPIECE

BY DOROTHY DAKE

The Potter's Masterpiece.

(Jer. 18:1-4.)

Words and Music by
DOROTHY DOBBINS DAKE

1. The Pot-ter de-sir-ed a master-piece Up-on the wheels to make; And
2. He sought like our Heav-en-ly Pot-ter—Him-self to be re-vealed, In
3. And then did the Pot-ter with grief look down Up-on the mass of clay. 'I was
4. Fashioned a-gain in the Potter's house And made a ves-sel rare Is

in-to his hand some clay he took— On it his hopes did stake. The
form-ing a ves-sel that un-to Him And all of his moulding would yield. But
crumbled and shat-tered—a bro-ken heap, But still in his hand it lay. The
what we need, for we're but clay, Bro-ken and marred—in dis-pair. A

Pot - ter looked not at the mass of clay In all of its worth - less - ness, But
ah! while he worked so faith - ful - ly Up - on the mas - ter - piece planned, His
Pot - ter at last, with hope re - vived Did fash-ion the ves - sel a - gain. 'Twas
mas - ter - piece in-deed we'll be If we our lives will lay In the

saw it the ves-sel that he had planned Of beauty and use - fulness.
hopes for the vessel were bro - ken—A - las! it was marred in his hand.—
beautifully finished—an emblem of The Potter's own work among men.—
hand of the Heaven-ly Pot - ter; Let Him mould us like pli - a - ble clay.

Of
A -
The
Let Him

beau - ty and use - ful - ness.
las! it was marred in his hand.
Pot - ter's own work a - mong men.
mould us like pli - a - ble clay.

The Potter's Masterpiece 2

382

LIKE A ROSE

By Dorothy Dake

LIKE A ROSE

D. D.

DOROTHY DAKE

1. I heard that the life of the Sav - ior Did blos - som like a rose;
2. At first I tho't blos-soms of beau - ty, Would send forth that fra-grance a - lone;
3. A - long with the buds in the gar - den, A blos-som in full I made,
4. But still I had not been a bless - ing, With fra-grance to shed a - broad;

I heard that His won - der - ful fra - grance, Was breathed by friends and foes.
But soon I. dis-cov-ered 'most hid - den, A thorn that caused me to moan,
I wel-comed the wa - ter from Heav - en, And hoped I would nev - er fade;
I want-ed to be like the Mas - ter, While He on this earth did trod;

The od - or was rare and ver - y sweet, It filled the air in house or street;
It pricked my hands un - til they bled, In grief I hum - bly bowed my head;
But ere the sum - mer came to end, My stur - dy stem be - gan to bend;
And then there came a friend a - long, And crushed me 'til I had no song,

rit.

And I prayed that my life to oth - ers, Would some-how be like a rose.
But when I was healed of my bruis - es, The price of my per - fume was known.
And lo! on the ground be - neath me, My pet - als their price had paid.
But af - ter the crush - ing my fra - grance, Was more like the breeze of God.

Order from Finis J. Dake, Shiloh Bible Institute, Zion, Ill. Price 10¢ - Postage 3c

DAKE AND DOCTRINE

A SIMPLE DECISION

Early in Dake's life he made a decision that molded and shaped his doctrine for the rest of his ministry. It was a very simple decision, yet it was one that would generate a great deal of controversy over the years. In understanding his Bible, Dake determined that he would take the Bible at face value. He would simply believe it. He often said while preaching:

> We are taking for a textbook the Bible itself. And we are going to believe everything that it says, about any particular question. Regardless of what it says we are going to believe it.

From the first editions of His *Dake Annotated Reference Bible*,[149] published in 1961, he continues to give his basic approach to the Word of God. In the preface of his Bible he wrote:

> The general principle adhered to throughout is that of literalizing instead of spiritualizing. Statements of fact and historical accounts are accepted as such. THE RULE OBSERVED IS: Take the Bible literally wherein it is at all possible; if symbolic, figurative or typical language is used, then look for the literal truth it intends to convey.

Thus Dake approached the Bible from a literal standpoint. The Bible was a document of truth and conveyed its message much like any other literal document. It was not a book of mystery or mysticism, but one of facts, truth, and simplicity. It was written in a language to the common man, to be understood by the simple and the masses of God's children. It was clear and plain so that all could understand its message of faith, hope and love to mankind. Indeed, while very educated and learned, Dake spent his life bringing the simplicity of the Bible message to God's children and the world.

---

[149] Finis J. Dake, *Dake Annotated Reference Bible*, (Lawrenceville, Georgia: Dake Publishing, Inc.)

SIMPLE YET COMPREHENSIVE

Dake understood that the Bible was an inspired revelation from God.[150] It was God speaking to his creation. Dake wrote:

> A revelation is an uncovering or unveiling so that all can see alike what was previously covered or hidden. The only excuse any man would have for not seeing something that was uncovered for him is his willful refusal to look. Anything that is revealed is clear, or the purpose of the revelation has failed.

God desired relationship and the communication of Himself and the pages of the Bible were His way of making himself known unto men. He would not lie or misrepresent Himself. The statements contained within the Bible were to be believed and understood like you would any other document of truth. It is to be trusted. The simplicity of the Bible was a hallmark of Dake's teaching. Often he would say:

> There is nothing hard in the Bible; I don't see anything hard about that passage; and if the Bible is hard to understand it is because men make it hard.

Dake wrote:

> The most simple beginners can understand the Bible one line at a time, for this is the way it was given, and it is the best way to understand it. The Bible is the most simple book to understand.

Yet this being said, Dake understood the Bible to be a very comprehensive book and a man would do well to invest himself in its pages for a lifetime of study. Dake said:

---

[150] In *God's Plan for Man*, page 20, Dake quotes two great men of God in regard to the Bible being a revelation from God. These quotes tell us of Dake's great love for and respect for the Word of God. *"All other books are of little importance in comparison with the Holy Scriptures, which are a revelation from God, and are given as the only rule of faith and practice"*—Alexander Cruden. *"The Bible is the Book of faith, and a Book of doctrine, and a Book of morals, and a Book of religion, of special revelation from God; but it is also a Book which teaches man his responsibility, his own dignity, and his equality with his fellow man"*—Daniel Webster.

No man can get all the vastness of the Bible at once. It is the seemingly infinite scope of truth that causes some men to think the Bible is hard to understand. It is like a man arguing that he cannot understand water because he cannot drink the ocean dry at one drink. Naturally, it takes time to get a simple knowledge of the whole Bible, but what we contend is this: that taking it a line at a time, verse at a time, or truth at a time, it cannot be hard to understand. If a man will do this he will find the Bible truths opening up beyond his fondest dreams.

FORMATION OF BIBLE DOCTRINE IS A HARMONY OF SCRIPTURES

In regard to the formulation of biblical doctrine, Dake required doctrine to be borne out and proved from the text of the Bible itself.[151] While Dake worked with and respected the teachings of the Church, the traditions of the Church held weight only as its traditions were proved from the Bible itself. Often he would say:

I'm not going to tell you anything tonight that you can't find in the Bible. And if I do, don't you believe it! And I am going to treat you the same way. If you tell me something that we can't find in the Bible, I am not going to believe it. But if what you believe is found in the Bible then we will have no problem at all.

This was a statement Dake lived his life by. For when men and the Bible came into disagreement, Dake concluded that men were wrong and the Bible was always correct and true.[152]

Doctrine was not to be determined by a selection of pet Scriptures, but, rather, a harmony of biblical teaching was to be sought out. Dake understood that the Bible was not a book of systematic discourses on any one subject, but it did give divine information on practically every subject. Dake said:

---

[151] *2 Corinthians 13:1 This is the third time I am coming to you. In the mouth of two or three witnesses shall every word be established.*

[152] *Romans 3:4 God forbid: yea, let God be true, but every man a liar; as it is written, That thou mightest be justified in thy sayings, and mightest overcome when thou art judged.*

One must collect together here and there all God's information through various writers in order to get the whole truth. When this is done, there is perfect harmony, and everything about the subject that man really needs to know is clear.

All Scriptures on any particular subject are to be collected and brought together for a clear picture of what the Bible was saying. Dake believed that:

Over and over the Bible repeats truth so that "in the mouth of two or three witnesses every word may be established." Any doctrine that is not plainly stated in Scripture is best left alone. If God did not say anything about a question, then man has no right to teach anything about it as though it were taught in the Bible. Anything that is not taught in the Bible should not be taught at all by the Bible teacher, as being in the Bible. He should limit his teachings to a "thus saith the Lord" or leave it alone. His opinion is of no value toward proving something the Bible does not teach.

A COMPOSITE OF BIBLE DOCTRINE

Dake's belief in the literal truth of the Bible, as well as his belief that God desired to communicate that truth, gave him a foundation to formulate doctrine that was simple to understand, easy to believe and— most importantly—Bible–based. In a discussion of the Devil's attempt to lead men away from sound doctrine, Dake wrote in his monumental book, *God's Plan for Man,* a paragraph which clearly states his position on many of the doctrines of the Bible. He also brought condemnation to those who would teach contrary to sound doctrine. That paragraph is excerpted here and broken down for clarity:

Any doctrine that denies or in any way causes doubt and unbelief concerning anything taught in Scripture is from demons. Any religion that denies the:

- Inspiration of the Bible;
- The reality of God as a person;

- The divine sonship of Jesus Christ as the only begotten Son of God;
- The virgin birth;
- The pre–existence of Jesus Christ;
- The divinity of Christ and His miraculous power and supernatural ministry;
- The death, burial, bodily resurrection, and the bodily manifestation of Christ after His resurrection;
- The bodily ascension to heaven and coming again of Jesus Christ to set up a kingdom in the world forever;
- The reality and power of the Holy Spirit and His ministry among men to convict of sin, to create men in Christ and to carry on the work of God among men;
- The reality of Christian experiences as the new birth, cleansing from sin, living free from sin, divine healing, the Spirit baptism, gifts of the Spirit, miracles and signs following believers, answers to prayer, fulfillment of the promises in getting health, happiness, prosperity, and the numerous other experiences of the New Testament;
- The reality of Satan, demons, sickness, sin, and the fall of man; the creation of all things by God;
- The free moral agency of men;
- The universality of sin and the depravity of man;
- The necessity of repentance and the born again experience;
- The penalty of sin as being eternal loss of the soul;
- The necessity of the atonement;
- The reality of heaven and eternal hell;
- The resurrection and judgment of all men;
- The immortality of the soul.

Any religion that teaches contrary to these and all other fundamental doctrines of Scripture is of the Devil and is for the purpose of causing the soul to be damned in eternal hell.[153]

---

[153] Finis J. Dake, *God's Plan for Man*, (Lawrenceville, Georgia: 1977), page 96.

ALWAYS OPEN TO BIBLE TRUTH

At times throughout his life, Dake was accused of being dogmatic. Often people felt as though they simply could not argue with Dake. But in reality, Dake welcomed various opinions from all. He enjoyed Bible discussion. He often said:

> I don't have any fear or any confusion. I don't have to worry about what you teach, what I teach, what this church teaches and what that church teaches. All I have to worry about is: if the Book says it, then where does it say it? If it says it, then that's all right with me. That's *final* with me. Anybody that will give me Scripture to contradict anything I say, I'll bless them any day. You won't make me mad! I've got something better if you give me something better than what I've got. I'll appreciate it!

OPPOSITION EXISTS

This short introduction gives us some understanding of Dake's respect, love for, and belief in the Bible and sound doctrine. We see here a man who regarded truth as one of the highest virtues. We also see the determination of a man who was willing to stand up against the tide of the day, the latest fad doctrines and the errors of the past, even if they were propagated by the established church of the day.

Today there are those who believe that the "church," "traditions," and "theories of men" rank higher than the simple statements of the Word of God. They become angry when men challenge their traditions and theories with a simple "thus saith the Lord," as found in Scripture. They seek to discredit those who do not agree with them. They malign and criticize those who do not adhere to their belief system. During the ministry of Finis Jennings Dake, he met his share of these kinds of critics. And as the ministry of his writings continue to circle the globe, there are still those who question Dake's method of understanding Scripture.

In an attempt to bring clarity to the arguments and criticisms that are occasionally raised, the next few pages will deal will some of the issues that Dake had to confront from time to time. It is not the author's intent to win every critic to Dake's way of believing and understanding the Bible. However, there are those who have only been given one side of the story—the side of the critics. These are honest people who genuinely want to know the truth of the arguments the critics present. So for this purpose, let us now turn our attention to some of the issues that seemed to have been misunderstood and criticized the most.

THE TRINITY

A MOST IMPORTANT DOCTRINE

Wayne Grudem writes:

> The doctrine of the trinity is one of the most important doctrines of the Christian faith. To study the Bible's teachings on the trinity gives us great insight into the question that is at the center of all of our seeking after God: What is God like in himself?[154]

It's easy to understand why the doctrine of the Trinity is one of the most widely–debated of all Christian doctrines. Throughout church history—from the time of Christ until today—men have struggled to gain a biblical understanding of God, who is indeed one and yet three persons—all at the same time. It is not difficult to see why the doctrine of the Trinity is one of the most *"asked about"* topics of which Dake wrote.

TRINITY DEFINITION

Let us approach the definition of the Trinity from a classical point of view. Here, we will turn to the definition as given by *H. Orton Wiley* in his widely acclaimed, *Introduction to Christian Theology:*

> The evangelical doctrine of the trinity as generally held in the Church is best expressed in the words of the ancient creeds and confessions of faith. The Athanasian Creed has the most explicit statement: "We worship one God in Trinity, and trinity in Unity; neither confounding the Persons, nor dividing the substance. For there is one Person of the Father, another of the Son, and another of the Holy Ghost; but the Godhead of the Father, of the Son, and of the Holy Ghost is all one, the glory equal, the majesty coeternal." The Thirty–nine Articles, as revised by John Wesley, declared that "in the unity of this Godhead,

---

[154] Wayne Grudem, *Systematic Theology*, (Grand Rapids, Michigan: Zondervan Publishing House, 1994), page 226.

there are three Persons of one substance, power, and eternity—the Father, the Son, and the Holy Ghost." Therefore, we may say that the evangelical doctrine affirms that the Godhead is of one substance, and that in the unity of this substance there are three subsistences or Persons; and further, that this must be held in such a manner as not to divide the substance or confuse the Persons.[155]

Now let us read Dake's definition of the Trinity as taken from *God's Plan for Man:*

TRINITY. This means the union of three persons—the Father, the Son, and the Holy Spirit in one (unified) Godhead or divinity—so that all three persons are one in unity and eternal substance, but three separate and distinct persons as to individuality (1 Jn. 5:7-8; Dan. 7:9-14; Mt. 3:16-17; 28:19; Acts 7:56-59).[156]

Note that Dake's definition of the Trinity includes all the elements of the classical definition. In fact, the similarity between Dake's and Wesley's definitions are striking. No doubt Dake gleaned his definition from Wesley.

THE MOODY HANDBOOK OF THEOLOGY

For a more detailed look at this definition, let us consult another classic work, *The Moody Handbook of Theology,* which points out the required elements of a biblical definition of the Trinity. The Moody Handbook states the following:[157]

1. God is one in regard to essence.
2. God is three with respect to Persons.
3. The three Persons have distinct relationships.
4. The three Persons are equal in authority.

Here again we can easily see that Dake's definition of the Trinity has

---

[155] Wiley, H. Orton, *Introduction to Christian Theology*, (Kansas City, Missouri: Beacon Hill Press, 1946), page 123.

[156] Ibid. *God's Plan for Man,* page 51.

[157] Paul P. Enns, *Moody Handbook of Theology,* (Chicago, Illinois: Moody Press, 1989), page 199.

all four of the basic requirements for a biblical definition of the Trinity. In fact, let's look at Moody's definition point by point for comparison. Let's also bring in a few other pages from Dake's works in order to gain a more complete understanding of his view of the Trinity:

Moody	Dake
1. God is one in regard to essence.	. . . all three persons are one in unity and eternal substance[158]
2. God is three with respect to Persons.	. . . the union of three persons[159]
3. The three Persons have distinct relationships.	. . . the Father, the Son, and the Holy Spirit . . . three separate and distinct persons as to individuality[160]
4. The three Persons are equal in authority.	. . . equality with God in Divinity is definitely stated[161]

Without doubt, Dake's view of the Trinity is compatible with the orthodox view as stated in Moody. There can be no argument here.

WESTMINSTER CONFESSION OF FAITH

Further confirmation that Dake's views on the Trinity are within the mainline discussion of the doctrine can be found in a simple statement from the historic Westminster Confession of Faith:

> In the unity of the Godhead there be three Persons, of one substance, power, and eternity: God the Father, God the Son, and God the Holy Ghost.[162]

---

[158] Ibid. *God's Plan for Man,* page 51.

[159] Ibid. *God's Plan for Man,* page 492.

[160] Ibid. *God's Plan for Man,* pages 373, 446, and 481.

[161] Ibid. *God's Plan for Man,* pages 371.

[162] G. I. Williamson, *The Westminster Confession of Faith,* (Philadelphia, Pennsylvania: Presbyterian and Reformed Publishing Company, 1964), page 199.

Again, an examination of Dake's definition of the Trinity, when compared to this definition by the Westminster Confession of Faith, shows that Dake's definition is well within the bounds of the orthodox view.

EASTON'S BIBLE DICTIONARY

So as not to be accused of being shallow we shall consult one last work on this definition of the Trinity. The *Easton's Bible Dictionary* gives the following definition:

> TRINITY a word not found in Scripture, but used to express the doctrine of the unity of God as subsisting in three distinct Persons. This word is derived from the Gr. *trias*, first used by Theophilus (A.D. 168–183), or from the Lat. *trinitas*, first used by Tertullian (A.D. 220), to express this doctrine. The propositions involved in the doctrine are these: 1. That God is one, and that there is but one God (Deut. 6:4; 1 Kings 8:60; Isaiah 44:6; Mark 12:29, 32; John 10:30). 2. That the Father is a distinct divine Person (hypostasis, subsistentia, persona, suppositum intellectuale), distinct from the Son and the Holy Spirit. 3. That Jesus Christ was truly God, and yet was a Person distinct from the Father and the Holy Spirit. 4. That the Holy Spirit is also a distinct divine Person.[163]

Here once again a comparison chart may be useful to see the Easton definition and the Dake definition side by side:

Easton	Dake
1. That God is one, and that there is but one God.	. . . three persons are one in unity and eternal substance . . . Elohim is not a divided Deity, but three persons in one God, or one Deity.[164]

---

[163] M. G. Easton M.A., D.D., *Easton's Illustrated Bible Dictionary*, (Nashville Tennessee: Thomas Nelson, 1897)

[164] Ibid. *God's Plan for Man*, page 51, 480 and 492.

2. That the Father is a distinct divine Person . . . distinct from the Son and the Holy Spirit.	. . . The Godhead consists of three separate and distinct Persons. This fact is simply stated in Scripture . . .[165]
3. That Jesus Christ was truly God, and yet was a Person distinct from the Father and the Holy Spirit.	. . . divine names and titles given to Jesus prove that He is by nature divine and a member of the Godhead. Jesus Christ is not the Father or the Holy Ghost.[166]
4. That the Holy Spirit is also a distinct divine Person.	. . . The Holy Spirit is pictured in Scripture as God, as a real person separate and distinct from both the Father and the Son.[167]

In addition to these definitions written by Dake, it is interesting to hear him define the doctrine of the Trinity in his normal conversational speech. He did this in response to questions that had been asked when he was host of his WGST radio program in Atlanta, Georgia, in 1954. On broadcast number 16, during a discussion of the "Truth About God," Dake said:

> The word "trinity" is often misunderstood. It simply means the union of three persons, the Father, the Son, and the Holy Spirit, in one; so it refers to the unified Godhead or the deity, so that all three persons in the one unity and eternal substance are really one in unity and yet three separate and distinct persons as to individuality.

Citations and comparisons could go on for a number of pages, but to the honest reader, the agreement between Dake's view of the Trinity and

---

[165] Ibid. *God's Plan for Man,* page 64 and 65.
[166] Ibid. *God's Plan for Man,* pages 370 and 373.
[167] Ibid. *God's Plan for Man,* pages 444.

mainline Christianity has been demonstrated. As with any writer who has chosen the doctrine of the Trinity as their subject matter, there may be fine points of doctrinal distinctions which could bring about a heated discussion among theologians, but none that separate Dake from a sound understanding of the Trinity and—more importantly—a biblical understanding of the doctrine. In fact, in an examination of over 75 theological texts that sit on my shelves, written by many well–known historic and modern theologians, I could easily find differences in doctrine between most on this subject, while at the same time most of them would still fall within the bounds of the classical view of the Trinity, just as Dake does.

TRI–THEISM

DEFINITION

Tri–theism is a word that some critics have used to describe Dake's understanding of the Trinity. However, nothing could be further from the truth. In its most simple sense, Tri–theism is the belief in polytheism, or the belief that there is more than one God. This is something Dake neither believed nor taught.

Henry C. Thiessen gives an excellent discourse on the subject in which he defines Tri–theism, as well as it's opposite extreme, Modalism.

> The doctrine of the trinity must be distinguished from both Tri–theism and Sabellianism. Tri–theism denies the unity of the essence of God and holds to three distinct Gods. The only unity that it recognizes is the unity of purpose and endeavor. God is a unity of essence as well as of purpose and endeavor. The three persons are consubstantial. Sabellianism held to a trinity of revelation, but not of nature. It taught that God, as Father, is the creator and lawgiver; as Son, is the same God incarnate who fulfills the office of redeemer; and as Holy Spirit, is the same God in the work of regeneration and sanctification. In other words, Sabellianism taught a modal trinity as distinguished from an ontological trinity. Modalism speaks of a threefold nature of God, in the same sense in which a man may be an artist, a teacher, and a friend, or as one may be a father, a son, and a brother. But this is in reality a denial of the doctrine of the trinity for these are not three distinctions in the essence, but three qualities or relationships in one and the same person.[168]

Notice Tri–theism denies the unity of the essence of God and holds to three distinct Gods. It recognizes a unity of purpose and endeavor, but not a unity of essence. As we have seen, Dake recognizes a unity of essence which Tri–theism denies. Dake's definition of the Trinity is as follows:

[168] Henry C. Thiessen, *Lectures in Systematic Theology*, (Grand Rapids, Michigan: William B. Eerdmans Publishing Company, 1949) page 90.

TRINITY. This means the union of three persons—the Father, the Son, and the Holy Spirit in one (unified) Godhead or divinity—so that all three persons are one in unity and eternal substance, but three separate and distinct persons as to individuality (1 Jn. 5:7-8; Dan. 7:9-14; Mt. 3:16-17; 28:19; Acts 7:56-59).[169]

DAKE DOES NOT TEACH TRI–THEISM

As we have seen, Tri–theism involves a belief in three separate, unrelated gods. Dake does not teach this. Dake teaches three separate *"persons"* in the one *"substance"* of the Godhead. This is completely orthodox. Nowhere in Dake's writings do we find him saying that there are *"three gods."* It is simply not there.

Theologian *Milliard Erickson* tells us:

Monotheism is deeply implanted in the Hebrew Christian tradition. God is one, not several. The unity of God may be compared to the unity of husband and wife, but we must keep in mind that we are dealing with one God, not a joining of separate entities. God is three persons at every moment of time.[170]

We find Dake in complete agreement with this quote. Dake's definition of the Trinity speaks both to the "threeness" and the "oneness" of God. In fact, since Dake declares that the Godhead is one in "unity and eternal substance*,"* no claim of Tri–theism could possibly be made, or as Ryrie puts it: "the phrase 'the same in substance' (or perhaps better, *essence*) protects against Tri–theism."[171]

COMBATING THE JESUS ONLY MOVEMENT

A popular teaching was "making the rounds" early in Dake's ministry. It was known then as the "Jesus Only*"* teaching, and later became known

---

[169] Ibid. *God's Plan for Man,* page 51.

[170] Millard J. Erickson, *Christian Theology*, (Grand Rapids, Michigan: Baker Book House, 1983), page 337.

[171] Charles C. Ryrie, *Basic Theology*, (Wheaton, Illinois: Chariot Victor Books, 1986) page 54.

as the "Oneness" movement. In his writings, Dake stressed the "three-ness" of God in an effort to combat the fallacies of the "Oneness" move-ment. Some have taken this emphasis to mean that Dake had theological leanings toward Sabellianism or Tri–theism. As we have seen above, this is not the case. Another citation from *God's Plan for Man* makes this even more clear. In regard to the plural name of God, *Elohim*, Dake writes:

> The one *Elohim* then is not one person, or one in number, but one in unity. *Elohim* is not a divided Deity, but three persons in one God, or one Deity.[172]

Take note, Dake says:

> . . . that *Elohim* is not a divided Deity, but three persons in one God, or one Deity.

After examining the facts, we see that Dake was not a tri–theist, nor did he believe in separating the divine essence or substance. For Dake, the choice was a biblical one: "Hear, O Israel: The Lord our God is one Lord" (Dt. 6:4).

---

[172] Ibid. *God's Plan for Man,* page 480.

The Mormon Doctrine of God

Time For A Good Laugh

On a few rare occasions there have been some who have suggested that Dake's view of God is the same as that of the Mormons. For those who have studied both the Dake writings and Mormon doctrine, the idea is laughable. But, in an effort to set the record straight, we will address this issue.

Mormons Believe The Trinity Doctrine Is False

Let us take a look at three elements of Mormon doctrine concerning God and the Trinity and compare them to clear statements by Dake, which refute such false teaching.

From *Decker's Complete Handbook on Mormonism*[173] we read the following:

> 1. Mormons are taught that the historic Christian position on the Trinity (three persons in one God) is false. Instead they believe that the first visions of Joseph Smith and subsequent "revelations" from Smith reveal that God the Father and God the Son are two separate gods.

Mormons believe the teaching of the Trinity is false. They also believe in more than one God. And while it is not the purpose of this work to go into detail concerning Mormon doctrine, it is interesting to note that Mormons believe that one day, they themselves will become a God! Contrary to this kind of teaching Dake writes:

> The whole Bible abundantly proves that there are three separate persons in the Godhead, or in the "one Lord" and "one God" or Deity; that these three persons are in absolute unity and "are one . . .[174]

---

[173] Ed Decker, *Decker's Complete Handbook on Mormonism*, (Eugene, Oregon: Harvest House Publishers, 1995) page 405.
[174] Ibid. *God's Plan for Man*, page 500.

MORMONS BELIEVE THAT GOD IS PRESIDENT

Decker's Complete Handbook on Mormonism also states:

> 2. . . . the Godhead is like the First Presidency of the church: a president and two counselors, the president being first in authority. God the Father being the president and the Son and Holy Spirit are His two counselors.

For the Mormon, no equality between the members of the Trinity exist. God is "president;" the Holy Spirit and Christ are merely counselors. Contrary to inequality of the Godhead, Dake writes:

> Equality with God in Divinity is definitely stated (Jn. 5:19-29; Phil. 2:5-11). [175]

MORMONS BELIEVE THE TRINITY DOCTRINE IS A PAGAN HERESY

Continuing with Decker's Handbook:

> 3. They regard the Trinity as a pagan heresy, much like Jehovah's Witnesses do (except from the other extreme).

Mormons do not accept the Trinity as a Christian doctrine. Contrary to this Mormon teaching, Dake lists over 500 Scriptures proving the Trinity to be a biblical doctrine.[176]

MORMONS BELIEVE IN AN INFINITE NUMBER OF GODS

Other writers also give us an understanding of the Mormon doctrine of God. Salam Kirban in his book *Mormonism* writes:

> "But in addition there is an infinite number of holy personages, drawn from worlds without number, who have passed on to exaltation and are thus gods. God was once less powerful, he grew until He attained the status of Godhead. (*The Gospel Through the Ages*, page 114–115)[177]

---

[175]   Ibid. *God's Plan for Man*, page 371.
[176]   Ibid. *God's Plan for Man*, pages 498–500.
[177]   Salem Kirban, *Mormonism*, (Huntingdon Valley, Pennsylvania: Salem Kirban Publisher, 1981) page 33.

Mormons teach that there are an *infinite* number of gods. Dake labels this idea as satanic in origin when he says that the idea of becoming "gods" is one of Satan's most effective appeals to a human.[178]

MORMONS BELIEVE THAT GOD HAS A FLESH AND BLOOD BODY

Latayne Colvett Scott in her book *The Mormon Mirage* writes that Mormon's teach the incredible doctrine that God has a body of flesh and bones and was once a man of mortal flesh:

> . . . the Mormon God has a body of flesh and bones. Mormons teach that He looks like a man, as indeed, He once was (*Doctrines and Covenants* 130:22). God is a natural man (*Journal of Discourses*, vol. 8, page 211). God was once a man in mortal flesh (*Journal of Discourses*, vol. 7, page 333).[179]

Dake, on the other hand, opposes such teachings. For in *God's Plan for Man* Dake wrote: "God has a 'spirit' body, not flesh and blood."[180]

And, in the notes of the *Dake Annotated Reference Bible*, Dake wrote: "God is not flesh and blood."[181]

MORMONS BELIEVE GOD HAD A BEGINNING

Kurt Van Corden in his book *Mormonism* tells us that Mormons believe that God had a beginning and was begotten in a previous world!

> Each god is born as a man and later progresses to the level of godhood. The Father, Son, and Holy Ghost, as distinct and separate entities born at different times and in different places, became gods at different times in different worlds. God our father was begotten on a previous heavenly world by his father. (*The Seer*, page 132)[182]

---

[178]   Finis J. Dake, *Dake Annotated Reference Bible*, (Lawrenceville, Georgia: Dake Publishing, 1961) Genesis 3:5 note j.

[179]   Laytayne Colvett Scott, *The Mormon Mirage,* (Grand Rapids, Michigan: Zondervan Publishing, 1979) page 169.

[180]   Ibid. *God's Plan for Man,* pages 56–57.

[181]   Ibid. *Dake Annotated Reference Bible*, Genesis 3:5 note j.

[182]   Kurt Van Gorden, *Mormonism*, (Grand Rapids, Michigan: Zondervan Publishers, 1995) page 39.

This is, of course, contrary to the Bible and Dake tells us that God had no beginning, but has always been God.[183]

It is easy to see that the Mormons have a very strange view of God and one that cannot in any way be reconciled with the God of the Bible. Dake's view of God is biblical and in no way reflects any semblance of the Mormon God.

---

[183] Ibid, God's Plan For Man, Page 381.

Personal Recollections

The following are personal recollections of Finis and Dorothy Dake by their children and grandchildren.

Finette Dake Kennedy – Daughter

What do I remember about Papa and Pampaw? . . .

I can remember sometimes when I was growing up and I would ask to go out, Dad, wanting to protect his oldest daughter at all costs, would hesitate, and then Mom would say, "Now, Finis, we've got good kids and it won't hurt to do this." Dad would get a big, yet hesitant, grin on his face and say, "Well, okay, since you'll are such good kids."

After I graduated from high school I often traveled with him. I didn't go to college until three years later. I sang at his meetings and although he had a gorgeous voice, he always left the singing up to me. One of my voice teachers told me that if he had Dad's voice to train, he could make an opera star out of him!

My greatest memories of Papa are those of him teaching and lecturing from the chart. He always included a question and answer period toward the end of the session that allowed him to interact more closely with the congregation. I was used to him being able to immediately answer ALL questions on the spot. But one time someone sitting way in the back got up and asked a Bible question that was so remote it stunned me, and in my mind I thought, "Dad, how in the world are you going to answer this one?" I wish I had had presence of mind to write the question down, but I didn't. I could tell that dad was also taken by surprise for a moment. To bide for time he started telling about his books that were for sale on the table in the back of the church. Then, in an instant, I saw it hit him (the answer from the Holy Spirit). He almost stopped in mid-sentence. I don't remember the exact Scriptures he gave, but what I do remember is the look of confidence on his face when the Holy Spirit gave him the answer, and the assurance with which he spoke when he responded. He said, "Now in 'such and such' a verse we find 'so and so' (he was quoting chapter and verse). Boy, did I breathe a sigh of relief. I had never seen this happen to my Daddy before . . . or since!

RHODA ANNABETH DAKE GERMAINE – DAUGHTER
(DECEASED)

One of my fondest memories about my Daddy was how he loved ice cream! His favorites were: chocolate, strawberry and black walnut. I remember that, about once a month—on Sundays—we would take a break from our regular Sunday dinner.

After church Daddy would go by "Miss Georgia's" ice cream place and buy four gallons of ice cream. Then we would all go home and eat that ice cream. We didn't eat it for dessert—it was our entire meal! On those special days, Daddy would let us eat as much as we wanted. And the truth is, Daddy enjoyed ice cream as much as any of us!

FINIS JENNINGS DAKE, JR. – SON

Long before I knew my dad was a cowboy and owned a horse, he was my hero. I am glad I did not know until later in life when I saw a photograph of him in cowboy chaps sporting, holster and gun.

Had I known as a child, listening to the radio's Lone Ranger, he would have been my hero in a different arena for a different reason. But he was my hero in the Biblical arena for being a preacher.

Along side this, I learned my dad loved God's animals. In the evening of the last day my dad had been scheduled in church meetings, he drove into our driveway. We all ran, hugged and greeted him, welcoming him home again. He then opened the trunk of his automobile to retrieve his luggage, and there on top was an Otter that had been stuffed by a taxidermist. Dad was smiling from ear to ear.

We all asked him, "What in the world is it?" which gave him the opportunity to educate us about the Otter. Evidently, someone in the church meetings had given it to him when he admired it.

Years later, in my teens now, he showed me a sample printing of several New Testament pages of a reference Bible he was planning to print and sell. It takes a lot to surprise a high school teen, but that day he did.

After I told him it was "great," in my mind I asked myself "Will anybody buy anything my dad wrote?"

Years later, I was thankfully amazed when sales grew and grew to become internationally known. Then people would ask me what it was like to be the son of Rev. Dake, the author of the Dake Bible.

I would tell the story about when dad showed me the sample of printed Bible pages, and then I would tell them, "1 didn't know, He was just my dad." I thought everybody in my neighborhood had a dad like mine.

DAVID GERMAINE – SON–IN–LAW
(DECEASED)

Finis Dake as I knew him was a most simple, quiet, and meek man. He could have ended up quite wealthy by some people's standards, instead, he was very much a middle–class type American who never desired anything but to teach the Word of God to anybody who would listen . . . either individually, or to a large body of people.

I never saw him in a new set of clothes or shoes for the last fifteen or so years of his life. His wife, Dorothy Dake, was the same way. They drove an inexpensive automobile, as long as driving was practical. After that time expired, family members helped by taking them whenever travel became necessary.

Both Finis and Dorothy Dake were a normal pair of grandparents who spent many hours of everyday instructing and praying with members of their family, as well as helping to promote the Dake writings. Up until the last week or two of their lives, each of them were brought up to the Dake Bible Sales office to be with us and to be cared for by us.

The final minutes of their lives were as peaceful as anybody would desire as they passed into Heaven to be with Jesus.

KIMBERLY D. KENNEDY – GRANDDAUGHTER

I was blessed to have been born into a strong, loving, close–knit family who loves God and His Word more than anything else. The two things that were most important to my grandparents were God (and teaching others about His Word) and family. These two things came before anything else. Back in 1971 my grandparents bought forty acres of land so they could have their business and ministry headquarters, as well as their entire family, all in the same location. Aunts, uncles, cousins and grandparents were never more than a quarter to a half–mile away from each other and from Dake Publishing. Some of our friends refer to it as "The Dake Compound."

When I think of my Papa, there are two images that come to mind. The first one is of him studying in his office—totally consumed in the moment—typing, reading or writing, surrounded by stacks of books on every side, covering almost every inch of his desk. If he was not at his desk, he would be sitting in front of my grandmother's desk beside the huge, wall–to–wall picture window, in a big, black leather rocking chair. Each day when I got off the school bus in the afternoon, I'd walk into the Dake Publishing office building to find Papa in one of these two places—every day—day in and day out.

Some people get aggravated or upset if they are deep in thought studying the Bible and they get interrupted, especially by a kid; but not my
Papa. When I, or any one of his grandchildren, would walk in—whether
it was at the office when he was working, or at home when he was relax-
ing and watching television—he would instantly drop everything he was
doing and give us his complete attention. His whole face would light up
and he would grin from ear to ear and reach out his arms to hug us. It
didn't matter what he was doing at that moment. If one of his grandkids
came in to see him, he would stop everything just to talk to us, for as long
as we wanted to. His family was his life—second only to his personal
relationship with God and his love for teaching and sharing God's Word.

Sundays were always special to me because my family attended the
same church as my grandparents. The rest of my aunts and uncles took
their families to different churches. Every week after the Sunday morning service we would drive to Northlake Mall and eat lunch together at
the Piccadilly cafeteria. Afterward, we would split up and go shopping
for a while. Papa and Pampaw would go one way, Mom and I would go
the other. Pampaw made most of her clothes by hand. She could afford
to buy new clothes if she wanted to, but she preferred to make them herself. She was great with a sewing machine. Their first stop was usually
at the Singer store so she could match up threads with the fabric she was
using to make her next dress. Papa was a real sweetheart. He would wait
patiently for all of us girls to finish our shopping, even though there were
probably a million other things he'd rather be doing with his Sunday afternoon. He never once fussed or complained.

My grandparents led peaceful, modest, simple lives. They were not
showy or pretentious. In fact, they were just the opposite. They were as
down–to–earth as anyone could be. Papa was accessible by the people.
Some were amazed that they could call Dake Publishing and actually get
to personally speak with Finis Dake himself! He loved reaching out and
talking to people and answering their Bible questions over the phone. In
fact, Papa was so kind and laid-back (and eager to talk about the Word)
that sometimes he would be at home on the phone answering Bible questions until well after midnight, and my grandmother would have to polite-
ly step in and interrupt the conversation and tell the other person that "the
man of God needs his rest and has to get off the phone now to go to bed
and get some sleep." Otherwise, Papa would've talked all night long.

Granted, he was not nearly as famous as most of the Pentecostal leaders in the body of Christ today. Clearly, that is what made it possible for him to talk to the average person one–on–one. His passion was teaching the Bible to anyone who would listen and simplifying Scripture so that the average person could understand it. This was the love of his life. Papa and Pampaw weren't interested in too many things apart from ministering and teaching God's Word, except maybe watching a little television at night after dinner. They liked to relax after dinner by eating a bowl of their favorite ice cream and watching a few sitcoms, like "The Cosby Show" or "Facts of Life." And my grandfather loved to watch wrestling, while my grandmother preferred to knit or sew in the evenings before bedtime.

When Papa was younger, his greatest desire was to be a cowboy and work on a ranch, riding horses and roping cattle. And when my cousin, Monique, and I were growing up, we both wanted a horse of our own from the time we were able to walk and talk. It was the greatest desire of our hearts. It was something we felt was born into us. It was a part of our nature or makeup—a part of who we were. When we got a little older and learned of Papa's dream to become a cowboy and live and work on a ranch, we concluded that we inherited this love of horses from our grandfather. One day our dreams came true, and we were each blessed with a horse of our very own to love and take care of. We used to ride everywhere! And whenever Papa would look out the window at the office and see us riding, he would stop working and come out to talk to us and pet our horses. Now that I am older and I realize just how strong his desire was to work as a cowboy on a ranch, I'm convinced that it gave him great pleasure to see that some of his grandchildren shared his same passion. Looking back, I'm sure he was thrilled to watch his very own granddaughters having so much fun with their own horses and following in his footsteps with the same love and desire that he had not so long ago.

We, the children and grandchildren of Finis and Dorothy Dake, are in awe when we realize that one man alone, with the anointing and guidance of the Holy Spirit, wrote the commentary notes to the Bible (with over 500,000 cross references and over 35,000 commentary notes), and one woman edited the entire project by hand—without the aid or assistance of a computer or any other modern machinery or technology. It is truly amazing. And it is indeed a remarkable gift from God.

They were the best parents and grandparents anyone could hope for and we all miss them greatly.

RHONDA G. WAGONER – GRANDDAUGHTER

As the first grandchild, I can truthfully say "thank you" to our Heavenly Father above for the privilege and blessing of having had Finis Dake, Sr. and Dorothy Dake as my grandparents. What humble and godly examples they were, and what a great heritage they left me!

My grandfather was big and tall in stature, but he had a quiet and humble spirit. He was a true gentleman. A giant in the Lord that would light up instantly like a light bulb, when you wanted to talk to him about Jesus. It was and is still so amazing, the gift God gave my grandfather of being able to quote Scriptures, one after the other as the Holy Spirit gave the utterance through him, at the different meetings we would attend.

The lifetime it literally took for my grandfather to write the commentary of the *Dake Annotated Reference Bible*, the books, chart, etc., with the help of my grandmother, still shows what Jesus the Master potter can do with His clay when it is pliable in His hands—an instrument that can accomplish anything if totally yielded to Him. These were my beloved grandparents I called Pampaw and Papa.

My grandparents had a little apartment at the end of our house. I would go down to be with them every chance I could get. My grandpa, grandma and myself, in the evening hours after dinner, would sit in their little bedroom and always have some laughs together—as I would love to read from the *Reader's Digest* (laughter is the best medicine). They loved it! Lots of Saturday evenings my grandpa and I would love to watch Saturday night wrestling on TV together.

Many times I would just walk into their apartment to talk to my grandparents. I will never forget seeing my grandfather's face and body completely flat on the floor, praying before God in his bedroom. My grandmother was also a great prayer warrior. There was not a day that went by that I didn't hear her softly speaking to the Lord and sometimes groaning and praying loud enough to hear on my end of the house. These are great memories I will never forget. It was cute to see Papa Dake wearing his favorite hard–top safari hat, as he went for outside walks. One thing that was funny—in the office when Papa Dake saw he might need to get involved in a conversation—he would flail his hands up in the air and say: "What's going on here?" He was funny even when he didn't mean to be. At the office of Dake Bible Sales, he was always diligently devouring the Word, that he loved! These are just some of the things I remember.

KEEL GERMAINE – GRANDSON

My grandfather and grandmother were some of the most generous and loving people that I have known. They would always try to help in every possible way.

When I was in high school, I would have our Fellowship of Christian Athletes Club come over to our house for a meeting or for Bible study. I would have him come down to our end of the house and help all of us young people get a better understanding of God's Word. We would ask the typical questions any teenager would and he would answer everyone, without hesitation. I think we even asked the same questions several times, just in different ways. But he never once made any of us feel inadequate.

They were the type of grandparents any kid would love to have. We were blessed to have been able to grow up with them as a close part of our lives.

DERRICK GERMAINE – GRANDSON

I lived all of my life in the same house as my Dake grandparents. At first, they had a house we shared in Atlanta, but when we moved to Lawrenceville, Georgia, in 1972, we lived in a house with an in–law suite. Their kitchen was on the other side of the wall of my bedroom. I always remember Papa smiling when any of us grandkids walked in. He was soft–spoken and had a very mild temperament. Whether people saw him differently in public, I don't know, but even in a public church setting he was proper, straight–forward, calm, and loved to communicate about God's Word.

As a matter of fact, a lot of conversation with him was minimal, except when it came to the Bible. Then he would enjoy sharing its contents and encouraging us to learn. I remember many times hearing my grandmother groan in prayer through the walls as she prayed—she wasn't playing around. She always had a sermon for me when I visited. They let me know there was something God wanted me to do and that He had a purpose for my life.

The story goes that around the age of 4 or 5, I was upset with my grandmother. One day I stuck my head in their room when she was by herself and said, *"Someone in here is a stupid idiot."* I can't remember that far back, but she made a point to remind me of it when I got older.

I remember the mega amount of hours during which he would study

God's Word, and I thought, surely, "Papa, you get tired of doing that, don't you?" When I would hear him speak, I remember people being amazed at his gift and often laughing throughout the service. I finally realized why they were laughing. It was because he could quote word–for–word, any chapter or verse, faster than you could follow with your eyes. I'm not talking about one or two verses, but chapters—big segments of Scripture, randomly throughout the Bible. I would even start laughing when I tried to follow him. As a child growing up, I was amazed at how he could answer questions, and have a scripture to back up everything.

When I was in my teens, I played around with my grandparents and would sneak into their kitchen. There used to be a small opening or window that was part of the wall that separated their bedroom and the kitchen. I would get vanilla wafer cookies and break pieces off, throwing them and hitting Papa Dake in the back of the head. He would look around, thinking a fly or a bug had hit him. I would do it again and again until they knew something was going on. He would say *"Come on now, what's going on in here?"* Then I would walk in to their room with a smile and visit for a while. I also remember playing a lot of Chinese Checkers with Pampaw Dake.

This may really mess with some people's minds, but nevertheless, in my grandfathers later years, he really enjoyed watching wrestling on TV. He loved to watch "Andre the Giant," as well as all the goofy things other wrestlers did while wrestling. Of course, wrestling has changed a lot since then. They also enjoyed, at a late age, some of the humor in television shows like *Sanford and Son* and *The Cosby Show*; but even then their television watching was very limited.

Some of the little funny things I noticed while visiting their part of the house would be things like: Papa would walk by the sink and see potato peelings or something Pampaw Dake had just left there while cooking. He would say, *"What is that doing in there?"* She would say: *"Oh I don't know, I guess it's laying eggs"*

One of the funniest things I remember as a teenager, was Papa Dake trying to kill a wasp in the kitchen, which was flying around the ceiling. Pampaw Dake would raise her hands and say out loud "Oh God, help this man. Oh Jesus, help this man. He is going to get me stung!" I laughed and laughed!

I also remember Papa Dake loved stuffed bell peppers, corn bread, beans, meat loaf, and anything that grew in a garden.

MONIQUE GERMAINE MILLER – GRANDDAUGHTER

This has been a long time coming with the thoughts and adoration that I have for him—the feelings of needing to put something down on paper to let the world know just who he was, from a grandchild's point of view. Allow me to take you briefly into the life that I knew of Finis Jennings Dake. He was a big man, not heavy—just strong. Standing about 6 ft. 3 and had hands and fingers that were so big it seemed like you could put 1 ½ of my adult fingers to his one. His presence was that of a gentle spirit, but bold in his stance. His heart was like mush that just poured out of his soul. He cried at the quiet times as he thought about the Lord and what He has done for him. Papa, as the grandkids fondly called him, was such a gentle man and so tenderhearted. He and my grandmother, Pampaw, lived in a separate living space connected onto our house all my life. My whole life is remembering them always being there and available. Always seeing the books and the typewriters that he worked on as I went into their house where we lived on Cascade Road in Atlanta. This is the place we lived until 1970. We then moved out to a little town called Lawrenceville where we built the Dake Publishing office building and warehouse, which is still present. The office had small living quarters within the building where they lived until our house was built, which had their living space connected onto it. Papa and Pampaw's dream was to have the entire family living on the same property together and that is what happened. My Aunt Finette and Uncle Finis, along with their families, built their houses on the property so that the entire family was within walking distance from one another. Although we were lucky enough to have Papa and Pampaw live with our family, my cousins were able to enjoy them on a daily basis as grandkids would. Everyday Papa would be at work, which was just a quarter–mile up the driveway, and he would be there until work was done. He would always be at his desk with books piled high from study. He loved the outdoors, but never went out. His breaks would consist of stepping out for a moment with his safari hat on and walking to the mailbox, or as my cousin, Kim, and I would ride our horses up to the huge windows at the front of the office building he would come out and pet them. He would just smile at us. I joked around with him several times about him getting back on a horse. He would just laugh. He loved horses so much and I know that is where my cousin and I get our passion for them. I used to tell him that I was going to get him back on one and I almost got to fulfill that promise. I brought my buggy horse home just months before he died. He and I had special moments together, one being a few weeks after Pampaw passed away I found out that I was pregnant with my first child. He was sitting in front of the windows at the office and I went over and knelt down in front of him. I looked at him and said, "Papa, I'm going to have a baby." He looked at me and just began to cry, so I leaned over and held him. He never got to see my son. I had him two months after he passed away.

I wish you could have known him personally. He loved his family and his grandchildren, but his passion was for God. His heart was to teach truth to all and to help people realize that the Bible was not some complicated book. He lived and breathed the Word of God and loved all people of all nations and all colors. He didn't see color. He only saw souls and human relationships.

MELANIE JEANNE DAKE PATTON – GRANDDAUGHTER

For most of our growing up years, we lived just a few miles from our Dake grandparents. I fondly remember "going to work" with Daddy. We would spend the day playing with all our Dake cousins. We were also in and out of the office where our grandparents and parents were working on the Dake Bible. I remember watching them type single letters on a typewriter: a, b, c, etc. then literally cutting and pasting the letters onto the working pages of the Bible. They would use tweezers to hold the tiny cut out letters. They were also on the phone a lot taking Bible orders from bookstores. I remember the unique smell of the warehouse full of cardboard boxes and Bibles. We would climb on the boxes and play hide and seek around the stacks of boxes and Bibles. It was a fun and uncommon environment to play in, but more than that it was a blessing to be around our grandparents and parents throughout the work day.

Sometimes we would spend the night with them too. At night, Papa and Pampaw would let Rhonda and me play "beauty parlor" with their hair. Pampaw had dark brown hair that fell to her waist when it wasn't in her customary bun. We would brush and brush her hair. It looked like a waterfall. Papa's hair was combed straight back from his forehead, so even though it came to his collar in the back, the front hair was several inches long. He would sit quietly talking with Pampaw and us, patiently letting us put his hair in a bunch of tiny ponytails sticking up all over his head, using real rubber bands from his desk in the office. I'm sure it hurt his head but he let us have our fun with his hair.

I remember sitting between my parents in church listening to Papa preach the word of God. I feel so blessed to have the heritage and the godly example that my grandparents and parents have given to me. I cherish my autographed Dake Bible that he gave to each of us grand-children. These are unique blessings for me as a Dake grandchild. But I was also very blessed with the ordinary talking and playing relationships between my grandparents and all of us grandchildren. The time they took to relax and focus on us was priceless too. I will always remember them in both of these ways; their ministry to world and their ministry to me.

Edward Finis Dake – Grandson

I knew him all my life as "Papa," my paternal grandfather. My father is Finis J. Dake, Jr. I am named after my maternal grandfather, "Edward" and my paternal grandfather, "Finis" Dake.

Some of my fondest memories of him were at Christmas time when he would dress up in a Santa outfit and bring all the grandchildren their toys. We always came together at one of my relatives homes for Christmas. It was a big family gathering. The highlight for the grandchildren was when "Santa" would arrive. He had a big red bag and it always contained the gifts for the boys and the girls. There were a number of us and usually the boys all received the same thing and the girls did as well. One year all the boys got those ice hockey games where you slide the players up and down the ice with a little pole under the rink . . .

I also remember his study at the Dake Publishing office. He had tons of books and stacks and stacks of *National Geographic* magazines. He had large hands and an always welcoming lap for me to climb up into. His smile was always quick and I really enjoyed visiting him as I continued to grow.

BIBLIOGRAPHY

BOOKS WRITTEN BY FINIS J. DAKE

The following list consist of books and a chart written by Finis J. Dake and available through Dake Publishing, Lawrenceville, Georgia.

Dake, Finis J. *God's Plan for Man*. Lawrenceville, Georgia: Dake Bible Sales, Inc. 1949.

_____. *The Plan of the Ages Bible Chart*. Lawrenceville, Georgia: Dake Bible Sales, Inc. 1949.

_____. *Revelation Expounded*. Lawrenceville, Georgia: Dake Bible Sales, Inc. 1950.

_____. *Bible Truths Unmasked*. Lawrenceville, Georgia: Dake Bible Sales, Inc. 1950.

_____. *Dake Annotated Reference Bible*. Lawrenceville, Georgia: Dake Bible Sales, Inc. 1963.

_____. *The Rapture and the Second Coming of Christ*. Lawrenceville, Georgia: Dake Bible Sales, Inc. 1977.

_____. *Help For Today*. Lawrenceville, Georgia: Dake Bible Sales, Inc. 1984.

_____. *Heavenly Host*. Lawrenceville, Georgia: Dake Bible Sales, Inc. 1995.

_____. *Another Time, Another Place, Another Man*. Lawrenceville, Georgia: Dake Bible Sales, Inc. 1997.

_____. *What The Bible Says: The Rapture*. Lawrenceville, Georgia: Armor Books. 2003.

_____. *What The Bible Says: Mystery Babylon*. Lawrenceville, Georgia: Armor Books. 2003.

_____. *What The Bible Says: The Great White Throne Judgment*. Lawrenceville, Georgia: Armor Books. 2003.

_____. *What The Bible Says: Daniel's 70 Weeks*. Lawrenceville, Georgia: Armor Books. 2003.

_____. *What The Bible Says: The Future Anti–Christ*. Lawrenceville, Georgia: Armor Books. 2003.

_____. *What The Bible Says: The Marriage Supper of the Lamb/ The Battle of Armageddon*. Lawrenceville, Georgia: Armor Books. 2003.

_____. *What The Bible Says: The Millennial Reign of Christ*. Lawrenceville, Georgia: Armor Books. 2003.

_____. *What The Bible Says: The Second Coming of Jesus.* Lawrenceville, Georgia: Armor Books. 2003.

_____. *What The Bible Says: The Tribulation.* Lawrenceville, Georgia: Armor Books. 2003.

BOOKS FINIS J. DAKE USED OFTEN IN HIS WRITINGS

The following list consists of some of the books and Bibles that Finis J. Dake used and quoted from in his writings.

General

Brewer, Cobham E. *Dictionary of Phrase and Fable.* New York, New York: Harper & Row Publishers, 1970. 1870 reprint.

Bullinger, Ethelbert W. *Figures of Speech Used in the Bible.* Grand Rapids, Michigan: Baker Book House, 1968. 1898 reprint.

_____. *Numbers in Scripture.* Grand Rapids, Michigan: Kregel Publications, 1980. 1894 reprint.

_____. *The Witness of the Stars.* Grand Rapids, Michigan: Kregel Publications, 1997. 1893 reprint.

Clarke, Adam. *Clarke's Commentary.* Nashville, Tennessee: Abingdon Press, 1967. 1826 reprint.

Finney, Charles G. *Finney's Lectures on Systematic Theology.* Grand Rapids, Michigan: WM. B. Eerdmans Publishing Company, 1878.

Henry, Matthew. *Matthew Henry's Commentary on the Whole Bible.* Minneapolis, Minnesota: Bethany House Publishers, 1985.

Hislop, Alexander. *The Two Babylons.* Neptune, New Jersey: Loizeaux Brothers, 1916.

Kenyon, Essek W. *Living Bible Studies.* Lynnwood, Washington: Kenyon's Gospel Publishing Society.

_____. *The Wonderful Name of Jesus.* Lynnwood, Washington: Kenyon's Gospel Publishing Society, 1964.

Larkin, Clarence. *Dispensational Truth or God's Plan and Purpose in the Ages.* Glenside, Pennsylvania: Rev. Clarence Larkin Estate, 1918.

_____. *Rightly Dividing the Word.* Glenside, Pennsylvania: Rev. Clarence Larkin Estate, 1920.

_____. *The Book of Daniel.* Glenside, Pennsylvania: Rev. Clarence Larkin Estate, 1929.

_____. *The Book of Revelation.* Glenside, Pennsylvania: Rev. Clarence Larkin Estate, 1919.

_____. *The Spirit World*. Glenside, Pennsylvania: Rev. Clarence Larkin Estate, 1921.

Pember, G. H. *Earth's Earliest Ages*. Grand Rapids, Michigan: Kregel Publications, 1942. 1876 reprint.

Scofield, C. I. *Rightly Dividing the Word of Truth*. Neptune, New Jersey: Loizeaux Brothers, 1896.

Torrey, R. A. *The New Topical Textbook*. Westwood, New Jersey: Fleming H. Revell Company, 1987.

_____. *The Treasury of Scripture Knowledge*. Old Tappen, New Jersey: Fleming H. Revell Company, 2002.

Wesley, John. 1703–1791. *The Works of Rev. John Wesley*. Nashville, Tennessee: Abingdon, 1988.

Histories

Herodotus. *The Histories*. Germany: Alfred A. Knopf, Inc., 1910.

Josephus, Flavious. *Josephus Complete Works*. Grand Rapids, Michigan: Kregel Publications, 1960. 79 A.D. reprint.

Judaeus, Philo. *Philo*. Translated by C. D. Yonge. Peabody, Massachusetts: Hendrickson Publishers, 1997. 50 A.D. reprint.

Pamphilus, Eusebius. *Eusebius' Ecclesiastical History*. Nicene and Post Nicene Fathers, 263–339 A.D. Hendrickson Publishers.

Bibles

Berkeley Version in Modern English. 1959. Grand Rapids, Michigan: Zondervan Publishing House, 1959.

Bullinger, Ethelbert W. *The Companion Bible*. Grand Rapids, Michigan: Kregel Publications, 1990. 1886 reprint.

Moffatt, James. *The Bible: James Moffatt Translation*. New York, New York: Harper Brothers Publishers, 1926. 1922 reprint.

Rotherham, Joseph B. *Rotherham's Emphasized Bible*. Grand Rapids, Michigan: Kregel Publications, 1994. 1902 reprint.

Scofield, C. I. *The Scofield Reference Bible*. New York, New York: Oxford University Press, 1909.

The Amplified Bible. Grand Rapids, Michigan: Zondervan, 1958.

The Holy Bible: King James Version 1611 Edition. Nashville, Tennessee: Thomas Nelson Publishers, 1611. (Dake's choice above all other versions.)

The Holy Bible: Revised Standard Version. New York, New York:

Thomas Nelson and Sons, 1952.

Young, Robert. *Young's Literal Translation Bible.* Grand Rapids, Michigan: Baker Book House, 1863.

CHARISMATIC AND PENTECOSTAL HISTORY AND DOCTRINE

The following list consists of books, periodicals and articles which may be of interest to those who desire to study Charismatic and Pentecostal history and doctrine.

Bartleman, Frank. *Azusa Street.* South Plainfield, New Jersey: Bridge Publishing, 1980.

Carey, Juanita S. *E. W. Bullinger: A Biography.* Grand Rapids, Michigan: Kregel Publications, 2000.

Conn, Charles W. *Like A Mighty Army: A History of the Church of God 1886–1976.* Cleveland, Tennessee: Pathway Press, 1977.

Dallimore, Arnold. *The Life of Edward Irving.* Carlisle, Pennsylvania: The Banner of Truth Trust, 1983.

Drummond, Lewis A. *The Life and Ministry of Charles G. Finney.* Minneapolis, Minnesota: Bethany House Publishers, 1985.

Gardiner, Gordon P. *Out of Zion Into All the World.* Shippenburg, Pennsylvania: Companion Press, 1990.

Harrell, Jr. David E. *All Things are Possible.* Bloomington, Indiana: Indiana University Press, 1975.

Hollenweger, Walter J. *The Pentecostals.* Peabody, Massachusetts: Hendrickson Publishers, 1972.

Hyatt, Eddie L. *2000 Years of Charismatic Christianity.* Lake Mary, Florida: Charisma House, 2002.

McIntosh, Ron. *The Quest for Revival.* Tulsa, Oklahoma: Harrison House, 1997.

McIntyre, Joe. *E. W. Kenyon and His Message of Faith: The True Story.* Orlando, Florida: Creation House, 1997.

Nienkirchen, Charles W. *A. B. Simpson and the Pentecostal Movement.* Massachusetts: Hendrickson Publishers, 1992.

Riss, Richard M. *A Survey of 20th Century Revival Movements in North America.* Peabody, Massachusetts: Hendrickson Publishers, 1988.

Robeck, Cecil M. *Charismatic Experiences in History.* Peabody, Massachusetts: Hendrickson Publishers, 1985.

Synan, Vinson. *Aspects of Pentecostal—Charismatic Origins.* Plainfield, New Jersey: Logos International, 1975.

_____. *The Century of the Holy Spirit.* Nashville, Tennessee: Thomas Nelson Publishers, 2001.

_____. *The Holiness Pentecostal Movement in the United States.* Grand Rapids, Michigan: William B. Eerdmans Publishing Company, 1971.

_____. *Voices of Pentecost.* Ann Arbor, Michigan: Servant Publications, 2003.

Wellman, Sam. *John Wesley.* Uhrichsville, Ohio: Barbour Publishing, 1997.

BOOKS USED BY THE AUTHOR NOT SITED ABOVE

Allen, David. *The Unfailing Stream.* Kent, Tennessee: Sovereign World Ltd., 1994.

Berkow, Robert. General Editor. *The Merck Manual of Medical Information.* Whitehouse Station, New Jersey: Merck Research Laboratories, 1997.

Burgess, Stanley M. ed. *Dictionary of Pentecostal and Charismatic Movements.* Grand Rapids, Michigan: Zondervan Publishing House, 1988.

Burke, Bob. *Like A Prairie Fire, A History of the Assemblies of God in Oklahoma.* Marceline, Missouri: The Oklahoma District of the Assemblies of God, 1994.

Corum, Fred T. and Hazel E. Bakewell. *The Sparkling Fountain,* Windsor, Ohio: Corum & Associates, Inc., 1989.

Decker, Ed. *Decker's Complete Handbook on Mormonism.* Eugene, Oregon: Harvest House Publishers, 1995.

Easton, M. A. ed. *Easton's Illustrated Bible Dictionary.* Nashville, Tennessee: Thomas Nelson, 1897.

Enns, Paul P. *Moody Handbook of Theology.* Chicago, Illinois: Moody Press, 1989.

Erickson, Millard J. *Christian Theology.* Grand Rapids, Michigan: Baker Book House, 1983.

Fletcher, John. *The Works of the Rev. John Fletcher,* Vol. 2. London: Printed for Thomas Allman, 1974 reprint.

Gorden, Kurt Van. *Mormonism.* Grand Rapids, Michigan: Zondervan Publishers, 1995.

Grudem, Wayne. *Systematic Theology.* Grand Rapids, Michigan: Zondervan Publishing House, 1994.

Kirban, Salem. *Mormonism.* Huntingdon Valley, Pennsylvania: Salem Kirban Publisher, 1981.

Lindsay, Gordon. *John Alexander Dowie—A Life Story of Trials Tragedies and Triumphs.* Dallas, Texas: Christ for the Nations, 1986.

Menzies, William and Stanley Horton. *Bible Doctrines: A Pentecostal Perspective.* Springfield, Missouri: Login Press, 1993.

Orton, Wiley, H. *Introduction to Christian Theology.* Kansas City, Missouri: Beacon Hill Press, 1946.

Schereth, Thomas J. *Victorian America.* New York, New York: Harper Pernnial, 1991.

Sumrall, Dr. Lester. *Pioneers of Faith.* Tulsa, Oklahoma: Harrison House, 1995.

Thiessen, Henry C. *Lectures in Systematic Theology.* Grand Rapids, Michigan: William B. Eerdmans Publishing Company, 1949.

Ryrie, Charles C. *Basic Theology.* Wheaton, Illinois: Chariot Victor Books, 1986.

Scott, Laytayne Colvett. *The Mormon Mirage.* Grand Rapids, Michigan: Zondervan Publishing, 1979.

Williamson, G. I. *The Westminster Confession of Faith.* Philadelphia, Pennsylvania: Presbyterian and Reformed Publishing Company, 1964.

Index

A

A.J. Holman Company 306
Allen, David 137
Annabeth Dake Germaine 5, 313, 408
Appleby, Sister Blanche 65
Archibald, Dorothy 176
Argue, Rev. Waston 133
Arkansas 62, 64, 122
  Eureka Springs 62
  Hot Springs 64

B

Bakker, Jim 331
Bamford, Annie 126
Baptist 12, 14, 23, 24, 28, 58, 91, 229, 234, 317, 330
Baptist Standard 317
Beckman, Dora 358
Bell, Arthur 172
Bell South 320
Bible Research Foundation 284, 285, 297, 299, 300, 307, 313, 320
Boer War 360
Bonaparte, Napoleon 360
Boom, Corrie Ten 331
Boucher, Sister Florence 127
Bowley, H.E. 79
Boyd, Frank M. 48
Boyer, K.J. 172
Bryan, William Jennings 9
Buffalo Bill 13
Bunyon, John 250
Byrd, Ralph 321

C

Cadwalder, Hugh H. 79
California 37, 47, 64, 75, 82, 331
  Anaheim 331
  Los Angeles 279, 353
  San Francisco 37, 38, 39, 45, 52, 173
  San Francisco: China Town 45
Cambridge University Press 306, 323
Canada 81, 260, 272
Carroll, William 274, 275, 276, 277, 278, 284, 285, 291, 292, 294, 300,
    301, 313, 314, 319, 320, 323
  Carroll Baking Company 273, 292, 295, 320
Carter, Howard 149, 209, 250
Chant, Barry 137
Cherokee Indian 9
Childers, Martha 15
China 45, 65, 81
Christenson, Larry 331
Christmas 39, 58, 179, 196, 213, 258, 311, 339, 417
Churches
  Assembly of God 54, 58, 62, 64, 71, 74, 124, 133, 151, 168, 212, 246,
    251, 321, 330
  Baptist 12, 14, 23, 24, 28, 58, 91, 229, 234, 317, 330
  Bethel Temple 174
  Christian Assembly 133, 135, 136, 143, 145, 147, 148, 149, 151, 152,
    155, 167, 168, 172, 173, 178, 185, 198, 210, 219, 245, 247, 248,
    249, 250
  Church of God 189, 257, 259, 260, 267, 268, 269, 271, 273, 300, 324,
    325, 330, 351, 422
  Congregational Holiness 334
  Faith Memorial Assembly of God 321
  Full Gospel Church 26, 172
  Hemphill Church of God 273, 274, 278
  Lawrenceville Church of God 330, 335
  Melody Land Christian Ctr. 331
  Methodist 12, 14, 23, 24, 28, 58, 330
  New Testament Church 284, 297-300, 301, 303, 308, 314, 320

Presbyterian 274, 278, 308, 330, 395
Reformed Adventist Church 353
The Stone Church 172
Wesleyan Methodist 317
Civil War 360
Colorado 21
Conn, Charles W. 324, 351
Contractor and Builder 10
Corden, Kurt Van 405
Craig, R.J. 37
Cunningham, E.F. 26, 48

D

Dake
    Arthur 14, 16, 24, 46, 54, 172, 189, 254, 326, 365
    Edward Finis Dake 417
    Finis Jennings Jr. 5, 73, 252, 253, 257, 313, 366, 408
    Flomarie Etta 12, 365
    George W. 12, 365
    James Henry 9, 10, 11, 12, 23, 365
    Joseph Franklin 16, 365
    Mary Ellen 9, 12, 13, 16, 25
    Steven Arthur 254, 255, 366
Dake Books
    Another Time Another Place Another Man 103, 348, 419
    Bible Truths Unmasked 303, 352, 419
    Dake Annotated Reference Bible 41, 45, 51, 69, 77, 147, 211, 212,
        247, 250, 303, 312, 313, 315, 316, 318, 323, 348, 350, 352, 357,
        359, 385, 405, 412, 419
    God's Plan of the Ages 68, 73, 95, 147, 173, 201, 203, 285
    Revelation Expounded 71, 96-99, 173, 285, 303, 305, 350, 352, 419
    Zondervan Expanded Concordance 323, 324
Davidson, James 246
Death 12, 16
Dobbins, Hattie May 57
Dobbins Sisters Evangelistic Party 61, 62, 65
Dorothy Dake 5, 67, 86, 91, 147, 155, 174, 202, 257, 259, 313, 381,
        383, 407, 409, 412

Dowie, John Alexander 135, 136, 137, 138, 139, 140, 141, 153, 165, 166, 167, 170, 172, 193, 215, 216, 219, 220, 221, 222, 227, 270, 343, 347, 348
Dutch 9, 273, 291, 295, 320
Du Plesis, David 331
Dyksterhuis, Rein 174

E

Erickson, John 172

F

Finette Dake Kennedy 5, 313, 407
Finis 1, 2, 5, 9, 15, 16, 24, 27, 28, 54, 66, 67, 71-73, 77, 79, 80, 95, 101, 103, 125, 126, 128, 129, 131, 135, 149, 172, 173, 188, 198, 202, 207, 209, 212, 215, 245, 252-254, 257, 266, 286, 292, 293, 295, 298, 300-302, 307, 313, 319, 321, 327, 328, 336, 338, 343, 348-350, 353, 365, 366, 373, 377, 385, 389, 390, 405, 407, 408, 409, 412, 417, 419, 420
Finis J. Dake 5, 27, 67, 77, 101, 128, 131, 135, 149, 172, 173, 188, 202, 207, 286, 292, 293, 295, 298, 321, 343, 349, 385, 389, 405, 417, 419, 420
Finis Jennings Dake Jr. 5, 252, 253, 366, 408
Fischer, H.A. 132
Fletcher, John 346
Flomarie Etta Dake 12, 365
Florida 26, 320, 422
Ford Philpot Evangelistic Association 330
Fort Dearborn 177
Fourche, Belle 64
France, Sister Lula 14
Freeman, J. Edgar 70, 76
French 9, 27, 54, 61, 146, 196, 360
French, Otto 27
Full Gospel Business Men's Fellowship 331

G

general store 10

George W. Dake 12, 365

Georgia 1, 2, 24, 28, 45, 67, 71, 72, 77, 101, 103, 136, 149, 273, 285, 292, 298, 299, 324, 325, 334, 335, 337, 357, 359, 385, 389, 397, 405, 408, 413, 419, 420

  Atlanta 136, 273, 276, 278, 279, 280, 285, 292, 293, 294, 297, 298, 299, 320, 321, 324, 329, 397, 413

  Atlanta: Belvedere Avenue 278, 313, 325, 329

  Atlanta: West Peachtree Street 294, 297, 320

  East Point 325

  East Point: Cleveland Avenue 325

  Gainesville 325

  Lawrenceville 1, 2, 24, 28, 45, 67, 71, 72, 77, 101, 103, 149, 329, 330, 335, 357, 359, 385, 389, 405, 413, 419, 420

  Lawrenceville: Martins Chapel Road 329

  Marietta 277

  Riverside 273

  Union Grove 334

Germaine

  Annabeth Dake 5, 249, 253, 254, 300, 307, 313, 329, 336, 338, 339, 366, 408

  Dave 329, 338, 409

  Derrick 413

  Keel 413

Goldsmith, Theodore 167

Gospel Publishing House 25, 65

Graham, Billy 334

Graham, Otto 175, 176

Great Lakes Naval Training Station 177

Gresham, Charles 318

Gring, Emma G. 167

H

Hall, John G. 207, 212, 223

Hamilton, Thomas 335

Harned, Mrs. 82, 87
Hart, Charles T. 176
Henry Dake 9, 10, 11, 12, 23
Heron, Mr. 358
Hicks, Amanda 221
Hindu 29
Holy sabbath 11
Hop-A-Long Cassidy 20
Hoyt, Earl 246
Humbard, Rex 331
Hunt, Dave 331
Hutsell, James 128

I

Iberia 9, 26, 63, 365, 366
Illinois 48, 49, 63, 65, 95, 133, 135, 138, 140, 141, 168, 172, 173, 174,
    185, 188, 201, 208, 212, 215, 246, 247, 250, 343, 347, 366, 394,
    400
  Belleville 172
  Chicago 49, 63, 140, 172, 174, 175, 177, 184, 210, 394
  Granite City 47, 48
  Joliet 49, 50, 63, 67
  Lab Villa 172
  Waukegan 167, 172, 177
  Zion 65, 131, 132, 133, 134, 135, 136, 138, 140, 141, 142, 143, 145,
    147, 149, 150, 151, 152, 153, 155, 165, 166, 170, 171, 172, 173,
    177, 185, 188, 190, 198, 199, 201, 207, 208, 210, 211, 212, 213,
    215, 216, 219, 220, 227, 245, 246, 249, 250, 251, 270, 272, 297,
    343, 347, 366, 422
  Zion: Elim Avenue 225
  Zion: Elizabeth Avenue 140, 225
  Zion: Emmaus Avenue 225
  Zion: Eschol 133, 136
  Zion: Shiloh Blvd. 141, 166
  Zion: Shiloh House and Cottage 141, 166, 167, 171, 172
Indiana 95, 173, 215, 331, 422
  South Bend 215, 217, 331

Irish 9
Israel 54, 111, 120, 156, 232, 241, 268, 330, 357, 364, 401
Iverson, Otto 37

J

J.H. Dake, Groceries Flour & Feed, Meat Market 10
James Henry 9, 365
Jamieson, S.A. 28
Jernigan, John C. 257, 260
Johansen, Julius 172
John C. Winston Company 306
Jones, Robert Ellis 174

K

Kansas 19, 20, 58, 62, 122, 394
  Chetopa 62
  Kansas City 19, 394
  Topeka 58
Keener, Otis R. 174
Kennedy
  Finette Dake 5, 73, 87, 95, 131, 150, 151, 245, 249, 252, 254, 261,
    272, 280, 300, 307, 313, 326, 336, 338, 340, 341, 366, 407
  Kimberly 409
Kentucky 221
  Clinton 221
Kerr, Elder D. 64
Kessel, Theodore A. 173
Kuhlman, Kathryn 331

L

Lett, Belva 59
Liddle, Cecil 175
Lockyer, Herbert 308
Logsdon, Glyndon 260

M

Marriage 70, 258, 284, 365, 366, 419
Mary Ellen Dake 9, 12, 13, 16, 25
McAfee 95
  Caleb 251
  Pauline 57, 58, 61, 95, 99, 182, 251, 253, 254, 271, 366
McCutchan, Robert 126, 127
McCutcheon, J.F. 76
Menzi, William W. 219
Methodist 12, 14, 23, 24, 28, 58, 317, 330
Mexico 23, 59, 194, 360
Michigan 63, 152, 307, 308, 314, 393, 399, 400, 405, 420, 421, 422, 423
  Detroit 152, 358
  Grand Rapids 63, 307, 393, 399, 400, 405, 420, 421, 422, 423
  Lake Michigan 138, 140, 177, 185
Millard, Glenn 121, 122, 127
Miller, John 260, 261
Miller, Monique Germaine 415
Miller County 9, 365, 366
Mills, Dick 331
Minnesota 358, 420, 422
Missouri 9, 16, 19, 45, 46, 51, 57, 59, 62, 63, 64, 65, 66, 95, 102, 176, 209, 220, 250, 259, 267, 353, 365, 366, 394, 423, 424
  Des Arc 65, 66
  Flat River 259
  Greenville 66
  Iberia 9, 26, 63, 365, 366
  Joplin 14, 57, 58, 59, 60, 62, 65, 366
  Marshfield 16
  Miller County 9, 365, 366
  Moffatt Avenue 57
  Springfield 9, 10, 12, 14, 17, 19, 23, 24, 25, 26, 46, 50, 51, 52, 64, 78, 126, 209, 220, 250, 353, 365
  St. Louis 9, 63, 246, 247, 248
Moody, W.E. 65

N

Nebraska 20, 63
  Milford 63
  Omaha 20, 21
Nelson, P.C. 91, 128
Nerr, D.W. 47
New Mexico 59, 74, 78, 79, 123, 124
New Mexico District Council 78
New York 10, 13, 19, 52, 63, 331, 420, 421
North Carolina 331
  Charlotte 331
Nuir, E.F. 75
Nye, George 93, 95

O

Oakley, Annie 13
Ohio 16, 48, 95, 423
Oklahoma 24, 37, 61, 65, 91, 92, 93, 94, 95, 102, 121, 125, 128, 150,
      174, 207, 208, 215, 246, 250, 337, 422, 424
  Enid 91, 102, 121, 122, 125, 128, 174, 208
  Sand Springs 92, 93, 94
  Tulsa 24, 25, 26, 27, 37, 39, 65, 70, 71, 76, 92, 93, 94, 95, 150, 215,
      246, 250, 337, 422, 424
  Tulsa: Boonville Street 14, 15
  Tulsa: Florida Street 26

P

Page, Charlie 94, 95
Parham, Charles 58
Patton, Melanie Dake Patton 416
Pearlman, Myer 52
Pennsylvania 167, 251, 252, 257, 259, 260, 267, 268, 269, 270, 272,
      395, 404, 420, 421, 422
  Newport 167

Saxton 257
Somerset 259
St. Paul 251, 253
Waynesboro 264, 266, 267, 268
Perkin, Noel 209
Perkins, Jonathan 70
Peterson, Paul B. 172
Phillips, J.B. 323
Philpot, Ford 330
Pierce, Willard 47
PTL Club 331

R

Religious 377
Rowen, Mrs. 353
Russia 81, 216, 362

S

Sayles, Annabel 174
Scharnick, R.L. 172
Schools
   Bowie Hall 16
   Central Bible Institute 15, 16, 46, 47, 48, 52, 53, 54, 64, 173, 250, 353
   Emerson School 60
   Glad Tidings Bible Institute 37, 38, 44, 64
   Great Lakes Bible Institute 247, 250
   Phillips University 174
   Sherwood School of Music 174
   Shiloh Bible Institute 168, 169, 170, 172, 178, 179, 188, 189, 193, 194, 195, 196, 197, 198, 202, 205, 207, 208, 212, 215, 219, 222, 245, 246, 247, 250, 272, 283
   Southwestern Bible School 91, 125, 128, 166, 173, 174, 176, 272
   Texico Bible School 74, 77, 78, 80, 82, 86, 91, 173, 176, 272
   University of Illinois 175

Washington High School 261, 262
West Texas State University 77
Schott, Fred 175
Schreffier, Ted 132
Scotch 9
SeRine, Lillian Evans 167
Shakarian, Demos 331
Shiloh Scroll 155, 193, 195, 197, 198, 199, 200, 201, 202, 203, 204
Smith, Wilbur 308
Solomon 32, 113, 368
South Dakota 64
South Fulton Hospital 325
Spicer, J.A. 172
Springfield 9, 10, 12, 14, 17, 19, 23, 24, 25, 26, 46, 50, 51, 52, 64, 78,
     126, 209, 220, 250, 353, 365, 424
St. Louis 9, 63, 246, 247, 248
Standard Publishing Foundation 318
Steveson, Earl 66
Sullivan, Eugene 248
Sumrall, Lester 149, 150, 215, 246, 250, 331, 337
Swank, Celia 126, 127
Swarztrauber, A.D. 172
Swinefurth, Mr. 358

T

Talcutt, Pastor 66
Tennessee 9, 252, 253, 254, 255, 257, 270, 271, 324, 349, 366, 396,
     420, 421, 422, 423
  Bristol 251, 252, 253, 254, 257, 270, 297, 366
  Cleveland 257, 324, 325, 349, 422
Texas 15, 70, 71, 72, 74, 75, 78, 79, 80, 122, 123, 124, 139, 174, 220,
     221, 317, 366
  Amarillo 70, 71, 72, 73, 76, 77, 366
  Dallas 74, 78, 80, 87, 139, 174, 220, 221, 317, 319
The Macmillan Company 305, 323
Thomas Nelson 305, 323, 396, 421, 422, 423

Thomsen, Neils P. 172
Tipton, B.E. 298

U

United States Census 9
Unruh, Louise 101
Utah 37
  Salt Lack City 37

V

Veach, H.R. 264, 265, 266, 267
Virginia 57, 251, 254, 366

W

Wagoner, Rhonda Germaine 412
Wallower, Edgar 61
Ward, C.M. 79
Washington 257, 260, 261, 262, 264, 267, 269, 270, 319, 362, 420
Welch, Mrs. 25
Wesley, Charles 346
Wilder, J.C. 79
Wilkerson, Ralph 331
Williams, E.S. 129
Williams, Ernest S. 209
Williams, J. Rodman 331
William Jennings Bryan 9
Wilson, Arthur 54
Wisconsin 131, 140, 172, 185, 246
  Kenosha 177, 246
  Oshkosh 172
  Sheboygan 131, 132
wooden sign 10

World Publishing Company 307
Wyoming 21

Z

Zondervan Publishing House 52, 91, 129, 149, 307, 323, 393, 421, 423

The powerful tools you know and trust are only a mouse-click away—thanks to the Dake Reference Library on CD-ROM. With its wealth of integrated information and intuitive interface, the Dake Reference Library lets you access a lifetime of insights in just seconds. Includes instant links from the Scripture text to Dake's notes, Greek and Hebrew word studies, and much more. Runs under Windows 98 and Windows XP. Also Available: The Dake Reference Library for Macintosh! Powered by Accordance©, the Macintosh version runs natively under OS X, as well as OS 8 and 9.

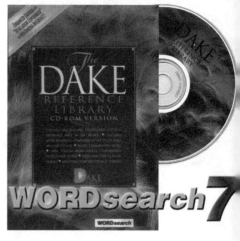

BOOKS

REVELATION EXPOUNDED

Of Dake's many contributions to a clear understanding of Scripture, perhaps his greatest achievement is in simplifying matters of prophecy. Unencumbered by the hype and sensationalism so often associated with Bible prophecy, Dake offers a straightforward exposition of the text, supporting his teaching with hundreds of Scriptures. Discover for yourself how eternal mysteries really can be simplified!

THE RAPTURE AND THE SECOND COMING OF CHRIST

As humanity steps into a new millennium, thoughts turn easily to questions of what the Bible has to say about our future. Will the Lord return soon? When will the rapture take place? Will the church endure the tribulation? Will the Antichrist rule the world? For years, believers have relied on Finis Dake to provide simple explanations of sound doctrine—especially in matters of Bible prophecy. Those who hunger for such truth will find solid meat in the pages of *The Rapture and The Second Coming of Christ.*

GOD'S PLAN FOR MAN

God's Plan for Man contains the very heart of Finis Jennings Dake's life work. In it, he unfolds the plans and purposes of God from the eternal past to the eternal future, exploring biblical prophecy and the privileges of life in Christ. He systematically discusses the nature of the Bible, principles of biblical interpretation, the Trinity and much more.

HEAVENLY HOSTS

Compiled from the writings of Finis Dake, *Heavenly Hosts* is more than just another book on angels. In the traditional Dake style, this is an exclusively biblical study of angels. Loaded with Scriptures that detail the nature, type, and work of angels, *Heavenly Hosts* balances the current popularity of the subject with a solid Scriptural foundation. Believers are thus encouraged to expect the help of these "...ministering spirits, sent forth to minister for them who shall be heirs of salvation."

ANOTHER TIME... ANOTHER PLACE... ANOTHER MAN

The first in a new doctrinal series based on the writings of the late Finis Dake, *Another Time... Another Place... Another Man* provides a biblical alternative to the traditional view of creation. Dake's unique approach removes much of the tension between Christianity and science with an insightful analysis of the Genesis account and relevant passages. The creation story takes on new meaning in this exciting and thought-provoking journey through the Scriptures.

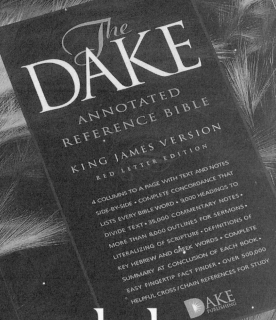

INTRODUCING
OFFERS

The Dake Annotated Reference Bible Is a Compact, One-Volume Library Featuring:

- 35,000 Commentary Notes
- Ancient Customs Explained
- Words of Christ in Red
- 500,000 Cross/Chain References
- 9,000 Headings Dividing Text
- Complete Concordance Lists Every Bible Word
- 8,000 Sermon Outlines
- Summary at End of Each Book
- Key Hebrew and Greek Words Defined

"Study to shew thyself approved unto God." Paul's words to Timothy still stir our hearts today. They're the reason study Bibles exist. And why more than twenty years of painstaking research were poured into the *Dake Annotated Reference Bible*. With 35,000 commentary notes, 500,000 cross references and 9,000 outline headings, the Dake Bible gives you more resources for personal study than you'll find in any other Bible. Period. Yet it's not just the number of notes, references and headings that set the Dake Bible apart. It's what those tools do for you.

Born in 1902, Finis Jennings Dake was a leader in the revival movements of the early twentieth century. His God-given ability to quote Scripture flawlessly without memorization earned him a reputation as the "Walking Bible." Throughout his eighty-four years he pastored several churches, started a Bible school, and lectured extensively. Amidst this busy ministry, he also wrote several books, including the huge volume of commentary notes in the Dake Annotated Reference Bible.

Thousands of passages are amplified. Obscure readings are made clear. Ancient customs are explained, along with matters of history, culture and geography. Greek and Hebrew words and idioms are presented. In addition, parables, types, symbols, allegories and figures of speech are discussed in detail. Dispensational issues are treated in a systematic fashion, along with hundreds of details of biblical prophecy.

HE BIBLE THAT
U MORE.

n other words, the Dake Bible is the ultimate tool to help you truly
nderstand Scripture and "rightly divide the word of truth."
No other study Bible is like it. No other study Bible gives you as much. The
Dake Annotated Reference Bible. It's the Bible that offers you more.

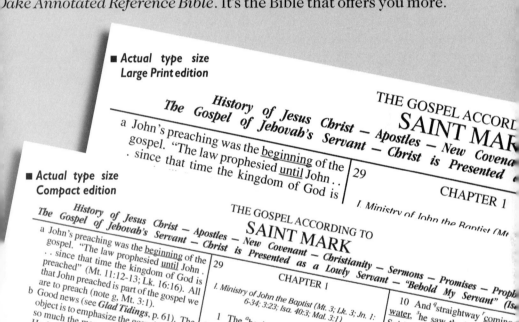

■ Actual type size
Large Print edition

History of Jesus Christ — Apostles — New Covena
The Gospel of Jehovah's Servant — Christ is Presented

a John's preaching was the beginning of the
gospel. "The law prophesied until John . .
. since that time the kingdom of God is | 29

THE GOSPEL ACCORD
SAINT MAR

CHAPTER 1

I. Ministry of John the Baptist (Mt.

■ Actual type size
Compact edition

History of Jesus Christ — Apostles — Christianity — Sermons — Promises — Proph
The Gospel of Jehovah's Servant — Christ is Presented as a Lowly Servant — "Behold My Servant" (Is.

THE GOSPEL ACCORDING TO
SAINT MARK

a John's preaching was the beginning of the
gospel. "The law prophesied until John .
. . since that time the kingdom of God is
preached" (Mt. 11:12-13; Lk. 16:16). All
that John preached is part of the gospel we
are to preach (note g, Mt. 3:1).
b Good news (see *Glad Tidings*, p. 61). The
object is to emphasize the gospel itself, not
so much the many events leading up to it.
He does not mention the birth or genealogy
of Christ and many other events about John

29

CHAPTER 1

I. Ministry of John the Baptist (Mt. 3; Lk. 3; Jn. 1:
6-34; 3:23; Isa. 40:3; Mal. 3:1)

1 The ᵃbeginning of the ᵇ gospel of Jesus
Christ, the ᶜSon of God;
★ 2 As it is written in the prophets, ᵈBehold,
I send my ᵉmessenger before thy face, which
shall prepare thy way before thee.

10 And ᵍstraightway ʳcoming
water, ʰhe saw the heavens open
Spirit like a ʲdove descending upo.
■ 11 And there came a voice fro
saying, "Thou art my beloved Son,
am well pleased.
12 And immediately the Spirit ᵛdri
into the wilderness.
13 And he was there in the wildern

■ type size
r edition

THE GOSPEL ACCORDING TO
SAINT MARK

tory of Jesus Christ - Apostles - New Covenant - Christianity - Sermons - Promises - Prophecies
Gospel of Jehovah's Servant -Christ is Presented as a Lowly Servant -"Behold My Servant" (Isa. 42: 1)

reaching was the beginning of
el. "The law prophesied until
ince that time the kingdom of
ached" (Mt. 11:12-13; Lk.
that John preached is part
el we are to preach (note g,

Glad tidings, p. 270). The
emphasize the gospel it-
much the many events
it. He does not mention
genealogy of Christ and
vents about John and Je-
1-3; Lk. 1-3. Such
e out of harmony with
his gospel, which is to
a servant of God. Gen-
ants are never given
16:16; Jn. 1:14
cy fulfilled in Mk.
Next, v 3
eings Used of both
cy fulfilled in Mk.
ext, 4:12

I Ministry of John the Baptist (Mt. 3; Lk. 3; Jn. 1:6-
34; 3:23; Isa. 40:3;Mal. 3:1)

THE ᵃbeginning of the ᵇgospel
of Jĕ′sus Christ, the ᶜSon
of God;
★ 2 As it is written in the prophets, ᵈBehold, I send my ᵉmessenger before thy face, which
shall prepare thy way before
thee.
★ 3 ᶠThe voice of one crying in
the wilderness, Prepare ye the
way of the Lord, make his paths
straight.
4 John did ᵍbaptize in the wilderness, and ʰpreach th
tism of repe

29

35

16 ᵏNow as he walked by the
sea of Găl′i-lee, he saw Sĭ′mon
and Ăn′drew his brother casting a net into the sea: for
they were fishers.
▶17 And Jĕ′sus said unto them,
Come ye after me, and I will
make you to become fishers of
men.
18 And ᵇstraightway they for-
sook their nets, and followed
him.

3 Call of James and John
(Mt. 4:21; Lk. 5:10)

19 And when he

a See notes on Mt. 4:18-22
b See note b, Mk. 3:6
c How many hired servants or how big
the fishing business was that they had
is unknown. The important thing is
that they obeyed Christ, and for doing
so they became the greatest men in
the greatest religion on earth (Eph. 2:
20-22)
d See note x, Mt. 11:23
e Gr. sunagoge, from sun, together,
and ago, I bring; a public assembly
of persons, or the place where they
assembled (Jas. 2:2). Synagogues were
numerous among Jews from the Bab-
ylonian captivity on. The
erected in all citie
the